Contents

KU-019-308

KAPLAN PUBLISHING

Paper Introduction

How to Use the Materials

These Kaplan Publishing learning materials have been carefully designed to make your learning experience as easy as possible and to give you the best chances of success in your examinations.

The product range contains a number of features to help you in the study process. They include:

(1) Detailed study guide and syllabus objectives

(2) Description of the examination

(3) Study skills and revision guidance

(4) Complete text or essential text

(5) Question practice

The sections on the study guide, the syllabus objectives, the examination and study skills should all be read before you commence your studies. They are designed to familiarise you with the nature and content of the examination and give you tips on how to best to approach your learning.

The **complete text or essential text** comprises the main learning materials and gives guidance as to the importance of topics and where other related resources can be found. Each chapter includes:

- The **learning objectives** contained in each chapter, which have been carefully mapped to the examining body's own syllabus learning objectives or outcomes. You should use these to check you have a clear understanding of all the topics on which you might be assessed in the examination.

- The **chapter diagram** provides a visual reference for the content in the chapter, giving an overview of the topics and how they link together.

- The **content** for each topic area commences with a brief explanation or definition to put the topic into context before covering the topic in detail. You should follow your studying of the content with a review of the illustration/s. These are worked examples which will help you to understand better how to apply the content for the topic.

- **Test your understanding** sections provide an opportunity to assess your understanding of the key topics by applying what you have learned to short questions. Answers can be found at the back of each chapter.

- **Summary diagrams** complete each chapter to show the important links between topics and the overall content of the paper. These diagrams should be used to check that you have covered and understood the core topics before moving on.

- **Question practice** is provided at the back of each text.

Icon Explanations

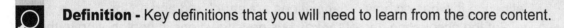 **Definition -** Key definitions that you will need to learn from the core content.

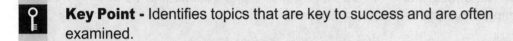 **Key Point -** Identifies topics that are key to success and are often examined.

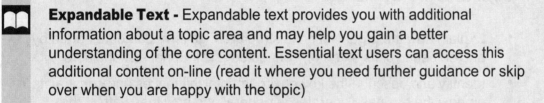 **Expandable Text -** Expandable text provides you with additional information about a topic area and may help you gain a better understanding of the core content. Essential text users can access this additional content on-line (read it where you need further guidance or skip over when you are happy with the topic)

Illustration - Worked examples help you understand the core content better.

Test Your Understanding - Exercises for you to complete to ensure that you have understood the topics just learned.

Tricky topic - When reviewing these areas care should be taken and all illustrations and test your understanding exercises should be completed to ensure that the topic is understood.

On-line subscribers

Our on-line resources are designed to increase the flexibility of your learning materials and provide you with immediate feedback on how your studies are progressing. Ask your local customer services staff if you are not already a subscriber and wish to join.

If you are subscribed to our on-line resources you will find:

(1) On-line referenceware: reproduces your Complete or Essential Text on-line, giving you anytime, anywhere access.

(2) On-line testing: provides you with additional on-line objective testing so you can practice what you have learned further.

(3) On-line performance management: immediate access to youron-line testing results. Review your performance by key topics and chart your achievement through the course relative to your peer group.

Paper introduction

Paper background

The aim of ACCA Paper F1, **Accountant in Business**, is to introduce knowledge and understanding of the business and its environment and the influence this has on how organisations are structured and on the role of the accounting and other key business functions in contributing to the efficient, effective and ethical management and development of an organisation and its people and systems.

Objectives of the syllabus

- Explain how the organisation is structured, governed and managed by and on behalf of its external, connected and internal stakeholders.

- Identify and describe the key environmental influences and constraints on how the business operates in general and how these affect the accounting function in particular.

- Describe the history, purpose, and position of accounting in the organisation and the roles of other functional areas.

- Identify and explain the functions of accounting systems and internal controls in planning, monitoring and reviewing performance and in preventing fraud and business failure.

- Recognise the principles of authority and leadership and how teams and individuals behave and are effectively managed, disciplined and motivated in pursuit of wider departmental and organisational aims and objectives.

- Recruit and develop effective employees, using appropriate work methods and procedures, while developing constructive relationships through effective communication and interpersonal skills.

Core areas of the syllabus

- Business organisational structure, governance and management
- Key environmental influences and constraints on business and accounting
- History and role of accounting in business
- Specific functions of accounting and internal financial control
- Leading and managing individuals and teams

- Recruiting and developing effective employees

Syllabus objectives

We have reproduced the ACCA's syllabus below, showing where the objectives are explored within this book. Within the chapters, we have broken down the extensive information found in the syllabus into easily digestible and relevant sections, called Content Objectives. These correspond to the objectives at the beginning of each chapter.

Syllabus learning objective Chapter	Chapter reference

A. BUSINESS ORGANISATIONAL STRUCTURE, GOVERNANCE AND MANAGEMENT

1. The business organisation and its structure

  (a) Identify the different types of organisation.[1]

      (i)   commercial

      (ii) not-for-profit

      (iii) public sector

      (iv) non-governmental organisations

      (v) cooperatives.   **1**

  (b) Describe the different ways in which organisations may be structured: entrepreneurial, functional, matrix, divisional, departmental, by geographical area and by product.[1]   **1**

  (c) Describe the roles and functions of the main departments in a business organisation: [1]

      (i)   research and development

      (ii) purchasing

      (iii) production

      (iv) direct service provision

      (v) marketing

      (vi) administration

      (vii) finance.   **1**

  (d) Explain the characteristics of the strategic, tactical and operational levels in the organisation in the context of the Anthony hierarchy.[1]   **1**

  (e) Explain the role of marketing in an organisation:[1]

      (i)   the definition of marketing

      (i)   the marketing mix

      (i)   the relationship of the marketing plan to the strategic plan.   **21**

  (f) Explain basic organisational structure concepts:[2]

      (i)   separation of direction and management

      (ii) span of control and scalar chain

      (iii) tall and flat organisations.   **2**

KAPLAN PUBLISHING

B. KEY ENVIRONMENTAL INFLUENCES AND CONSTRAINTS ON BUSINESS AND ACCOUNTING

1. Political and legal factors

2. Macro-economic factors

D. SPECIFIC FUNCTIONS OF ACCOUNTING AND INTERNAL FINANCIAL CONTROL

KAPLAN PUBLISHING

KAPLAN PUBLISHING

2. Techniques for improving personal effectiveness at work and their benefits

3. Features of effective communication

4. Training, development and learning in the maintenance and improvement of business performance

5. Review and appraisal of individual performance

The superscript numbers in square brackets indicate the intellectual depth at which the subject area could be assessed within the examination. Level 1 (knowledge and comprehension) broadly equates with the Knowledge module, Level 2 (application and analysis) with the Skills module and Level 3 (synthesis and evaluation) to the Professional level. However, lower level skills can continue to be assessed as you progress through each module and level.

The examination

Examination format

The syllabus is assessed by paper or computer-based examination. Questions will assess all parts of the syllabus and will test knowledge and some comprehension or application of this knowledge. The examination will consist of:

	Number of marks
Forty 2-mark questions	80
Ten 1-mark questions	10
	———
Total time allowed: 2 hours	90

Paper-based examination tips

Divide the time you spend on questions in proportion to the marks on offer. One suggestion **for this exam** is to allocate 1 and 1/3 minutes to each mark available, so a 2-mark question should be completed in approximately 2 minutes and 40 seconds.

If you **get completely stuck** with a question, leave space in your answer book and return to it later.

Multiple-choice questions: Read the questions carefully and work through any calculations required. If you don't know the answer, eliminate those options you know are incorrect and see if the answer becomes more obvious. Guess your final answer rather than leave it blank if necessary.

Computer-based examination (CBE) – tips

Be sure you understand how to use the software before you start the exam. If in doubt, ask the assessment centre staff to explain it to you.

Questions are **displayed on the screen** and answers are entered using keyboard and mouse. At the end of the exam, you are given a certificate showing the result you have achieved.

Do not attempt a CBE until you have **completed all study material** relating to it. **Do not skip any of the material** in the syllabus.

Read each question very carefully.

Double-check your answer before committing yourself to it.

Answer every question – if you do not know an answer, you don't lose anything by guessing. Think carefully before you guess.

With a multiple-choice question, eliminate first those answers that you know are wrong. Then choose the most appropriate answer from those that are left.

Remember that **only one answer to a multiple-choice question can be right**. After you have eliminated the ones that you know to be wrong, if you are still unsure, guess. But only do so after you have double-checked that you have only eliminated answers that are definitely wrong.

Don't panic if you realise you've answered a question incorrectly. Getting one question wrong will not mean the difference between passing and failing.

Study skills and revision guidance

This section aims to give guidance on how to study for your ACCA exams and to give ideas on how to improve your existing study techniques.

Preparing to study

Set your objectives

Before starting to study decide what you want to achieve - the type of pass you wish to obtain. This will decide the level of commitment and time you need to dedicate to your studies.

Devise a study plan

Determine which times of the week you will study.

Split these times into sessions of at least one hour for study of new material. Any shorter periods could be used for revision or practice.

Put the times you plan to study onto a study plan for the weeks from now until the exam and set yourself targets for each period of study - in your sessions make sure you cover the course, course assignments and revision.

If you are studying for more than one paper at a time, try to vary your subjects as this can help you to keep interested and see subjects as part of wider knowledge.

When working through your course, compare your progress with your plan and, if necessary, re-plan your work (perhaps including extra sessions) or, if you are ahead, do some extra revision/practice questions.

Effective studying

Active reading

You are not expected to learn the text by rote, rather, you must understand what you are reading and be able to use it to pass the exam and develop good practice. A good technique to use is SQ3Rs - Survey, Question, Read, Recall, Review:

(1) **Survey the chapter** - look at the headings and read the introduction, summary and objectives, so as to get an overview of what the chapter deals with.

(2) **Question** - whilst undertaking the survey, ask yourself the questions that you hope the chapter will answer for you.

(3) **Read** through the chapter thoroughly, answering the questions and making sure you can meet the objectives. Attempt the exercises and activities in the text, and work through all the examples.

(4) **Recall** - at the end of each section and at the end of the chapter, try to recall the main ideas of the section/chapter without referring to the text. This is best done after a short break of a couple of minutes after the reading stage.

(5) **Review** - check that your recall notes are correct.

You may also find it helpful to re-read the chapter to try to see the topic(s) it deals with as a whole.

Note-taking

Taking notes is a useful way of learning, but do not simply copy out the text. The notes must:

- be in your own words
- be concise
- cover the key points
- be well-organised
- be modified as you study further chapters in this text or in related ones.

Trying to summarise a chapter without referring to the text can be a useful way of determining which areas you know and which you don't.

Three ways of taking notes:

Summarise the key points of a chapter.

Make linear notes - a list of headings, divided up with subheadings listing the key points. If you use linear notes, you can use different colours to highlight key points and keep topic areas together. Use plenty of space to make your notes easy to use.

Try a diagrammatic form - the most common of which is a mind-map. To make a mind-map, put the main heading in the centre of the paper and put a circle around it. Then draw short lines radiating from this to the main sub-headings, which again have circles around them. Then continue the process from the sub-headings to sub-sub-headings, advantages, disadvantages, etc.

Highlighting and underlining

You may find it useful to underline or highlight key points in your study text - but do be selective. You may also wish to make notes in the margins.

Revision

The best approach to revision is to revise the course as you work through it. Also try to leave four to six weeks before the exam for final revision. Make sure you cover the whole syllabus and pay special attention to those areas where your knowledge is weak. Here are some recommendations:

Read through the text and your notes again and condense your notes into key phrases. It may help to put key revision points onto index cards to look at when you have a few minutes to spare.

Review any assignments you have completed and look at where you lost marks - put more work into those areas where you were weak.

Practise exam standard questions under timed conditions. If you are short of time, list the points that you would cover in your answer and then read the model answer, but do try to complete at least a few questions under exam conditions.

Also practise producing answer plans and comparing them to the model answer.

If you are stuck on a topic find somebody (a tutor) to explain it to you.

Read good newspapers and professional journals, especially ACCA's **Student Accountant** - this can give you an advantage in the exam.

Ensure you **know the structure of the exam** - how many questions and of what type you will be expected to answer. During your revision attempt all the different styles of questions you may be asked.

Further reading

You can find further reading and technical articles under the student section of ACCA's website.

1

The business organisation

Chapter learning objectives

Upon completion of this chapter you will be able to:

- define the term organisation
- explain the need for a formal organisation
- distinguish between different types of organisation
- summarise the main areas of responsibility for different functions within an organisation
- explain how different departments co-ordinate their activities
- explain the nature and process of strategic planning
- explain the purpose of each level of organisational management.

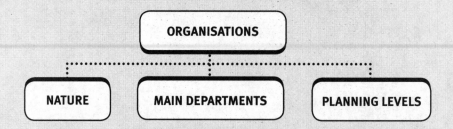

1 The nature of organisations

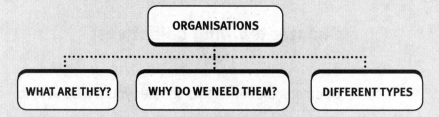

1.1 What is an organisation?

'Organisations are social arrangements for the controlled performance of collective goals.' (**Buchanan and Huczynski**)

The key aspects of this definition are as follows:

- collective goals
- social arrangements
- controlled performance.

Expandable text - defining organisations

As yet there is no widely accepted definition of an organisation. This is because the term can be used broadly in two ways:

- It can refer to a group or institution arranged for efficient work.
- Organisation can also refer to a process, i.e. structuring and arranging the activities of the enterprise or institution to achieve the stated objectives.

There are many types of organisations, which are set up to serve a number of different purposes and to meet a variety of needs, including companies, clubs, schools, hospitals, charities, political parties, governments and the armed forces.

What they all have in common in summarised in the definition given by **Buchanan and Huczynski:**

'Organisations are social arrangements for the controlled performance of collective goals.'

(a) 'Collective goals' – organisations are defined primarily by their goals. A school has the main goal of educating pupils and will be organised differently from a company where the main objective is to make profits.

(b) 'Social arrangements' – someone working on his own does not constitute an organisation. Organisations have structure to enable people to work together towards the common goals. Larger organisations tend to have more formal structures in place but even small organisations will divide up responsibilities between the people concerned.

(c) 'Controlled performance' – organisations have systems and procedures to ensure that goals are achieved. These could vary from ad-hoc informal reviews to complex weekly targets and performance review.

For example, a football team can be described as an organisation because:

- It has a number of players who have come together to play a game.

- The team has an objective (to score more goals than its opponent).

- To do their job properly, the members have to maintain an internal system of control to get the team to work together. In training they work out tactics so that in play they can rely on the ball being passed to those who can score goals.

- Each member of the team is part of the organisational structure and is skilled in a different task: the goalkeeper has more experience in stopping goals being scored than those in the forward line of the team.

- In addition, there must be team spirit, so that everyone works together. Players are encouraged to do their best, both on and off the field.

Test your understanding 1

Which of the following would be considered to be an organisation?

(i) A sole trader

(ii) A tennis club

(iii) A hospital

A (i), (ii) and (iii)

B (i) and (ii) only

C (ii) and (iii) only

D (i) and (iii) only

1.2 Why do we need organisations?

Organisations enable people to:

- share skills and knowledge
- specialise and
- pool resources.

The resulting synergy allows organisations to achieve more than the individuals could on their own.

As the organisation grows it will reach a size where goals, structures and control procedures need to be formalised to ensure that objectives are achieved.

These issues are discussed in further detail below.

Illustration 1 – The nature of organisations

When families set up and run restaurants, they usually do not have to consider formalising the organisation of their business until they have five restaurants. After this stage responsibilities have to be clarified and greater delegation is often required.

Expandable text

Organisations exist primarily because they are more efficient at fulfilling needs than individuals who attempt to cater for all their requirements in isolation and without assistance from others. The main reason for this is the ability that organisations have of being able to employ the techniques of specialisation and the division of labour.

- Specialisation is perhaps the oldest organisational device. It occurs when organisations or individual workers concentrate on a limited type of activity. This allows them to build up a greater level of skill and knowledge than they would if they attempted to be good at everything. The advantage of arranging work in this way lies in the fact that, by concentrating on one type or aspect of work, it is possible to become much more efficient. By concentrating its expertise into a limited range of activities, the organisation plans and arranges its output to achieve the most efficient use of its resources. A key aspect of specialisation involves the division of labour.

- The division of labour developed as industrialisation advanced, and larger organisations became more popular. It was first used in car production at Ford and is associated with the work of Taylor, which we will be discussing later. The car production process was broken down into many separate tasks and each worker was required to specialise in only one small aspect of the total process. This benefits the manufacturer in three ways:
    - Simple tasks encourage the use of highly specific equipment, e.g. power wrenches that speed up the manufacturing operation.
    - Semi-skilled labour can be employed rather than highly skilled operatives.
    - Workers are only responsible for one process and so are able to develop a high level of expertise and increase their output per period.

Modern industrialised economies make great use of specialisation and the division of labour, but for organisations to gain the full benefits of these techniques they also employ another organisational device known as **hierarchy.** We will be examining this further when we discuss the distribution of authority, responsibility and accountability within the organisation.

Test your understanding 2

Suppose you are organising a student ball. What advantages could be gained by forming a committee to manage the process and ultimate event?

1.3 Classifying organisations by profit orientation

Organisations can be classified in many different ways, including the following:

Profit seeking organisations

Some organisations, such as companies and partnerships, see their main objective as maximising the wealth of their owners. Such organisations are often referred to as 'profit seeking'.

The objective of wealth maximisation is usually expanded into three primary objectives:

- to continue in existence (survival)
- to maintain growth and development
- to make a profit.

Not-for-profit organisations

Other organisations do not see profitability as their main objective. Such not-for-profit organisations ('NFPs or NPOs') are unlikely to have financial objectives as primary.

Instead they are seeking to satisfy particular needs of their members or the sectors of society that they have been set up to benefit.

Illustration 2 – NFP organisations

NFPs include the following:

- government departments and agencies (e.g. HM Revenue and Customs)
- schools
- hospitals
- charities (e.g. Oxfam, Red Cross, Red Crescent, Caritas) and
- clubs.

The objectives of NFPs can vary tremendously:

- Hospitals could be said to exist to treat patients.

- Councils often state their 'mission' as caring for their communities.

- A charity may have as its main objective 'to provide relief to victims of disasters and help people prevent, prepare for, and respond to emergencies'.

- Government organisations usually exist to implement government policy.

One specific category of NFPs is a mutual organisation. Mutual organisations are voluntary not-for-profit associations formed for the purpose of raising funds by subscriptions of members, out of which common services can be provided to those members.

Mutual organisations include

- some building societies
- trade unions and
- some working-men's clubs.

Expandable text - financial objectives and constraints in NFPs

Many NPOs view financial matters as constraints under which they have to operate, rather than objectives.

For example,

- Hospitals seek to offer the best possible care to as many patients as possible, subject to budgetary restrictions imposed upon them.

- Councils organise services such as refuse collection, while trying to achieve value for money with residents' council tax.

- Charities may try to alleviate suffering subject to funds raised.

1.4 Classifying organisation by ownership/control

Public sector organisations

The public sector is that part of the economy that is concerned with providing basic government services and is thus controlled by government organisations.

The composition of the public sector varies by country, but in most countries the public sector includes such services as:

- police
- military
- public roads
- public transit
- primary education and
- healthcare for the poor.

Private sector organisations

The private sector, comprising non-government organisations, is that part of a nation's economy that is not controlled by the government.

Illustration 4 – Public sector organisations

This sector thus includes:

- businesses
- charities and
- clubs.

Within these will be profit-seeking and not-for-profit organisations.

Co-operatives

A co-operative is an autonomous association of persons united voluntarily to meet their common economic, social and cultural needs and aspirations through a jointly owned and democratically controlled enterprise.

(The International Co-operative Alliance Statement on the Co-operative Identity, Manchester 1995)

Co-operatives are thus businesses with the following characteristics:

- They are owned and democratically controlled by their members – the people who buy their goods or use their services. They are not owned by investors.

- Co-operatives are organised solely to meet the needs of the member-owners, not to accumulate capital for investors.

Illustration 5 – Retail co-operatives

For example, a retail co-operative could comprise a group of people who join together to increase their buying power to qualify for discounts from retailers when purchasing food.

Expandable text - co-operatives v mutuals

Co-operatives are similar to mutual organisations in the sense that the organisations are also owned by the members/clients that they exist for. However, they tend to deal in primarily tangible goods and services such as agricultural commodities or utilities rather than intangible products such as financial services.

Test your understanding 3

Some building societies have demutualised and become banks with shareholders. Comment on how this may have affected lenders and borrowers.

Test your understanding 4

Which of the following are usually seen as the primary objectives of companies?

    (i)   To maximise the wealth of shareholders

    (ii) To protect the environment

    (iii) To make a profit

A   (i), (ii) and (iii)

B   (i) and (ii) only

C   (ii) and (iii) only

D   (i) and (iii) only

Test your understanding 5

Many schools run fund-raising events such as fêtes, where the intention is to make a profit. This makes them 'profit-seeking'.

True or False?

2 The roles and functions of the main departments in a business organisation

2.1 The main functions within an organisation

The main departments in a business organisation are as follows:

Department	Role	Key concerns
Research and development	• Improving existing products • Developing new products	• Anticipating customer needs • Generating new ideas • Testing • Cost
Purchasing	• Acquiring the goods and services necessary for the business	• Price and payment terms • Quality • Stock levels/delivery schedules
Production	• Converting raw materials into finished goods	• Quality (of materials and finished goods) • Costs • Wastage/efficiency • Stock levels/production schedules
Direct service provision	• Providing services to clients (e.g. accountancy firm)	• Quality • Time sheets/scheduling

Department	Role	Key concerns
Marketing	<ul><li>Identifying customer needs</li><li>Market research</li><li>Product design</li><li>Pricing</li><li>Promotion</li><li>Distribution</li></ul>	<ul><li>Customer needs</li><li>Quality</li><li>Promotional strategy</li><li>Distribution channel strategy</li><li>Pricing strategy</li></ul>
Administration	<ul><li>Administrative support</li><li>Processing transactions</li></ul>	<ul><li>Efficiency</li><li>Information processing</li></ul>
Finance	<ul><li>Bookkeeping</li><li>Financial reporting</li><li>Financial controls</li><li>Budgeting</li><li>The raising of capita</li></ul>	<ul><li>Accuracy and completeness of record keeping</li><li>Monthly management reporting</li><li>Annual financial reporting</li></ul>
Human Resources	<ul><li>Job analysis and job design</li><li>Recruitment and selection</li><li>Performance appraisal</li><li>Rewards (e.g. setting pay)</li><li>Training and development</li><li>Grievances and discipline</li></ul>	<ul><li>Staff competence</li><li>Staff commitment/motivation</li><li>Cost</li><li>Staff welfare (e.g. stress)</li><li>Compliance (e.g. equal opportunities legislation)</li></ul>

Test your understanding 6

Which of the following is not part of the responsibility of a research and development department?

A   Improving existing products.

B   Developing new products.

C   Researching new technologies for application to future products.

D   Researching market demand for products.

2.2 Co-ordination

It is vital that effective co-ordination is achieved between different departments and functions.

The main way this is achieved is through the budget-setting process, e.g. to ensure that production make enough products (subject to stock policies) to meet predicted sales figures from marketing. Both the production and marketing budgets will be based on the same set of assumptions.

Other mechanisms for co-ordination include the following:

- regular planning meetings between the managers
- effective and regular communication between departments to confirm deadlines, target activity levels, etc.
- clear, well-documented reporting lines
- supervision.

Expandable text - Achieving co-ordination

Co-ordination is achieved in one or more of the following ways; the relative complexity of the work affects the method chosen:

- **Standardised work processes** – the work is specified, and everybody works in the same way.

- **Standardised outputs** – through such things as product or service specifications. Whilst the results are standardised, the means are not.

- **Standardised skills and knowledge** – even though each job is performed independently. This is an important co-ordinating mechanism in professional activities and specifies the kind of training needed to perform the work.

- **Direct supervision** – exists throughout the hierarchy where individuals issue instructions and monitor performance. One person has a specific co-ordinating role.

- **Mutual adjustment** – co-ordination results from internal communication and through informal contact between the people performing their organisational roles. This exists in simple structures where people work closely together. It also applies to some complex tasks, e.g. in a research project if the outcome is uncertain, colleagues will adjust their activities in the light of new findings.

Test your understanding 7

An over-keen sales person promises a new product to a major client before production anticipates manufacturing it.

What problems could this cause and how could it have been avoided?

---

3 Strategic, tactical and operational planning levels in the organisation

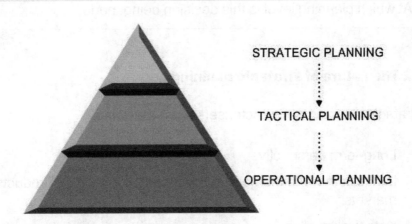

3.1 Different levels of planning

- Strategic planning is long-term, looks at the whole organisation and defines resource requirements.

- Tactical planning is medium-term, looks at the department/ divisional level and specifies how to use resources.

- Operational planning is very short-term, very detailed and is mainly concerned with control.

Strategic plans will have to be translated into medium-term tactical plans, which in turn need to be converted into detailed performance targets and budgets.

Illustration 6 – Strategic, tactical and operational planning

The above planning levels could be applied to a farmer as follows:

- Strategic planning would look at deciding which crops should be grown and how much land should be allocated for crops, livestock, etc. These decisions would be based on consumer trends, the actions of competitors, changes in EU Common Agricultural Policy, etc.

- Tactical planning would then look at how best to use specified resources such as fields. This would include issues such as crop rotation.

- Operational planning would include organising extra staff for harvesting, etc.

Test your understanding 8

A hospital is considering whether to have specialist wards or multi-disciplinary wards.

At which planning level is this decision being made

3.2 The nature of strategic planning

Strategic planning is characterised by the following:

- Long-term perspective.

- Looks at the whole organisation as well as individual products and markets.

- Sets the direction of the whole organisation and integrates its activities.

- Considers the views of all stakeholders, not just the shareholders' perspective.

- Analyses the organisation's resources and defines resource requirements.

- Relates the organisation to its environments.

- Looks at gaining a sustainable competitive advantage.

3.3 The strategic planning process

The rational approach to strategic planning breaks down the process into three distinct steps.

1 Strategic analysis – three key areas

- External analysis of markets, competitors, the business environment, etc. to identify opportunities and threats.

- Internal analysis of the firm's resources, competences, etc. to identify strengths and weaknesses.

- Stakeholder analysis – to understand stakeholder expectations/influence in order to clarify objectives and define the mission of the organisation.

2 Strategic choice – again three key angles to consider

- What is the basis of our strategy? In particular how are we going to compete – high quality, low costs?

- Where do we want to compete? Which markets, countries, products?

- How do we want to get there? Organic growth, acquisition or some joint arrangement such as franchising?

3 Strategic implementation

- Once determined, the long-term strategy needs to be translated into plans for marketing, human resources management, IT, production, organisational structure, etc.

- The strategy may involve major changes so these will also have to be managed.

Test your understanding 9

Give three strategic issues that should be considered by the headmaster of a school as part of strategic analysis.

Chapter summary

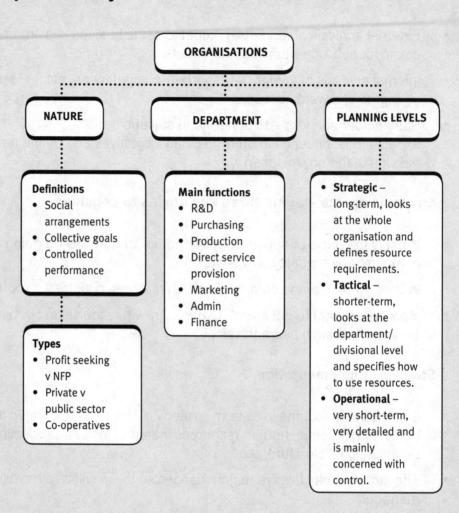

ORGANISATIONS

NATURE

DEPARTMENT

PLANNING LEVELS

Definitions
- Social arrangements
- Collective goals
- Controlled performance

Types
- Profit seeking v NFP
- Private v public sector
- Co-operatives

Main functions
- R&D
- Purchasing
- Production
- Direct service provision
- Marketing
- Admin
- Finance

- **Strategic** – long-term, looks at the whole organisation and defines resource requirements.
- **Tactical** – shorter-term, looks at the department/ divisional level and specifies how to use resources.
- **Operational** – very short-term, very detailed and is mainly concerned with control.

Test your understanding answers

Test your understanding 1

C

A sole trader would normally be someone working on their own, so there would be no collective goals.

Test your understanding 2

The committee would give the following benefits:

- It would help overcome your limitations by pooling knowledge, ideas and expertise.
- It would enable individuals to specialise in particular roles.
- It would save time through joint effort.
- It would enable synergy to be gained.
- It would satisfy social needs.

All these should result in a more successful ball.

Test your understanding 3

Mutual building societies exist for the benefit of their members. This is reflected in setting:

- interest rates for borrowers as low as possible
- interest rates for savers as high as possible.

The aim is not to make a profit so the borrowing and saving rates are moved as close as possible with a small margin sufficient to cover costs.

Once it becomes a bank the building society must then seek to maximise shareholder wealth and become profit seeking. This is done by increasing borrowing rates and reducing saving rates.

Members will thus find that the terms offered by the building society become less attractive.

However, when demutualising most building societies give their members windfalls of shares so members become shareholders, thus benefiting from dividends and share price increases.

Test your understanding 4

D

While protecting the environment is to be encouraged and is reinforced within statute to some degree, it is not a primary objective of the company. Companies exist primarily to maximise the return to its owners.

Test your understanding 5

False

Schools run fund-raising activities to help pay for extra books, e.g. to improve the quality of education given to pupils. The primary objective is educational, not profit. The money made at the fête is thus a means not an end.

KAPLAN PUBLISHING

Test your understanding 6

D

Demand would be assessed by a market research function within the marketing department.

Test your understanding 7

The problems this will cause are:

- either the firm will let down its major customer, with resulting loss of goodwill and impact on future orders or
- the firm will incur extra costs to advance production to meet the deadline set.

This could have been avoided by the following:

- better communication between sales and production
- ensuring that sales staff are briefed by their supervisor regarding delivery and production schedules
- having an IT system where all sales staff can verify stock and anticipated production times before confirming orders.

Test your understanding 8

Tactical – the issue is how best to use existing resources (i.e. wards).

Test your understanding 9

Strategic issues could include the following:

Internal analysis

- Review of Ofsted reports to identify areas for improvement.
- Review of government league tables.
- An assessment of each member of staff to identify strengths and weaknesses.
- A review of assets, including buildings and equipment.

External analysis

- Local birth rates to anticipate likely future student numbers.
- Numbers of graduates going into teaching to anticipate future supply of teachers.
- Proposed government legislation relating to schools, e.g. funding.

Stakeholder analysis

- Feedback from PTA groups and other parent groups.
- Feedback from school governors.

Organisational structure

Chapter learning objectives

Upon completion of this chapter you will be able to:

- explain the different ways in which an organisation might be structured
- list advantages and disadvantages of each type of organisational arrangement
- define the terms scalar chain and span of control
- what factors influence the span of control
- give reasons why ownership and management of the organisation are often separated
- explain what is meant by tall and flat organisational structure
- explain what is meant by centralised/decentralised structure
- list advantages and disadvantages of centralised/decentralised structure
- explain the nature of the 'informal organisation'
- what are the advantages and disadvantages of the informal organisation
- identify what impact the informal organisation has on the business
- how can managers foster the benefits of the informal organisation while at the same time reducing its potential disadvantages.

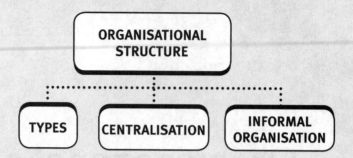

1 Organisational structure

1.1 Different types of structure

Definition

Organisation structure is concerned with the way in which work is divided up and allocated, and how coordination to achieve objectives is achieved.

It outlines the roles and responsibilities of individuals and groups within an organisation.

A typical pattern of structural change can be represented by the following sequence.

Entrepreneurial

- This type of structure is built around the owner manager and is typical of small companies in the early stages of their development.

- The entrepreneur often has specialist knowledge of the product or service

- Example owner/managed business

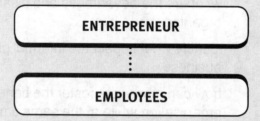

Advantages	Disadvantages
• Fast decision making. • More responsive to market. • Goal congruence • Good control. • Close bond to workforce.	• Lack of career structure. • Dependant on the capabilities of the manager/owner • Cannot cope with diversification/growth.

Expandable text - advantages and disadvantages of

Advantages

- There is only one person taking decisions – this should lead to decisions being made quickly.

- As soon as an element of the market alters, the entrepreneur should recognise it and act quickly.

- A lack of a chain of command and the small size of the organisation should mean that the entrepreneur has control over the workforce and all decisions within the organisation leading to better goal congruence.

Disadvantages

- This type of structure is usually suited to small companies where due to the size; there is no career path for the employees.

- If the organisation grows, one person will not be able to cope with the increased volume of decisions etc.

Functional structure

- This type of structure is common in organisations that have outgrown the entrepreneurial structure and now organise the business on a functional basis.

- It is most appropriate to small companies which have few products and locations and which exist in a relatively stable environment.

- For example a business making one type of electrical component for use in a car manufacturing company.

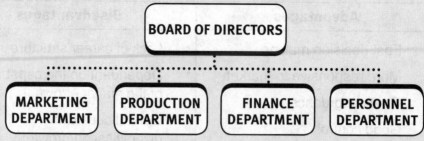

Advantages	Disadvantages
• Economies of scale.	• Empire building.
• Standardisation.	• Slow.
• Specialists more comfortable.	• Conflicts between functions.
• Career opportunities.	• Cannot cope with diversification.

Expandable text - advantages and disadvantages of functional

Advantages

- This organisational structure relates to an organisation which has outgrown the entrepreneurial stage. Rather than duplicating roles in different parts of the company, similar activities are grouped together so leading to:
    - lower costs
    - standardisation of output/systems, etc.
    - people with similar skills being grouped together and so not feeling isolated.

- Due to the larger size of the organisation and the grouping into functions, there is a career path for employees – they can work their way up through the function.

Disadvantages

- Managers of the functions may try to make decisions to increase their own power/be in the best interest of their function rather that work in the best interest of the company overall, leading to empire building and conflicts between the functions.

- Due to the longer chain of command, decisions will be made more slowly.

- This style of structure is not suited to an organisation which is rapidly growing and diversifying – the specialists in for example the production function would not be able to cope with making gas fires and radios.

Product/Division/Department

- Organisation structured in accordance with product lines or divisions or departments.

- They are headed by general managers who enjoy responsibility for their own resources.

- Divisions are likely to be seen as profit centres and may be seen as strategic business units for planning and control purposes.

- Some departments, e.g. accounts will be centralised.

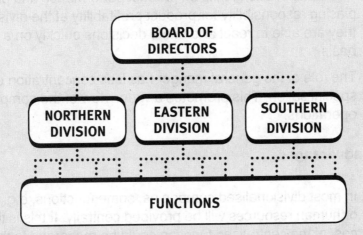

Advantages	Disadvantages
• Enables growth.	• Potential loss of control.
• Clear responsibility for products/divisions.	• Lack of goal congruence.
• Training of general managers.	• Duplication.
• Easily adapted for further diversification.	• Specialists may feel isolated.
• Top management free to concentrate on strategic matters.	• Allocation of central costs can be a problem.

 Expandable text - advantages and disadvantages of divisional

Advantages

- If an organisation wants to grow and diversify, the functional structure cannot cope, so instead the divisional structure should be adopted. Should the company want to diversify further, it is easy to 'bolt on' another division.

- It encourages growth and diversity of products, e.g. by adding additional flavours etc to capture other segments of the market. This in turn promotes the use of specialised equipment and facilities.

- Due to the break down of the company's activities into the divisions, it should mean that the divisional managers can clearly see where their area of responsibility lies and it should leave the top management free to concentrate on strategic matters, rather than to get involved in the day to day operations of each division – although this can lead to a lack of control over the activities of the division and possible lack of goal congruence.

- The focus of attention is on product performance and profitability. By placing responsibility for product profitability at the division level, they are able to react and make decisions quickly on a day to day basis.

- The role of the general manger has less concentration upon specialisation. This promotes a wider view of the company's operations.

Disadvantages

- In most divisionalised companies, some functions, e.g. accounting or human resources will be provided centrally. If this is the case, the cost of the centralised function could be recharged to those divisions using e.g. the human resource function. There are different ways of calculating the recharge and divisional managers may complain if the profitability of their division is reduced by an amount that they perceive as being arbitrary.

Geographically structured

- Grouping activities on the basis of location.
- Common in organisations that operate over a wide geographic area.
- Often, some departments e.g. accounts will be centralised.
- For example Kaplan.

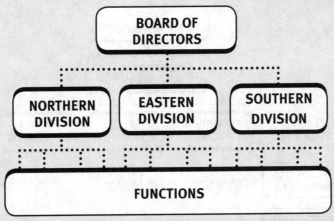

Advantages	Disadvantages
• Enables geographic growth. • Clear responsibility for areas. • Training of general managers. • Top management free to concentrate on strategic matters.	• As for divisional structure above.

Expandable text - product v geographic divisional structure

Product divisionalisation is generally preferred over say geographic divisionalisation when the product is relatively complex and requires a high cost of capital equipment, skilled operators, etc., e.g. the car industry.

Matrix

- A matrix structure aims to combine the benefits of decentralisation (e.g. speedy decision making) with those of co-ordination (achieving economies and synergies across all business units, territories and products).

- It usually requires employees from various departments to form a group to achieve a specific target.

- They require dual reporting to managers and the diagram shows a mix of product and functional structures.

- For example in a university, a lecturer may have to report to both subject and department heads.

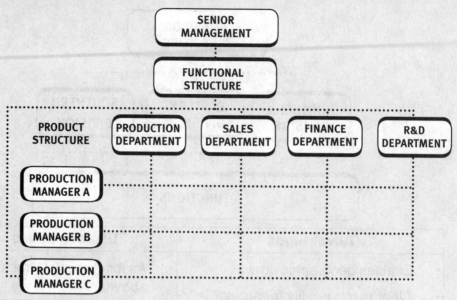

Advantages	Disadvantages
• Advantages of both functional and divisional structures. • Flexibility. • Customer orientation. • Encourage teamwork and the exchange of opinions and expertise	• Dual command and conflict. • Dilution of functional authority. • Time-consuming meetings. • Higher admin costs.

Expandable text - advantages and disadvantages of matrix

Advantages

- In todays rapidly changing environment, there is a need for effective coordination in very complex situations. If a car manufacturer wants to design, produce and market a new model, the process involves most parts of the organisation and a flexible/adaptable system is needed to achieve the objectives. The more rigid structure experienced in a divisional company would not have the flexibility to be able to coordinate the tasks and the people, whereas the matrix structrure can cope.

- The production managers could be replaced with customer managers, in which case the whole team will be focussed on meeting the needs of the customer.

Disadvantages

- Where the matrix structure can cause difficulty is in the lines of control. These may become ambiguous and conflict with each other. A team member may be answerable to the product manager **and** to a functional head, and this may cause confusion and stress. Time consuming meetings may be required to resolve the conflict, so resulting in higher administration costs.

Test your understanding 1

Food plc is a company that manufactures dried packet and tinned soups and tinned vegetables and is about to start making specialist soups for sale in small delicatessens as hot, healthy 'food on the go'. They have recently recruited a specialist from 'Gourmet Soups' to help them with their new venture. The packet and tinned soups are sold to 2 major supermarkets, the tinned vegetables to many outlets. Design an organisational structure for Food plc.

1.2 Further aspects of organisational structure

Ownership and management of larger organisations are often separated. One of the main reasons for this is that the managers do not have access to sufficient funds and therefore they rely on banks and the market (the owners) to provide the investment.

In order to ensure that managers are managing the business in the best interests of the owners, many safeguards/controls etc are put in place, which will lead to for example formal organisational structures being set up for an organisation.

The divorce of ownership and management (control) is dealt with in more detail in chapter 16.

Test your understanding 2

In a small company there is usually a divorce of ownership and control. True or false?

Scalar chain

This is defined as the line of authority which can be traced up or down the chain of command, and thus relates to the number of management levels within and organisation.

Span of control

A manager's span of control is the number of people for whom he or she is directly responsible.

Test your understanding 3

The scalar chain relates to the number of people over whom a manager has authority. True or false?

A tall structure has many managerial levels (hierarchies) and a 'narrow' span of control.

A flat structure has few managerial levels and a 'wide' span of control.

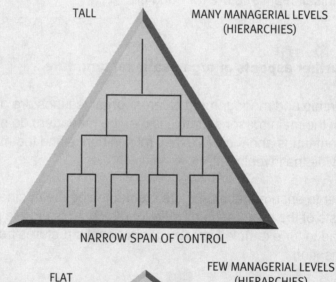

TALL — MANY MANAGERIAL LEVELS (HIERARCHIES)

NARROW SPAN OF CONTROL

FLAT — FEW MANAGERIAL LEVELS (HIERARCHIES)

WIDE SPAN OF CONTROL

> **Test your understanding 4**
>
> If a managerial structure has many levels of management, is it likely to have a narrow or wide span of control at each level of management?

The factors that influence the span of control include:

- nature of the work – the more repetitive the work, the wider the span of control
- type of personnel – the better managers and personnel are, the wider the span of control
- location of personnel – the more widely spread the personnel the narrower the span of control.

> **Test your understanding 5**
>
> What other factors could influence the span of control within an organisation?

> **Test your understanding 6**
>
> Haulage is an established haulage company operating nationwide, specialising in moving pallets. It has three levels of employee: directors, managers and drivers and its organisation chart shows a corresponding three tier structure. What factors will influence the span of control of the managers?

1.3 Centralisation and decentralisation

Another method of analysing structures is by reference to the level at which decisions are made.

- In a centralised structure, the upper levels of an organisation's hierachy retain the authority to make decisions.
- In a decentralised structure the authority to take decisions is passed down to units and people at lower levels.

The factors that will affect the amount of decentralisation are:

- Management style.
- Ability of management/employees.
- Locational spread.

- Size of the organisation/scale of activities.

Test your understanding 7

A multi national company is likely to have a _____ structure.

Fill in the blank with:

- centralised, or
- decentralised

Test your understanding 8

How does the ability of the employees affect the level of decentralisation?

The advantages and disadvantages of decentralisation are:

Advantages	Disadvantages
• Senior management free to concentrate on strategy. • Better local decisions due to local expertise. • Better motivation due to increased training and career path. • Quicker responses/flexibility, due to smaller chain of command.	• Loss of control by senior management. • Dysfunctional decisions due to a lack of goal congruence. • Poor decisions made by inexperienced managers. • Training costs. • Duplication of roles within the organisation. • Extra costs in obtaining information.

Test your understanding 9

A company has found in a recent survey that their staff are demotivated as they are bored and not using all the skills they have been given. Should the company consider increasing or decreasing the level of centralisation in the company?

Test your understanding 10

A disadvantage of decentralisation can be increased costs. How can these arise?

Handy's Shamrock

In modern business environments there has been an increasing trend towards workforce flexibility. This can include

- **Functional** flexibility so employees can be redeployed to other tasks if necessary - e.g. through multi-skilling

- **Numerical** flexibility to adjust the number of employees to match fluctuations in demand

- **Temporal** flexibility to match employees' work patterns with demand - e.g. through having some workers "on call".

One way for achieving numerical flexibility is described by **Handy's shamrock**

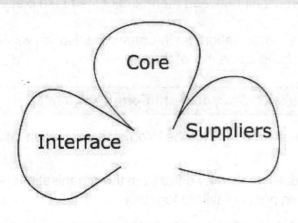

- *core emloyees* who have critical and scarce skills - they deliver the core competencies of the firm. They receive good promotion, security and status prospects relative to others and are often managers, team leaders, professional staff, skilled technicians and skilled employees.

  These workers are becoming increasing less dominant.

- *Interface workers (flexible labour force)* are low skilled and form a buffer in relation to fluctuations in demand. These include temporary, part-time, seasonal and standby staff.

- *Suppliers (contractual fringe)* such as contractors, temporary and self-employed staff with the general skills needed. Many are created by contracting out, a process where the firm trims headcounts and then re-employs them as consultants on more flexible hours.

Handy also considered adding "customers" as a fourth leaf because in many service organisations custoemrs are asked to do some of the work (e.g. filling in forms, self-service).However, he decided to exclude them as they are not paid by the organisation and so cannot be considered part of the formal structure.

1.4 The informal organisation and its relationship with the formal organisation

So far, we have been looking at formal organisational structures - they have been designed by management to try and ensure that an organisation can meet its goals

We now look at the informal organisation. This organisation evolves over time and is a network of relationships that exist within an organisation. The relationships arise due to common interests or friendships. These relationships can be across divisions and it is through these relationships that daily interactions between members of staff take place.

Within a formal organisation, an informal organisation will be present and all organisations have some mix of the two.

Expandable text - Reasons for informal organisation

There are many reasons for the informal organisation, including.

- individuals' goals may differ from the organisations – workers with the same goals gravitate together.

- personal relationships may arise between individuals.

- a group of individuals may share common interests, e.g. football and so form an informal group.

- certain members of the organisation may be natural leaders and so lead a group, even though they have no formal managerial place.

- workers find new ways of doing things which save them time.

Test your understanding 11

Informal relationships are shown on organisational charts. True or false?

The advantages and disadvantages of informal organisation are:

Advantages	Disadvantages
• better motivation • better communication	• inefficient organisations • opposition to change can be intensified • the 'grapevine effect'

Expandable text - advantages and disadvantages of informal

Advantages

- If managers can work with the informal groups within their department, there should be higher levels of motivation and productivity.

- Interdivisional communication should be better through the informal network. This could lead to increased innovation which should help the company succeed.

Disadvantages

- If the formal structure is in conflict with the informal structure, the organisation may end up being inefficient at meeting its objectives. This can arise due to, e.g. formal lines of communication being blocked as informal lines of communication are more efficient and become more important.

- If managers try to implement change, they may find opposition from not only the formal but also the informal organisation e.g. change in one division, may lead to company wide unrest as word of the changes spread through the informal network, and other divisions start to be concerned that 'they will be next' (the grapevine effect).

Test your understanding 12

Social relationships within an organisation can be across divisions. True or false?

1.5 The impact of the informal organisation on the business

The informal organisation can either enhance or hold back the business. Managers need to be aware of the informal structure and ensure that they

- adapt the formal structure to complement the informal one
- maintain a looser formal structure so that the informal structure can thrive.
- at the very least take account of the informal structure in decision making.

Expandable Text

If a manufacturing department has split itself into two informal 'cliques' and output is in decline, the declining output could have nothing to do with the formal structure, but be due to lack of integration of the whole division due to the cliques. Rather than changing the formal structure, management could for example mix members of the two 'cliques' on training courses, and so try and reduce the impact of the informal organisation.

In his studies at the Hawthorne works of the Western Electric Company in Chicago between 1924 and 1927, Elton Mayo concluded that informal groups exercised strong social controls over workers' habits and attitudes, e.g. an individual productivity bonus scheme failed as workers were unwilling to show up their less capable colleagues.

Test your understanding 13

What other methods could be employed to integrate a department and reduce the impact of the informal organisation as in the last example above?

Chapter summary

```
                    ┌─────────────────┐ ········· ┌──────────────┐
                    │  ORGANISATIONAL │          │  INFORMAL    │
                    │    STRUCTURE    │          │ ORGANISATION │
                    └─────────────────┘          └──────────────┘
           ┌──────────────┬──────────────┐
   ┌──────────────┐  ┌──────────┐  ┌──────────────┐
   │   TYPES OF   │  │ ASPECTS  │  │ CENTRALISED / │
   │  STRUCTURE   │  │          │  │ DECENTRALISED │
   └──────────────┘  └──────────┘  └──────────────┘
```

- Enterpreneurial
- Functional/Department
- Divisional/Product
- Geographical
- Matrix

Divorce of
ownership
and control

Scaler
chain/span
of control

Test your understanding answers

Test your understanding 1

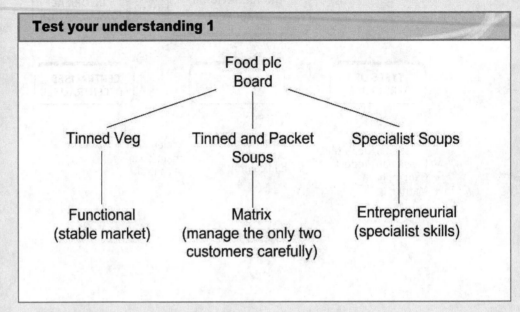

Test your understanding 2

False – They tend to be owner managed

Test your understanding 3

False

Test your understanding 4

Narrow

Test your understanding 5

Other factors could include:

Management style

Level of organisational support for routine tasks

The nature of the work

Test your understanding 6

The work of the drivers is not particularly complex and drivers will not need much guidance

Modern technology means that meetings between managers and drivers will not often be necessary.

Each manager will have a wide span of control.

Test your understanding 7

Decentralised

Test your understanding 8

The more able the employees, the more decisions they can be entrusted with, and the greater the level of decentralisation.

Test your understanding 9

Decreasing

Test your understanding 10

Poor decisions/lack of goal congruence, leading to increased costs.

Training costs

Duplication of roles leading to increased personnel costs

Extra costs of gathering information form various sources/locations

Test your understanding 11

False

Test your understanding 12

True

Test your understanding 13

Methods could include:

Away days, ensuring that teams for the activities are picked with members from both cliques.

Change shift patterns so that the cliques are broken up on the production line.

Change break times, so that one 'clique' does not take its break together.

3

Organisational culture

Chapter learning objectives

Upon completion of this chapter you will be able to:

- define the term organisational culture
- identify the components of organisational culture
- what factors influence the company culture
- describe Schein's approach to organisational culture
- describe Handy's four cultural types
- describe how organisational culture is influenced by national cultures using the Hofstede approach.

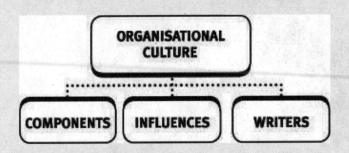

1 Defining organisational culture

1.1 Definition

Culture is expressed by **Handy** as being: 'the way we do things around here'. By this **Handy** means the sum total of the belief, knowledge, attitudes, norms and customs that prevail in an organisation.

- Organisations have distinctive cultures, and behaviour acceptable in one organisational culture may be inappropriate in another – think about the different cultures in the different accountancy firms.

- Also cultures develop over time or can change instantly as a result of a single major event, e.g. death of company founder, threatened takeover, etc.

1.2 Components of culture

The key elements of organisational culture are:

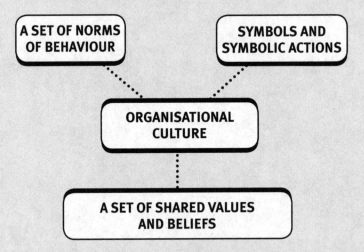

- Norms guide people's behaviour, suggesting what is or is not appropriate (the 'done thing'.) - e.g. informal dress codes

- Symbols or symbolic action, e.g. rituals such as buying the office a cake on your birthday.

- Beliefs underlie the culture by identifying what is important, e.g. a belief in the importance of people as individuals.

2 The factors that shape the culture of the organisation

The six major influences on the culture of an organisation are as follows:

- Size
- Technology
- Diversity
- Age
- History
- Ownership

Expandable text - the main factors that shape culture

- **Size** – How large is the organisation – in terms of turnover, physical size, employee numbers?

- **Technology**– How technologically advanced is the organisation – either in terms of its product, or its productive processes?

- **Diversity** – How diverse is the company – either in terms of product range, geographical spread or cultural make-up of its stakeholders?

- **Age** – How old is the business or the managers of the business – do its strategic level decision makers have experience to draw upon?

- **History** – What worked in the past? Do decision makers have past successes to draw upon; are they willing to learn from their mistakes?

- **Ownership** – Is the organisation owned by a sole trader? Are there a small number of institutional shareholders or are there large numbers of small shareholders?

Expandable text - other influences on culture

There are other, more subtle influences.

- The degree of individual initiative – is it encouraged or are decisions always referred upwards?

- The degree of risk tolerance – are managers only allowed to follow low-risk strategies?

- Clarity of direction – is there a clear focus; are these clear objectives and performance expectations?

- The degree of integration between groups – are different units encouraged to work together? Are management aloof or approachable; is communication clear to lower level staff?

- The reward system – are individuals rewarded for succeeding, i.e. are rewards based on performance criteria?

- Conflict tolerance – are employees encouraged to air grievances?

- Communication patterns – is there a formal hierarchy or an informal network?

- Formalisation of clothing and office layout – are there strict rules over this?

- The kind of people employed (graduates, young, old, etc.).

3 Writers on culture

There are three writers you need to have knowledge of: **Schein**, **Handy** and **Hofstede.**

3.1 Schein

Schein argues that the first leaders of a company create the culture of an organisation. Once the culture exists, the attributes/criteria for the later leaders are determined by the culture. Thus the link between culture and leadership is very strong.

Schein further commented that it if leaders are to lead, it is essential that they understand the culture of the organisation. In order to try and define culture, **Schein** described three levels:

- **Artefacts** – these are the aspects of culture that can be easily seen, e.g. the way that people dress.

- **Espoused values** – these are the strategies and goals of an organisation, including company slogans etc.

- **Basic assumptions and values** – these are difficult to identify as they are unseen, and exist mainly at the unconscious level.

New employees find the last level of culture the most difficult to understand, and lack of understanding of the basic values is one of the main contributors to failure when trying to implement change.

Test your understanding 1

Schein said that leadership and culture were totally divorced from one another. True or false?

Test your understanding 2

State three aspects of culture that could be classified as artifacts.

3.2 Handy

Handy popularised four cultural types.

- **Power** culture (denoted by the Greek god "Zeus") - Here there is one major source of power and influence. For example, in a small owner-managed business the owner may strive to maintain absolute control over subordinates. There may be few procedures and rules of a formal kind as staff take direction directly from the owner.

- **Role** culture (denoted by the Greek god "Apollo") - In this version of culture, people describe their job by its duties, not by its purpose, so job descriptions dictate "the way we do things around here". This would be seen in a bureaucratic organisation, where the structure determines the authority and responsibility of individuals and there is a strong emphasis on hierarchy and status.

- **Task** culture (denoted by the Greek god "Athena") - The emphasis here is on achieving the particular task at hand and staff may need to be flexible to ensure deadlines are met. People thus describe their positions in terms of the results they are achieving. Nothing is allowed to get in the way of task accomplishment. This is best seen in projects teams that exists for a specific task.

- **Person** culture (denoted by the Greek god "Dionysius") - This is characterised by the fact it exists to satisfy the requirements of the particular individual(s) involved in the organisation. The person culture is to be found in a small, highly participatory organisation where individuals undertake all the duties themselves, for example, a barrister in chambers.

Test your understanding 3

Describe what **Handy** meant by a task culture. Can you think of two disadvantages this may create for an organisation?

3.3 Hofstede

Hofstede looked for national differences between over 100,000 of IBM's employees in different parts of the world, in an attempt to find aspects of culture that might influence business behaviour.

He found five traits or cultural dimensions:

- **Individualism (vs. collectivism)** – looks at the extent to which people are integrated into groups. Some cultures are more cohesive than others. e.g. Anglo Saxon cultures are generally more individualistic than the collectivist cultures of South America.

- **Uncertainty avoidance index** – deals with a society's tolerance for uncertainty and ambiguity - e.g. France and Japan use bureaucracy to reduce uncertainty because they dislike it.

- **Power distance index** – the extent to which the less powerful members of organizations and institutions (like the family) accept and expect that power is distributed unequally. e.g. In South American societies, differences in power were tolerated more than in North European cultures.

- **Masculinity (vs. femininity)** – a masculine culture is one where the distinction between the roles and values of the genders is large and the males focus on work, power and success (e.g. in Japanese culture) whereas in feminine cultures such as Finland, the differences between the gender roles is much smaller.

- **Long term orientation (based on Confucianism dynamism)** – values associated with Long Term Orientation (e.g. China) are thrift and perseverance; values associated with Short Term Orientation (e.g. Germany) are respect for tradition, fulfilling social obligations and protecting one's 'face'.

Test your understanding 4

Looking at the **Hofstede** traits, choose the classification that most closely fits Great Britain.

Individualistic or collective?

Large power distance or small?

Masculine or feminine roles?

Chapter summary

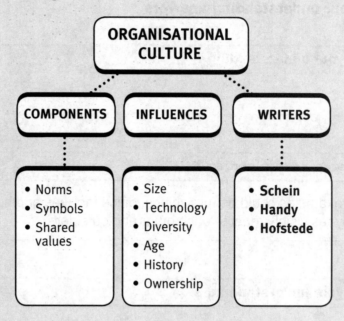

ORGANISATIONAL CULTURE

COMPONENTS
- Norms
- Symbols
- Shared values

INFLUENCES
- Size
- Technology
- Diversity
- Age
- History
- Ownership

WRITERS
- **Schein**
- **Handy**
- **Hofstede**

Test your understanding answers

Test your understanding 1

False

Test your understanding 2

Other examples could be furnishings, office facilities and how employees visibly react to each other and outsiders.

Test your understanding 3

A task culture is one where nothing is allowed to get in the way of completing the task.

Disadvantages could be:

- high levels of stress
- quality compromised in an effort to get the job finished on time
- people feeling that their individual needs are surpassed by the needs of the task, e.g. feeling pressurised to work late.

Test your understanding 4

Although the points can be debated, and the culture is changing, Great Britain probably:

Individualistic

Small power distance

Masculine roles

KAPLAN PUBLISHING

4

Leadership, management and supervision

Chapter learning objectives

Upon completion of this chapter you will be able to:

- define the term leadership

- define the term management

- define the term supervision

- explain the difference between a leader and a manager

- distinguish between the role of the manager and the role of a supervisor

- explain the classical approach to management using theories of **Fayol and Taylor**

- explain the main duties of a manager according to **Fayol**

- outline the relevance of classical approach to modern data practices

- explain the nature of the human relations school – **Mayo**

- describe the modern school of management with reference to the theories of **Mintzberg** and **Drucker**

- describe the three managerial roles as per work of **H Mintzberg**

- explain what is meant by authority

- explain what is meant by the term responsibility

- identify the main sources of authority

- explain the relationship between authority and responsibility

- summarise the trait theory of leadership

- explain the situational approach to leadership using **Adairs's** theory

- explain the contingency approach using **Fiedler's** leadership theory

- explain the differences between transactional and transformational leadership referring to the **Bennis** theory

- describe the phases of the change process referring to **Kotter** theory

- explain the **Heifetz** leadership theory

- explain the five scores on the **Blake** and **Mouton** managerial grid

- outline the usefulness of the Blake and Mouton grid

- describe the four leadership styles as per **Ashridge.**

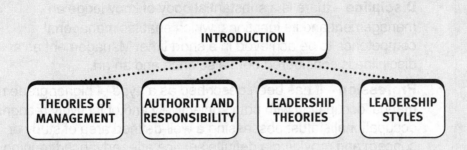

1 Introduction

1.1 Leadership

A basic definition of a leader is 'someone who exercises influence over other people'. This can be expanded into a more complex definition: 'Leadership is an interpersonal influence directed toward the achievement of a goal or goals'.

- Interpersonal – between people.
- Influence – the power to affect others.
- Goal – something that we need/want to achieve.

Leadership is a conscious activity and is concerned with setting goals and inspiring people to provide commitment to achieve the organisation's goals.

1.2 Managers

All managers have in common the overall aim of getting things done, delegating to other people rather than doing everything themselves.

Management can be defined as 'the effective use and co-ordination of resources such as capital, plant, materials and labour to achieve defined objectives with maximum efficiency'.

Expandable text - what is management?

Management can be considered as a:

- **Function** – the responsibility for directing and running an organisation.
- **Process** – it incorporates activities by which internal and external resources are combined to achieve the objectives of the organisation. These resources include people, money, machines and materials.

- **Discipline** – there is a substantial body of knowledge on management and its functions, which enables managerial competence to be achieved in a short time. Management as a discipline is considered both a science and an art.

- **Profession** – it has been described as a 'type of higher grade non-manual occupation with both subjectively and objectively recognised occupational status; possessing a well-defined area of study or concern and providing a definite service after advanced training and education'.

A leader can be a manager, but a manager is not necessarily a leader. If a manager is able to influence people to achieve the goals of the organisation, without using formal authority to do so, then the manager is demonstrating leadership.

Illustration 1 – Differences between managers and leaders

The manager administers; the leader innovates.

The manager relies on control; the leader inspires trust.

The manager has his eye on the bottom line; the leader has his eye on the horizon.

1.3 Supervision

The supervisor is part of the management team.

- The supervisor is a person given authority for planning and controlling the work of their group, but all they can delegate to the group is the work itself.

- A supervisor, therefore, is a type of manager whose main role is to ensure that specified tasks are performed correctly and efficiently by a defined group of people.

- In general, supervisors will also be doing operations work and giving advice to others to help solve problems. If the more senior manager is absent, the supervisor will take over the role.

Illustration 2 – The role of a supervisor

Supervisors divide their time between supervisory duties and a detailed task. For example a supervisor in purchasing may also regularly complete some clerical work like raising purchase orders.

Managers must ensure that supervisors understand organisational objectives and communicate the power and limits of the supervisor's authority. Supervision is an important part of the task and process of management.

The role of the supervisor requires direct contact with and responsibility for the work of others.

- The supervisor is the interface between the management and the workforce.
- Front line – resolving problems first hand where the work is done, and often having to resolve problems quickly.
- They often need to have direct knowledge of employment legislation.
- Often have responsibility for negotiation and industrial relations within the department.
- Management tasks and operational work to perform.
- Day-to-day detailed internal information (manager – medium-term internal and external information).

Test your understanding 1

Briefly explain in general terms the responsibilities of a supervisor.

2 Theories of management
2.1 The classical school

Both **Taylor and Fayol** shared the belief that individuals must subordinate themselves to the needs of the organisation. In return the organisation was obliged to provide job security and good remuneration.

- **Taylor and Fayol** believed in 'one best way', the optimum way to:
  - organise the firm
  - do the individual job
- emphasis on the task to be done rather that the person doing it.
- some of the main features of their approach were as follows:
  - belief in one controlling central authority
  - specialisation of tasks
  - fair pay and good working conditions, decided by management
  - clear lines of command.

Illustration 3 – Theories and management

Scientific thinking on motivation in the workplace included a belief that reward for effort was a key consideration.

Test your understanding 2

Which of the following statements best describes the classical approach to management?

A   No one best approach.

B   Communication should be encouraged.

C   One best approach.

D   An employee is considered an input to the organisational system.

Fayol argued that management may be split into five broads areas: forecasting and planning, organisation, command, co-ordination and control.

Forecasting & Planning
- Set objectives
- Evaluation & choice of action to reach objectives

Control
- Setting targets
- Measure the outcomes and compare with target
- Taking remedial action to deal with divergences of actual from target performance

Co-ordination
- Ensure all staff are working towards common goals (goal congrunce)

THE MANAGER ACCORDING TO FAYOL

Organisation
- Divide the work into tasks and projects
- Appoint subordinates responsible for each element of work
- Ensure staff have the necessary skills and resources they need

Command
- Give instructions to subordinates to carry out the task
- Delegate authority to subordinates so that they can command others

Expandable text - Fayol's rules of managerial conduct

Fayol applied 14 rules of managerial conduct. These are:

- **Division of work** – to improve practice and familiarity and become specialised.
- **Authority** – the right to give orders, linked with responsibility.
- **Discipline** – respect in accordance with the agreement between the firm and its employees.
- **Unity of command** – each subordinate answerable to only one superior.
- **Unity of direction** – only a single head and plan for a set of activities.
- **Subordination to the general interest** – the general good prevails over individual or sectional interests.
- **Remuneration** – should be fair to both the recipient and the firm.
- **Centralisation** – inevitable in organisations, but the degree should be appropriate.
- **Scalar chain** – graduated lines of authority should exist from the top to the bottom of the organisation.
- **Order** – workers and materials should be in their prescribed place.
- **Equity** – combining clemency with justice.
- **Tenure of personnel** – adequate time for settling into jobs should be allowed.
- **Initiative** – should be encouraged within the boundaries of authority and discipline.
- **Esprit de corps** – harmony and teamwork should be encouraged in the organisation.

Fayol believed that a manager obtained the best performance from his workforce by leadership qualities, by his knowledge of the business and his workers, and by his ability to instil a sense of mission.

Test your understanding 3

Which of the following are elements of management as identified by **Fayol.**

A   Control.

B   Motivation.

C   Communication.

D   Compromise.

The implications of **Taylor's** scientific management are as follows:

- Workers should be set high targets, but should be well rewarded for achieving them.

- Working methods should be analysed 'scientifically', including the timing of work.

- Management should plan and control all the workers' efforts, leaving little discretion for individual control over working methods.

While there may be areas where these principles are still relevant, most modern theorists would argue that a more progressive approach is needed where:

- It is recognised that there is not always a 'best' way of doing a particular job.

- Employees can often have considerable insight into a job and can make important suggestions for improvements.

- Many workers can be motivated by other methods than tight control and financial reward.

These issues are discussed in more details later in this chapter.

Illustration 4 – Theories of management

The classical approach is still being utilised today since this is the principle applied in most call centres: targets are set for the number of calls to be taken in a predetermined time period and reward is based on the achievement of the target.

Test your understanding 4

Which one of the following statements is closest to the beliefs of the classical school?

A Emphasis on social groups.

B Emphasis on the task to be done rather than the person doing it.

C Emphasis on the person rather than the task.

D Emphasis on encouraging people to reach their full potential.

2.2 The human relations school

Research carried out by **Mayo** at the General Electric Company in Chicago concluded that group relationships and management- worker communication were far more important in determining employee behaviour than were physical conditions (e.g. lighting and noise) and the working practices imposed by management. Also, wage levels were not the dominant motivating factor for most workers.

Further research established the following propositions of the human relations school.

- Employee behaviour depends primarily on the social and organisational circumstances of work.

- Leadership style, group cohesion and job satisfaction are major determinants of the outputs of the working group.

- Employees work better if they are given a wide range of tasks to complete.

- Standards set internally by a working group influence employee attitudes and perspectives more than standards set by management.

The usefulness of the human relations approach

The school explicitly recognised the role of interpersonal relations in determining workplace behaviour, and it demonstrated that factors other than pay can motivate workers. However, the approach possibly overestimates the commitment, motivation and desire to participate in decision making of many employees.

Test your understanding 5

Which one of the following statements is closest to the beliefs of the human relations school?

A   Emphasis on social groups.

B   Emphasis on the task to be done rather than the person doing it.

C   Emphasis on one best approach.

D   Emphasis on hierarchy of management.

2.3 Modern writers

Contributions made by modern writers on management include:

- **Contingency approach ('no one best approach')** – contingency theorists do not ignore the lessons learnt from earlier theorists, but adapt them to suit particular circumstances.

- **Behaviouralism** – concerned with the personal adjustment of the individual within the work organisation and the effects of group relationships and leadership styles.

- **Systems theory** - expresses a manger's role as being a co-ordinator of the elements of a system, of which people are only one part.

Expandable Text - systems theory

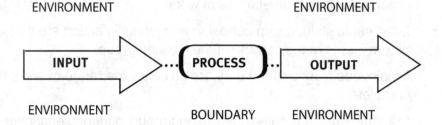

KEY FEATURES OF A SYSTEM

Systems theory takes the view that an organisation is a social system, consisting of individuals who co-operate together within a formal framework, drawing resources from their environment and putting back into that environment the products they produce or the services they offer:

- in doing so the input is converted into the final product or service, hopefully with value being added

- an organisation does not exist in a vacuum. It depends on its environment and is part of larger systems, such as society, the economic system and the industry to which it belongs.

Examples of the other systems include an information system, production system and a communication system.

Drucker identified five basic operations in the work of a manager. Managers:

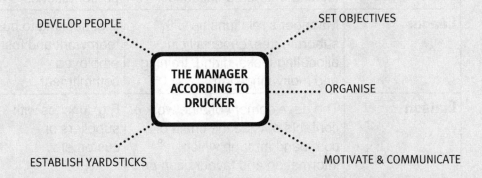

DEVELOP PEOPLE

SET OBJECTIVES

THE MANAGER ACCORDING TO DRUCKER

ORGANISE

ESTABLISH YARDSTICKS

MOTIVATE & COMMUNICATE

Expandable text

- **Set objectives** – determining what they should be and what the goals in each area should be. They decide what has to be done to reach these objectives and make them effective by communicating them to the people who are going to perform them.

- **Organise** – analysing the activities, decisions and relations needed. They classify the work, divide it into manageable activities and further divide the activities into manageable jobs. They group the units and jobs, and select people for the management of the units and for the jobs to be done.

- **Motivate and communicate** – making a team out of the people that are responsible for various jobs.

- **Establish yardsticks** – by making measurements available, which are focused on the performance of the whole organisation and which, at the same time, focus on the work of the individual and help them to do it. Managers analyse, appraise and interpret performance.

- **Develop people**, including themselves.

Mintzberg identified ten skills which managers need if they are to develop greater effectiveness, and grouped them together under three categories, interpersonal, informational and decisional.

Interpersonal		
Figurehead	Symbolic role, manager obliged to carry out social, inspirational, legal and ceremonial duties.	E.g. receiving visitors and making presentations.
Leader	Manager's relationship with subordinates, especially in allocating tasks, hiring, training and motivating staff.	E.g. seeking to build teamwork and foster employee commitment.
Liaison	The development of a network of contacts outside the chain of command through which information and favours can be traded for mutual benefits.	E.g. lunches with suppliers or customers.
Informational		
Monitor	The manager collects and sorts out information which is used to build up a general understanding of the organisation and its environment as a basis for decision making.	E.g. reading reports and interrogating subordinates.
Disseminator	To be a disseminator means to spread the information widely.	E.g. passing privileged information to subordinates.
Spokesperson	Managers transmit information to various external groups by acting in a PR capacity, lobbying for the organisation, informing the public about the organisation's performance, plans and policies.	E.g. a sales presentation to prospective customers.
Decisional		
Entrepreneur	Managers should be looking continually for problems and opportunities when situations requiring improvement are discovered.	E.g. launching a new idea or introducing procedures such as a cost reduction programme.
Disturbance handler	A manager has to respond to pressures over which the department has no control.	E.g. strikes.
Resource allocator	Choosing from among competing demands for money, equipment, personnel and management time.	E.g. approving expenditure on a project.

Negotiator	Managers take charge when their organisation must engage in negotiating with others. In these negotiations, the manager participates as figurehead, spokesperson and resource allocator.	E.g. drawing up contracts with suppliers.

Test your understanding 6

Is the following statement in line with **Mintzberg's** approach?

'The manager in the informational role combines being a spokesperson and disseminator with being a monitor of information.'

3 Managerial authority and responsibility

Authority refers to the relationship between the participants in an organisation.

- Authority is the right to give orders and the power to exact obedience **(Fayol).**

- Authority is the right to do something, or ask someone else to do it and expect it to be done.

- Authority is thus another word for legitimate power.

Illustration 5 – Managerial authority and responsibility

When analysing the types of authority which a manager or department may have the following terms are often used:

- **Line authority** – the authority a manger has over a subordinate, down the vertical chain (or line) of command.

- **Staff authority** – is the authority one manager or department may have in giving specialist advice to another manager or department, over which there is no line authority. (HR department advising the accounts manager on interviewing techniques.)

- **Functional authority** – is a hybrid of line and staff authority, whereby a manager setting policies and procedures for the company as a whole has the authority in certain circumstances, to direct, design or control activities or procedures of another department. (A finance manager has authority to require timely budgetary control reports from other departmental/line managers.)

Test your understanding 7

If a manager justifies an instruction to a subordinate by saying 'because I am your superior' the manager is relying on which of the following bases of authority?

A   Functional

B   Staff

C   Line

Responsibility is the liability of a person to be called to account for his or her actions.

- Responsibility expresses the obligation a person has to fulfil a task, which he or she has been given. A person is said to be responsible for a piece of work when he or she is required to ensure that the work is done.

- Responsibility is the obligation to use delegated powers.

- The important point is that managers and supervisors are ultimately responsible for the actions of their subordinates; the term 'accountable' is often used.

- It is accountability for the performance of specified duties or the satisfactory achievement of defined company objectives.

- Because responsibility is an obligation owed, it cannot be delegated.

- No superior can escape responsibility for the activities of subordinates, for it is the supervisor who delegates authority and assigns the duties.

Test your understanding 8

Which of the following statements could be a definition of responsibility?

A   Liability to be called to account.

B   Accountability for actions.

C   An obligation owed.

John French and Bertram Raven identified five sources or bases of power.

- **Reward** power – is based on one person having the ability to reward another person for carrying out orders or meeting other requirements.

- **Coercive** power – is based on one person's ability to punish another for not meeting requirements, is the negative side of reward power.

- **Expert** power – is based on the perception or belief that a person has some relevant expertise or special knowledge that others do not.

- **Referent** power – is based on one person's desire to identify with or imitate another.

- **Legitimate** power – the power derived from being in a position of authority within the organisational structure – according to the position they hold within the organisation.

Illustration 6 – Managerial authority and responsibility

If a manager justifies an instruction to a subordinate by saying 'because I am a qualified accountant' the manager is relying on which of the following bases of power?

A   Referent

B   Reward

C   Legitimate

D   Expert

Solution

D

Test your understanding 9

If a manager justifies an instruction to a subordinate by saying 'because I am your superior' the manager is relying on which of the following bases of authority?

A   Referent

B   Reward

C   Legitimate

D   Expert

In every position authority and responsibility should correspond (principle of correspondence):

- **Having responsibility without authority** – supervisor may be held responsible for time keeping but does not have the authority to discipline subordinate for poor time-keeping. The supervisor is powerless to achieve the levels upon which his or her performance is being judged. This supervisor is likely to become frustrated, stressed and demotivated. Performance is likely to suffer.

Conflict will occur if the supervisor fails the task due to lack of co-operation caused by lack of authority.

- **Having authority without responsibility** – personnel department employ an individual but will have no responsibility for the employee; they are in a position of false security. Managers not held accountable for their authority may exercise their authority in an irresponsible way, which may not be to the benefit of the organisation. They may take unacceptable risks, because the consequences of decisions will not rebound on them.

The control mechanisms of the organisation depend on accountability.

Test your understanding 10

John has just joined a small accounts department. The financial controller is taken ill. John has been told that he needs to prepare the management accounts and requires information regarding salaries. The payroll department are not happy about giving John the information required. What is the underlying cause of the problem?

---

4 Theories of leadership approaches

4.1 Trait theories (also called the 'qualities approach')

Early studies of leadership were based on the assumption that leaders were born and not made.

- They tried to pick out the common personality characteristics (or traits) so that they had a basis on which to recognise actual and potential leaders by knowing their traits and comparing them with the traits of known leaders.

- Lists of leadership qualities were compiled that included.
    - Physical traits – drive, energy, appearance.

–   Personality traits – adaptability, enthusiasm and self-confidence.

–   Social traits – co-operation, tact, courtesy.

Test your understanding 11

Can you think of any other traits essential in a leader?

4.2 The action-centred approach (Adair)

- **Adair** suggests that any leader has to strive to achieve three major goals while at the same time maintaining a position as an effective leader.

- **Adair's action** – centred leadership model looks at leadership in relation to the needs of the task, individual and group.

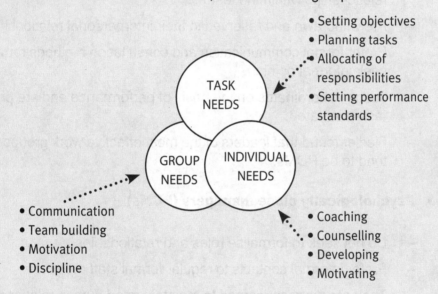

Test your understanding 12

The table below includes needs that managers have to action. Suggest whether they are likely to be associated with individual, task or group needs.

Need	Task/group/individual
Decision making	
Peace keeping	
Training	

4.3 The contingency approach (Fiedler)

Contingency theory sees effective leadership as being dependent on a number of variable or contingent factors. There is no one right way to lead that will fit all situations; rather it is necessary to lead in a manner that is appropriate to a particular situation.

Fiedler's contingency theory

- **Fiedler** studied the relationship between style of leadership and effectiveness of the work group. Two styles of leader were identified.

  Psychologically distant managers (PDMs).

  - Maintain distance from their subordinates by formalising roles and relationships within the team.

  - Are withdrawn and reserved in their interpersonal relationships.

  - Prefer formal communication and consultation methods rather than seek informal opinion.

  - Judge subordinates on the basis of performance and are primarily task-orientated.

  - Fiedler found that leaders of the most effective work groups actually tend to be PDMs.

  Psychologically close managers (PCMs)

  - Do not seek to formalise roles and relationships.

  - Prefer informal contacts to regular formal staff meetings.

  - They are more concerned to maintain good human relationships at work to ensure that tasks are carried out efficiently.

  - **Fiedler** concluded that a structured (or psychologically distant) style works best when the situation is either very favourable or very unfavourable to the leader.

  - On the other hand, a supportive (or psychologically close) style works best when the situation is moderately favourable to the leader.

  - He further suggested that group performance would be contingent upon the appropriate matching of leadership styles and the degree of favourableness of the group situation for the leader.

Fiedler went on to develop his contingency theory in 'A theory of leadership effectiveness', in which he argued that the effectiveness of the workgroup depended on the situation. The leadership situation is made up of three key variables:

- The relationship between the leader and the group (trust, respect and so on).

- The extent to which the task is defined and structured.

- The power of the leader in relation to the group.

Illustration 7 – Theories of leadership approaches

Fiedler suggested that a situation is favourable to the leader when the leader is liked and trusted by the group, the tasks of the group are clearly defined and the power of the leader to reward and punish the team, with organisational backing, is high.

Test your understanding 13

The accounts manager holds a departmental meeting every Monday at 10.00am. How would **Fiedler** define this manager?

4.4 Transformational leadership (Bennis)

Some of the values used to distinguish between managers and leaders have also been identified as:

- Transactional leaders – see the relationship with their followers in terms of a trade: they give followers the rewards they want in exchange for service, loyalty and compliance.

- Transformational leaders – see their role as inspiring and motivating others to work at levels beyond mere compliance. Only transformational leadership is said to be able to change team/organisational cultures and create a new direction.

Expandable Text

Bennis is an influential American author on leadership and change. He focuses on the need to inspire change rather than imposing it. He identifies five 'avenues of change':

- Dissent and conflict – top management impose change by means of their position of power, the result being rancour amongst those affected.

- Trust and truth – management must gain trust, express their vision clearly, and persuade others to follow.

- Cliques and cabals – cliques have power, money and resources; cabals have ambition, drive and energy. Unless the cliques can co-opt the cabals, revolution is inevitable.

- External events – forces of society can impose change, e.g. by new government regulation or through overseas competition.

- Culture or paradigm shift – changing the corporate culture is the most important avenues of change.

Test your understanding 14

When organisational change requires a change in structure and/or culture would the organisation require a transformational or transactional leader?

4.5 Managing change (Kotter)

Kotter set out the following change approaches to deal with resistance:

Participation and involvement	E.g. this approach aims to involve employees, usually by allowing some input into decision making.	Employees are more likely to support changes made and give positive commitment as they 'own' the change.
Education and communication	E.g. this approach aims to keep employees informed, usually through presentations about the reasons for the required change.	This approach relies on the hopeful belief that communication about the benefits of change to employees will result in their acceptance of the need to exercise the changes necessary.
Facilitation and support	E.g. training, counselling.	Employees may need help to overcome their fears and anxieties about change.
Manipulation and co-optation	E.g. the information that is disseminated is selective and distorted to only emphasise the benefits of the change.	Involves covert attempts to sidestep potential resistance.

Negotiation and agreement	E.g. this approach enables several parties with opposing interests to bargain.	This bargaining leads to a situation of compromise and agreement.

Test your understanding 15

Training in the use of a new information system is a means of overcoming resistance to change by:

A   Facilitation and support.

B   Education and communication.

C   Participation and involvement.

D   Negotiation and agreement.

4.6 Leadership to mobilise (Heifetz)

Heifetz argues that the role of the leader is to help people face reality and to mobilise them to make change. **Heifetz** suggests that the old approach to leadership was that leaders had the answers, the vision and then needed to persuade people to sign up for the change. Heifetz believes that leaders provide direction but do not have to offer definite answers and should mobilise people to tackle the tough challenges for themselves.

Leaders have two choices when resolving a situation:

- Technical change – the application of current knowledge, skills and or tools to resolve a situation.

- Adaptive change – is required when the problem cannot be solved with existing skills and knowledge and requires people to make a shift in their values, expectations, attitudes or habits of behaviour. This is often required to ensure organisational survival.

Expandable Text

Heifetz suggests four principles for bringing about adaptive change:

- Recognition that the change requires an adaptive approach and understanding the values that need to be shifted and the issues that need to be resolved to make the shift possible.

- Adaptive change causes unhappiness in the people being led; adaptive change requires the right level of stress to be applied: too little stress and people do not appreciate the need for change: too much stress and there will be no 'buy-in'.

- Keep focused on the real issue of realising the change; do not spend too much time on stress-reducing distractions.

- Ensure the people who need to make the change take responsibility and face the reality of doing the work of change for themselves. Leaders provide the direction, posing well-structured questions, rather than offering definite answers.

5 Leadership styles

5.1 Blake and Mouton

Robert Blake and Jane Mouton carried out research into managerial behaviour and observed two basic dimensions of leadership: concern for production (or task performance) and concern for people.

Based on the results of staff questionnaires, managers can then be plotted on **Blake and Mouton's grid.**

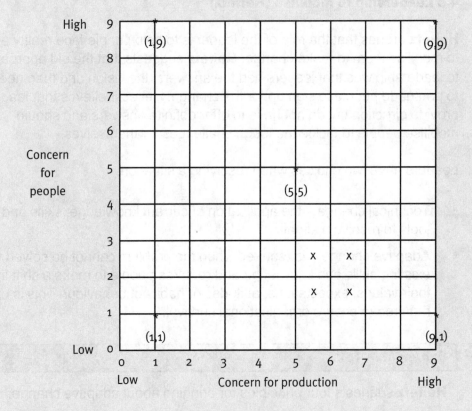

1.1 Management impoverished – this manager only makes minimum effort in either area and will make the smallest possible effort required to get the job done.

1.9 'Country Club' management – this manager is thoughtful and attentive to the needs of the people, which leads to a comfortable friendly organisation atmosphere but very little work is actually achieved.

9.1 Task management – this manager is only concerned with production and arranges work in such a way that people interference is minimised.

5.5 'Middle of the road management'- this manager is able to balance the task in hand and motivate the people to achieve these tasks.

9.9 Team management - this manager integrates the two areas to foster working together and high production to produce true team leadership.

Blake and Mouton's grid can be used to assess the current behavioural style of a manager and then plan appropriate training and development to enable them to move towards 9.9.

Test your understanding 16

Using the scores shown on the above grid, make suggestions as to how this particular manager could improve his/her managerial style.

Benefits	Drawbacks
• The grid shows areas where management faults can be identified and can then provide the basis for training and for management development. • As an appraisal and management development tool to inform managers that attention to both task and people is possible and desirable. • Managers can determine how they are viewed by their subordinates.	• The grid assumes that leadership style can be categorised into the two dimensions and that results can be plotted on the grid. • The position of team management is accepted as the best form of leadership. This may not be practical or indeed advisable. In many industries, concern for the task may be more important than concern for people, and visa versa and will always depend on the individual situation.

5.2 Ashridge

The research unit at **Ashridge Management** College distinguished four different management styles.

Tells (autocratic) – the manager makes all the decisions and issues instructions which must be obeyed without question.

Strengths:

- Quick decisions can be made when required.
- The most efficient type of leadership for highly-programmed work.

Weaknesses:

- Communications are one-way, neglecting feedback and potential for upward communication or team member input.
- Does not encourage initiative or commitment from subordinates, merely compliance.

Sells (persuasive) – the manager still makes all the decisions, but believes that team members must be motivated to accept them in order to carry them out properly.

Strengths:

- Team members understand the reason for decisions.
- Team members may be more committed.
- Team members may be able to function slightly better in the absence of instruction.

Weaknesses:

- Communications are still largely one-way.
- Team members are not necessarily motivated to accept the decision.
- It still doesn't encourage initiative or commitment.

Consults (participative) – the manager confers with the team and takes their views into account, although still retains the final say.

Strengths:

- Involves team members in decisions, encouraging motivation through greater interest and involvement.
- Consensus may be reached, enhancing the acceptability of the decision to team members.
- The quality of the decision may benefit from the input of those who do the work.
- Encourages upward communication.

Weaknesses:

- May take longer to reach decisions (especially if consensus is sought).
- Team member input may not enhance the quality of the decision.
- Consultation can be a façade for a basic 'sells' style.

Joins (democratic) – the leader and the team members make the decision together on the basis of consensus.

Strengths:

- Can provide high motivation and commitment from team members.
- Empowers a team member to take the initiative (e g. in responding flexibly to customer demands and problems).
- Shares other advantages of the 'consults' style (especially where team members can add value).

Weaknesses:

- May undermine the authority of the manager.
- May further lengthen the decision-making process.
- May reduce the quality of the decision because of the politics of decision making.

Test your understanding 17

For each of the statements made by managers listed below, choose an Ashridge leadership style that best describes the statement.

Statement	Style
'Produce this report immediately because HR have an urgent need for the information.	
'What would you like to include in this report?'	
'Produce this report immediately or else.'	
'What do you think we should include in the report?'	

Chapter summary

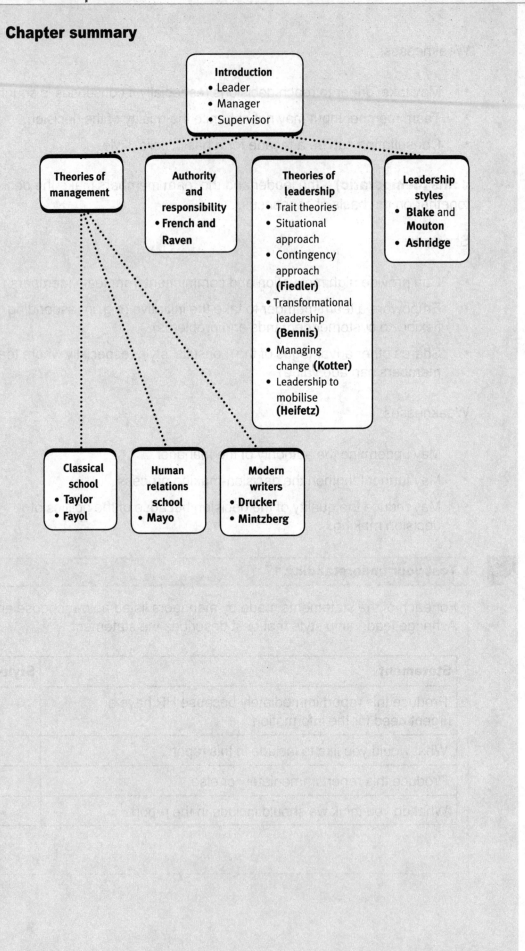

Test your understanding answers

Test your understanding 1

- Planning the work of the department.
- Ensuring by adequate supervision that the work is completed as far as possible according to plan.
- Maintaining discipline in the department.
- Undertaking the task when required.
- Having knowledge and ability in all aspects of health, safety and employment legislation that applies to his or her subordinates.

Test your understanding 2

C

Test your understanding 3

A only

Test your understanding 4

B

Test your understanding 5

A

Test your understanding 6

Yes

Test your understanding 7

C

Test your understanding 8

A, B and C

Test your understanding 9

C

Test your understanding 10

John has been given the responsibility for completing a task but without the authority.

Test your understanding 11

Examples could include: ambition, fairness, integrity, and initiative.

Test your understanding 12

Need	Task/group/individual
Decision making	Task
Peace keeping	Group
Training	Individual

Test your understanding 13

Psychologically distant manager.

Test your understanding 14

Transformational.

Test your understanding 15

A

Test your understanding 16

The manager illustated in the above grid is showing good concern for production (although this can be strengthened further) but is weak in terms of concern for employees. Further investigation would then be carried out to determine why this is the case and in what ways such a lack of concern is exhibited. Then rectifying action can be taken.

For example:

- Attend a training course on people skills and motivation.

- Involve staff in more decisions.

- Treat staff as valuable assets; adopt an open door policy.

Test your understanding 17

Statement	Style
'Produce this report immediately because HR have an urgent need for the information.	Sells
'What would you like to include in this report?'	Joins
'Produce this report immediately or else.'	Tells
'What do you think we should include in the report?'	Consults

Individual and group behaviour in business organisations

Chapter learning objectives

Upon completion of this chapter you will be able to:

- define the term behaviour

- explain what factors influence the way individuals act

- describe the characteristics of passive, aggressive and assertive behaviour

- give reasons why working in teams is more effective than working as an individual

- outline the contribution teams make to the organisational success

- what factors are required in order to make a cohesive group?

- distinguish between different approaches necessary to organise work around an individual and around the work group.

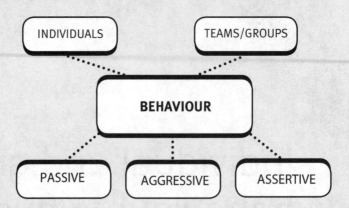

1 The main characteristics of individual and group behaviour

Although individual behaviour patterns may vary significantly, the process of behaviour is the same for all people. Behaviour can be caused, motivated and is goal directed.

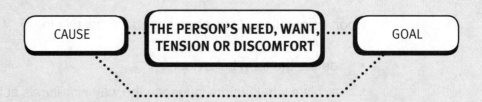

For each individual there are many factors that affect behaviour and performance at work:

- **Motivation level** - why people choose to do one thing rather than another and also with the amount of effort or intensity of action people use.

- **Perception** - individuals select, organise and interpret the stimuli they receive. No matter how hard a manager tries to send a clear message, the message is still subject to distortion. The subordinate will select parts of the message, interpret it in the light of experience and organise the information in a form that makes sense to them.

- **Attitudes** - persistent feelings and behaviour tendencies directed towards specific persons, groups, ideas or objects.

- **Personality** - Influences an individuals' behaviour and performance.

When you are dealing with other people there are different types of behaviour that can be adopted.

- Assertive behaviour - is direct, honest and professional communication. It is insisting on your rights without violating the rights of others. E.g. "I would like you to rework this report there are several mistakes in it."

- Aggressive behaviour - violates another person's rights and can lead to conflict. E.g. " I do not know how you have the nerve to submit this report it has so many mistakes in it."

- Passive behaviour - is giving in to another person in the belief that their rights are more important than one's own. E.g. "The mistakes in the report are probably my fault for not explaining it properly."

Test your understanding 1

A colleague telephones you when you are working on some invoices that you particularly want to finish. He says he wants to talk about next weeks safety meeting. You prefer to discuss it later. Give both an assertive response and an aggressive response.

Test your understanding 2

Explain the inappropriateness of aggressive behaviour. Explain the appropriateness of assertive behaviour.

2 The contribution of individuals and teams to organisational success.

One person cannot do everything, but a team can combine all the main areas of skill and knowledge that are needed for a particular job.

- **Synergy** describes the phenomenon in which the combined activity of separate entities has a greater effect than the sum of the activities of each entity working alone - often described as a way of making 2 + 2 = 5.

Within organisations there has been an implicit belief that people working as members of a group or team perform more effectively than if they are organised as individuals. There are, of course, many work situations where the group is the best means to get work done, such as:

- When working co-operatively, rather than working individually, gives a better end result in terms of speed, efficiency or quality.

- Where the task requires a mixture of different skills or specialisms.

- Where competition between individuals leads to less effectiveness rather than more.

- Where the task requires the co-ordination of activities.

Test your understanding 3

Identify some differences between the contribution of the individual to the organisation and the contribution of the team to the organisation.

The advantages associated with cohesive groups include:

- improved teamwork and problem solving
- greater creativity
- provide support for individuals within the group
- improved communication through participation
- satisfaction of social needs
- provides a forum for conflict resolution.

Expandable text

- **Atmosphere** - an effective, cohesive group will work in an informal, relaxed atmosphere.

- **Participation** - the group will discuss the work.

- **Commitment** - as a result of effective communication and acceptance of the objective, there will be a degree of commitment and desire to complete the task(s).

- **Communication** - there will be a good rapport between group members.

- **Leadership** - informal leaders are more likely to have the total support of the group.

- **Progress** - the group monitors its progress and quality, always trying to perform better.

Test your understanding 4

Explain how teams can help to deliver organisational success.

KAPLAN PUBLISHING

The factors required to make a cohesive group could include;

- **Leadership** - The leader should use an appropriate leadership style in order to promote co-operation and to motivate individuals towards the task and ensure that work is properly organised.
    - Creating a climate of communication and mutual trust.
    - Creating a climate in which people speak their minds.

- **Right mix of skills** - A mixed balance of individuals each able to perform the role required.

- **Clear objectives and commitment to shared goals** - the task must be clearly defined and everyone must understand their contribution to the task.

- **Team identity** - the sense of being a team.

- **Team solidarity** - loyalty to the group, so that team members put in extra effort for the group and in support of its norms and values.

> **Test your understanding 5**
>
> Suggest three ways in which a leader can build cohesiveness.

3 Individual and team approaches to work

One of the key points that mangers need to grasp is that an effective group is one, which not only achieves its task objectives, but satisfies the needs of its members as well.

For each individual there are many factors that affect behaviour and performance at work

Motivation

- Physical and working conditions.
- Safety.
- Monetary rewards.
- Recognition.
- Many of the factors that motivate individuals to perform are social in nature; groups can bring out the best in people and can be essential for the delivery of social needs.

Perception

Developing a group means identifying distinct roles for each of its members. Any individual can have several roles, varying between different groups and activities. The role adopted a will affect the individual's attitude towards other people.

- A role is the expected pattern of behaviours associated with members occupying a particular position within the structure of the organisation. It also describes how individuals perceive their own situation.

- An individual's perceptions of other people and interactions with other people will be influenced by the different roles. The role they adopt will affect their own behaviour, as well as their attitude towards other people.

There are several terms associated with role theory.

- **Role ambiguity** arises when individuals are unsure what role they are to play, or others are unclear of that person's role and so hold back co-operation. This can arise, for example, when a new member joins an established group.

- **Role conflict** arises, when individuals find a clash between differing roles that they have adopted. A company finance officer who uncovers fraud by senior management may feel a conflict between the roles of professional confidentiality and honest citizenship.

- **Role incompatibility** occurs when individuals experience expectations from outside groups about their role that are different from their own role expectations.

- **Role signs** are visible indications of the role. Style of dress and uniform are clear examples of role signs. These may be voluntary (a male accountant wearing a grey or blue suit and a tie) or mandatory (in military, police and hospital occupations, variations in uniform denote status).

- **Role set** describes the people who support a lead person in a major role, e.g. the clerk and junior barristers would form part of a senior barrister's role set.

- **Role behaviour** - certain types of behaviour can be associated with a role in an office or works. For instance, the 'crown prince' behaving as if they are heir apparent to a senior position.

Chapter summary

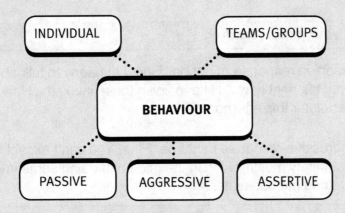

Test your understanding answers

Test your understanding 1

An assertive response might be "Fine. I'm happy to talk about the safety meeting, but right now I'd like to finish these invoices. How about ringing me back later this afternoon?"

An aggressive response might be "Fine. You can't expect me to think about a safety meeting. I'm in the middle of doing some invoices. You'll have to ring me back later?"

Test your understanding 2

Aggressive behaviour

- Counter-productive, may allow someone to get their way immediately but in the long term it leads to broken relationships resentment and hostility.

- Often leads to escalation of conflict.

- Often leads to guilt feelings on the part of the aggressor.

Assertive behaviour

- It defuses the potential for conflict

- It maintains a good working relationship as it displays a willingness to deliver a mutual compromise as an aid to achieving a clear objective.

Test your understanding 3

Individual Contribution	Team Contribution
• One set of skills	• A mix of skills
• One point of view	• A number of different views
• Innovative ideas based on the individual's expertise	• Innovative ideas based on the ombination of expertise

Test your understanding 4

- The delivery of organisation objectives more effectively (2+2=5).
- If social needs are meet increases motivation.
- A mixed balance of skills and expertise might increase the chance of success.

Test your understanding 5

- Clear communication of the group's task objective and the contribution each member can make to delivery of the task.
- Strive to create a cooperative atmosphere and style, based on trust.
- Good communication through facilitating openness and honesty, information sharing, ideas generation and constructive feedback.

6

Team formation, development and management

Chapter learning objectives

Upon completion of this chapter you will be able to:

- explain what is meant by a group
- explain what is meant by a team
- distinguish between a group and a team
- what is the purpose of the team
- explain the different roles people play in a team with reference to Belbin's theory
- explain the stages of team development as per Tuckman's theory
- what factors make a team ineffective
- identify the criteria necessary for a successful team as per Peters and Waterman
- what criteria is used to evaluate team's success.

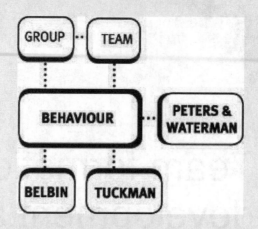

1 The differences between a group and a team

A group is any collection of people who perceive themselves to be a group. Groups have the following attributes.

- A sense of identity - there are acknowledged boundaries of the group, who is in and who is out.

- Loyalty to the group - acceptance within the group that bind the group together.

- Purpose and leadership - express purpose, choose individuals to lead them towards their goals.

Practically all individual effort takes place in association with other people in groups.

- Informal groups - individuals join groups to meet their social and security or safety needs. Membership is normally voluntary. Individual members are dependent on each other, influence each other's behaviour and contribute to each other's needs, e.g. the group of employees who sit together and chat at lunchtime.

- Formal groups - organisations use groups to carry put tasks, communicate and solve problems. Membership is normally formal, often determined or constrained by the organisation into departments or divisions, e.g. a project team put together to deliver a new payroll system.

Test your understanding 1

Would a number of people waiting for a bus be described as a formal or informal group?

An effective team can be described as 'any group of people who must significantly relate with each other in order to accomplish shared objectives'.

In order to ensure that the group is truly an effective team, team members must have a reason for working together. They must need each other's skills, talent and experience in order to achieve their mutual goals.

A team is a formal group. It has a leader and a distinctive culture and is geared towards a final result.

Teams

- share a common goal
- enjoy working together
- commitment to achieve goals
- diverse individuals
- loyalty to the project
- attain a team spirit.

Test your understanding 2

Would an orchestra be considered a team?

We can establish the differences between groups and teams by observing their behaviour.

In teams:

- there is more openness and trust
- feelings are expressed more freely
- there are common objectives
- process issues are part of the work
- conflict is worked out
- decisions are by consensus
- commitment can be very high.

In groups:

- people accommodate each other
- people negotiate
- objectives may be modified
- the process issues are often covert
- politics are rife
- commitment can be high.

As a way to ensure that the team welds together to become an effective unit, you might look for evidence of successful team-building.

Expandable text

Woodcock has described some features of effective teamwork, which include the following:

- There is the right balance of skills, ability and aspiration.
- Mistakes are faced openly and there is no 'scape-goating'.
- There is pride in success, support and trust in personal relationships.
- There is a high level of task achievement.
- Openness and honesty is present.
- There is healthy competition.
- There is a happy feel to the place and good relationships with other departments.

Illustration 1 – The differences between a group and a team

What is a team?

A small number of people with complimentary skills who are committed to a common purpose, performance goals and approach for which they hold themselves basically accountable.

Test your understanding 3

Outline some of the characteristics that identify a team.

2 The purposes of a team

The basic purpose of a team is to solve complex problems through

- A diverse team of specialists.
- The concept of synergy 2+2=5 - the sum of the whole is greater than the sum of the individual parts.

3 The role of the manager in building a team

3.1 Belbin's theory of group roles

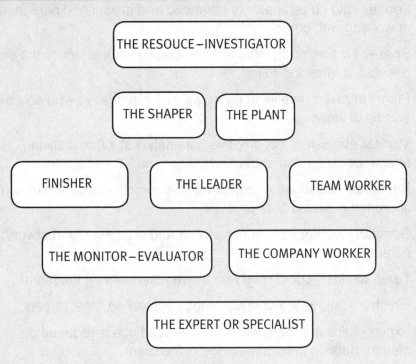

Leader	Co-ordinator
Shaper	Promotes activity- dominant, extrovert
Plant	Thoughtful and thought provoking, ideas person
Monitor-evaluator	Criticises others ideas, brings the team down to earth
Resource-investigator	Extrovert, networker, looks for alternative solutions
The Company worker	Administrator, organiser
The Team worker	Concerned with relationships within the groups
The Finisher	The progress chaser
The Expert	As required by the project

- Belbin suggested that a group needs a balance of the above roles to be effective.

Expandable text

- Leader - the co-ordinator, a balanced and disciplined person, good at working with others.

- Shaper - a dominant, extrovert personality, task driven to the point of passion, a force for action.

- Plant - introvert, intellectually bright and imaginative who acts as a source of ideas.

- Monitor-evaluator - not creative but analytical, often tactless, examines ideas and spots flaws.

- Resource-investigator - popular social member of the team, a useful source of contacts but not ideas.

- Company worker - the administrator and organiser, a trustworthy person.

- Team-worker - concerned with the maintenance of the team.

- Finisher - enjoys the detail, pushes the team to meet targets.

- Expert - joins the team when specialist advice is required on matters outside the competence of the team.

Test your understanding 4

Neville is in charge of a group of 12 people involved in complex work. This is of an on going nature. The group has been working together amicably and successfully for a considerable time. Its members value Neville's leadership and the back-up given by Olivia. She elaborates on Neville's instructions and deals on his behalf with group members queries, especially when he is absent on the group's business.

Much of the success of the group has been due to Peter, who is creative at problem solving, and Rosalinde who has an encyclopaedic knowledge of sources of supply and information. Quentin is an expert on charting and records, and Sheila is invaluable at sorting out disagreements and keeping everyone cheerful. The remaining members of the group also have roles, which are acceptable to themselves an to the others.

Requirement

Which of Belbin's role classifications do the following group members most closely comply with?

Neville
Olivia
Peter
Rosalind
Quentin
Sheila

Test your understanding 5

From Belbin's model, explain any three roles that members of a team might perform?

3.2 Tuckman's stages of group development

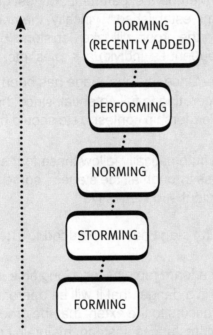

Forming	Awareness
Storming	Conflict
Norming	Co-operation
Performing	Productivity
Dorming	Adjournment

Expandable text

Tuckman helps identify what needs to be done to weld the team together. The stages are:

- **Forming** - At this initial stage, the group is no more than a collection of individuals who are seeking to define the purpose of the group and how it will operate.

- **Storming** - most groups go through this conflict stage. In this stage norms of attitude, behaviour, etc., are challenged and rejected. Members compete for chosen roles within the group. If successful, this stage will have forged a stronger team with greater knowledge of each other and their objectives.

- **Norming** - This stage establishes the norms under which the group will operate. Members experiment and test group reaction as the norms become established. Typically, the norming stage will establish how the group will take decisions, behaviour patterns, level of trust and openness, individual's roles, etc.

- **Performing** - Once this final stage has been reached, the group is capable of operating to full potential, since the difficulties of adjustment, leadership contests, etc should have been resolved.

All groups do not automatically follow these four stages in this sequence. Not all groups pass through all the stages - some get stuck in the middle and remain inefficient and ineffective.

More recently a fifth stage has been added to Tuckman's original four.

- **Dorming** - If a team remains for a long time in the performing phase, there is a danger that it will be operating on automatic pilot. 'Groupthink' occurs to the extent that the group may be unaware of changing circumstances. Instead, maintaining the team becomes one of its prime objectives.

Test your understanding 6

Following on from TYU above, suppose the following has occurred:

- Recently, Olivia resigned for family reasons.

- Because the workload has been increasing, Neville recruited four new people to the group.

- Neville now finds that various members of the group complain to him about what they are expected to do and about other people's failings.

- Peter and Rosalinde have been unusually helpful to Neville, but have had several serious arguments between themselves and with others.

Requirement

Relating your answer to Tuckman, analyse the situation before and after the changes.

Test your understanding 7

Describe Tuckman's stages of team development.

4 The characteristics of an effective team

Blockages to an effective team:

- inappropriate leadership
- unqualified membership
- unconstructive climate
- unclear objectives
- poor achievement
- ineffective work methods
- insufficient openness and confrontation
- undeveloped individuals
- low creative capacity
- unconstructive relationships between team members.

Test your understanding 8

Consider the type of behaviour characterising an ineffective group.

Peters and Waterman define the five key aspects of successful task-force teams as:

- The numbers should be small; inevitably each member will then represent the interest of their section/ department.

- The team should be of limited duration, and exist only to resolve this particular task.

- Membership should be voluntary.

- Communication should be informal and unstructured, with little documentation and no status barriers.

- It should be action-oriented. The team should finish with a plan for action not 'just a form of words'.

Test your understanding 9

List some of the characteristics of effective teams.

5 Evaluating team effectiveness

The organisation could measure

- effectiveness - the degree to which objectives are achieved

- efficiency - the use of resources in achieving the objectives

- team-member satisfaction - the motivational climate

- observe and rate the teams behaviour

- interview the team about performance

- send out a questionnaire to team members.

Test your understanding 10

High labour turnover is a characteristic of effective teams. True or false?

Chapter summary

```
GROUP    TEAM
          │
      BEHAVIOUR ···· PETERS &
          │          WATERMAN
   BELBIN    TUCKMAN
```

Key aspects of successful teams
- small
- limited duration
- membership voluntary
- informal, unstructured
- action oriented

Group roles
- Leader
- Shaper
- Plant
- Monitor/evaluator
- Resource investigator
- Company worker
- Team worker
- Finisher
- Expert

Stages of development
- Forming
- Storming
- Norming
- Performing
- Dorming

Test your understanding answers

Test your understanding 1

Consider group attributes

- There would be no sense of identity as there are no acknowledge boundaries of the group.

- The loyalty only comes from the norms that might be expected - orderly queue (not always adhered to)

- While they share common individual aims (to catch a bus), there is no collective objective (e.g. I will still get on the bus even if there is no room for others).

- The people are unlikely to choose a leader

In conclusion, they would be considered as a random crowd rather than a group. If they know each other or have to wait a long time, then they could develop into an informal group.

Test your understanding 2

Yes. An orchestra is a team made up of brilliant individuals. The conductor attempts to blend them together to make a superlative team performance.

Test your understanding 3

- Share a common goal
- enjoy working together
- commitment to achieve goals
- diverse individuals
- loyalty to the project
- attain a team spirit.

KAPLAN PUBLISHING

Test your understanding 4

Neville - Leader

Olivia - Shaper

Peter - Monitor-evaluator and innovator

Rosalinde - resource-investigator

Quentin - Company worker

Sheila - Team worker

Test your understanding 5

- Leader - the co-ordinator, a balanced and disciplined person, good at working with others.
- Shaper - a dominant, extrovert personality, task driven to the point of passion, a force for action.
- Plant - introvert, intellectually bright and imaginative who acts as a source of ideas.
- Monitor-evaluator - not creative but analytical, often tactless, examines ideas and spots flaws.
- Resource-investigator - popular social member of the team, a useful source of contacts but not ideas.
- Company worker - the administrator and organiser, a trustworthy person.
- Team-worker - concerned with the maintenance of the team.
- Finisher - enjoys the detail, pushes the team to meet targets.
- Expert - joins the team when specialist advise is required on matters outside the competence of the team.

Test your understanding 6

Before the changes - the team could be described as at the performing stage of team development

After the changes - the recruitment of four new people to the group has taken the team back to the forming and storming stages.

Test your understanding 7

Forming - meeting the members, find out more about one another and the task.

Storming - conflict of ideas, responsibilities and roles.

Norming - routines become established.

Performing - the team is able to perform effectively.

Dorming - the team becomes complacent and loses interest in the task.

Test your understanding 8

- Tense atmosphere
- no clear objectives
- members not listening to each other
- dominating characters
- group pressure - individuals feeling they need to agree with decisions even when they believe them to be wrong
- conflict is avoided - Tuckman suggests conflict is required and needs to be managed in order to develop team norms.

Test your understanding 9

- Absenteeism will below
- output and productivity will be high
- quality of output will be high
- stoppages and interruptions to work flow will be low
- communication will be free and open
- opinions will be based on consensus
- job satisfaction will be high.

Test your understanding 10

False.

7

Motivating individuals and groups

Chapter learning objectives

Upon completion of this chapter you will be able to:

- explain what is meant by the term motivation, distinguishing between motivation and satisfaction

- explain why motivation is important

- explain what is meant by the content and process theories

- explain the content theory put forward by Maslow

- suggest the weakness of Maslow theory

- explain Herzberg two-factors theory

- explain the three methods of job design

- explain what is meant by McGregor Theory X and Theory Y

- explain the process theory put forward by Vroom

- explain what is meant by intrinsic and extrinsic rewards

- describe the management objectives for an effective reward system

- explain the differences between long-term and short-term incentive schemes.

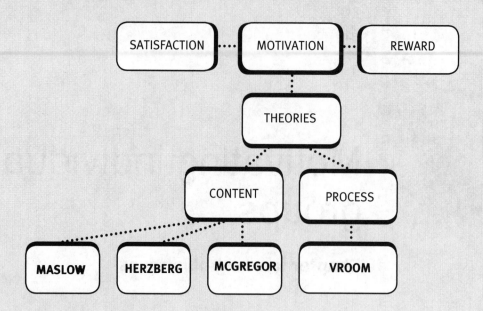

1 Introduction

A distinction should be made here between

- motivation (how hard you are willing to work) and
- satisfaction (being content with your job and not looking for another).

In the short run you can have one without the other but in the long run there is usually congruence.

Consider someone working for a very aggressive manager who constantly shouts at them. They may work very hard to avoid further abuse from their boss but would probably be looking for another job. In the longer term the poor working conditions would also dampen their motivation.

Expandable text

Satisfaction

Job satisfaction is seen to be present when an individual or group has a favourable attitude towards the company. Satisfaction therefore relates to contentment. Thus a person could have a high level of job satisfaction with the company but a low level of motivation for the job.

Characteristics of a satisfied worker

- The employee has a high degree of trust in the company. He will tend to accept rather than challenge company rules and requirements.
- The worker takes pride in belonging to the company. He identifies with the company image and defends its reputation.

- The satisfied worker identifies with the company aims and feels a part of the overall enterprise.

Benefits of job satisfaction

- high staff loyalty and low staff turnover;
- better timekeeping and attendance;
- good general morale;
- pleasant working relationships, helpful to colleagues with a high level of trust.

From the organisation's perspective it is highly desirable to have motivated workers, as they

- work harder
- make fewer mistakes
- generate less waste
- want more feedback
- make more suggestions
- are more likely to be satisfied with their jobs and
- don't waste time.

Expandable text

Success is dependent on three factors

(1) Innate ability
(2) Acquired skills and experience
(3) Motivation

1 and 2 can be ensured by good recruitment and training. No. 3 requires more input from managers.

Together these should result in higher quality, improved productivity and lower costs.

Test your understanding 1

Discuss why an organisation is looking for motivated employees as oppose to satisfied employees.

Test your understanding 2

For each of the following characteristics listed below, indicate whether they are due to satisfaction or motivation:

- low staff turnover
- fewer mistakes
- higher productivity
- higher levels of trust.

Teams

Motivation is also key to the efficient running of teams. Apart from the benefits outlined above, motivated employees are also

- more likely to co-operate and
- put team interests first.

Individuals

From an individual's perspective being motivated should result in

- greater job satisfaction
- improved health (less stress)
- improved career prospects and
- finding the job more interesting.

Test your understanding 3

Is the manager of an accounts department correct in believing that the high levels of productivity currently being achieved by his workforce is due to the high level of satisfaction the employees get from their job?

Test your understanding 4

Discuss how useful motivation is as a concept.

2 Content and process theories of motivation.

Content Theories	Process Theories
• Ask the question **'What'** are the things that motivate people? They are also referred to as **"need theories"** and assume that human beings have a set of needs or desired outcomes which can be satisfied through work. • Content theories assume that everyone responds to motivating factors in the same way and that there is one best way to motivate everybody.	• Ask the question **'how'** are people motivated. They attempt to explain how individuals start, sustain and direct behaviour and assume that individuals are able to select their own goals and means of achieving those goals through a process of calculation. • **Process theories** change the emphasis from needs to the **goals** and **processes** by which workers are motivated.

Expandable text

Content and process theories today

If we consider the relevance and applicability of content and process theories, especially the expectancy theory, to management in the 2000s, there are several features to support their use.

Together they claim to give a comprehensive view of the motivational process. They take account of the ways the individual judges their situation and the link to effective performance.

They imply that job satisfaction (intrinsic) follows from, rather than precedes, effective job performance. Expectancy theory has led to the re-design of work, giving emphasis to intrinsic job satisfaction (to a degree the motivating factors of Herzberg's hygiene-motivation theory).

Further, in a world of increased emphasis on cost-efficiency, minimum manning levels and employee flexibility, they provide a fruitful direction for managers to take.

2.1 Maslow's hierarchy of needs.

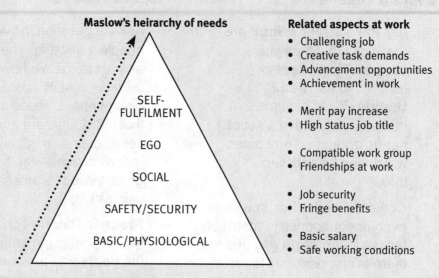

Maslow's heirarchy of needs

SELF-FULFILMENT

EGO

SOCIAL

SAFETY/SECURITY

BASIC/PHYSIOLOGICAL

Related aspects at work
- Challenging job
- Creative task demands
- Advancement opportunities
- Achievement in work

- Merit pay increase
- High status job title

- Compatible work group
- Friendships at work

- Job security
- Fringe benefits

- Basic salary
- Safe working conditions

Expandable text

Maslow's theory may be summarised and simplified by saying that everyone wants certain things throughout life, and these can be placed in five ascending categories, namely:

- Basic or physiological needs - The things needed to stay alive: food, shelter and clothing. Such needs can be satisfied by money.

- Safety or security needs - People want protection against unemployment, the consequences of sickness and retirement as well as being safeguarded against unfair treatment. These needs can be satisfied by the rules of employment, i.e. pension scheme, sick fund, employment legislation etc

- Social needs - The vast majority of people want to be part of a group and it is only through group activity that this need can be satisfied. Thus the way that work is organised, enabling people to feel part of a group, is fundamental to satisfaction of this need.

- Ego needs - These needs may be expressed as wanting the esteem of other people and thinking well of oneself. While status and promotion can offer short-term satisfaction, building up the job itself and giving people a greater say in how their work is organised gives satisfaction of a more permanent nature. An example might be being asked to lead groups on a course.

- Self-fulfilment needs - This is quite simply the need to achieve something worthwhile in life. It is a need that is satisfied only by continuing success, for example opening and running a new office.

KAPLAN PUBLISHING

Test your understanding 5

Violet is the managing director of a successful design company. Assess her motivation using Maslow's hierarchy.

Test your understanding 6

Which of the needs listed below do not feature explicitly on Maslow's hierarchy?

(a) Salary

(b) Sense of achievement

(c) Recognition

(d) Bonus

(e) Interpersonal relationships.

Criticisms of Maslow's hierarchy

- Individuals have different needs and not necessarily in the same order
- Individuals may seek to satisfy several needs at the same time
- Not all of these needs are or can be satisfied through work

Test your understanding 7

Why might a graduate starting a new job who had already satisfied the basic needs on Maslow's hierarchy then seek to satisfy needs in a different order.

2.2 Herzberg's two factor theory of motivation

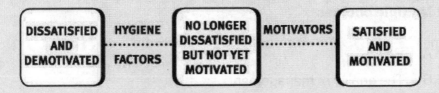

Herzberg's needs based theory identified two sets of factors on the basis that they "motivate" in different ways.

Hygiene factors must be addressed to avoid dissatisfaction and include

- Policies and procedures for staff treatment
- Suitable level and quality of supervision
- Pleasant physical and working conditions
- Appropriate level of salary and status for the job
- Team working

Hygiene factors are concerned with extrinsic factors these are separate from or external to the job itself.

However, in themselves hygiene factors are not sufficient to result in positive motivation.

Motivators include

- Sense of achievement
- Recognition of good work
- Increasing levels of responsibility
- Career advancement
- Attraction of the job itself

The main motivation factors are thus not in the environment but in the intrinsic value and satisfaction gained from the job itself. Most are non-financial in nature.

Test your understanding 8

Which of the following factors can be both a hygiene factor and a motivator for employees?

Multiple choices

A   Pay

B   The quality of management

C   Working conditions

D   The level of responsibility the individual is given

Herzberg defines three ways that management can attempt to improve staff satisfaction and motivation

- **Job enrichment** (sometimes called 'vertical job enlargement') - a deliberate, planned process to improve the responsibility, challenge and creativity of a job. Typical examples include delegation or problem solving. For instance, where an accountant's responsibilities for producing quarterly management reports end at the stage of producing the figures, they could be extended so that they included the preparation of them and the accountant could submit them to senior management. This alteration in responsibilities could not only enrich the job but also increase the workload, leading to delegation of certain responsibilities to clerks within the department, the cascading effect enriching other jobs as well.

- **Job enlargement** - widening the range of jobs, and so developing a job away from narrow specialisation. There is no element of enrichment. Argyris calls this 'horizontal job enlargement'. Herzberg contends that there is little motivation value in this approach.

- **Job rotation** - the planned rotating of staff between jobs to alleviate monotony and provide a fresh job challenge. The documented example quotes a warehouse gang of four workers, where the worst job was tying the necks of the sacks at the base of the hopper after filling; the best job was seen as being the fork-lift truck driver. Job rotation would ensure that equal time was spent by each individual on all jobs. Herzberg suggests that this will help to relieve monotony and improve job satisfaction but is unlikely to create positive motivation.

Test your understanding 9

Modern trends in job design have been aimed at the quality of working life for the worker and labour flexibility. Which of Herzberg's three definitions would these be attributed to?

2.3 McGregor's Theory X/Y

McGregor presented **two opposite sets of assumptions** made by managers about their staff. These assumptions, which he called **Theory X** and **Theory Y,** are implicit in most approaches to supervision,. These theories are opposite ends of a continuum.

Theory X assumptions:

- people dislike work and responsibility
- people must be coerced to get them to make an effort
- subordinates prefer to be directed, wish to avoid responsibility, have relatively little ambition, and want security above all.

Theory Y assumptions:

- physical and mental effort in work is as natural as play or rest

- the average human being does not inherently dislike work, because it can be a source of satisfaction

- people can exercise self-direction and self-control to achieve objectives to which they are committed.

- people can learn to enjoy and seek responsibility

Expandable text

Theory X/Y and management styles

Based on their assumptions, supervisors will adopt a corresponding management style:

- If you believe that you have Theory X workers, then you adopt an authoritarian, repressive style with tight control. Effectively the workforce are a problem that needs to be overcome by management.

- If you believe that you have Theory Y workers, then you adopt a participative, liberating, developmental approach. Employees will be viewed as assets who need to be encouraged and empowered.

Test your understanding 10

According to Douglas McGregor

A   Theory X people "dislike work need direction and avoid responsibility.

B   Theory Y people dislike work, need direction and avoid responsibility.

C   People trying to satisfy ego needs dislike work, need direction and avoid responsibility.

D   Hygiene factors determine whether people like work, need direction or take responsibility.

2.4 The Vroom expectancy model

Vroom believes that people will be motivated to do things to reach a goal if they believe in the worth of that goal and if they can see that what they do will help them in achieving it.

Vroom's theory may be stated as:

Force	= **valence x expectancy**
where	
Force	= the strength of a person's motivation
valence	= the strength of an individual's preference for an outcome
expectancy	= the probability of success

Test your understanding 11

Sonya lacks confidence. Her boss wants to motivate her by showing her that she has regularly exceeded targets in the past. Which aspect of the Vroom model is being focused on here?

3 Intrinsic and extrinsic rewards

Rewards offered to the individual at work may be of two basic types

- **Extrinsic** - are separate from (or external to) the job itself, and is dependent on the decisions of others (that is, external to the control of the workers themselves). Pay, benefits, non-cash incentives and working conditions. Herzberg hygiene factors are examples.

- **Intrinsic** - are those which arise from the performance of the work itself. Intrinsic rewards include the satisfaction that comes from the job itself, the feeling of achievement that comes from doing a difficult job.

Intrinsic rewards include

- Job design
  - Job enrichment
    - Higher level decision making
    - Greater empowerment

  - Job enlargement
    - Increasing task variety by increasing the number of operations

  - Job rotation
    - Transferring staff from one job to another to increase task variety.

Test your understanding 12

Which one of the following is an intrinsic reward?

A   Company car

B   Extra holiday entitlement

C   On the job training of new recruits

D   Bonus payment.

4 Reward systems

Management action is required to keep staff highly motivated in order to deliver high performance. Achievement of high performance may be delivered through positive rewards. It is important that in setting the reward system goal congruence is achieved (e.g. higher productivity may be at the expense of quality when using a piece-rate system)

These rewards should help to

- Attract and retain staff.

- Demonstrate care for employees.

- Improve company image - being seen as a company who is socially responsible.

- To encourage desirable behaviour (motivation).

- Provide a fair and consistent basis for motivating and rewarding employees.

- To further company objectives through an externally based fair system.

- To reward progression or promotion through developed pathways.

- To recognise the various factors apart from performance such as job size, contribution, skills and competences.

- To control salary costs.

Incentive schemes

An incentive scheme ties pay directly to performance and the reward should encourage improvements in performance. It can be tied to the performance of an individual or a team of employees. The scheme should link performance to organisational goals.

There are three main types of incentive schemes

- Performance related pay (PRP)
    - Piecework - reward related to the pace of work or effort. The faster the employee works, the higher the output and the greater the reward.
    - Management by objectives (MBO) - key results are identified for which rewards will be paid on top of salary.
    - Points system - this is an extension to MBO reward systems where a range of rewards is available based on a point system derived from the scale of improvement made such as the amount of cost reduction achieved.
    - Commission - paid on the performance of an individual typically paid to salaried staff in sales functions, where the commission earned is a proportion of total sales.
- Bonus schemes - usually a one off as oppose to PRP schemes which are usually a continual management policy
- Profit sharing
    - Usually available to a wide group of employees (often company wide) where payments are made in the light of the overall profitability of the company.
    - Share issues may be part of the scheme.

Incentives need to encourage effort or action towards the delivery of organisational objectives there can be potential conflict when contrasting long and short term objectives. (e.g. sales staff offering discounts to customers to win extra orders this year to get a bonus, at the expense of next year's sales)

- Long-term incentive schemes will be those that are designed to continually motivate and deliver organisational objectives.
- Short-term incentive schemes will be those that motivate in he short-term but do not deliver on-going motivation and are often achieved at the detriment of longer term objectives.

Test your understanding 13

Discuss the objectives of reward management.

Chapter summary

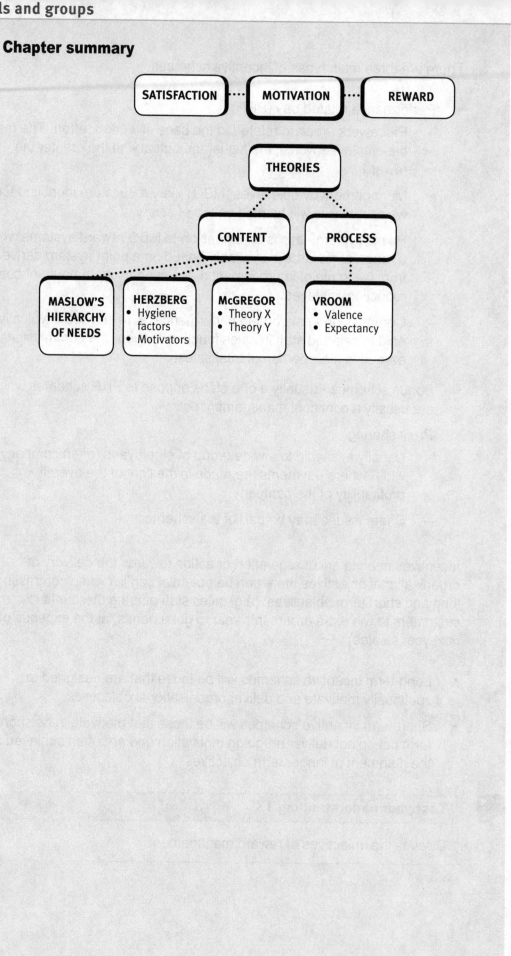

Test your understanding answers

Test your understanding 1

The point at issue is the way in which the job is done. It is suggested that if individuals can be "motivated" by one means or another,

- They will work more effectively and productivity will rise.
- They will produce a better quality of work.
- They will exercise their creativity and initiative in the service of organisational goals.

Test your understanding 2

Statements	Satisfaction	Motivation
Low staff turnover	✓	
Fewer mistakes		✓
Higher productivity		✓
Higher levels of trust	✓	

Explanation: a satisfied worker will be more content with their job and will trust their employer. Motivation is required for the employee to work harder and take more care over their work.

Test your understanding 3

There is no evidence that job satisfaction can lead to increased productivity. To increase productivity the employees need to be motivated. (see motivational theories)

Test your understanding 4

It could be argued that if a person is employed to do a job, he will do that job and motivation should not arise. The point that we need to consider is the way in which the job is done. If individuals are motivated they will work more efficiently and productivity will rise. They may produce a better quality of work. Motivation may ensure that they exercise their creativity and initiative in the service of organisational goals.

Test your understanding 5

Statements	Satisfied	Not Satisfied	Explanation
Self-achievement needs	✓		Self-achievement needs should be satisfied by the succuss of the business.
Ego needs	✓		Ego needs should be satisfied by being MD.
Social needs	✓		Social needs are met by being part of the Board of Directors (Note: you could have argued that some MDs may feel isolated and that the Board is against them.)
Safety/ security needs	✓		Security needs will be met by a generous pension scheme and a long notice period.
Basic/ physiological needs	✓		Basic needs are satisfied by a high salary.

Test your understanding 6

(a) **Salary**

(b) Sense of achievement = self fulfilment needs

(c) Recognition = ego needs

(d) **Bonus**

(e) Interpersonal relationships = social needs

Rationale: Salary and bonus are second order factors and may contribute towards first order needs but do not appear on the hierarchy.

Test your understanding 7

A graduate might then seek to meet social needs before worrying about job security and long term security of pension arrangements.

Test your understanding 8

A

Explanation

Herzberg argued that the quality of management and working conditions are hygiene factors, and the level of responsibility is a motivator. He also argued that pay is a hygiene factor, particularly basic pay. However, pay can also be used as an incentive/motivator, for example by offering the prospect of a cash bonus for achieving a performance target.

Test your understanding 9

Labour flexibility would include functional flexibility (multi-skilling) which would allow employees to move around the organisation depending on demand required in each department, this could be linked to job rotation.

Test your understanding 10

Answer = A

McGregor suggested the ideas of Theory X and Y so the answer has to be A or B.

Test your understanding 11

Expectancy - the perceived profitability of success is being modified, not the value of the reward.

Test your understanding 12

Answer = C

This would be considered as increased responsibility therefore an intrinsic value.

Test your understanding 13

- To attract and retain suitable employees.
- To maintain and improve levels of employee performance.
- To comply with legislation and regulation.

Information technology and information systems in business

Chapter learning objectives

Upon completion of this chapter you will be able to:

- explain how organisations deploy information systems in their operations

- describe the advantages computerisation will bring to a company

- list the attributes of good quality information

- explain how the type of information differs and the purposes for which it is applied at different levels of the organisation: strategic, tactical and operational

- list the internal and external sources of information

- identify what information organisation can obtain from internal/external sources

- describe the main features of information systems used within the organisation

- explain the features of:
    - transaction processing systems
    - management information systems
    - executive information systems
    - decision support systems
    - expert systems
    - spreadsheet and database software.

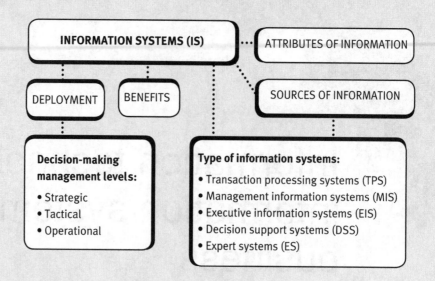

1 Information technology and information systems

Information is different from data.

Data consists of numbers, letters, symbols, raw facts, events and transactions, which have been recorded but not yet processed into a form that is suitable for making decisions.

Data can also be classified as:

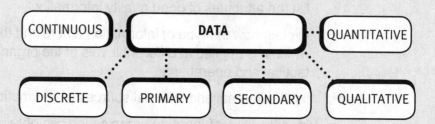

Expandable text

Quantitative data is that capable of being measured numerically, e.g. the standard labour hours required to produce one unit of output.

Qualitative data is not capable of being measured numerically but may reflect distinguishing characteristics, e.g. the grade of labour used to produce the unit of output.

Data is said to be discrete when it can only take on specific fixed values, e.g. the actual number of vehicles through a car wash per day could be 35 but not 35.3. Whereas continuous data takes on any numerical value and we could, in an eight hour day, measure the throughput of cars as 4.375 per hour, i.e. 35 cars / 8 hours.

KAPLAN PUBLISHING

Data needs to be collected and summarised to the form required by the user.

Primary data is collected for a particular enquiry, for example by observation, employees would be observed performing a 'value adding' activity when establishing a standard time for the activity.

Data collected by a trade association from a number of firms and comprising trade association statistics would become secondary data when used by a firm in the sector making an enquiry of its own.

Information is data that has been processed in such a way that it has a meaning to the person who receives it, who may then use it to improve the quality of decision-making.

It is a vital requirement within any business and is required both internally and externally. Management requires information:

- to provide records, both current and historical
- to analyse what is happening within the business
- to provide the basis of decision making in the short-term andlong-term
- to monitor the performance of the business by comparing actual results with plans and forecasts.

Various third parties require information about the business, including:

- the owners, e.g. shareholders
- customers and suppliers
- the employees
- government agencies such as tax authorities.

Data processing is the conversion of data into information, perhaps by classifying, sorting or producing total figures. The conversion process may be manual or automated. In general, data may be transformed into information by:

- bringing related pieces of data together
- summarising data
- basic processing of data
- tabulation and diagrammatic techniques
- statistical analysis
- financial analysis.

Information technology (IT) describes any equipment concerned with the capture, storage, transmission or presentation of information

The IT is the supporting hardware that provides the infrastructure to run the information systems.

 Information systems (IS) refer to the provision and management of information to support the running of the organisation.

1.1 Deploying information systems in the organisation

Information systems are a combination of planned procedures, suitably designed forms, an appropriate organisation structure and managers who are capable of using the output that is produced to assist them in the administration and use of available resources.

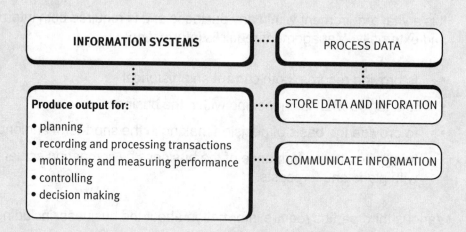

The output from the systems falls into two groups:

- routine reports or transaction documents are those required to conform to business conventions, such as payslips, invoices sent to customers, purchase orders sent to suppliers and works orders sent to the factory, day book listings or standard letters

- management information in the form of reports which are summaries of or extracts from the data which has been processed, e.g. labour cost analyses, sales analyses, stock reports.

 Illustration 1 – Information technology and information systems

In cost accounting the accounting system records a large number of facts (data) about materials, times, expenses and other transactions. These facts are then classified and summarised to produce accounts, which are organised into reports that are designed to help management to plan and control the organisation's activities.

KAPLAN PUBLISHING

Test your understanding 1

A typical market research survey employs a number of researchers who interview a sample of the target market and ask them a number of questions relating to the product or service. Several hundred questionnaires may be completed and they will then be processed.

Why does the data need processing and what processing operations will be carried out?

Test your understanding 2

Twenty five employees from the finance department of a large organisation took an introductory course in Computing. The test at the end of the course resulted in the marks shown below. The marks were out of 50 and the pass mark was 20 out of 50. Can you process this data so that the manager of the finance department can make decisions based on the results?

12	19	8	21	32
25	34	22	30	20
43	21	16	45	32
27	38	39	21	18
33	11	28	26	27

1.2 The advantages computerisation will bring to a company

Most aspects of our economy, from the music industry to manufacturing, banking, retailing and defence, are now totally dependent on modern information processing systems. Developments in information technology provide companies with new opportunities, e.g:

- internet
- access to corporate databases
- mobile computing

- improved telecommunication structure.

The value of computer systems in handling and processing business data cannot be underestimated.

Computers have revolutionised information systems for the following reasons:

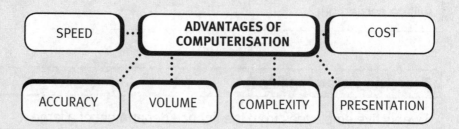

Expandable text

The advantages of computerisation include the following:

- **Speed** – Computers are ideal for dealing with repetitive processes. The limiting factors, for example, in processing a payroll by computer are not the speed of calculation by the computer, but the speed with which data can be input and the speed of the printer at the output.

- **Accuracy** – In general, computers do not suffer from errors, or lapses of concentration but process data perfectly. Any mistakes that computers make nowadays are not caused by electronic error, but by human error, for example at the input stage, or in designing and programming software.

- **Volume** – Not only do computers work fast, but they do not need to rest. They can work twenty-four hour days when required. They are therefore able to handle vast volumes of data.

- **Complexity** – Once subsystems are computerised they can generally function more reliably than human beings. This makes it easier to integrate various subsystems. Computers are therefore able to handle complex information systems efficiently. However, one of the problems with this is that when the computer does fail, there is often a major breakdown in the system, with many personnel unable to perform their work functions.

- **Cost** – All the above advantages mean that computers have become highly cost-effective providers of information. The process of substituting computers for human beings has revolutionised information-oriented industries such as accountancy, banking and insurance and this process is continuing.

- **Presentation** – More recently, emphasis has been placed on displaying information in as 'user-friendly' a way as possible. Modern packages containing sophisticated word processors, spreadsheets and graphics combined with the development of colour printers now enable boring reports to be presented in new and exciting ways!

Note – It is necessary, however, to remember the advantages that people have as providers of information. Chief amongst these is judgement of reasonableness. People can usually see when an item of information looks unreasonable. Although it is possible to program limited reasonableness tests into computer systems, it is still very difficult to program judgement. The computer remains a highly trained idiot, which is particularly apparent when a programming error is made or it is subject to a computer virus.

Test your understanding 3

Why does a computer system process information better than a manual system?

Information systems are also seen as a valuable strategic resource which can help an organisation gain competitive advantage, e.g. those instances where the information system:

- links the organisation to customers or suppliers

- creates effective integration of the use of information in a value-adding process

- enables the organisation to develop, produce, market and deliver new products and/or services based on information

- gives senior management information to help develop and implement strategy.

Illustration 2 – Information technology and information systems

For example, strong links with suppliers can be forged by the use of computerised Just-In-Time stock systems. Customers can be 'tied in' to a company's products or services by being given an IT link for after-sales service. Computerised systems can also can help not only by mechanising production systems but also by making the planning of production more efficient.

2 The qualities of information

Good information is information that helps in the decision-making process, is useful to the recipient and can be relied upon. The information supplied to management must add to the understanding of a situation and display the following qualities of good information. You can remember these qualities by means of the mnemonic ACCURATE

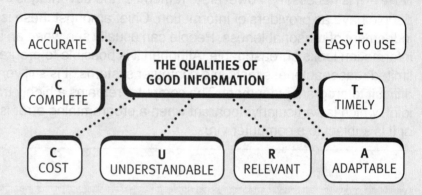

- Accurate – information should be sufficiently accurate for its intended purpose and the decision-maker should be able to rely on the information.

- Complete – the more complete information is, the more reliable it will be.

- Cost – the information should not cost more to obtain than the benefit derived from it.

- Understandable and user friendly information is much more readily acted upon.

- Relevant – the information provided should concentrate on the essentials and ignore trivia.

- Adaptable – information should be tailored to the needs and level of understanding of its intended recipients.

- Timely – information that is out-of-date is a waste of time, effort and money.

- Easy to use – information should be clearly presented and sent using the right medium and communication channel.

Test your understanding 4

Why is it important for information for decision-making to be complete, relevant, timely, accurate and significant?

3 Management structure and information requirements

The levels of decision-making and the information required to support it have been analysed into three levels – strategic, tactical and operational, as discussed in chapter 1.

An organisation's information systems must be organised in such a way as to meet the information needs of these various levels of management.

- The strategic level of management requires information from internal and external sources in order to plan the long-term strategies of the organisation. Internal information – both quantitative and qualitative – is usually supplied in a summarised form, often on an ad-hoc basis.

- The tactical level of management requires information and instructions from the strategic level of management together with routine and regular quantitative information from the operational level of management. The information would be in a summarised form, but detailed enough to allow tactical planning of resources and manpower.

- The operational level of management requires information and instructions from the tactical level of management. The operational level is primarily concerned with the day-to-day performance of tasks and most of the information is obtained from internal sources. The information must be detailed and precise.

The following chart outlines the characteristics of information at each of the levels of management/decision-making in an organisation

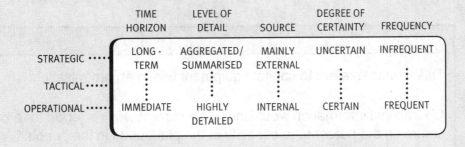

3.1 The type of information used at each level of the organisation

Typical information used at each of the management levels include:

Strategic	Tactical	Operational
• expected government policy • overall profitability • competitor analysis • profitability of divisions/ segments of the business • future market prospects • availability and cost of capital • total cash needs • resource levels • capital equipment requirements	• productivity measurements • budgetary control reports • variance analysis • stock turnover • cash flow forecasts • short-term purchasing requirments • labour turnover statistics within a department/ factory	• employee hours worked • raw materials input to a production process • hours spent on each individual job • reject rate • stock levels

Illustration 3 – Management structure and information

This example refers to capital equipment use in an organisation:

Operational information would include a current week's report for a cost centre on the percentage capacity of the plant used in the period.

Tactical information could include the short-term budget for 12 months and would show the budgeted machine use in terms of machine hours for each item of plant. The total machine hours being predetermined from the production budget for the period.

Strategic information would relate to the longer-term strategy on the company's market share, which in turn informs the production plan. This plan would be used to predetermine the level of investment required in capital equipment in the longer term. This process would also lead to investigating new methods and technology.

Test your understanding 5

The information used at lower levels of the management hierarchy may be characterised as routine, complete, structured, detailed, computational and short term.

How would you characterise the information used at strategic levels of management?

4 Sources of information

4.1 Internal/external sources of information

A great deal of interpreted information is disseminated within an organisation, and used by its members. The organisation as an information-processing entity is shown in the figure below.

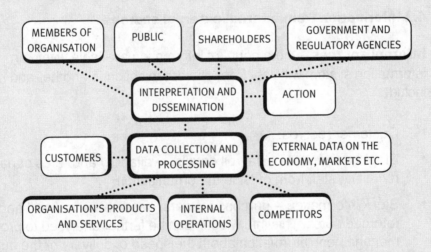

Data and information collected by an organisation may be internal (from the organisation itself) or external (from outside the organisation).

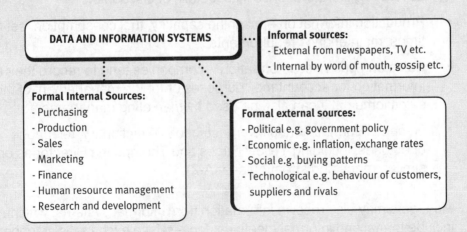

Internal data/information will relate to activities or transactions performed within the organisation, e.g.:

- administrative tasks
- the production of products and services
- the sale of those products.

Often these activities generate costs and revenues, so much of the internal data/information collected will be quantitative.

External data/information will come from customers, suppliers and potential suppliers. The phrase environmental scanning is often used to describe the process of gathering external information, relating to the outside world or the 'environment' of the organisation, which is available from a wide range of sources.

4.2 Information from internal/external sources

Internal sources – the amount of information available within an information system will vary from one organisation to another and may include.

- Customer records.

- Employee records – payroll details, availability and rates of pay, cost of recruiting staff from outside the organisation.

- Stock information – purchase orders, goods received and goods returned notes. This information can be further analysed to provide management information about the speed of delivery or the quality of supplies.

- Product or service details and specifications – nominal ledger codes, advertising literature, price lists, details of discounts.

- Production information – machine capacity, fuel consumption, set up times, maintenance requirements.

- Sales and purchase information – companies tend to record their sales information for accountancy purposes or for the management of the sales force but it can also be used by marketing management.

- General information and reference books – dictionary, telephone directories, including Yellow Pages and Thompsons Directories or similar, maps and street guides (A-Z).

Managers may also receive information from informal systems, which include formal and informal meetings, face-to-face exchanges, telephone conversations, ad hoc memoranda and 'grapevine' rumours.

External sources – an organisation's files will be full of information received from customers and suppliers, e.g.:

- invoices
- letters
- stock price quotations
- catalogues
- advertisements.

Systems for obtaining external information include.

- Market research and analysis of competitors' prices
- Legal and regulatory update information: changes to company law, tax law, employment law, accounting standards, environmental protection, etc.
- Government data on economic and financial conditions
- Research intelligence: information about technology changes or new discoveries that may have an impact on the organisation
- Other forms of market intelligence: for example the formal collection of feedback forms from customers, salesmen and others 'in the field', such as maintenance staff.

Illustration 4 – Sources of information

A company is thinking of adding a new baby milk substitute to its existing range of baby foods and is considering only secondary sources of information for its market research. Possible sources of secondary information include:

- Past market research – it is quite probable that the company will have undertaken relevant research in connection with similar products.
- Existing sales – will indicate current consumer preferences that together with past sales may show trends.
- Government health departments/agencies may have significant information regarding baby foods together with its current advice to parents.
- Milk Marketing Boards may have undertaken relevant research or have useful information regarding trends.
- Supermarket/baby food retailers may have analyses regarding consumer choices and apparent preferences.

Other sources of information include trade organisations, universities and colleges, welfare organisations and specialist consumer groups.

Test your understanding 6

What sort of data is collected by staff in a purchasing department?

5 Information systems used within an organisation

A modern organisation needs a wide range of systems to process, analyse and hold information. We have already noted that the different management decision-making levels within an organisation need different types of information and in this section we look at how the information systems vary accordingly.

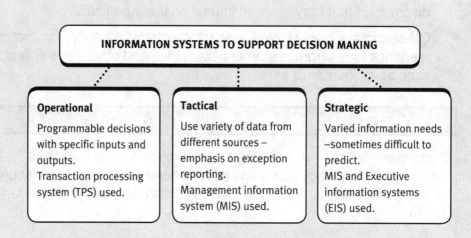

There are five main types of information processing system:

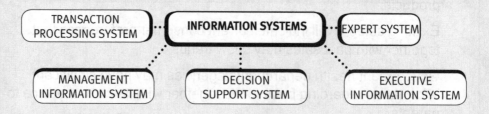

Transaction processing systems (TPS)

Definition and purpose	Examples of use
(1) Records all daily routine transactions in an organisation (2) Used mainly by operational level managers (3) Supplies summary data to DSS and MIS	(1) Sales/marketing systems. Record sales transactions and provide details on marketing and promotional activities. (2) Manufacturing production systems. Records details of purchases, production and shipping of goods. (3) Finance/accounting systems. Maintenance of financial data in organisation. (4) Human resources – maintain details of employees.

Test your understanding 7

A friend of yours owns a small supermarket. He has told you that he plans to introduce an electronic point-of-sale system soon and he would like to know what the benefits would be to the stock control process.

Make a list of the benefits that you would explain to your friend.

Management information systems (MIS)

Definition and purpose	Examples of use
(1) Converts data into information and communicates that information in an appropriate form to managers at all levels. (2) Enables managers to make timely and effective decisions for planning and controlling the activities for which they are responsible. (3) Used extensively by tactical users.	(1) Product information – on-line categorised information at a keystroke. (2) Sales ledger – information relating to customer turnover and payment records. Trend analysis to identify customers whose business is growing/declining. (3) Supplier information – such as amount spent and reliability indicators to use when negotiating and making strategic decisions.

Within most management information systems there are four system types.

- Database systems which process and store information which becomes the organisation's memory.

- Direct control systems which monitor and report on activities such as output levels, sales ledger and credit accounts in arrears.

- Enquiry systems based on databases which provide specific information such as the performance of a department or an employee.

- Support systems which provide computer-based methods and procedures for conducting analyses, forecasts and simulations.

Decision support systems (DSS)

Definition and purpose	Examples of use
(1) An integrated, computer-based, user-machine system that provides information for supporting operations and decision-making functions. (2) Assists tactical or management level decision makers. (3) No typical system – depends on requirements in company.	(1) Supports structured decision making. (2) Provides online access to TPS to obtain summary data. (3) May provide external information on competitors. (4) Basic statistical analysis normally found in a DSS.

Executive information systems (EIS)

Definition and purpose	Examples of use
(1) A system for total business modelling. (2) Monitors internal and external environment.	(1) Company performance data on sales, production, earnings, budgets and forecasts. (2) Internal communications such as personal correspondence, reports and meetings. (3) Environmental scanning for news on government regulations, competition, etc.

Expert systems (ES)

Definition and purpose	Examples of use
(1) A form of DSS that allows users to benefit from expert knowledge and information (2) Not part of normal 'hierarchy' of information systems but provides useful information to any management level (3) Uses a knowledge base from which a piece of software determines solutions to user questions.	(1) Process loan applications (2) Legal advice (3) Forecasting of economic or financial developments or of market and customer behaviour

The application of these to different aspects of the business are covered in Chapter 11.

Expandable Text

We can identify five different types of information system:

(1) Transaction Processing Systems (TPS)

A transaction processing system gathers source data relating to individual monetary transactions (purchases, sales, costs) and summarises them so that they can be reported on a routine basis. These systems represent the lowest level in an organisation's use of information systems. They are used for routine tasks in which data items or transactions must be processed so that operations can continue.

The function of transaction processing is concerned with recording, processing and communicating data relating to the activities involved in converting input resources into goods and services to meet customers' needs.

Examples of common TPS are the purchase ledger, sales ledger and payroll systems.

(2) Management Information Systems (MIS)

Management information systems (MIS) convert data from a TPS into information for monitoring performance, maintainingco-ordination and providing background information about the organisation's operation. Typical users are managers at the tactical level for planning, controlling and making unstructured orsemi-structured decisions.

The information within a system is used in three basic ways:

- to keep records (historic details)
- to supply management information (up-to-date information)
- to forecast (predictions, planning, etc.).

A sales transaction processing system stores transaction data (name of salesperson, customer name and address, name and quantity of item sold, line sales amount, total sales amount, form of payment) on every sale made. The MIS then generates reports (the frequency of the report being specified by users) such as:

- total sales for each item
- total sales for region
- sales for each salesperson.

(3) Decision Support Systems (DSS)

Decision support systems are computer-based systems that help decision-makers confront ill-structured problems through direct interaction with data and analysis models.

A good DSS should have balance among the following three capabilities:

- it should be easy to use to support the interaction withnon-technical users
- it should have access to a wide variety of data.
- it should provide modelling and analysis in many ways.

This report could come from a decision support system used by marketing staff in planning corporate entertainment events. It shows a real-time weather forecast for the region in which the event is to be held.

KAPLAN PUBLISHING

(4) Executive Information Systems (EIS)

Executive Information Systems (EIS) provide managers with flexible access to information at the tactical and strategic levels, for monitoring operating results and general business conditions. They monitor both the internal and external environment of the company and highlights information that the executive should be made aware of. In some ways they resemble, in outcomes, the DSS, but whereas the DSS provided tools that required significant expertise to use, the EIS is designed to help managers find the information they need whenever they need it, and in the most appropriate format. For both DSS and EIS, the TPS/database will be the source of raw information. The EIS is a high cost facility, and therefore its use is likely to be limited to high-level management functions.

A typical screen-based report from an EIS would combine many types of data on the same screen.

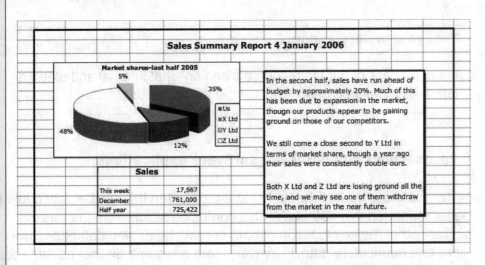

The introduction of an EIS should negate the necessity for a great majority of manual reports. The executive would have faster access to information and would be able to 'drill-down' to gain more detailed information if required.

(5) Expert systems (ES)

Expert systems hold specialist (expert) knowledge and allow non-experts to interrogate the system for information, advice and recommended decisions.

There are many examples of expert systems in such areas of business as credit control, engineering and recruitment. Even something as simple as the control panel of a photocopier can be considered an expert system, as it allows the operator to diagnose the cause of a machine breakdown and to fix the machine.

They are used widely in the following areas:

- law (e.g. conveyancing)
- taxation (e.g. personal tax)
- banking (e.g. granting credit)
- medicine (e.g. diagnosis of symptoms)
- defence (e.g. aircraft recognition).

Expert systems can be used at a variety of different levels. At the simplest level they can give factual answers to technical questions. At a more complex level they can suggest how a decision should be made, recommending a course of action. In this respect they go further than decision support systems.

Test your understanding 8

In the process of human resource planning what internal and external information may be used to assist the management?

6 Spreadsheet and database software applications

Many users use spreadsheets to store data, even though the data could be better managed in a database. This confusion stems from the basic similarity that the key function of both spreadsheets and databases is to store and manipulate data. However, there are some distinct advantages and disadvantages to both spreadsheets and databases that define their usefulness as a data management tool.

6.1 Spreadsheets

Spreadsheets are designed to analyse data and sort list items, not for long-term storage of raw data. A spreadsheet should be used for 'crunching' numbers and storage of single list items. They also include graphing functions that allow for quick reporting and analysis of data.

Advantages	Disadvantages
• Spreadsheet programs are relatively easy to use, • require little training to get started and • most data managers are familiar with them.	• You have to re-copy data over and over again to maintain it in separate data files. • Inability to efficiently identify data errors, • Spreadsheets lack detailed sorting and querying abilities • There can be sharing violations among users wishing to view or change data at the same time. • Additionally, spreadsheets are restricted to a finite number of records, and can require a large amount of hard-drive space for data storage.

6.2 Databases

To store large amounts of raw data, it is best to use a database. This is especially true in circumstances where two or more users share the information.

Advantages	Disadvantages
• The most important benefit gained by using a database is the ease of reporting and sharing data. • Databases require little or no duplication of data between information tables • Changes made to the data do not corrupt the programming (e.g. at the cell level of a spreadsheet where calculations are running) • Databases offer better security to restrict users from accessing privileged information, and from changing coded information in the programming.	• Requires the user to learn a new system • Requires a greater investment in training and software. • The initial time and cost of migrating all of the data into a new database system

Test your understanding 9

Which of the following is not an advantage that databases have over spreadsheets:

A   Less training required

B   Better security

C   Less duplication of information

D   Greater ease of sharing information.

Chapter summary

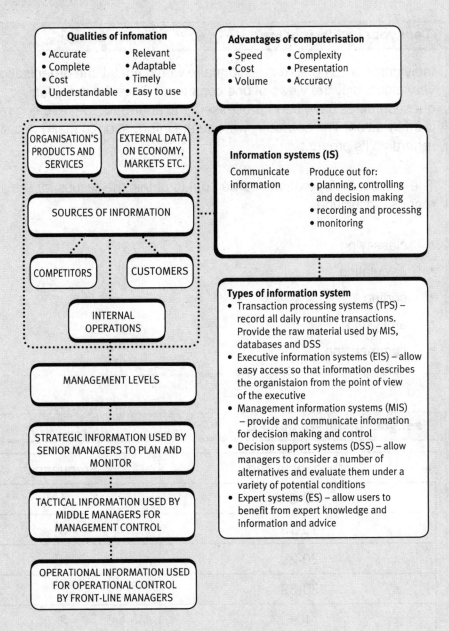

Qualities of infomation
- Accurate
- Complete
- Cost
- Understandable
- Relevant
- Adaptable
- Timely
- Easy to use

Advantages of computerisation
- Speed
- Cost
- Volume
- Complexity
- Presentation
- Accuracy

ORGANISATION'S PRODUCTS AND SERVICES

EXTERNAL DATA ON ECONOMY, MARKETS ETC.

SOURCES OF INFORMATION

COMPETITORS

CUSTOMERS

INTERNAL OPERATIONS

MANAGEMENT LEVELS

STRATEGIC INFORMATION USED BY SENIOR MANAGERS TO PLAN AND MONITOR

TACTICAL INFORMATION USED BY MIDDLE MANAGERS FOR MANAGEMENT CONTROL

OPERATIONAL INFORMATION USED FOR OPERATIONAL CONTROL BY FRONT-LINE MANAGERS

Information systems (IS)

Communicate information

Produce out for:
- planning, controlling and decision making
- recording and processing
- monitoring

Types of information system
- Transaction processing systems (TPS) – record all daily routine transactions. Provide the raw material used by MIS, databases and DSS
- Executive information systems (EIS) – allow easy access so that information describes the organistaion from the point of view of the executive
- Management information systems (MIS) – provide and communicate information for decision making and control
- Decision support systems (DSS) – allow managers to consider a number of alternatives and evaluate them under a variety of potential conditions
- Expert systems (ES) – allow users to benefit from expert knowledge and information and advice

Test your understanding answers

Test your understanding 1

Individually a completed questionnaire would not tell the organisation very much, only the views of one consumer. Once the individual questionnaires have been processed and analysed, the resulting report is information. The company will use the information to make decisions regarding its product.

The processing operations carried out to obtain the results for the reports will include:

- classifying
- calculating
- sorting
- analysing
- summarising.

Test your understanding 2

Marks obtained	Frequency
0-9	1
10-19	5
20-29	10
30-39	7
40+	2

This chart shows that the 19 employees that pass the test (achieve 20+) are in the top 3 class intervals and those that fail – 6 employees – are in the bottom two intervals.

There are many ways that the data could have been processed and presented but, because we are not aware of the specific requirements, this type of general chart could form the basis for further processing if required.

Test your understanding 3

The functions of computers in information processing include:

- processing information more quickly
- handling bigger volumes of processing
- undertaking complex operations
- processing information more reliably, i.e. with less chance of errors and mistakes
- processing information at less cost than a manual system
- improving the scope and quality of management information.

Test your understanding 4

It is important for information for decision-making to have the following qualities:

- completeness – if a decision is being made details of all possible options should be available for consideration
- relevance – only that information which is useful to the decision making process should be included
- timeliness – unless the information is up to date and produced in time for the decision to be made it is unlikely to be useful
- accuracy – the information must be sufficiently accurate for the purposes of the decision being made, but any greater levels of precision may reduce its overall value
- significance – to ensure that the information is meaningful to the person using it should concentrate on the points that are needed by the decision maker.

Test your understanding 5

At strategic levels of management the most useful information can be characterised as subjective, incomplete, unstructured, summary, ad hoc and long term.

Test your understanding 6

The data will be related to:

- Suppliers – the standing of the organisation (you do not want to be dealing with a company that is on the verge of bankruptcy), the quality of their service, the discounts they offer, theirafter-sales service, the delivery charges and times etc.

- Products and services – the prices, availability, quality assurance and the quantities supplied.

Test your understanding 7

The benefits, which would be gained from using electronic point-of-sale terminals in the stock control process, include:

- update of inventory records – as soon as goods are sold, the inventory records are updated. This means they will always show the correct inventory balance. This will enable him to order the precise inventory it requires, rather than using an element of guesswork with partly out of date information from the old system

- decrease in input errors – details of stock movements will be taken directly from bar codes, or a similar input system, attached to each stock line. This should decrease the number of input errors compared to a manual input system. The stock records should also provide more accurate information concerning the items in stock.

- provision of additional management information – concerning sales of individual product lines will be easily collected for each day; changes in quantity sold resulting from a change in the price charged for goods will also be shown. This information can be used by the manager in determining the price for goods, and will assist in the marketing strategy by ensuring products are sold at similar prices to the local competition.

Test your understanding 8

Internal data to assist	External data to assist
• Employee gender, age, qualification, skill and experience • Categories of staff • Staff suitable for promotion or redeployment • Overtime levels and trends • Labour turnover analysis and reasons • Absence level categories and trends • Productivity ratios and trends	• Regional employment and unemployment trends • Demographic projections • Education levels and proposals • Transport planning and proposals • Labour mobility and immigration • Growth of competing firms in the area

Test your understanding 9

A

Database systems are generally considered to be more complex than spreadsheets.

9

Political and legal factors

Chapter learning objectives

Upon completion of this chapter you will be able to:

- define what factors of the external environment influence an organisation

- explain how political systems and governmental policy affect the organisation

- identify the governmental organisations that influence national and regional policy setting

- explain the difference between data protection and data security

- outline the main principles of data protection

- outline the potential risks to data held in the organisation and possible counter measures

- briefly describe the different types of hazards commonly found in the workplace

- outline the main features of health and safety legislation

- identify who is responsible for compliance with legislation.

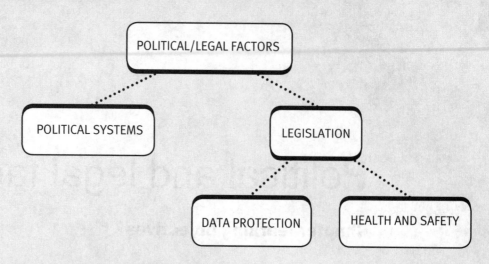

1 Introduction to PEST analysis

1.1 Environmental analysis

As discussed in chapter 1, firms will carry out external analysis as part of their strategic planning. This is to identify potential threats and opportunities.

This external analysis should encompass the following factors:

- Political / legal factors – covered in this chapter.
- Economic factors – covered in chapter 10.
- Social / demographic factors – covered in chapter 11.
- Technological factors – covered in chapter 11.
- Competitive factors – covered in chapter 12.

The first four of these are sometimes referred to as a PEST analysis.

Expandable text

This same categorisation of environmental factors is sometimes referred to as

- PESTL analysis – where legal is separated from political.
- STEP analysis – PEST reordered!
- PESTLE analysis – political, economic, social, technical, legal and ecological/environmental.

The **political** environment includes taxation policy, government stability and foreign trade regulations.

The **economic** environment includes interest rates, inflation, business cycles, unemployment, disposable income and energy availability and cost.

The **social/cultural** environment includes population demographics, social mobility, income distribution, lifestyle changes, attitudes to work and leisure, levels of education and consumerism.

The **technological** environment is influenced by government spending on research, new discoveries and development, government and industry focus of technological effort, speed of technological transfer and rates of obsolescence.

The **legal** environment covers influences such as taxation, employment law, monopolies legislation and environmental protection laws.

The **ecological** environment, sometimes just referred to as 'the environment' considers ways in which the organisation can produce its goods or services with the minimum environmental damage.

Illustration 1 – Introduction to pest analysis

For example, a haulage firm might monitor the following factors:

Political

- Fuel tax.
- Government steps to reduce pollution from lorries.
- Congestion charges in cities.
- Plans to build new roads.
- Road blockades due to strikes (e.g. in France).

Economic

- State of the economy – a downturn would result in less trade.
- Fuel is a major cost so oil price movements will be seen as significant.
- Most hauliers borrow to purchase trucks, so a rise in interest rates would increase costs.

Social

- Predicted car numbers and usage would affect likelihood of traffic jams and hence journey times.
- Public concerns over safety could result in lorries being banned from certain routes or/and reductions in speed limits.

Technological

- Developments in route planning software.
- Anti-theft devices.
- Tracking systems to monitor driver hours.
- Developments in tyre technology.

Competitive

- Competitive rivalry from other hauliers.
- Threat from substitutes – e.g. haulage by rail.
- Threat of new firms entering the market.

Test your understanding 1

List the factors that a farmer might consider as part of their external strategic analysis.

2 Political systems and government policy

2.1 Political systems

A political system is a complete set of

- institutions
- political organisations
- interest groups (such as trade unions, lobby groups)
- the relationships between those institutions and
- the political norms and rules that govern their functions (constitution, election law).

Firms have to take account of political systems at three levels

(1) Global – e.g. WTO, EU legislation.

(2) National – national government policy, national legislation, government departments.

(3) Local – local government departments, councils.

As with all external analysis, the factors considered may present firms with opportunities or threats.

2.2 Government policy

Governments can influence firms through legislation (section 2.3 below) and government policy decisions. For example,

Illustration 2 – Political systems and government policy

Housing

- New housing developments can give opportunities to house building firms and will create new communities that will demand shops, leisure facilities, etc, giving opportunities for firms in these industries.

Crime

- Crime policy can affect firms that specialise in security.

Education

- Education policy can affect the availability of suitable potential employees for firms.

Defence

- Defence policy will primarily affect arms manufacturers.
- Closure of a military base could have serious implications for local suppliers.

Healthcare

- Healthcare policy has obvious implications for drugs and equipment manufacturers and private hospitals.

Energy

- Policy regarding choice of energy sources (e.g. nuclear) will be critical to power generators.

Environmental

- Targets on greenhouse gas emissions will affect major manufacturers.

Farming

- Government support through subsidies is critical for many farmers.

Town planning

- National plans to build new roads could influence business location.
- On a local level firms need to obtain planning permission for a new factory or to open new shops or build new houses.

Domestic

- A government may use regional development grants to attract new employers to areas of high unemployment.

Foreign

- Protectionism.
- Trade relations with other countries, e.g. a ban of the sale of arms to Iran.

2.3 Legislation

Organisations need to ensure that they comply with legislation. Failure to do so could result in fines, closure, bad publicity and/or loss of customers.

Most industries have specific legislation that must be complied with, e.g. food labelling in the food industry.

Key areas of legislation that affect all firms include:

- protecting employee rights
- protecting consumers
- protecting the environment
- health and safety
- data protection.

These are covered in detail below.

Test your understanding 2

In September 2006 the State of California in the USA issued a lawsuit against six major car manufacturers over their contribution to global warming and its impact on California.

This is clearly a threat to the six manufacturers concerned. Give examples of two firms for which this gives an opportunity.

Test your understanding 3

Suppose a government decided to introduce a new tax whereby home owners were taxed on all profits made when buying and selling houses. Give an example of a firm for which this is an opportunity and a firm for which this is a threat.

2.4 Sources of legal authority

Sources of legal authority include the following:

Supra-national

- United Nations resolutions.

- International Court of Justice.

- Other international agreements that apply to signatories (e.g. The World Trade Organisation sets rules on trade between member states).

- European Parliament.

- European Courts.

National

- National Governments through Acts of Parliament.

- Senior Courts (e.g. House of Lords in UK, The Supreme Court in the USA).

- Other major courts through the principles of case law and the setting of precedents.

Regional

- Regional / federal Government (e.g. Welsh assembly in the UK, State Government in the USA).

- Local councils can issue bye-laws in many countries.

The Kyoto Protocol to the United Nations Framework Convention on Climate Change is an amendment to the international treaty on climate change, assigning mandatory targets for the reduction of greenhouse gas emissions to signatory nations.

Would this be an opportunity or a threat to a factory owner in the USA (a country that has not signed up to the protocol)?

3 The principles of data protection and security

3.1 Data protection and data security

Data protection is concerned with protecting individuals against the misuse of information about them held by organisations.

This is necessary because of:

- Easy interrogation of large files – especially from outside.
- Speed of response – entire files can be copied or transmitted in seconds.
- Computer systems can be cross-linked to obtain personal profiles.
- An individual's records can be selected easily through the search facilities.

Data security is concerned with keeping data safe from various hazards that could destroy or compromise it.

These include:

- Physical risks- impact on the physical environment in which the system exists, e.g. fire or flood.
- Human risks – access is gained to the system by an unauthorised user, either physically or remotely, e.g. hacking, virus infection and fraud.

Illustration 3 – The principles of data protection and security

In 2003 two hackers broke into Riverside County, California court computers and electronically dismissed a variety of pending cases. Both William Grace, 22, and Brandon Wilson, 28, were sentenced to nine years in jail after pleading guilty to 72 counts of illegally entering a computer system and editing data, along with seven counts of conspiracy to commit extortion.

3.2 The main principles of data protection

The principles of data protection vary from country to country but a typical policy could incorporate the following:

(1) Personal data shall be obtained and processed fairly and lawfully, and in particular shall not be processed unless at least one of the following is met:

- The data subject has given his or her consent; or, processing is necessary; or

- For the performance of a contract to which the data subject is party (or to take steps to enter into a contract at the request of the data subject); or

- To comply with any legal obligation of the data controller; or

- For the administration of justice; or

- For the exercise of any function conferred by or under enactment; or for any other function in the public interest.

- For the processing of 'sensitive personal data', data controllers have to meet additional requirements including:

- The data subject has given explicit consent; or

- The data relates to ethnic origin and the processing relates to the company's maintenance of equal opportunity standards.

(2) Personal data shall be obtained for one or more specified and lawful purposes, and shall not be further processed in any manner incompatible with those purposes.

(3) Personal data shall be adequate, relevant and not excessive in relation to the purpose or purposes for which it is processed.

(4) Personal data shall be accurate and kept up-to-date.

(5) Personal data should not be kept for longer than is necessary.

(6) Personal data shall be processed in accordance with the rights of data subjects.

(7) A data user is responsible for the security and protection of data against unauthorised access, alteration, destruction, disclosure or accidental loss.

(8) Restrictions on the transfer of data to other countries

Expandable text

In the UK the Data Protection Act sets out seven rights of individuals with respect to information stored about them:

(1) Right of subject access – upon making a written request and paying a fee, individuals are entitled to be told whether the data controller or someone on their behalf, holds personal data about them and if so to be given:

    – A description of the personal data;

    – The purposes for which they are being processed; and

    – Those to whom they may be disclosed.

(2) Right to prevent processing likely to cause damage or distress.

(3) Right to prevent processing for the purposes of direct marketing.

(4) Rights in relation to automated decision making (no decision is taken against an individual by purely automated means – the individual has 21 days to require the data controller to reconsider the decision or to take the decision on a different basis).

(5) Right to take action for compensation for damages caused by the data controller.

(6) Right to take action to rectify, block, erase or destroy personal data – through application by an individual to the Courts.

(7) Right to request that the Commissioner assesses whether any contravention of the Act has occurred.

Illustration 4 – The principles of data protection and security

A survey of US consumers in 2005 revealed that one in five immediately terminated their accounts with vendors that lost their information.

Test your understanding 6

In July 2006 a post office in Southampton in the UK discarded papers, revealing names, addresses and national insurance numbers of customers, into a city centre waste bin.

Comment.

3.3 Data Security

The main risks to computer systems and the data they contain include the following:

Potential threats	Counter measures
Physical damage, due to • fire • flooding • terrorist acts • power failures • other environmental – heat, cold, humidity,dust.	• Well documented fire procedures. • Staff training. • Provide fire extinguishers and smoke/heat detectors, fire-doors. • Computer equipment might be located in a segregated area in which air conditioning and dust controls operate effectively. • Back-up generators. • Off-site facilities to cater for the possibility of total destruction of the in-house computer equipment • Off-site back-up copies of data files.
Human Damage caused by human interference, such as unauthorised access resulting in theft, piracy, vandalism.	• Restricted access to the computer room (e.g. PIN codes). • Closed circuit TV and security guards. • Hardware can be physically or electronically tagged to sound an alarm if it is removed from the building. • Hardware can be locked down.
Operational problems, such as program bugs and user operational errors.	• Thorough testing of new programs • strict operating procedures • adequate training of all staff members.
Data corruption, e.g. viruses, hackers.	• Anti-virus and firewall software • passwords and user number limits • off-site back-up copies of data files.
Data theft, e.g. fraud, industrial espionage, loss of confidentiality.	• Data encryption techniques • passwords and user numbers • physical access controls.

Illustration 5 – The principles of data protection and security

Second Life (a 3D digital on-line world)

In September 2006 all Second Life users were asked to change their password following a successful attack on one of the virtual world's core databases.

Test your understanding 7

In one survey it was revealed that some high profile companies in London were maintaining their off-site back-ups of data in buildings on the same street as their offices.

Comment on this data security practice.

4 Health and safety in the workplace

4.1 Health and safety hazards

Typical hazards might include:

- desks/chairs too near to doors
- unsafe electric plugs
- trailing wires, cables and leads
- torn carpets
- unlit or poorly lit corridors and stairs
- top-heavy filing cabinets
- untrained operators using machinery
- unmarked plate glass doors
- wet floors.

Test your understanding 8

'Health and safety law is concerned with eliminating risks.'

Comment

4.2 Health and safety legislation

Many countries have detailed legislation covering health and safety in the workplace.

The law typically puts the responsibility for health and safety on BOTH the employer and employee.

Employer's responsibilities

The employer has a duty to provide the following:

- Safe ways in and out of the place of work.
- A safe working environment.
- Safe equipment and procedures.
- Arrangements for the safe use, handling, storage and transport of articles and substances.
- Adequate information, instruction, training and supervision.
- Adequate investigation of accidents.

Employees' responsibilities

The employee has a duty to:

- Be responsible for his or her own health and safety.
- Consider the health and safety of other people who may be affected by his or her actions.
- Co-operate with anyone carrying out duties under the act (this includes his or her employer).

Breach of health and safety provisions

- Employers must ensure safe and healthy working conditions for their employees. If they do not do so they may be in breach of a common law or statutory duty enabling the employee to make a civil claim against them. Alternatively, they may be guilty of a criminal offence and be open to prosecution.
- If employees have been injured at work they may have action against their employer for damages.

Test your understanding 9

Why should firms have certificates of testing of electrical appliances?

Test your understanding 10

While Dave was running down a staircase at work, he tripped and injured himself. Who is responsible for this accident?

Chapter summary

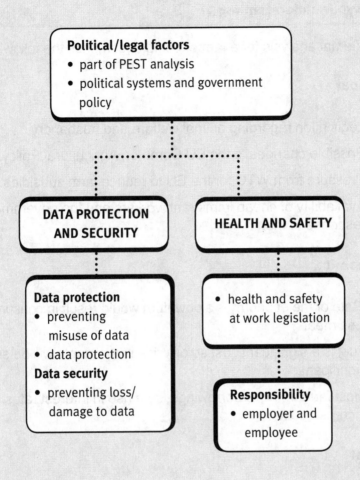

Political/legal factors
- part of PEST analysis
- political systems and government policy

DATA PROTECTION AND SECURITY

HEALTH AND SAFETY

Data protection
- preventing misuse of data
- data protection

Data security
- preventing loss/ damage to data

- health and safety at work legislation

Responsibility
- employer and employee

Test your understanding answers

Test your understanding 1

An external analysis for a farmer could encompass the following issues:

Political

- Legislation regarding animal welfare and husbandry
- Possible changes to the EU Common Agricultural Policy (CAP)
- Pressure from WTO for the EU to reduce farm subsidies
- Availability of cheap immigrant workers and the government's response to them.

Economic

- State of the economy – a downturn would result in consumers buying less meat
- Fuel is a significant cost so oil price movements will be seen as significant.
- Most farmers have borrowings, so a rise in interest rates would increase costs.

Social

- Public concerns over food health in the light of BSE, avian flu, etc.
- Public concerns over animal welfare, e.g. battery chickens.
- Public attitudes to organic food.
- Public attitudes to eating meat v vegetarianism.

Technological

- Ability to process vegetables at point of picking them (e.g. freeze-dried peas).
- Processes to increase the shelf life of fruit.
- Developments in pesticides (subject to public response).
- Genetically modified crops (subject to public response and government policy).

Competitive

- The main problem facing most farmers is the high buyer power of supermarkets.

- Competitive rivalry from other farmers.

- Threat of cheap imports.

Test your understanding 2

Opportunities would arise for:

- lawyers!

- manufacturers of environmentally friendly cars (e.g. electric)

- providers of public transport – if the suit is successful, then car manufacturers could face huge fines which will ultimately be reflected in higher car prices.

Test your understanding 3

The tax is likely to prevent people moving as often so will impact firms as follows:

- opportunity – DIY firms (people will improve their existing properties rather than moving), builders specialising in extensions

- threats – estate agents, house builders, conveyancing firms.

Test your understanding 4

The simple answer is neither, as mandatory targets will not apply to the US company. However, if competitors are based in countries where the protocol has been signed then it will affect the US firm as follows:

- Initially it will be an opportunity as the competitor will experience higher costs associated with compliance.

- In the longer term the US firm may lose business as customers chose more environmentally friendly competitors.

Test your understanding 5

Data protection – there is no indication of the market research firm obtaining the information through hacking or other underhand means.

Test your understanding 6

The post office concerned had failed to protect its customers' data, leaving them vulnerable to identity fraud. The Data Protection Act 1998 in the UK states that a data user is responsible for the security and protection of data against unauthorised access, alteration, destruction, disclosure or accidental loss.

Test your understanding 7

This approach is seriously flawed as a terrorist attack or plain crash or even an extensive fire could compromise both the original and copied data.

Test your understanding 8

While the media can sometimes give this impression, health and safety is about taking practical actions to control real risks, not about trying to eliminate risk altogether. It is impossible to eliminate all risk.

Test your understanding 9

- To comply with the law!
- To ensure that all electrical equipment is safe, reducing the risk of accident or fire.
- To ensure that equipment has been checked by qualified electricians.

KAPLAN PUBLISHING

Test your understanding 10

Dave's employer is responsible for ensuring that there are safe ways in and out of the place of work and that Dave has a safe working environment. Unless there was a problem with the staircase (e.g. poorly lit, uneven steps) it would appear that the employer has fulfilled their responsibility.

Dave is also responsible for his own safety and shouldn't have been running.

10

Macroeconomic factors

Chapter learning objectives

Upon completion of this chapter you will be able to:

- define macroeconomic policy
- identify the factors that influence the level of business activity:
  - confidence
  - demand
  - availability of capital
  - use of resources
  - government policy
  - exchange rate movements
- using the trade cycle model, explain what impact variations in the level of business activity have on individuals, households and businesses
- explain the impact of economic issues on the individual, the household and the business:
  - inflation
  - unemployment
  - stagnation
  - international payments disequilibrium
- describe the different types of economic policy commonly used by the government:
  - fiscal versus monetary
  - demand versus supply side

- give examples of governmental actions aimed at maximising economic welfare:
  - growth
  - unemployment
  - inflation
  - balance of payments.

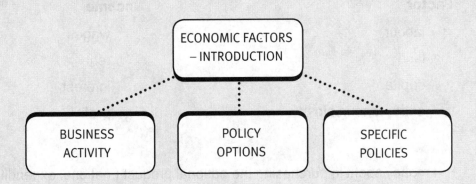

1 Defining macroeconomic policy

1.1 Environmental analysis

Part of a firm's external PEST analysis will involve assessing the economic factors within the industry environment. As discussed above the key issue is to identify potential opportunities and threats.

1.2 Defining macroeconomics

Economics can be defined in various ways, including:

- 'the study of how society allocates scarce resources, which have alternative uses, between competing ends'
- 'the study of wealth creation'.

It is useful to distinguish between two aspects of economics:

- **Microeconomics** is the study of the economic behaviour of individual consumers, firms, and industries.
- **Macroeconomics** considers aggregate behaviour, and the study of the sum of individual economic decisions.

Macroeconomics thus focuses on the workings of the economy as a whole, including:

- the overall ('aggregate') demand for goods and services
- the output of goods and services ('national output' or 'national product')
- the supply of factors of production
- total incomes earned by providers of factors of production ('national income')

Factor	Income
labour	wages
land	rent
capita	interest
entrepreneurship	profit

- money spent in purchasing the national product ('national expenditure')
- government policy – see below.

Expandable text

The problem of scarce resources

Given that resources are limited ('scarce'), it is not possible to make everything everyone would want ('unlimited wants'). All societies are thus faced with a fundamental economic problem:

- What goods and services should be produced?

- In what quantities?

- Who should make them?

- Who gets the output?

The market economy is one approach to dealing with this problem.

In a market economy interaction between supply and demand (market forces) determines what is made, in what quantity, and who gets the output. Patterns of economic activity are determined by the decisions made by individual consumers and producers.

In its purest form this would imply no government intervention in the economy. In reality most modern economies are a mix of free markets and government intervention to provide public services such as health and education.

1.3 Macroeconomic policy

Typically, governments will have four macroeconomic policy objectives:

- Economic growth – how can productive capacity be increased?

- Inflation – how can we ensure that general price levels do not increase?

- Unemployment – how can we ensure that everyone who wants a job has one?

KAPLAN PUBLISHING

- Balance of payments – how should we manage our relationship and trade with other countries?

These are discussed in more detail below.

Test your understanding 1

Which of the following is NOT an objective of macroeconomic policy?

A   Economic growth

B   Control of Inflation

C   Lower levels of taxation

D   A balanced balance of payments

---

2 The level of business activity in the economy

2.1 Introduction

While the level of activity within a particular industry will depend on specific PEST issues, the overall level of activity in an economy can be anticipated and explained by reference to generic (mainly economic) factors.

2.2 Factors that influence the level of business activity

Factors that influence the overall level of business activity include the following:

Confidence

- Greater consumer confidence will result in higher demand for products.

- Higher business confidence will result in higher levels of investment in new factories, machinery, etc. and new firms being set up by entrepreneurs.

- Confidence can be reduced by a wide range of factors such as political instability, disasters (e.g. hurricanes), likelihood ofunemployment and high inflation.

Aggregate demand

- Aggregate demand is the total demand for a country's output and consists of Consumer spending (C) + Investment by firms (I) + Government spending (G) + demand from exports (X) – imports (M)

$$AD = C + I + G + X - M$$

- Higher demand can result in firms increasing output (e.g. by employing more staff) to meet the demand.

- Higher demand can also result in inflationary pressure.

Capital

- Firms need to raise finance to invest in new projects. Greater availability of finance will result in higher levels of investment.

- Lower interest rates will make capital cheaper.

- Government policy on cheap loans (e.g. regional development grants).

Use of resources

- New technology and more efficient working practices can improve productivity and lower costs – key elements of firms' output decisions.

- Advances in levels of education can also give a more productive workforce.

Government policy

- Governments can increase or decrease the level of aggregate demand through fiscal policy (the blend of government spending and taxation).

- Investment in the infrastructure of the economy (e.g. better roads) can attract investment.

Exchange rate movements

- A strengthening currency will make a country's exports more expensive and will thus dampen demand for those exports. Imports, on the other hand get cheaper.

Illustration 1 – Factors that influence the level of business activity

(a) Hurricane Katrina

In 2005 US economists predicted that Hurricane Katrina could have the effect of slowing US economic growth by around a half-percentage point that year. However, the stimulus to the economy from rebuilding efforts was predicted to raise growth by half a percentage point in 2006.

(b) Should the UK join the Euro?

One of the main arguments used by proponents of the Euro is that the current system of floating exchange rates stifles business confidence and restricts economic growth.

Test your understanding 2

How would a cut in interest rates affect the level of activity in the economy?

Test your understanding 3

Would tax cuts boost the level of domestic economic activity? Justify your answer.

2.3 Trade cycles

Many economies exhibit fluctuations in economic activity over time with an underlying trend of output growth.

Some economists argue that one role of governments is to smooth out this pattern to avoid 'boom and bust' years.

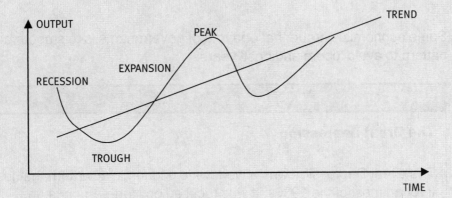

- A recession starts when demand begins to fall. Firms respond to the fall in demand by reducing their output, causing a decline in purchases of raw materials and an increase in unemployment, as workers are laid off.

- The reduction in demand will feed through into households' incomes, causing these to fall too, resulting in a further reduction in demand.

- The economy will quickly move into a slump, with low business confidence, depressed 'animal spirits' and little incentive to carry out investment.

- Once in the slump, it can take a long time before the economy begins to recover. One of the most difficult things to restore is business and consumer confidence.

- Eventually, though, economic activity begins to pick up. It may be a new invention that tempts entrepreneurs to invest, it may be that replacement investment can be put off no longer or a war may force the government to inject expenditure into the economy.

- The extra investment will push up incomes, which will persuade consumers to spend and this will induce yet more investment, reducing unemployment.

- The economy will expand, pushing upwards into a boom. After some time, however, full capacity will be reached and demand will become stable. The reduction in investment starts off the downward spiral once again.

Some economists argue that one role of governments is to smooth out this pattern to avoid 'boom and bust' years.

Illustration 2 – Trade cycles

The Great Depression

The Great Depression was a worldwide economic downturn that lasted through most of the 1930s. It was focused on North America and Europe, but had knock-on effects around the world.

- Construction virtually stopped in many countries as demand fell sharply.

- Unemployment and homelessness soared.

- Cities based on heavy industry suffered particularly badly.

- Rural areas and farmers suffered as prices for crops fell by 40-60%.

> * Mining and logging areas were also hit hard as there was little alternative economic activity.

Test your understanding 4

Why is a 'boom and bust' economy a problem?

3 The impact of economic issues

3.1 Stagnation and economic growth

Most governments want economic growth. Growth should result in the following:

* more goods being demanded and produced
* people earn more and can afford more goods
* more people should have jobs.

On the face of it, therefore, growth should result in an improved standard of living in a country and higher profitability for businesses.

However, growth is not without its problems.

* Is economic growth fast enough to keep up with population growth?
* Growth rates have to exceed inflation rates for benefits to arise (i.e. real growth has to occur).
* Growth may be in 'demerit' goods, such as illegal drugs.
* Growth may be at the expense of the environment or through exploitation of the poor.
* The gap between rich and poor may grow, as the benefits from growth are not evenly distributed.
* Measurement of growth is difficult given the black market and goods that are excluded from national income calculations.
* Rapid growth means rising incomes and this often 'sucks in' imports, worsening the balance of trade, rather than benefiting domestic producers.

3.2 Inflation

Most governments want stable prices and low inflation. The main reasons given include the following:

* Inflation causes uncertainty and stifles business investment.

- Not all incomes rise in line with inflation – the poor and those on fixed incomes suffer the most.

- In extreme cases of inflation, the function of money may break down, resulting in civil unrest and even war.

- Inflation distorts the working of the price mechanism and is thus a market imperfection.

Note that high inflation can affect savings in different ways:

- people who save to spend later (a "transactions motive") will save less to avoid the purchasing power of their money being eroded.

- people who save in case something bad happens (a 'precautionary motive') will save more due to the uncertainty inflation creates.

3.3 Unemployment

Even in a healthy economy some unemployment will arise as people change jobs. However, mass unemployment is a problem due to the following:

- The government has to pay out benefits to the unemployed at a time when its tax receipts are low. This can result in the government having to raise taxes, borrow money and cut back on services.

- Unemployment has been linked to a rise in crime, poor health and a breakdown in family relationships.

- Unemployment is a waste of human resources and can restrict economic growth.

High unemployment could give firms higher bargaining power allowing them to pay lower wages to prospective employees.

3.4 Balance of payments

In the long-term government seeks to establish a broad balance between the value of imports into, and exports from, the country.

To run a persistent surplus or deficit can have negative macroeconomic effects.

- A long-term trade deficit has to be financed. The financing costs act as a major drain on the productive capacity of the economy.

- A long-term trade surplus can cause significant inflationary pressures, leading ultimately to a loss in international confidence in the economy and a lack of international competitiveness.

Test your understanding 5

Which of the following statements is/are true?

A   Economic growth always brings benefits to all members of a society.

B   Economic growth can lead to an increase in imports.

C   Inflation does not affect those on fixed incomes as much as those in employment.

D   Inflation encourages investment in a national economy.

Test your understanding 6

Which of the following are consequences of unemployment?

A   Less pressure for government to increase taxes. YES/NO

B   Reduced economic output. YES/NO

C   Greater inflationary pressure in the economy. YES/NO

4 Economic policy options

4.1 Fiscal policy options

- Fiscal policy refers to a government's taxation and spending plans and is usually understood within the context of demand side policies (see section 4.3 below).

A balanced budget

- In the medium- to long-term it is suggested that a government should aim to achieve a balanced budget, i.e. one in which government expenditure is matched by government income.

- For a number of macroeconomic reasons that are explored in this chapter, government may decide to run either a budget deficit or a budget surplus.

Government income < expenditure = budget deficit

Government income > expenditure = budget surplus

Government income = expenditure = a balanced budget.

Note: Don't confuse a balanced budget with the balance of payments. The former refers to the relationship between government income (from taxation) and spending, while the latter refers to the flow of funds into and out of a country.

Expandable text

Problems with closing a deflationary gap

Whilst running a budget deficit to close a deflationary gap sounds straightforward, the approach is not without its problems:

- Unemployment is assumed to be caused simply by a lack of demand in the economy. If it has a structural cause, injecting money will simply boost demand but the economy will be unable to produce additional goods and services and unemployment is unlikely to fall (workers in the wrong place with the wrong skills). The most likely consequences will be inflation and/or an increase in imports.

- The injection may have limited effect, as much of the money may be spent on imports, or be saved, which will prevent effective operation of the multiplier.

- It is very difficult to determine the extent of the deflationary gap and therefore the size of the budget deficit required to close it. This is not helped by the significant time lag that can exist between injections being made and their effects being visible in the economy.

- Many economists now believe the concept of full employment to be unrealistic. Regardless of the strength of the economy or the effectiveness of government policy there will always be a residual level of unemployment.

Running a budget deficit

- If a government intends to run a budget deficit, then this has to be financed through borrowing – this borrowing is referred to as the Public Sector Net Cash Requirement (PSNCR).

- Running a budget deficit has frequently been used to promote economic growth and reduce unemployment by closing a 'deflationary gap'.

- A deflationary gap is said to exist in the economy when the current equilibrium level of national income is too low to provide employment opportunities for all those seeking work.

- By running a budget deficit, the government is injecting more into the economy than it is taking out and can boost aggregate demand and reduce unemployment. This known as an 'expansionary' policy.

KAPLAN PUBLISHING

Running a budget surplus

- If aggregate demand lies above the level necessary to generate full employment, this can lead to inflation (too much money chasing too few goods). In this situation an 'inflationary gap' is said to exist.

- Fiscal policy can also be used to control inflation. If an inflationary gap exists, government can seek to reduce aggregate demand by running a budget surplus, effectively taking money out of the economy. This is known as a 'contractionary policy'.

4.2 Monetary policy options

- Monetary policy refers to the management of the money supply in the economy and is usually understood within the context of monetarism (see section 4.3 below).

- Monetary policy can involve changing interest rates, either directly or indirectly through open market operations, setting reserve requirements for banks, or trading in foreign exchange markets.

- Like fiscal policy, monetary policy can be described as expansionary or contractionary. An expansionary policy increases the total supply of money in the economy, and a contractionary policy decreases the total money supply. Expansionary policy is traditionally used to combat unemployment in a recession by lowering interest rates, while contractionary policy has the goal of raising interest rates to combat inflation.

Money supply

- The term "money supply" refers to the total amount of money in the economy. There are many measures of the money supply, including the following:

  M0 Notes and coins in circulation and balances at the country's Central Bank.

  M4 Notes and coins and all private sector sterling bank/building society deposits (96% of which are deposits).

Note: you will not be examined on the different ways of measuring the money supply.

Reserve requirements

- Typically banks operate a fractional reserve system, i.e. only a part of their deposits are kept in cash on the assumption that not all customers will want their money back at the same time. The proportion of deposits retained in cash is known as the reserve asset ratio or liquidity ratio.

Illustration 3 – Monetary policy options

Imagine a simple example where banks have to keep 10% of their deposits in cash and everyone who borrows money immediately redeposits it with the bank.

A citizen has just returned from working abroad with $1,000 in cash in their wallet. As soon as they land at the airport, the money supply measure M0 increases by $1,000. This money is then deposited with a branch of a local bank.

This bank then lends 90% of the money to another person. What has happened to money supply?

M4 (notes and coins and all private sector sterling bank/building society deposits) has increased by $1,900, i.e. the bank has a $1,000 deposit and there is $900 in cash in circulation.

If this money is then redeposited with the bank it can be lent out again and so on.

This process cannot be repeated infinitely, as 10% of the cash has to be retained by the bank each time it makes a loan. The overall impact on money supply can be calculated using the following formula:

$$\text{Change in money supply} = \frac{1}{\text{Liquidity ratio}} \times \text{intial cash deposit}$$

In our example the total increase in the money supply could be 1/0.10 x 1,000 = $10,000.

Open market operations

- By buying and selling its own bonds the government is able to exert some control over the money supply.

- For instance, by buying back its own bonds it will release more cash into circulation. Conversely, when it sells bonds it receives cash in return, reducing the amount of money in circulation thus restricting the ability of banks to lend.

Interest rates

- High interest rates suppress demand for money due to the increased cost of borrowing. Over a period of time the money supply will then react to this reduced demand for money by contracting. Monetarists view interest rate manipulation as a key control over inflation.

- In some countries, such as the UK, the setting of interest rates is the responsibility of the Central Bank. In others it may be a government minister.

4.3 Demand and supply side policies

Managing a national economy that interacts fully with the global economy is complex and full of uncertainty. Different theories exist regarding how to manage the economy. Three of the most important are outlined below.

The classical view (do nothing)

- Classical economic theory involved doing nothing – a 'leave it alone' approach.

- It was thought that the economy would automatically move to equilibrium with full employment.

- In the event of a depression, for instance, the price of factors of production would fall. This would increase demand for them, leading to their utilisation and the re-establishment of economic growth.

- This theory was severely challenged by the Great Depression in the 1920s and 30s when, despite wages falling significantly, the economy did not respond by growing. During the Great Depression the economy seemed unable to stimulate itself to grow. Out of this failure grew the more interventionist approach advocated by John Maynard Keynes.

The Keynesian view (demand side)

- Keynes believed that an economy could become stuck at many different equilibrium points, ones that did not necessarily involve full employment. He cited the Great Depression as evidence for this, where the global economy got stuck in low gear and was unable to grow.

- He argued that it was government's role to move the economy to a better equilibrium, i.e. one closer to full employment.

- Simply put, this involved government borrowing money and injecting it into the economy to stimulate economic growth. Increased future tax revenues would then allow the government to repay this money.

- Conversely, if an economy was growing too fast and experiencing inflation, government could slow the economy down by increasing levels of taxation, reducing the amount of money in the economy.

- Effectively, Keynes argued for manipulation and management of aggregate demand in the economy (demand side economics).

The monetarist view (supply side)

- Monetarists revived the earlier classical view and believe that there is only one true equilibrium point in the national economy. Equilibrium will only occur when supply is equal to demand in all markets in an economy.

- Monetarists believe that the economy will automatically gravitate towards this 'natural' equilibrium unless hindered by market imperfections.

- Thus it is the role of government to 'free up' the economy by removing these imperfections. Once this is done the role of government should be minimal.

- Market imperfections include the following:
  - inflation
  - government spending and taxation
  - price fixing
  - minimum wage agreements
  - regulation of markets
  - abuses of monopoly power.

- Monetarist solutions to economic problems are often described as supply side economics as they focus on improving the supply of factors of production in an economy.

Illustration 4 – Demand - and supply-side policies

Between 1979 and 1984 the number of people claiming unemployment benefit in the UK rose from just over 1 million to nearly 2.9 million people. The Conservative Government of the time following monetarist supply-side policies, adopted the following policies:

- Freed up markets for both factors and goods and services. This involved reducing the power of the trade unions and a reduction in the number of state-owned monopolies.

- Provided government-funded worker retraining schemes.

- Improved information provided by job centres and employment agencies.

- Provided financial support and advice for workers willing to relocate.

- Provided assistance and incentives for firms willing to relocate to areas of high unemployment.

- Lowered state benefits to make it less attractive to depend on state benefits rather than working.

KAPLAN PUBLISHING

- Reformed taxation with less emphasis on direct taxes (argued to act as a disincentive to work, effort and the supply of enterprise) and more emphasis on indirect taxes.

Test your understanding 7

Which of the following statements is compatible with supply side policies?

- Reduction in unemployment benefit. **yes/no**

- A cut in funding of retraining schemes. **yes/no**

- Direct manipulation of the economy to increase supply of goods and services in an economy. **yes/no**

- Improvements in job centres. **yes/no**

- Reducing the power of the unions. **yes/no**

Test your understanding 8

Which ONE of the following would cause a fall in the level of aggregate demand in an economy?

A   A decrease in the level of imports.

B   A fall in the propensity to save.

C   A decrease in government expenditure.

D   A decrease in the level of income tax.

5 Achieving policy objectives

The above (and other) policy options discussed can be blended to achieve economic objectives as follows.

5.1 Growth

Policies to promote growth include the following:

Cutting interest rates

- This can be interpreted either as part of Keynesian demand management (cutting interest rates should boost aggregate demand) or monetarism (to boost the money supply).

Running a budget deficit

- The classic Keynesian response to a recession.
- Monetarists would argue that the way the government finances the increase will have a negative effect elsewhere (e.g. higher taxation), thus reducing its effectiveness.

Expandable text

The multiplier

It is difficult to see how a government injection of funds into the economy could lead to prolonged economic growth. If the government borrows $50 million and injects it into the economy, it will at some point have to pay this money back. It will do this by taking $50 million out of the follow through taxation. the net effect on aggregate demand and therefore national income would appear to be zero as the initial injection is counterbalanced by leakage in the form of taxation.

This analysis is incomplete as it neglects the fact that the injection of $50 million is spent many times in the economy, boosting national income by more than $50 million.

Example

Imagine the government funds a road construction project. The construction workers then spend their wages in the domestic economy. The shop owners who sold them goods then spend their income and so on. This effect is known as the multiplier.

The multiplier cannot continue infinitely as some of the extra income may be saved or spent on imported goods or paid back to the government in taxes.

Supply-side policies

- Increasing the availability of skilled labour through training schemes, childcare vouchers, etc.

Other

- Regional development grants and tax incentives to boost investment.
- Protectionist measures to reduce imports (e.g. quotas).
- Creating a stable economy to boost confidence (e.g. by achieving low inflation).

5.2 Unemployment

Reducing unemployment is not straightforward. At any moment in time unemployment may have a variety of causes, each of which may require a different and incompatible solution.

Cyclical unemployment

- This is sometimes referred to as demand-deficient, persistent or Keynesian unemployment.
- In this case unemployment is caused by the fact that aggregate demand in the economy is too small to create employment opportunities for all those willing, and able, to work.
- Keynesian economists refer to this as a deflationary gap and would seek to remove it by boosting aggregate demand.
- Monetarists would seek to reduce cyclical unemployment by appropriate supply-side measures as they would argue that cyclical unemployment does not really exist.

Frictional unemployment

- This refers to those people who are short-term unemployed as they move from one job to another.
- While not seen as a problem, it can be reduced by the provision of better information through job centres and other supply-side policies.

Structural and technological unemployment

- This is caused by structural change in the economy, leading often to both a change in the skills required and the location where economic activity takes place.

Illustration 5 – Unemployment

In the 1980s the UK experienced a huge decline in its traditional heavy industries in the north. At the same time new high technology industries were established in the south.

Workers in the former heavy industries were at a double disadvantage. Not only were they in the wrong location but they also had the wrong skills required by the new industries.

- Boosting aggregate demand (a demand-side policy) is likely to have little impact on structural unemployment. Supply-side policies are likely to be more effective, including:
  - government funded retraining schemes
  - tax breaks for redevelopment of old industrial sites
  - grant aid to encourage relocation of industry
  - business start-up advice and soft loans
  - help with worker relocation costs
  - improved information on available employment opportunities.

Seasonal unemployment

- Demand for some goods and services is highly seasonal, e.g. demand for fruit pickers. This in turn creates highly seasonal demand for workers. This can create regional economic problems in areas where a significant proportion of the workforce is employed in these seasonal industries.

Real wage unemployment

- This type of unemployment can occur in industries that are highly unionised. By keeping wages artificially high by the threat of strike action and closed shops, the number of people employed in the industry is reduced.

- Monetarists would see this as a prime example of a market imperfection and would address it by reducing union powers and abolishing minimum wage agreements.

KAPLAN PUBLISHING

Test your understanding 9

Identify which type of unemployment is being described in the following statements

A   A worker loses their job because of the introduction of new technology.

B   After the Wall Street Crash, millions of Americans were unable to find work.

C   Jobs in the car industry have been reduced due to a strong union and high wages.

D   A management accountant has just been made redundant but is due to start a new job in three weeks' time.

E   Bar staff are out of work in November in a Spanish holiday resort.

Expandable text

Unemployment

Keynesians view unemployment as being largely demand deficient, i.e. the equilibrium national income is too small to generate employment opportunities for all those wishing to work. The solution to this is for government to boost aggregate demand. In response to this, the economy will move to a new equilibrium closer to full employment.

For example, in response to falling aggregate demand during a recession Keynesian economists would advocate an increase in government spending to boost aggregate demand. This should then feed through into increased employment opportunities as firms respond by increasing the supply of goods.

Monetarists would react differently. They would advocate cuts in interest rates to encourage business investment. Further, they would seek to improve the operation of markets by removing government subsidies, freeing up labour markets by reducing the power of unions, and encouraging people into work by keeping unemployment benefits low.

Fundamentally, Keynesian economics does not allow for the co-existence of inflation and unemployment. Keynesian economists would argue that if unemployment exists there is insufficient demand in an economy whereas inflation indicates excessive demand.

In the mid-1970s many countries experienced high and growing levels of unemployment, together with record levels of inflation. This combination of economic variables was called stagflation and could not be explained by Keynesian economics.

Monetarists recognise a concept called the natural rate of unemployment. Even if an economy is at capacity, significant unemployment can still exist due to imperfections in the labour market, including:

- workers having the wrong skills relative to those demanded by the economy

- workers being located in the wrong place relative to economic activity

- workers having inadequate information about job opportunities

- occupational immobility due to trade unions and other restrictive working practices.

The natural rate of unemployment essentially has a structural cause. Boosting aggregate demand will do nothing to remove this problem. Inappropriate boosting of demand when the economy cannot respond for structural reasons will lead to inflation and will not decrease unemployment, i.e. stagflation.

Monetarists view the role of government as one of reducing or removing these labour market imperfections, i.e. reduction in the natural rate of unemployment.

Whilst monetarists recognise that demand-deficient unemployment can occur they would not seek to manipulate aggregate demand directly. Typical monetarist policies aimed at removing demand deficient unemployment would involve:

- cutting interest rates to encourage business investment

- providing business start-up advice and support

- providing low-cost finance for business start up

- offering tax incentives for research and development

- offering incentives to encourage inward investment in the national economy.

5.3 Inflation

Inflation has a number of causes and solutions.

Demand-pull inflation

- If demand for goods and services in the economy is growing faster than the ability of the economy to supply these goods and services, prices will increase – the classic case of too much money chasing too few goods.
- Demand-side policies would focus on reducing aggregate demand through tax rises, cuts in government spending and higher interest rates.

Cost-push inflation

- If the underlying cost of factors of production increases, this is likely to be reflected in an increase in output prices as firms seek to maintain their profit margins.

Imported inflation

- In an economy in which imports are significant, a weakening of the national currency will increase the cost of imports and could lead to domestic inflation.
- This can be reduced by policies to strengthen the national currency (see below).

Monetary inflation

- Monetarists argue that inflation can result from an over expansion of the money supply. In effect increasing the money supply increases purchasing power in the economy, boosting demand for goods and services. If this expansion occurs faster than expansion in the supply of goods and services inflation can arise.
- The main monetarist tool for controlling such inflation is to reduce the growth in the money supply through higher interest rates.

Expectations effect

- If anticipated levels of inflation are built into wage negotiations and pricing decisions then it is likely that the expected rate of inflation will arise. Whilst the expectations effect is not the root cause of inflation it can contribute significantly to an inflationary spiral, particularly when underlying levels of inflation are high and rising.

- This spiral can be managed by a 'prices and incomes' policy where manufacturers agree to limit price rises in response to union agreements to limit wage claims.

Illustration 6 – Inflation

In 1975 the UK had inflation of nearly 25%. This reflected a number of factors:

- Poor macroeconomic management by government. In seeking to reduce unemployment the government had injected significant sums into the UK economy. However, due to growing structural problems the economy was unable to grow and the net result of this increased demand was to trigger an inflationary spiral.

- The effects of the quadrupling of the oil price in 1973/74 were still being felt in the UK economy.

- Strong unions and weak management led to poor control over wage demands.

In summary the high inflation was a mix of both cost push and demand pull.

Illustration 7 – Inflation

After the collapse of communism in the former Soviet Union, inflation in Russia during the early 1990s reached 5,000%, according to some estimates. This was due to the government policy of financing redevelopment through a rapid growth in the money supply.

Test your understanding 10

What type of inflation is each phrase describing?

A   Workers seek above inflation pay rises.

B   Growth in demand for new homes has outstripped supply.

C   Retailers have increased their prices in advance of inflation figures to be published next month.

D   Copper prices have more than doubled on the world market this year, increasing the cost of electrical cables.

Test your understanding 11

- If a deflationary gap exists, what kind of unemployment is most likely to exist in the economy?

- Will running a budget deficit successfully reduce all types of unemployment in an economy?

Expandable text

Inflation and unemployment combined

Most governments wish both to reduce unemployment and keep inflation low. However, there is fundamental conflict between the two objectives. Research by **Phillips** indicated that there is an inverse relationship between inflation and unemployment, i.e. during periods of low inflation unemployment was high and vice versa. The suggestion here is that during times of low unemployment labour can command higher wages as it is in relatively short supply.

5.4 Balance of payments

The balance of payments records all of the transactions that have taken place between residents of a country and overseas residents during the period of a year. Just like any bookkeeping system, each transaction has a debit and a credit entry and overall the system should balance.

The balance of payments is split into three parts:

- current account (goods and services),
- capital account (e.g. buildings) and
- financial account (e.g. cash flows)

Exporting goods for cash would give rise to a debit in the financial account and a credit in the current account.(This is similar to sales being a credit in the income statement).

When discussing debits and credits we conventionally look at the current account, hence exports are a credit entry and imports a debit.

Balance of payments deficits

If a country is said to have a deficit on its balance of payments this means that there is a net outflow of funds from the country, for example through importing more than it exports. Clearly, this outflow cannot continue as a country cannot keep spending more than it earns in foreign currency – eventually it will run out of reserves and other countries will cease to be willing to loan it money.

Government can seek to reduce a balance of payments deficit in a number of ways. Traditionally the strategies that can be used are divided into:

- expenditure-reducing strategies
- expenditure-switching strategies.

Expenditure-reducing strategies

- This involves the government deliberately shrinking the domestic economy. By reducing overall demand in the domestic economy a government will be able to reduce demand for imports.

- Reducing demand in the home economy should also reduce inflationary pressures, reducing export prices and making them more competitive.

- Conversely, suppressing demand in the home economy could lead to an increase in unemployment.

- Examples of such strategies include contractionary monetary policy (see above) and contractionary fiscal policy.

Increasing interest rates

- Increasing interest rates will reduce demand for imports as domestic consumers and firms will have less money to spend.

- However, it will also discourage investment in the home economy as the cost of borrowing increases.

- It can cause a country's currency to strengthen (appreciate) due to demand for sterling from overseas investors. This can actually worsen the deficit as it increases the price of UK exports, whilst making imports cheaper.

Expenditure-switching strategies

In this case the government seeks to change expenditure patterns of consumers by encouraging expenditure on domestically-produced rather than imported goods.

Import controls

Government could seek to restrict imports. This could be achieved by:

- direct imposition of tariffs or quotas
- or through exchange controls limiting the supply of sterling available to buy overseas currencies to pay for imports.

The imposition of trade barriers is highly controversial, however, and is likely to breach WTO regulations.

Boost exports

A government could seek to boost exports in a number of ways:

- Provide subsidies to exporters to allow them to reduce export prices.
- Extend export credit guarantees to more countries, reducing the risk for exporters of non-payment.

Lower the exchange rate

- In the case of a fixed exchange rate this is referred to as a devaluation. Where exchange rates are floating it is referred to as a depreciation. This strategy has the effect of making imports more expensive and exports cheaper (in their own currency) to an overseas buyer.
- This policy has a number of problems associated with it often making it a last choice of government. These problems include:
    - It may not work if it results in competitive depreciations or devaluations.
    - It may not work as the rise in import prices triggers domestic inflation.

Test your understanding 12

Which of the following policies for correcting a balance of payments deficit is an expenditure-reducing policy?

A   Cutting the level of public expenditure.

B   Devaluation of the currency.

C   The imposition of an import tax.

D   The use of import quotas.

Test your understanding 13

Which of the following might cause a country's exports to decrease?

A   A fall in the exchange rate for that country's currency.

B   A reduction in other countries' tariff barriers.

C   A decrease in the marginal propensity to import in other countries.

D   A rise in that country's imports.

Test your understanding 14

Which of the following would not correct a balance of payments deficit?

A   Revaluing the currency.

B   Raising domestic interest rates.

C   Deflating the economy.

D   Imposing import controls.

Chapter summary

Economic factors
- Part of PEST analysis to identify opportunities and threats
- Macroeconomic objectives focus on growth, unemployment, inflation and balance of payments

BUSINESS ACTIVITY
Level influenced by
- Confidence
- Aggregate demand
- Government policy
- Supply of resources
- Capital
- Exchange rate movements

POLICY OPTIONS

Fiscal policy
- Mix of G and T
- Budget deficit, surplus or balanced

Monetary policy
- Control of money supply

Demand side
- Manipulate aggregate demand to move economy

Supply side
- Remove market imperfections to free up economy

SPECIFIC POLICIES

Growth
- Expansionary – e.g. increase G, cut interest rates

Unemployment
- Cyclical
- Structural
- Seasonal
- Frictional
- Real wage

Inflation
- Demand pull
- Cost push
- Imported
- Expectations
- Growth in money supply

Balance of payments
- Correct a deficit by expenditure reducing and expenditure switching policies

Test your understanding answers

Test your understanding 1

C

Lower taxation is not a policy objective. Rather it is a policy instrument that could be used to encourage economic growth.

Test your understanding 2

A cut in interest rates is likely to boost economic activity:

- Low interest rates will encourage firms to increase investment.
- Low interest rates will boost confidence.
- Low interest rates will make mortgages cheaper, giving consumers more disposable income to spend in the economy.

Test your understanding 3

Tax cuts would be expected to boost economic activity due to:

- A fall in corporation tax will give businesses more profit to finance reinvestment.
- A fall in income tax will give consumers more money to spend, increasing aggregate demand.
- A tax cut may boost consumer confidence.

However, there are counter-arguments:

- A fall in government tax income may result in a drop in government expenditure, reducing aggregate demand.
- Consumers may spend extra income on imported rather than domestic goods.
- Consumers may save the extra money rather than spending it.

Test your understanding 4

The main implications of 'boom and bust' are:

	Boom	Bust
Individuals and households	On the whole a boom time will be good for households: • low unemployment • rising house prices • high levels of confidence • increasing consumer spending. But: • People may be tempted to over-stretch borrowings. • Possible inflation, the main problem with 'boom and bust'.	The main problem with 'boom and bust' is the 'bust': • job losses • people losing their homes when unable to pay mortgages • fall in labour mobility due to negative equity • bankruptcy • low confidence.
Firms	• growth in profitability • extra competition as new firms are established.	• corporate failures • fall in profits • excess capacity.

Most people and firms would prefer steady growth without the high risks associated with the extremes of 'boom and bust'.

Test your understanding 5

A   FALSE

The benefits of economic growth are often very unevenly spread across a population. Those missing out on growth can experience a relative decline in their standard of living.

B   TRUE

Rising incomes that accompany economic growth can lead to an increase in imports as consumers choose to spend their income on foreign rather than domestically-produced goods.

C   FALSE

Fixed incomes do not increase in line with inflation, e.g. 10% on $10,000 savings will not increase if a country is experiencing inflation. Those in employment would expect to receive pay rises broadly in line with inflation ensuring that the spending power of their income is not eroded.

D   FALSE

Inflation tends to discourage investment in a national economy in a number of ways. This includes a loss in confidence by both domestic and international investors.

Test your understanding 6

A   Less pressure for government to increase taxes. **NO**

During periods of unemployment government tax receipts will be low but its expenditure (on unemployment and other benefits) will be high. There is therefore increased pressure on government to raise taxes to fund these obligations.

B   Reduced economic output. **YES**

Unemployed people are not economically active and are not adding to the output from the economy. Further, their longer-term ability to contribute may decline as their skills become outdated.

C   Greater inflationary pressure in the economy. **NO**

Lower levels of demand for goods and services are unlikely to put upward pressure on the price of goods and services. Equally, unemployment reduces upward pressure on wages as there is in effect an oversupply of labour.

Test your understanding 7

- Reduction in unemployment benefit: **yes**

  This acts as an incentive for people to return to work and therefore improves the supply of labour.

- A cut in funding of retraining schemes: **no**

  Training schemes are compatible with supply-side economics as they are an attempt to equip workers with the skills demanded by the economy, hence increasing the supply of labour.

- Direct manipulation of the economy to increase supply of goods and services in an economy: **no**

  Remember, supply-side policies refer to attempts to improve the supply of factors in an economy and not goods and services.

- Improvements in job centres: **yes**

  Improving the quality of information available to those seeking work should improve the supply of labour as those out of work are able more easily to identify relevant employment opportunities

- Reducing the power of the unions: **yes**

  Unions can distort the operation of markets by effectively restricting the supply of labour. Reducing their power removes this market imperfection and is consistent with a monetarist approach.

Test your understanding 8

C

$$AD = C + I + G + (X - M)$$

- Reducing government expenditure will decrease aggregate demand.
- Reducing imports, savings and tax will all act to increase aggregate demand.

Test your understanding 9

A   A worker loses their job because of the introduction of new technology – structural.

B   After the Wall Street Crash, millions of Americans were unable to find work – cyclical.

C   Jobs in the car industry have been reduced due to a strong union and high wages – real wage.

D   A management accountant has just been made redundant but is due to start a new job in three weeks time – frictional.

E   Bar staff are out of work in November in a Spanish holiday resort – seasonal.

Test your understanding 10

A   Workers seek above inflation pay rises: cost push.

Above inflation pay rises lead to cost push inflation as wages are part of the factor cost of production.

B   Growth in demand for new homes has outstripped supply: demand pull.

Where demand is exceeding supply consumers will be prepared to pay higher prices to obtain the goods or services they require. This type of inflation is known as demand pull.

C   Retailers have increased their prices in advance of inflation figures to be published next month: expectations effect.

This type of inflation is occurring due to the expectations effect.

D   Copper prices have more than doubled on the world market this year, increasing the cost of electrical cables: cost push.

Increase in copper prices represents an increase in the cost of input and would be classified as cost-push inflation.

Test your understanding 11

- When a deflationary gap exists the current equilibrium level of national income is too low to provide employment opportunities for all those seeking work. In other words there is insufficient demand in the economy, i.e. cyclical or demand-deficient unemployment exists.

- Government injection of funds will not have any affect on structural unemployment. Simply stimulating demand under these circumstances will lead to inflation as the additional demand will not be met by an increase in economic output. Alternatively, additional income will simply be spent on imports.

Test your understanding 12

A

The other three are expenditure-switching policies which will make imported goods either more expensive or hard to obtain.

Test your understanding 13

C

A fall in the exchange rate for a country's currency will encourage exports as they will become relatively cheaper to the foreign importer, hence A is incorrect. B is also wrong since reducing tariff barriers will open up export markets giving exporting countries more opportunities. A rise in a country's imports is not clearly related to changes in the same country's exports.

Test your understanding 14

A

Revaluing the currency would worsen the balance of payments deficit by making exports more expensive and imports cheaper.

11

Social and technological factors

Chapter learning objectives

Upon completion of this chapter you will be able to:

- explain, with examples, the effect social and demographic trends have on the economy

- explain the effect of changes in social structure, values, attitudes and tastes on the organisation

- state the measures government can take in response to demographic changes and explain their impact.

- describe the effect of technological change on the structure of the organisation

- explain the following terms: downsizing, delayering, outsourcing

- explain the ways in which information technology and information systems development is influencing the business processes:
  - products
  - production
  - marketing.

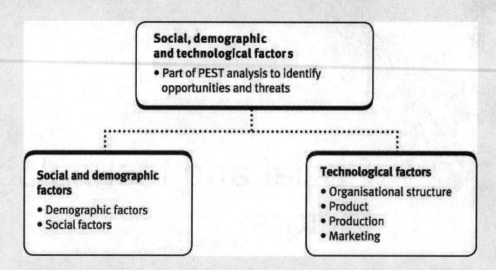

1 Demographic and social trends

1.1 Environmental analysis

Part of a firm's external PEST analysis will involve assessing the social and demographic factors within the industry environment. As discussed above the key issue is to identify potential opportunities and threats.

Key social and demographic issues include:

- population – size, location, density and composition

- wealth – income, distribution

- education and training

- health

- social structure, attitudes, values and tastes.

1.2 Demographic trends

Population size

- Many firms monitor forecasts for population size as a growing population often results in a growing market.

- Population growth (or decline) is the result of a combination of factors including birth rates, death rates, immigration and emigration

- The world average fertility rate is 2.59 children per adult woman with 2.1 being seen as the replacement rate in most industrialised nations (i.e. to maintain a stable population)

- Singapore has a fertility rate of 1.06 - one of the lowest in the world – whereas many African countries have rates in excess of six.

Population composition

- The relative sizes of birth and death rates will change the age composition of the population.

- In Ireland over 36% of the population is aged under 25 making it an attractive market for firms seeking a large workforce.

- On the other hand many countries face a pensions timebomb due to an ageing population.

- The percentage of the UK population aged over 65 has risen from 13% in 1971 to 16% in 2006 and is predicted to reach 20% by 2021.

Population location

- In 1950 30% of the world's population lived in cities. That figure has risen to 50% in 2006 and is predicted to reach 60% by 2030.

- Given that space is more at a premium in cities it is likely that people will be living in smaller houses and apartments, thus creating an opportunity for firms specialising in space-saving furniture.

Wealth

- Economic growth often results in higher disposable incomes with the knock an effect of greater demand for (most) products.

- The four fastest growing economies in the world are the "BRIC" countries (Brazil, Russia, India and China)

Education

- An educated workforce is a key driver of economic growth, e.g. in China 99% of the youth population is now literate compared with 70% in the 1980s.

- Increasing standards of education generally and greater access to IT have made the Internet a major channel for selling and advertising.

Health

- In many western countries the population is becoming increasingly overweight. This places greater demands on healthcare providers.

- More than 12% of South Africans are infected by HIV. South Africa's declining life expectancy (currently 51 years) is a major concern, especially as the population structure has changed with fewer people in their middle ages. This is normally the most economically active and skilled group who support the elderly and younger groups.

Test your understanding 1

Give three demographic changes of interest to a firm of funeral directors.

Test your understanding 2

A greater percentage of teenagers in the UK are going on to university than ever before with the government putting forward a target figure of 50% by 2010.

Give examples of three firms who will be affected by this and state whether they face an opportunity or a threat.

1.3 Social trends

Social structure

- Many countries are finding the demand for housing growing faster than the population.

- The population of the UK grew by 7.7% between 1971 and 2006. Over the same period the number of dwellings grew by 35%.

- This is partly explained by increasing wealth but also by changes in social structure. For example, the proportion of one person households may be increasing, due to a range of factors such as, e.g. higher divorce rates.

Values

- An increasing concern about greenhouse gases and the ozone layer, testing of products on animals and generally greater social awareness could spell disaster in the future for those firms unwilling to embrace this cultural shift.

- Many women are choosing to pursue careers first before having children, so the average age of a mother on the birth of their first child has risen in many countries. Such older mothers are often wealthier and more demanding of the baby products they buy resulting in an increase in demand for better-quality clothing, prams, etc.

- A widespread change in lifestyle has been the shift away from the historic '9 to 5' working day to a more flexible form. Supermarkets are now open throughout the night and the internet and other forms of IT allow people to shop or bank in the middle of the night as a response to this trend.

Attitudes

- A change in attitudes is taking place across the EU at present in relation to willingness to seek compensation from organisations for alleged wrongs. The potential costs of this 'compensation culture' could be huge and may lead to some corporate casualties. The culture has, to a certain extent, been imported from the United States.

- Changes in public attitudes to recycling have resulted in opportunities for recycling firms.

- People are far more comfortable with computers and using the internet. In the UK the proportion of households with a broadband connection rose from 8 per cent to 31 per cent between April 2003 and July 2005. This has created huge opportunities for online firms and many conventional retailers have set up websites to sell their products.

Tastes

- Culturally, changes in tastes and fashions can have a damaging effect on organisations that fail to anticipate the changes. Clothing is an excellent case in point, and Marks & Spencer has in recent times experienced decline for this very reason. Even cars and furniture are susceptible to changes in trends and tastes.

Test your understanding 3

Give two examples of organisations for which the trend towards increased materialism is a threat.

Test your understanding 4

In 2001 it was announced that chicken tikka masala was the UK's favourite culinary dish, reflecting the huge increase in demand for such products in the 1990s. Give three reasons why this growth has occurred.

Expandable text

According to **Johnson and Scholes** the social influences that should be monitored include the following.

Population demographics – a term used to describe the composition of the population in any given area, whether a region, a country or an area within a country.

Income distribution – will provide the marketer with some indication of the size of the target markets. Most developed countries, like the UK, have a relatively even distribution spread. However, this is not the case in other nations.

Social mobility – the marketer should be aware of social classes and the population distribution among them. The marketer can use this knowledge to promote products to distinct social classes within the market.

Lifestyle changes – refer to our attitudes and opinions towards things like social values, credit, health and women. Our attitudes have changed in recent years and this information is vital to the marketer.

Consumerism – one of the social trends in recent years has been the rise of consumerism. This trend has increased to such an extent that governments have been pressured to design laws that protect the rights of the consumer.

Levels of education – the level of education has increased dramatically over the last few years. There is now a greater proportion of the population in higher education than ever before.

1.4 Government policy

For many firms the impact of social and demographic change is primarily through government responses to trends. For example:

Population structure

- Governments of countries with low birth rates often introduce tax advantages and other financial incentives to encourage women to have more children. This is the case in Singapore for example. Another common policy is to encourage immigration. Both Canada and Australia have been promoting this for over a decade.

- Governments in countries with rapidly rising populations often put in place policies to discourage large families, e.g. the 'one child' policy adopted by China.

- The increasing percentage of the population aged over 65 is creating a pensions crisis in many countries. The main concern is that the taxes received from a smaller proportion of workers will be insufficient to meet the pension demands of a growing retired population without huge increases in income tax rates. Typical government responses include raising the retirement age and encouraging private and occupational pension schemes.

Housing

- Increasing demand for new housing, in many countries has resulted in governments setting out plans for new developments, creating further demand for builders.

Employment

- The percentage of single-parent families in the UK rose from 7% in 1971 to 23% in 2005. The UK government has focused on enabling single parents to return to work through a mixture of childcare vouchers and tax credits. Among others this has created extra demand for childcare services and after-school clubs.

Health

- Concerns over the effects of smoking has resulted in bans on tobacco advertising on television in many countries. Concerns over obesity are giving rise to increasing pressure on government to legislate in a similar way in the fast food industry.

- In South Africa the government has put in place many initiatives to raise awareness of AIDs and sexual health. The global community is under great pressure to provide cheap drugs to help.

- Some governments have also taken steps to improve the nutritional value of school meals with obvious implications for the suppliers of those meals.

Test your understanding 5

Given increasing health concerns there is pressure for some governments to legislate for more detailed food labelling. Give an example of a firm for whom this will be an opportunity and one for whom this will be a threat.

Test your understanding 6

The average price paid by first-time house buyers in the UK doubled between 1998 and 2004. This has led to a shortage of affordable housing resulting in shortages of key staff such as nurses and teachers in many areas. To counter this, there have been national and local government initiatives to ensure that new housing developments include affordable housing.

What implications does this have for a house building firm?

2 Technological factors

2.1 Introduction

Technological changes can affect a firm in many different ways.

- Organisational, e.g. employees working from home but still able to access files and systems at work.

- Product developments, e.g. turntables were effectively replaced by CD players which in turn are being replaced by mp3 players.

- Production changes, e.g. computer-controlled machinery.

- Marketing, e.g. using the internet to sell the product.

2.2 Impact on organisational structure

Technological change has affected organisational structure in a number of key ways:

- Some administrative and managerial roles have been replaced by more effective IT systems.

- Some production roles have been replaced by the use of robots and automated production lines. This has also reduced the need for as many supervisors.

- Improved communications (email, use of secure intranets, wireless networks) mean that employees can work out of the office/at home allowing more flexible work arrangements.

These have resulted in downsizing and delayering in firms.

Downsizing

- Downsizing is a term used for reducing the number of employees in an organisation without necessarily reducing the work or the output.

- Downsizing has been a feature of the 1980s and 1990s and many organisations, large and small alike, believe that they have become 'leaner' and 'fitter' as a result.

Delayering

- Often linked to downsizing, delayering is the process of removing layers of management.

- This is usually to change the organisation from one with a rigid hierarchical framework with numerous layers of supervisory grades into a 'flatter' organisation with minimal layers of management. Such organisations tend to emphasise team working, with people taking on different roles in different teams.

Outsourcing

- Outsourcing means contracting-out aspects of the work of the organisation, previously done in-house, to specialist providers.

- In some cases suppliers are given access to the firm's records so they can review production schedules and stock records to ensure that supplies are delivered before they run out.

Illustration 1 – Impact on organisational structure

Wal-Mart, the US store chain, makes its sales data immediately available to its suppliers, through the internet. This sales data allows the suppliers to make their own forecasts of expected future demand for their products through Wal-Mart and plan their production schedules on the basis of these forecasts, rather than waiting for an actual purchase order from Wal-Mart before making any scheduling decisions.

Test your understanding 7

An audit firm has decided to eliminate the role of supervising senior and split the workload between other existing staff. What type of change is being described here?

Test your understanding 8

Comment on why technological changes have resulted in an increase in outsourcing.

2.3 Impact of technological change on products

- Technological advances allow many products to become increasingly more sophisticated, e.g. mobile phones are now smaller, can record images and video and be used to access the internet.

- New technology can lead to the emergence of substitutes, e.g. the cinema industry went into decline in the early 1980s as a result of the emergence of the video.

- Some industries have seen their business model completely transformed, e.g. online banking has reduced barriers to entry allowing supermarkets, among others, to move into banking.

- Customer support is often provided by call centres in countries where wage rates are lower. However some firms have reinstated call centres into their home countries after concerns over customer care.

2.4 Impact of technological change on production processes

- The most obvious way that technology has affected production is the use of robots and automated production lines.

- However, IT systems have also been used for more efficient scheduling and monitoring of production, resulting in lower inventory levels, higher quality, elimination of bottlenecks and lower costs.

Expandable text

Two specific applications of IT to production are MRP and ERP.

Manufacturing resource planning (MRP)

MRP is a push-based system, pushing work through production. The focus of the computer based technology is to draw together the appropriate resources to meet demand. Functions include:

- Identifying firm orders and forecasting future orders with confidence.
- Translating these into capacity requirements.
- Determining the timing of material requirements.
- Calculating purchase orders based on stock levels.
- Automatically placing purchase orders.
- Scheduling labour and materials for future production.

Benefits include:

- Reduced stock holding.
- Improved ability to meet orders.
- Reliable quotations of delivery times.

- Improved facilities utilisation.
- Less time spent on emergency orders.
- Better supplier relationships.

MRPII systems provide a central database through which the planning process can extend to incorporate other departments such as engineering, finance and marketing into a cohesive organisational system.

Enterprise resource planning (ERP)

ERP is a management system that integrates all aspects of the business into a single computer-based system to meet the needs of all organisational users. Its scope moves into HR applications, logistics, sales, marketing and comprehensive management accounting as well as an Extranet to co-ordinate those outside of the organisation.

2.5 Impact of technological change on marketing

As well as the product issues mentioned above, technology has affected all parts of the marketing function.

- Pricing – many retailers monitor competitors' prices to ensure that they are not being undercut. Most 'price watch' schemes are IT-based.
- Promotion – the obvious issue here is the use of websites but promotional methods also include viral and banner advertisements.
- Distribution, e.g. the internet has created a huge opportunity for many firms to sell direct to a wider range of potential customers.
- Market research, e.g. customer databases.

Test your understanding 9

Comment on how technological changes have affected the demand for holiday travel agents.

2.6 Impact of technological change on society as a whole

Society is becoming more dependent upon computer and communications technology. Many would argue that we have left the industrial age behind, and the information age has taken over. Key issues are:

- E-commerce
  - (i) www advertising
  - (ii) www ordering of products
  - (iii) www financial transactions
  - (iv) Electronic data interchange
- Home shopping
- Home banking
- Home learning
- Home entertainment
- Teleworking/telecommuting.

Some industries may disappear, but new ones are emerging. Employment patterns will change.

For example, sales staff and retail jobs could be reduced as home shoppers order directly from centralised warehouses. The new skills needed, will be that of web authoring and new languages such as JAVA to create attractive and interactive interfaces for the customers.

Chapter summary

SOCIAL, DEMOGRAPHIC AND TECHNOLOGICAL FACTORS

- Part of PEST analysis to identify opportunities and threats

DEMOGRAPHIC FACTORS

- Population size, composition and location
- Wealth
- Education
- Health

Social factors

- Social structure
- Values
- Tastes

Govenment responses

TECHNOLOGICAL FACTORS

Organisational structure

- Downsizing
- Delayering
- Outsourcing

Product

- More sophisticated
- Replaced
- Change in business model

Production

- Robotics, automation
- Scheduling, planning

Marketing

- Price watch
- Internet selling
- Websites
- Viral, banner ads

Test your understanding answers

Test your understanding 1

Demographic factors could include the following:

- life expectancy
- death rates by age group, social group and geographic region
- number of people aged over 65
- wealth distribution among older people – could they afford more expensive funerals?

Test your understanding 2

- Firms who rent out properties in university towns and cities – opportunity.
- Providers of stationery and study aids – opportunity.
- Student loan providers – opportunity.
- Any firm which typically takes staff on after school – threat as there will be fewer suitable candidates available. The number of graduate applicants for jobs may rise, but they may expect higher starting salaries.

Test your understanding 3

Organisations for which the trend towards increased materialism is a threat could include:

- sellers of basic goods, such as black and white televisions, as consumers will want more luxurious alternatives
- charities, as people prefer to spend their income on themselves.

Test your understanding 4

- A rise in the population of ethnic groups with Indian and Bangladeshi heritage, resulting in more restaurants selling chicken tikka masala.

- More diverse social tastes toward foods generally.

- A reduction in the number of parents staying at home, increasing demand for takeaway food generally.

Test your understanding 5

Opportunity – food labelling specialists (!), sellers of high quality unprocessed foods.

Threats – smaller businesses which cannot afford expensive labelling technology.

Test your understanding 6

The initiatives will be viewed as threats to profitability as the firm will have to rent out or sell properties at below the market rate. It may also have to reduce the prices on other houses in the development because of a perceived fall in their exclusivity.

The trend may, however, present an opportunity. If competitors are unable or unwilling to meet the criteria set out for new developments, then the firm which can will gain approval on more planning applications.

Test your understanding 7

Given that one level of management is being removed, this could be described as delayering.

(Note: It would also be downsizing if existing supervising seniors are made redundant.)

Test your understanding 8

Firms have always had the option of outsourcing. Many chose to bring production in-house to ensure that supply met demand and to avoid stock-outs. Advances in technology, such as allowing suppliers access to intranets, have allowed firms to outsource without losing these scheduling advantages.

Test your understanding 9

- Demand for travel agents grew hugely when technology allowed agents to explore availability and book flights from their premises in the 1970

- More recently the internet has allowed customers to do this from the comfort of their own homes, reducing the demand for agents.

- There has also been an increase in the number on online agents, such as Expedia.co.uk offering to build bespoke holidays.

Competitive factors

Chapter learning objectives

Upon completion of this chapter you will be able to:

- briefly explain **Porter's** ideas on competitive advantage:
    - differentiation
    - cost leadership
    - focus

- briefly explain the factors that influence the level of competitiveness in an industry using Porter's five forces model:
    - competitive rivalry
    - power of buyers
    - power of suppliers
    - threat from substitutes
    - threat of new entrants

- using **Porter's** value chain, describe how a firm's competitiveness is affected by the following departments' activities:
    - purchasing
    - production
    - marketing
    - service.

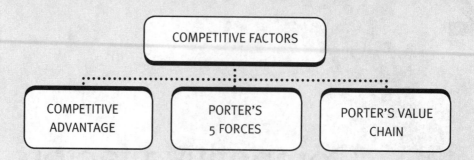

COMPETITIVE FACTORS

COMPETITIVE ADVANTAGE

PORTER'S 5 FORCES

PORTER'S VALUE CHAIN

1 Competitive advantage

1.1 Environmental analysis

Part of a firm's external analysis will involve assessing the degree and sources of competition within the industry. The key issue here is whether the firm has a sustainable competitive advantage.

This will be analysed in three steps:

- the different ways a firm can achieve a competitive advantage
- the main competitive forces in an industry
- how different activities and departments within the firm contribute to its competitiveness.

1.2 Competitive advantage

Michael Porter stated that a firm wishing to obtain a competitive advantage over its rivals is faced with two choices.

Choice one (Cost leadership versus differentiation)

- Is the company seeking to compete by achieving lower costs than its rivals for similar products and services?
- If so, then it can either undercut competitors on price, or charge similar prices and enjoy superior margins.

OR

- Is the company wishing to differentiate itself by offering a better product than competitors?
- Here the customer is prepared to pay a premium price for the added value which the customer perceives in the product.
- The firm thus enjoys a greater margin than the undifferentiated product.

Choice two (Degree of focus)

- What is the scope of the area in which the company wishes to obtain competitive advantage?

- Is it industry-wide or is it restricted to a specific niche?

The answers to these two choices leave the organisation faced with three 'generic' strategies:

- cost leadership

- differentiation

- focus.

Porter argues that trying to be both a cost leader and a differentiator usually results in the firm becoming 'stuck in the middle' with no clear competitive advantage – a recipe for disaster.

	BASIS OF COMPETITION	
	Lower Cost	**Differentiation**
Broad target	Cost leadership	Differentiation
COMPETITIVE SCOPE		
Narrow target	Cost focus	Differentiation focus

Illustration 1 – Competitive advantage

In the car industry one can identify the following strategies:

- differentiation – e.g. BMW, Jaguar, Mercedes
- cost leadership – e.g. Nissan, Ford, Honda
- focus – e.g. Ferrari, Rolls Royce.

Expandable text

Cost leadership

For companies competing in a 'price-sensitive' market, this generic strategy calls for being the low-cost producer in an industry for a given level of quality. This does not mean that products are 'cheap and cheerful' – merely that competitors' quality is matched rather than bettered.

The firm sells its products either at average industry prices to earn a profit higher than that of rivals, or below the average industry prices to gain market share. In the event of a price war, the firm can maintain some profitability while the competition suffers losses. Even without a price war, as the industry matures and prices decline, the firms that can produce more cheaply will remain profitable for a longer period of time. The cost leadership strategy usually targets a broad market.

Some of the ways that firms acquire cost advantages are by improving process efficiencies, gaining unique access to a large source of lower cost materials, making optimal outsourcing and vertical integration decisions, or avoiding some costs altogether. If competing firms are unable to lower their costs by a similar amount, the firm may be able to sustain a competitive advantage based on cost leadership.

Differentiation

A differentiation strategy calls for the development of a product or service that offers unique attributes that are valued by customers and that customers perceive to be better than or different from the products of the competition. In the differentiation focus strategy, a business aims to differentiate within just one or a small number of target market segments. The special customer needs of the segment mean that there are opportunities to provide products that are clearly different from competitors who may be targeting a broader group of customers. The important issue for any business adopting this strategy is to ensure that customers really do have different needs and wants – in other words that there is a valid basis for differentiation – and that existing competitor products are not meeting those needs and wants.

Differentiation strategies may be successful if a company can:

- reduce the ongoing cost to the customer of using the product (e.g. manufacture a better-quality product, easier to use, cheaper to run, etc.)

- increase customer satisfaction with the product (e.g. manufacture a product that performs better than its rivals)

KAPLAN PUBLISHING

- modify the customer's perception of value (this is very common in industries such as clothes manufacturing where brand names are marketed).

Focus

A focus strategy concentrates on a narrow segment (a particular buyer group, market segment, geographical region, service need, product feature or section of the product range) and within that segment attempts to achieve either a cost advantage or differentiation. The premise is that the needs of the group can be better serviced by focusing entirely on it. A firm using a focus strategy often enjoys a high degree of customer loyalty, and this entrenched loyalty discourages other firms from competing directly.

An important advantage of focus strategies is that they may be the only way into a market for a small company competing against larger companies.

Test your understanding 1

Identify examples of the three generic strategies in the food retail industry.

Test your understanding 2

What type of generic strategy is adopted by EasyJet? What are the key drivers of its success?

2 Porter's five forces analysis

2.1 Introduction

A PEST analysis is particularly good at identifying whether and why certain markets will be expected to grow in the future. However, just because a market is growing, it does not follow that it is possible to make money in it.

Porter's 5 forces approach looks in detail at the firm's competitive environment by analysing five forces.

Together these forces determine the overall profit potential of the industry. Looking at an individual firm, its ability to earn higher profit margins will be determined by whether or not it can manage the five forces more effectively than competitors.

2.2 Porter's five forces model

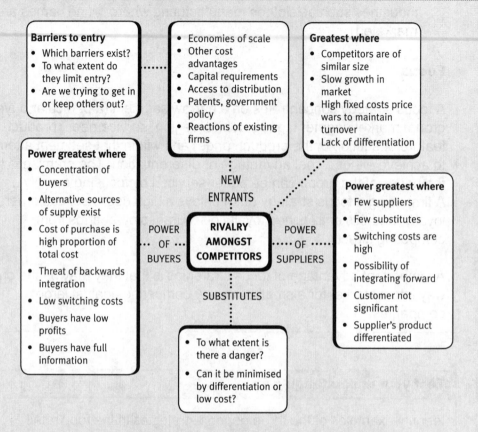

Barriers to entry
- Which barriers exist?
- To what extent do they limit entry?
- Are we trying to get in or keep others out?

- Economies of scale
- Other cost advantages
- Capital requirements
- Access to distribution
- Patents, government policy
- Reactions of existing firms

Greatest where
- Competitors are of similar size
- Slow growth in market
- High fixed costs price wars to maintain turnover
- Lack of differentiation

Power greatest where
- Concentration of buyers
- Alternative sources of supply exist
- Cost of purchase is high proportion of total cost
- Threat of backwards integration
- Low switching costs
- Buyers have low profits
- Buyers have full information

NEW ENTRANTS

POWER OF BUYERS

RIVALRY AMONGST COMPETITORS

POWER OF SUPPLIERS

SUBSTITUTES

Power greatest where
- Few suppliers
- Few substitutes
- Switching costs are high
- Possibility of integrating forward
- Customer not significant
- Supplier's product differentiated

- To what extent is there a danger?
- Can it be minimised by differentiation or low cost?

Expandable text

PORTER'S FIVE FORCES MODEL

Competitive rivalry

High competitive rivalry will put pressure on firms to cut prices and/or improve quality to retain customers. The result is reduced margins.

Intensity of existing competition will depend on the following factors:

- Number and relative strength of competitors – where an industry is dominated by a few large companies rivalry is less intense (e.g. petrol industry, CD manufacture).

- Rate of growth – where the market is expanding, competition is low key.

- Where high fixed costs are involved companies will cut prices to marginal cost levels to protect volume, and drive weaker competitors out of the market.

- If buyers can switch easily between suppliers the competition is keen.

- If the exit barrier (i.e. the cost incurred in leaving the market) is high, companies will hang on until forced out, thereby increasing competition and depressing profit.
- An organisation will be highly competitive if its presence in the market is the result of a strategic need.

Threat of entry

New entrants into a market will bring extra capacity and intensify competition. The threat from new entrants will depend upon the strength of the barriers to entry and the likely response of existing competitors to a new entrant. Barriers to entry are factors that make it difficult for a new entrant to gain an initial foothold in a market.

There are six major sources of barriers to entry.

- Economies of scale, where the industry is one where unit costs decline significantly as volume increases, such that a new entrant will be unable to start on a comparable cost basis.
- Product differentiation, where established firms have good brand image and customer loyalty. The costs of overcoming this can be prohibitive.
- Capital requirements, where the industry requires a heavy initial investment (e.g. steel industry, rail transport).
- Switching costs, i.e. one-off costs in moving from one supplier to another (e.g. a garage chain switching car dealership).
- Access to distribution channels may be restricted (e.g. for some major toiletry brands 90% of sales go through 12 buying points), i.e. chemist multiples and major retailers. Therefore it is difficult for a new toiletry product or manufacturer to gain shelf space.
- Cost advantages independent of scale, e.g. patents, special knowledge, favourable access to suppliers, government subsidies.

Threat of substitute products

This threat is across industries (e.g. rail travel versus bus travel versus private car) or within an industry (e.g. long-life milk as a substitute for delivered fresh milk). Porter explains that, 'substitutes limit the potential returns … by placing a ceiling on the price which firms in the industry can profitably charge'. The better the price-performance alternative offered by substitutes, the more readily customers will switch.

Bargaining power of customers

Powerful customers can force price cuts and/or quality improvements. Either way margins are eroded. Bargaining power is high (as, for instance, Sainsbury and Tesco in relation to their suppliers) when a combination of factors arises.

Such factors could include the following.

- Where a buyer's purchases are a high proportion of the supplier's total business or represent a high proportion of total trade in that market.

- Where a buyer makes a low profit.

- Where the quality of purchases is unimportant or delivery timing is irrelevant, prices will be forced down.

- Where products have been strongly differentiated with good brand image, a retailer would have to stock the complete range to meet customer demands.

Bargaining power of suppliers

The power of suppliers to charge higher prices will be influenced by the following:

- the degree to which switching costs apply and substitutes are available

- the presence of one or two dominant suppliers controlling prices

- the extent to which products offered have a uniqueness of brand, technical performance or design not available elsewhere.

Illustration 2 – Porter's five forces model

Porter's five forces can be applied to the house building industry as follows:

Competitive rivalry – very high

- large number of domestic and international firms

- it is difficult to differentiate your product

- firms typically have high fixed costs.

Threat of entry – high

- For new firms entering the industry the main barriers are as follows:
    - capital requirements are low – construction is labour intensive, most equipment can be hired if necessary
    - some economies of scale – e.g. purchasing bricks
    - need initial finance to acquire land
    - need good relationships with planning offices to get planning permission
- overall these barriers are low, resulting in a high threat of entry.

Threat of substitutes – high

- Main threat is the availability of second-hand property for rent or purchase.
- This will depend on the country concerned – some countries have housing shortages (e.g. Turkey) whereas others have booming housing property markets.

Power of suppliers – low for materials, higher for land and planning permission

- Material suppliers have low power – numerous suppliers, undifferentiated products.
- Suppliers of prime land sites are in a strong position and can command high prices.
- Local planning office has very high power.

Power of customers – low

- In the housing sector customers have more choice but individually have low buying power.

Summary: key issue is competitive rivalry.

Test your understanding 3

Use **Porter's** five forces to identify the most important competitive force for a burger chain, such as McDonalds.

Test your understanding 4

Discuss why a generic competitive strategy of differentiation makes sense by reference to **Porter's** five forces model.

Test your understanding 5

Would low industry profitability be a barrier to entry?

3 Porter's value chain

3.1 Introduction

Porter developed his value chain to determine whether and how a firm's activities contribute towards its competitive advantage.

3.2 The value chain

The approach involves breaking the firm down into five 'primary' and four 'support' activities, and then looking at each to see if they give a cost advantage or quality advantage.

Primary activities

Activity	Description	Example
Inbound logistics	Receiving, storing and handling raw material inputs.	A just-in-time stock system could give a cost advantage.
Operations	Transformation of the raw materials into finished goods and services.	Using skilled craftsmen could give a quality advantage.
Outbound logistics	Storing, distributing and delivering finished goods to customers.	Outsourcing deliveries could give a cost advantage.
Marketing and sales	Market research + 4Ps.	Sponsorship of a sports celebrity could enhance the image of the product.

KAPLAN PUBLISHING

Service	All activities that occur after the point of sale, such as installation, training, repair.	Marks & Spencer's friendly approach to returns gives it a perceived quality advantage.

Support activities

Activity	Description	Example
Firm infrastructure	How the firm is organised.	Centralised buying could result in cost savings due to bulk discounts.
Technology development	How the firm uses technology.	The latest computer-controlled machinery gives greater flexibility to tailor products to individual customer specifications.
Human resources development	How people contribute to competitive advantage.	Employing expert buyers could enable a supermarket to purchase better wines than competitors.
Procurement	Purchasing, but not just limited to materials.	Buying a building out of town could give a cost advantage over High Street competitors.

Results of analysis

The results of the analysis are often summarised in the following diagram.

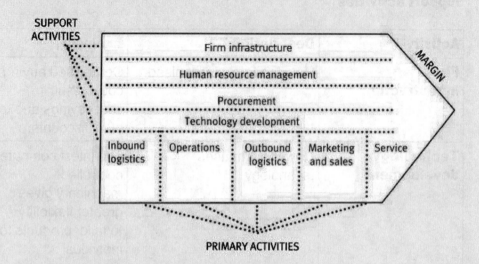

3.3 How different departments contribute to competitive advantage

Porter's value chain can now be used to explain how different departments contribute to competitiveness as follows:

Purchasing

- Cost advantages – sourcing cheaper materials, bulk discounts, centralised buying.

- Quality advantages – sourcing higher quality materials, employing expert buyers.

Production

- Cost advantages – mass production lines, standardisation, employing workers just above the minimum wage, keeping stock levels low.

- Quality advantages – using better quality materials, more quality control procedures, employing highly-skilled staff, flexible manufacturing systems, use of technology to ensure better consistency, ongoing training of staff.

Marketing

- Cost advantages – word-of-mouth promotion, sell direct to cut distribution costs.

- Quality advantages – market research can help tailor products to meet customer needs, large promotional budgets, sponsorship, perceived quality pricing, brand development.

Service

- Cost advantages – outsourcing (?), not offering service provision, low paid staff.

- Quality advantages – outsourcing (?), highly-skilled staff.

Test your understanding 6

How would a flexible manufacturing system affect competitiveness?

Test your understanding 7

The marketing department of a High Street clothes retailer plans to introduce a loyalty card scheme. How would this affect the firm's competitiveness?

Test your understanding 8

Rather than centralising purchasing, a food retailer is planning to allow local shop managers to source some of their own supplies. How could this affect competitive advantage?

Test your understanding 9

Human Resources (HR) is set up as a service department with a firm. How can this department contribute towards competitive advantage?

Chapter summary

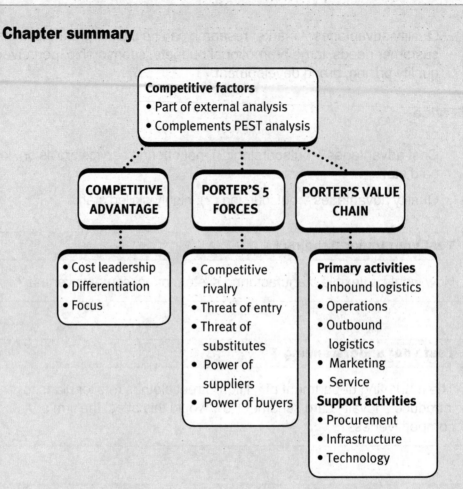

Competitive factors
- Part of external analysis
- Complements PEST analysis

COMPETITIVE ADVANTAGE
- Cost leadership
- Differentiation
- Focus

PORTER'S 5 FORCES
- Competitive rivalry
- Threat of entry
- Threat of substitutes
- Power of suppliers
- Power of buyers

PORTER'S VALUE CHAIN

Primary activities
- Inbound logistics
- Operations
- Outbound logistics
- Marketing
- Service

Support activities
- Procurement
- Infrastructure
- Technology

Test your understanding answers

Test your understanding 1

- Differentiation – e.g. Marks and Spencer, Harrods Food Hall.

- Cost leadership – e.g. Tesco, ASDA.

- Focus – e.g. traditional stores such as a local delicatessen, fruit and vegetable shop, fishmonger, butcher.

Test your understanding 2

EasyJet is adopting a cost leadership strategy.

Low costs are achieved by cheap airport fees (e.g. by not operating out of major airports), quick turnaround facilities, no free drinks or food in flight, and efficient booking and operating procedures (e.g. no tickets or boarding cards).

Note: you could argue that EasyJet also has a degree of focus as it only operates on more popular short-haul routes.

Test your understanding 3

Competitive rivalry – very high

- Many major competitors – e.g. Burger King.

Threat of entry – low

- Significant barriers to entry include economies of scale, capital investment required and strength of incumbents' brand names.

Threat of substitutes – medium

- Many substitutes – e.g. sandwiches, pizzas, etc.

Power of customers – low

- Customers have low switching costs and can easily go elsewhere BUT have very low individual buying power.

Power of suppliers – low

- McDonalds buys from small suppliers all over the world.

Summary: key issue is competitive rivalry.

Test your understanding 4

Threat of entry

The differentiation will be based on high quality and/or a strong brand name. These increase the development and marketing costs of new entrants and create switching barriers.

Competitive rivalry

Rivalry is reduced as competitors do not have comparable products at the price. Taken further, differentiation can enable the firm to carve out its own niche in the industry.

Threat of substitutes

The high quality associated with differentiation makes substitutes less attractive.

Power of buyers

Customer bargaining power is reduced as they will have to buy inferior goods if they switch to competitors.

Power of suppliers

Supplier power is only affected if suppliers want to be associated with the differentiator's high profile brand name.

Test your understanding 5

NO

While low profitability may make an industry unattractive, it does not make it more difficult for firms to enter should they wish to do so.

Test your understanding 6

A flexible manufacturing system will allow a firm to make bespoke products in response to differing customer needs. This additional focus on customer requirements will give a quality advantage.

Test your understanding 7

A loyalty card will make customers feel that they are getting 'something extra' so would contribute towards perceived quality.

Test your understanding 8

Local purchasing could result in the loss of bulk discounts, eroding a strategy of cost leadership.

However, managers may choose to buy local produce which could be perceived as better by customers.

Test your understanding 9

HR can contribute towards competitive advantage through selection, recruitment, training and appraisal schemes. These can all contribute towards lower staff turnover and greater motivations, which in turn will save costs and improve quality and productivity.

KAPLAN PUBLISHING

Stakeholders

Chapter learning objectives

Upon completion of this chapter you will be able to:

- explain the term stakeholder
- list the internal stakeholders of an organisation and explain their relationship with the organisation
- distinguish between internal, external and connected stakeholders
- list the external stakeholders of an organisation
- explain what impact each of the stakeholder groups has on the organisation
- identify the main stakeholder groups of an organisation
- list the objectives of each stakeholder group
- explain how different stakeholder groups interact with each other
- explain the nature of conflict between different stakeholder groups
- identify how the conflict between different stakeholder groups can be resolved.

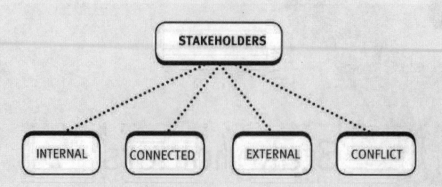

A stakeholder is a group or individual, who has an interest in what the organisation does, or an expectation of the organisation. It is important that an organisation understands the needs of the different stakeholders.

Expandable text

An important part of the strategic manager's job is to understand the contribution that relationships with stakeholders can make to the well-being of the organisation. Assessing the expectations of stakeholders enables an organisation to gauge whether its objectives will provide the means of satisfying the demands of the various stakeholders.

Stakeholders can be broadly categorised into three groups: internal, e.g. employees; connected, e.g. shareholders; external, e.g. government.

1 Internal stakeholders

Internal stakeholders are intimately connected to the organisation, and their objectives are likely to have a strong influence on how it is run.

Internal stakeholders include:

Stakeholder	Need/expectation	Example
Employees	pay, working conditions and job security	If workers are to be given more responsibility, they will expect increased pay.
Managers/directors	status, pay, bonus, job security	If growth is going to occur, the managers will want increased profits, leading to increased bonuses.

KAPLAN PUBLISHING

Test your understanding 1

Internal stakeholders have little influence over the way an organisation is run. True or false?

Test your understanding 2

Will the needs/expectations of the managers and employees always be the same?

2 Connected stakeholders

Connected stakeholders can be viewed as having a contractual relationship with the organisation.

The objective of satisfying shareholders is taken as the prime objective which the management of the organisation will need to fulfil, however, customer and financiers objectives must be met if the company is to succeed.

Stakeholder	Need/expectation	Example
Shareholders	steady flow of income, possible capital growth and the continuation of the business	If capital is required for growth, the shareholders will expect a rise in the dividend stream.
Customers	satisfaction of customers' needs will be achieved through providing value-for-money products and services	Any attempt to for example increase the quality and the price, may lead to customer dissatisfaction.
Suppliers	paid promptly	If a decision is made to delay payment to suppliers to ease cash flow, existing suppliers may cease supplying goods.
Finance providers	ability to repay the finance including interest, security of investment	The firm's ability to generate cash.

3 External stakeholders

External stakeholders include the government, local authority etc. This group will have quite diverse objectives and have varying ability to ensure that the organisation meets their objectives

Stakeholder	Need/expectation	Example
Community at large	The general public can be a stakeholder, especially if their lives are affected by an organisation's decisions.	E.g. local residents' attitude towards out-of-town shopping centres.
Environmental pressure groups	The organisation does not harm the external environment.	If an airport wants to build a new runway, the pressure groups may stage a 'sit in'.
Government	Company activities are central to the success of the economy (providing jobs and paying taxes). Legislation (e.g. health and safety) must be met by the company.	Actions by companies could break the law, or damage the environment, and governments therefore control what organisations can do.
Trade unions	Taking an active part in the decision-making process.	If a department is to be closed the union will want to be consulted, and there should be a scheme in place to help employees find alternative employment.

KAPLAN PUBLISHING

Test your understanding 3

In an article on stakeholders, Bob is surprised at how many stakeholders there are and the 'stake' they have in the organisation. He is finding it difficult to distinguish between the various groups. What are the needs/expectations of the following stakeholders and which of the following would not be described as a connected stakeholder?

Customers
Suppliers
Employees
Shareholders

Test your understanding 4

R is a high class hotel situated in a thriving city. It is part of a worldwide hotel group owned by a large number of shareholders. Individuals hold the majority of shares, each holding a small number, and financial institutions own the rest. The hotel provides full amenities, including a heated swimming pool, as well as the normal facilities of bars, restaurants and good quality accommodation. There are may other hotels in the city, all of which compete with R. The city in which R is situated is old and attracts many foreign visitors, especially in the summer season.

Who are the main stakeholders with whom relationships need to be established and maintained by managament? Explain why it is important that relationships are maintained with each of these stakeholders.

Test your understanding 5

Would competitors be classified as external or connected stakeholders and what are their needs/interests/expectations?

4 Stakeholder conflict

The needs/expectations of the different stakeholders may conflict. Some of the typical conflicts are shown below;

Stakeholders	Conflict
Employees versus managers	Jobs/wages versus bonus (cost efficiency)
Customers versus shareholders	Product quality/service levels versus profits/dividends
General public versus shareholders	Effect on the environment versus profit/dividends
Managers versus shareholders	Growth versus independence

Expandable text

One problem with analysing stakeholders is that they tend to belong to more than one group and will change their groupings depending on the issue in hand, e.g. marketing and production departments could be united against dropping a certain product but be in opposition regarding plans to buy a new product for the range.

Test your understanding 6

How could a conflict arise between shareholders and bankers?

It is important that an organisation meets the needs of the most dominant stakeholders, but the needs of the other stakeholders need to be considered – nearly every decision becomes a compromise. For example, the firm will have to earn a satisfactory return for its shareholders whilst paying reasonable wages.

If an organisation is having difficulty deciding who the dominant stakeholder is, they can use Mendelow's power-interest matrix.

		Level of intrest	
		Low	**High**
Level of Power	**Low**	Minimal effort	Keep informed
	High	Keep satisfied	Key players

By plotting each stakeholder according to the power they have over the organisation and the interest they have in a particular decision, the dominant stakeholder(s), i.e. the key players can be identified. The needs of the key players must be considered during the formulation and evaluation of new strategies.

Expandable text

Although the other stakeholders may be fairly passive, the managers must be aware that stakeholder groups can emerge and move from quadrant to quadrant as a result of specific events, so changing their position in the matrix.

Expandable text

Sources of stakeholder power include:

Hierarchy – provides people or groups with formal power over others.

Influence – may arise from personal qualities (leadership).

Control of the environment – knowledge, contact and influence of the environment can be a source of power if they are able to reduce the uncertainty experienced by others.

Test your understanding 7

Consider the following three organsiations:

Contract cleaning company

Accountancy training company

Local public library service.

In each case, the company is considering bringing down costs by reducing wages and making employees work more flexible shifts. In each case, who are the main employees who will be affected and classify them according to **Mendelow's** power interest matrix.

Chapter summary

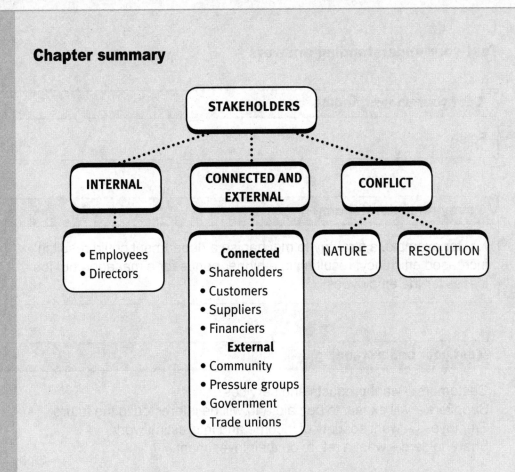

Test your understanding answers

Test your understanding 1

False

Test your understanding 2

No, for example, a strategy to mechanise a department could result in increased efficiency, resulting in a higher bonus for a manager, but job losses for the employees.

Test your understanding 3

Customers – want products and services.
Suppliers – will expect to be paid and will be interested in the future.
Employess – want security of income and interesting work.
Shareholders – want a return on their investment.

Employees are not connected stakeholders.

Test your understanding 4

Internal stakeholders

The employees and managers of the hotel are the main link with the guests and the service they provide is vital to the hotel as the quality of the guests' experience at the hotel will be determined by their attitude and approach.

Managers should be ensure that employees achieve the highest level of service are well trained and committed.

Connected stakeholders (shareholders, guests, suppliers)

The shareholders of the hotel will be concerned with a steady flow of income, possible capital growth and continuation of the business. Relationships should be developed and maintained with the shareholders, especially those operating on behalf of institutions. Management must try to achieve improvements in their return on investment by ensuring that customers are satisfied and willing to return.

Each guest will seek good service and satisfaction. The different types of guest will have different needs (business versus tourist) and management should regularly analyse the customer database to ensure that all customer needs are being met.

Suppliers must be selected very carefully to ensure that services and goods provided (e.g. food/laundry) continue to add to the quality of the hotel and customer satisfaction. They will be concerned with being paid promptly for goods, and maintaining a good relationship with the suppliers will ensure their continued support of the hotel.

External stakeholders (the government and the regulatory authorities)

The management of the hotel must maintain close relationships with the authorities to ensure they comply with all legislation – failure to do so, could result in the hotel being closed down.

Test your understanding 5

Connected stakeholder

Interests: customers being poached, possible takeover.

Test your understanding 6

The shareholders may be willing to take more risks in return for higher profits/returns, whereas the bankers will be more concerned with low risk/security.

Test your understanding 7

Contract cleaning company – main employees affected are the cleaners themselves. They are relatively easily replaced as they are unskilled and will have high interest but low power.

Accountancy training company – main employees affected are the lecturers. They are difficult to replace and will have high interest and high power.

Local public library service – main employees affected are the library staff. Although easily replaced, they are likely to be heavily unionised, and the power of the union will affect the decision-making process and will have high interest and power.

Committees in the business organisation

Chapter learning objectives

Upon completion of this chapter you will be able to:

- explain what is meant by a committee
- explain the purposes of committees in an organisation
- describe different types of committees used in the organisation
- explain their roles and purpose committee plays in the organisation
- list advantages and disadvantages of committees
- explain the roles of the chair and secretary of a committee.

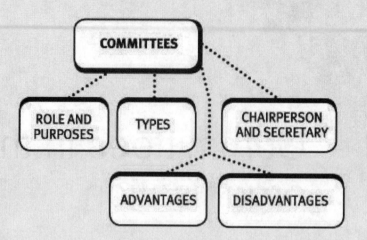

1 What is a committee?

A committee is a group of people to which some matter is committed.

- Ad hoc committees are usually temporary, as they are created for a specific purpose or to solve short-term problems.

- Formal committees are established as part of the organisational structure, with specifically delegated duties and authority.

Unlike teams (which are often established to tackle individual problems or projects), committees:

- are more likely to be permanent, or at least longer term

- have authority

- follow well established procedures

- provide a well tried way of resolving difficult decisions because all individuals and departments are formally involved in the decision-making process.

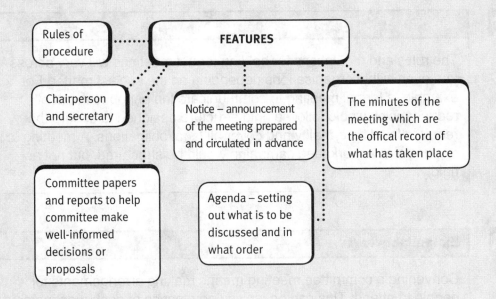

Test your understanding 1

Why might the notice of a forthcoming committee meeting also have the agenda and the minutes of the previous meeting attached to it?

There is usually a fairly rigid procedure about:

- Speaking
- Voting rights
- Proposing the motion and meetings
- Rights of attendance
- The construction of the agenda
- Adding emergency items to the agenda
- Quorum

1.1 The rules of procedure

The rules are designed:

- to promote the smooth running of a committee
- to ensure that consistency and fair play are maintained
- to enable both sides in an argument to state their case
- to help to minimise the effect of bullying tactics
- to ensure a proper record of all the proceedings is kept.

Illustration 1 – What is a committee?

The rules and regulations for holding formal meetings will vary across and even within organisations depending on the subject matter. For example, a formal meeting to communicate the announcement of redundancies would follow a rigid structure designed to ensure the required level of formality and cover all legal obligations. A meeting to discuss a new marketing campaign would be structured, but not as rigidly.

Expandable text

Convening a committee meeting means making arrangements for people to attend. This can be by issuing a notice of each meeting or, if the meeting is one of a series of similar gatherings, e.g. a regular monthly project status review meeting, it can be convened automatically. A formal meeting should be convened in accordance with any regulations laid down in the Articles of Association. Otherwise the proceedings may be challenged on the basis that procedures have not been followed.

A meeting may only proceed if it has been properly constituted, i.e. meets criteria laid down regarding attendance and conduct. Regarding attendance, the organisation may specify the minimum number of people that must be present for certain types of meeting. This is called a quorum. If there is no quorum, or the quorum is 'lost' during the meeting by people leaving, the Chair has two options:

(1)　To make the meeting a discussion group, with no authority to take decisions or agree actions.

(2)　To adjourn the meeting to a later date.

Procedures may also be defined regarding the conduct of the meeting. Each item of business may be required to be put before the meeting as a proposal or motion. This usually requires a proposer and a seconder. If it is carried (or approved), the motion becomes a resolution (or decision). The original motion is sometimes amended (or altered) in the course of debate and may then be carried in altered form as a 'substantive motion'. An amendment is a proposal to alter a motion that has been put before the meeting, but has not yet been put to the vote. An amendment which simply adds words to the original motion is called an addendum.

The participants will vote for or against a motion. This can be by a show of hands, a poll, a ballot or a voice vote.

A point of order is an objection about a perceived irregularity in the convening, constitution or conduct of the meeting. It is made to the chairperson, who makes an immediate ruling. Points of order are designed to ensure that regulations are observed, so that the proceedings cannot be disputed later as invalid.

Members are protected from attempts to manipulate procedures, for example by giving inadequate notice or voting without the right to do so.

There may be procedural problems over who is permitted to speak at a formal meeting. For example, at some meetings proxies, or 'stand ins' for absent members, have the right to be present but not to speak.

Test your understanding 2

You are chairing a meeting at work where a vote will be necessary. In trying to find out the best way of doing it you are surprised to find so many different methods. Which of the following methods would you be unlikely to use and why?

- A ballot
- A poll
- A division
- A voice vote
- A show of hands

1.2 The size and success of a committee

It is difficult to create a truly efficient committee but the following factors will help to foster efficiency.

The size of a committee is important:

- too large a committee may not give individuals time to give their point of view but if everyone spoke it would waste valuable time
- too few in the group may mean a lack of breadth of expertise, or decisions may be made with insufficient deliberation.

To be successful a committee should:

- be representative of all interests

- have a chairperson (sometimes called the chair) with the qualities of leadership to coordinate and motivate the other committee members and the ability to handle the group firmly and fairly
- choose suitable subjects for action and make precise proposals by agenda
- circulate reports prior to the meeting
- have clear cut terms of reference, wit areas of responsibility, timescales of operations and purpose specified in writing
- have the necessary skills and experience
- be worth the cost of its operation.

Test your understanding 3

Your friend Sally is arranging the first committee meeting for the project to implement a new business system. Her manager is helping her by suggesting the groups of people she should consider. From the list below decide which three would be considered when drawing up the list of attendees.

- Individuals who will be working with the new business system.
- Individuals who have an interest or concern in the outcome of the meeting.
- A person with the authority to ratify and enforce decisions taken by the meeting.
- Individuals with a balanced combination of qualities.
- A person who is working on the current business system.

2 The purpose of committees in an organisation

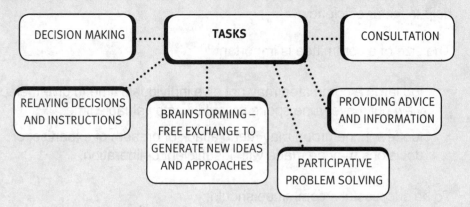

The purpose of the committee might be to:

- gather information

- disseminate information or instructions

- generate ideas

- make or implement decisions

- coordinate the efforts of a number of people from divergent disciplines

- act as a delaying mechanism

- oversee a function or procedure, e.g. the primary aim of a public oversight board is to eliminate or minimise any actual or potential breaches of legislative requirements and to ensure compliance with regulations applicable to organisations within their terms of reference.

Test your understanding 4

How can a committee act as a delaying mechanism?

3 Types of committees used in the organisation

Committees may be classified according to the power they exercise, distinguishing between those that have the power to bind the parent body and those without such power. Other ways of categorising them include:

- standing committees – are formed for a particular purpose on a permanent basis

- ad hoc committees – are formed to complete a particular task

- audit committees – review the company's accounting policies and internal controls, annual financial statements and the audit report with the company's external auditors.

Test your understanding 5

Are committee meetings suitable for all types of organisation?

4 Examples of committees

4.1 Board of directors

A board of directors is a group of people legally charged with the responsibility to govern a company

In a public company the board is a committee elected by shareholders and responsible to them. Its purpose is to:

- lay down strategy, general policy and broad sectional policies
- ensure legal standards are met and the company is operating in accordance with its Articles of Association
- sanction capital expenditure and the method of disposal of profits
- ensure sufficient capital is available and maintain an efficient system to control the affairs of the company.

4.2 Steering committee

The purpose of a steering committee is to oversee a major project, generally IT based, within an organisation. It is often involved in deciding how to allocate scarce IT resources and planning for future system development. Its role is to:

- ensure that all the IT activities are in line with the strategic plans of the organisation as a whole
- provide leadership at senior level for the exploitation and management of IT
- ensure that resource allocation decisions are effective
- co-ordinate requirements in any organisational restructuring
- create the terms of reference for the project teams
- monitor the progress of the various projects.

4.3 Works safety committee

This is an advisory committee, which meets regularly to discuss action required about unsafe working conditions or methods.

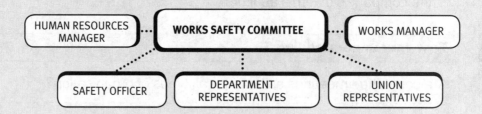

4.4 The Accounting Standards Board (ASB)

The Accounting Standards Board (ASB) took over the role of setting accounting standards from the Accounting Standards Committee (ASC) in August 1990.

The ASB aims to promote consistency in corporate reporting by creating financial reporting standards to which major businesses are expected to adhere.

4.5 Ethics committees

An increasing number of organisations have instituted ethics committees, which oversee the working practices and procedures in an organisation with respect to:

- conflicts of interest
- confidential information
- complaints of customers
- transactions involving related parties of the company.

Test your understanding 6

A steering committee is formed to monitor and control the feasibility study for the introduction of a management information system in a medium sized company. Who might be a member of this committee?

5 The advantages and disadvantages of committees

In the light of all this formality, what are the benefits and disadvantages of committees?

Advantages	Disadvantages
Responsibilities are shared	Slower decision making
Ability to undertake a larger volume of work than individuals working alone	Decisions may represent compromise solutions rather than optimum solutions
Decisions are based on a group's assessment of facts and ideas	Waste time and resources
Pools talent, judgement and allows specialisation	Managers may abdicate their personal responsibility for decision making
Improves coordination between work groups	Some 'experienced' committee members may dominate
Provides a focal point for information and action within organisation.	Excess procedural matters reduces the time available for the discussion of substantive matters.

Improves communication	Can not act quickly and flexibly to meet sudden changes in a situation

Expandable text

These advantages are particularly important in two respects. Firstly, the sheer size and complexity of modem enterprises make it increasingly impossible for isolated individuals or small groups to meet the decision-demands of their organisations. Secondly, the growing pressures from all sections of the workforce for a greater say in the decision- making processes of their organisations are creating expectations that decision-making will become more open and democratic. Committees are likely to be even more in demand as a result of these two factors.

Some of the disadvantages of committees can be overcome by applying the following guidelines for more effective communication.

Authority – the committee's authority should be spelled out so that members know whether their responsibility is to make decisions, make recommendations, or merely deliberate and give the chairperson some insights into the problem under discussion.

Size -the complexity of interrelationships greatly increases with the size of the group. If the group is too large, there may not be enough opportunities for adequate communication among its members. On the other hand, if the group consists of only three persons, there is the possibility that two may form a coalition against the third member. No precise conclusions can be drawn here about the appropriate size. As a general rule, a committee should be large enough to promote deliberation and include the breadth of expertise required for the job but not so large as to waste time or foster indecision. Research indicates that the ideal committee size may be five when the five members possess adequate skills and knowledge to deal with problems they are facing. It is obvious that the larger the group, the greater the difficulty in obtaining a 'meeting of the minds' and the more time necessary to allow everyone to contribute.

Membership – the members of the committee must be selected carefully. If a committee is to be successful, the members must be representative of the interests they are intended to serve. They must also possess the required authority and be able to perform well in a group. Finally, the members should have the capacity for communicating well and reaching group decisions by integrated group thinking rather than by inappropriate compromise.

Subject matter – committee work should be limited to subject matter that can be handled in group discussion. Certain kinds of subjects lend themselves to committee action, while others do not. Jurisdictional disputes and strategy formulation, for example, may be suitable for group deliberation, while certain isolated, technical problems may be better solved by an expert in the specialised field. Committees will be more effective if an agenda and relevant information are circulated well in advance so that the members can study the subject matter before the meeting.

Minutes – effective communication in committees usually requires circulating minutes and checking conclusions. At times, individuals leave the meeting with varying interpretations as to what was agreed. This can be avoided by taking careful minutes of the meeting and circulating them in draft form for correction or modification before the committee approves the final copy.

Cost effectiveness – it may be difficult to count the benefits, especially such intangible factors as morale, enhanced status of committee members, and the committee's value as a training device to enhance teamwork. But the committee can be justified only if the costs are off¬set by tangible and intangible benefits.

Test your understanding 7

How might a committee be misused?

6 The roles of the chair and secretary of a committee

6.1 The chair

One person at the meeting will act as chairperson and guide proceedings.

This person has responsibility for the following:

- Keeping the meeting to a schedule and to the agenda – to ensure issues relevant to the purpose are discussed.

- Maintaining order. Only one person at a time should speak. If there is conflict, the Chair decides who is to speak.

- Ensuring correct procedure is observed in convening and constituting the meeting, and during the meeting.

- Ensuring impartiality and giving all parties a reasonable opportunity to express their views.

- Ascertaining 'the sense of the meeting' (the consensus view or decision of the meeting) by summing up, or putting the issue to the vote and declaring the result.

- Depending on the level of formality of the meeting – checking and signing the minutes.

The skills and knowledge that the effective chairperson must have include:

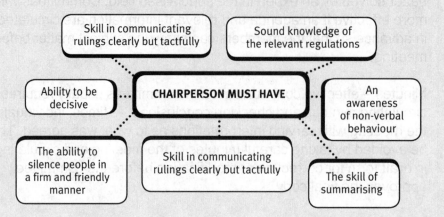

Skill in communicating rulings clearly but tactfully

Sound knowledge of the relevant regulations

Ability to be decisive

CHAIRPERSON MUST HAVE

An awareness of non-verbal behaviour

The ability to silence people in a firm and friendly manner

Skill in communicating rulings clearly but tactfully

The skill of summarising

Expandable text

The chairperson sets the tone of the meeting, integrates the ideas, and keeps the discussion from wandering. When chairing a meeting, it is useful to summarise the objectives of the meeting at the beginning. This will help to focus the attention of the attendees on the job in hand. It may also be necessary to remind the meeting of its objectives at various stages, to stop the meeting drifting out of control.

Other techniques that a chairperson can adopt include asking 'opening questions' to stimulate the thoughts of the group as a whole and asking a specific question to a particular participant to encourage participation and ensure those with specialist knowledge contribute when appropriate.

The chairperson will use summaries to consolidate points agreed on as a basis for moving on. The objective of summarising is to check on the level of understanding and give an opportunity to sort out misunderstandings. There are two different ways of accomplishing this objective.

(1) At intervals in the conversation, to give a summary of the salient points as you have understood them.

(2) To test understanding by inviting someone else to summarise and check that their summary accords with the one that you would have given at that stage in the proceedings. If a number of people are present, invitations to summarise can be shared around rather than become the prerogative of one person. This is a splendid incentive for people to listen hard since they never know when they might be called upon to paraphrase what they have heard.

Summarising reduces ambiguity by pointing things out explicitly and helps to reduce the likelihood that people are agreeing to different things.

RESPONSIBILITY OF SECRETARY TO THE COMMITTEE MEETING		
Before the meeting • fixing the date and time of the meeting • booking the venue • preparing and issuing the agenda and other relevant documents	**During the meeting** • assisting the chairperson • making notes • advising the chairperson on points of procedure	**After the meeting** • preparing minutes • acting on and communicating decisions • dealing with correspondence

Test your understanding 8

You have been asked to draw up a role description and person specification for the voluntary role of the secretary to the Management Committee in a local charity organisation. The commitment will be about three hours per month.

Chapter summary

```
                        ┌─────────────────┐
                        │   COMMITTEES    │
                        └─────────────────┘
```

FORMALITY FEATURES

Types
- Board of directors
- Works committee
- Employee representatives committee
- Steering committee
- Audit committee
- Governance/ethics committee

Rules of procedures
- Rights of attendance
- Voting rights
- Quorum
- Proposing motions and meetings

Role and purpose
- Decision making
- Information gathering
- Consultation
- Problem solving
- Brainstorming
- Delay tactics
- Advisory
- Overseeing
- Co-ordinating
- Generating
- ideas

- Notice
- Minutes
- Agenda
- Committee papers and reports

CHAIR AND SECRETARY

ADVANTAGES AND DISADVANTAGES

- Guide proceedings
- Maintain order
- Keep to schedule
- Sign minutes

- Prepare and issue agenda
- Assist Chair in meetings
- Prepare minutes

- Pooled authority
- Blurring responsibility
- Combined abilities
- Improved communication
- Co-ordinated actions

- Slower decision making
- Compromised solutions
- Wasting time/ resources
- Abdication of personal responsibilites
- Cannot act quickly

Test your understanding answers

Test your understanding 1

The agenda, i.e. the items of business to be discussed at the meeting, is often attached to the notice so that:

- Everyone knows what is to be covered, and can prepare speeches, questions etc. accordingly.

- All are aware of the order of business, and can if necessary arrange to attend only the relevant session of the meeting.

- The Chairperson can keep the meeting to a schedule, and within a framework of which everyone is already aware.

The minutes are the written record of the proceedings at the meeting, approved by those present. Because they provide a source of reference, particularly with regard to decisions and action points agreed by participants, the minutes of the previous meeting might also be attached to the agenda so that any queries or objections relating to them may also be prepared.

Test your understanding 2

There are two methods in the list that would be unlikely ways of voting in a committee meeting at work. The first is a ballot, which is generally where each voter completes an individual voting paper (out of the view of others) and puts it into a ballot box to be counted later. Parliamentary and local government elections follow this procedure. The second is a division, where those present at the meeting rise from their places and walk into separate 'lobbies' ('For' and 'Against') where their numbers are counted. This method is associated with parliament voting procedures and not with an organisation.

The other methods in order of suitability are the poll, the show of hands and the voice vote.

The poll is a popular company voting procedures. Each person entitled to vote does so in writing on an individual voting paper or on a polling list. The number of votes a person is entitled to cast may vary (eg by shareholding). With the show of hands, at the invitation of the Chair those 'In favour' raise a hand and then 'Those against'. The Chair declares the result of the count. This is a 'one person, one vote' system, requiring the presence of the individual or an appointed proxy. A voice vote, or 'vote by acclamation' is where the Chair calls for those in favour to say 'Aye' and those against to say 'No'. The volume of votes determines the result. This is used for conventional votes of thanks, or matters on which there is almost certainly unanimous feeling.

Test your understanding 3

The three that Sally would consider are those who have an interest or concern in the outcome of the meeting, someone with the authority to ratify and enforce decisions taken by the meeting and individuals with a balanced combination of qualities. The mix of attendees should comprise an effective problem-solving and task-oriented group with creativity, enthusiasm, analysis and 'people' skills.

Test your understanding 4

A committee can be used to gain time. For example, a manager may set up a committee to investigate a problem when he or she wants to delay a decision, or a company may refer a labour relations problem to a committee to defer a crisis with a trade union.

Test your understanding 5

On balance, committees are probably best suited to large-scale organisations that are bureaucratic in style, or which have a high degree of public accountability. Smaller-scale enterprises, on the other hand, would probably benefit more from the greater flexibility obtainable from less formal, and perhaps less thorough, forms of decision-making, such as informal management meetings and temporary project groups.

Test your understanding 6

Management requires as much detailed information as possible to make the correct decision. A computer manufacturer or a management consultant is often asked to carry out a feasibility study, but neither is likely to be familiar with the structure and working of the company.

Therefore a team (the steering committee) composed of people from within the company and those with computer experience could perform the feasibility study and produce a report for senior management. Generally, this is a standing committee, whose membership reflects the project being dealt with. For this type of project, the members are likely to comprise:

- the director of finance (or perhaps the deputy chief executive) as chairperson

- the director of management services

- the head of the IT department

- the chief analyst

- the chief programmer

- the management representatives of the user department(s)

- external consultants (if utilised).

Membership is bound to vary in accordance with the kind of project involved. Some members may only attend meetings relevant to their specialist areas, eg the chief programmer may only attend meetings where programming aspects will be considered. The project leader will also attend to report progress.

Test your understanding 7

A committee may be misused for a number of purposes that are 'wrong'. Examples include those used to:

- replace managers – a committee cannot do all the tasks of management, e.g. leadership and therefore cannot replace them entirely

- make unimportant decisions – this would be expensive and time-consuming

- carry out research work – a committee may be created to generate new ideas but work on those ideas cannot be done effectively by a committee itself

- coordinate activities when the problem is the organisation structure. Committees are accused of 'papering over the cracks' in a badly designed organisation

Test your understanding 8

Role description and person specification

The role of the Secretary is:

- to support the Chairperson in ensuring the smooth functioning of the Management Committee.

The Secretary's tasks include:

- ensure responsible administration
- to note all correspondence (in and out) on the agenda for the forthcoming meeting
- to ensure up-to-date records are kept of committee membership
- to keep minute book safe – it must never be destroyed
- to convene meetings and prepare agendas in consultation with the Chairperson (and chief officer)
- to circulate agendas and any supporting papers in good time
- to check that quorum is present
- to record names of those in attendance and apologies for non-attendance
- to minute meetings and circulate the draft minutes to all committee members
- to ensure that the chairperson signs the minutes once they have been approved
- to check that committee members and staff have carried out action (s) agreed
- to circulate agendas and minutes of the annual general meeting (AGM) and any special or extraordinary general meetings
- to ensure arrangements for meetings are met (booking the room, arranging for equipment and refreshments, and organising facilities for those with special needs, etc.)

Qualities and Skills required.

- Organisational ability.
- Experience of committee work and procedures.
- Minute-taking experience (if this is not being delegated to staff).
- Good communication and interpersonal skills.
- Impartiality, fairness and the ability to respect confidences.
- Approachable and sensitive to the feelings of others.

- Well organised and an eye for detail.
- Ability to work well with the chairperson.
- Good time-keeping.

Time Commitment Required

- The role of Secretary requires an estimated commitment of about 3 hours per month.

15

Business ethics and ethical behaviour

Chapter learning objectives

Upon completion of this chapter you will be able to:

- define the term 'business ethics'
- explain why business ethics is important for an organisation and the individual
- explain what criteria determine whether a decision made by the organisation is seen as ethical
- explain what is meant by a profession
- identify the factors that distinguish a profession from other occupations
- explain what role an accountant plays in ensuring the organisation acts in an ethical manner
- explain the purpose of international codes of ethics
- explain the purpose of the organisations such as IFAC and ACCA with regard to ensuring codes of conduct are adhered to.

THE MEANING OF BUSINESS ETHICS

HOW A PROFESSIONAL ACCOUNTANT ACCEPTS THE
RESPONSIBILITY TO ACT ETHICALLY AT ALL TIMES

RELEVANT CODES OF ETHICS ISSUED BY
THE ACCA, IFAC, ETC.

1 Definition of business ethics

- Ethics is the analysis of right and wrong, and associated responsibility.

- Business ethics is the application of ethical values to business behaviour.

It is possible to distinguish between business ethics (the discipline described above) and an ethical business (such as The Co-operative Bank) that has decided to place high ethical standards on an equal priority to the pursuit of profit.

Approaches to deciding what is "right" or "wrong" include discussion of the following:

(1) The consequences - "the end justifies the means"

(2) The motivation of the parties concerned

(3) Guiding principles - e.g."treat others as you would like to be treated"

(4) Duties - e.g. based on religious codes

(5) Key values - e.g. the importance of human rights

These are often, but not always, incorporated into legislation.

Expandable text

'Ethics' can be divided into three areas:

- meta-ethics – the study of what is ethical behaviour
- normative ethics – how to arrive at practical standards of ethical behaviour
- applied ethics – applying ethical ideas to specific controversial issues.

Any study of ethics ties in with the religious and cultural background of the society. For example 'Thou shalt not steal' is one of the Ten Commandments of the Christian faith. Meta-ethics would consider whether such a statement is always absolutely true, or whether it is only true relative to some society or culture (was Robin Hood wrong to 'steal' from the rich to give to the poor in medieval England?).

Proponents of business ethics are generally less concerned with meta-ethics and more interested in solving practical business problems. Business ethics is therefore a normative discipline whereby particular standards are set out and obligations are placed on participants in a commercial relationship. Experts in applied ethics can then test whether the normative rules are effective in particular circumstances.

Illustration 1 – Definition of business ethics

You discover that a colleague at work has been stealing from the company. What do you do? Do you report them to management which might lead to their dismissal and the loss of a friend? Do you keep quiet and risk being punished yourself if your knowledge of the situation later becomes clear? Do you urge the colleague to confess what they've done? Does it depend on the size of the theft, e.g. a $1 pad of paper, or a $1,000 piece of machinery? Does it depend on how friendly you are with the colleague?

You can see that ethical problems require moral judgements that can be extremely difficult and depend on many different factors.

Test your understanding 1

Business ethics and legal requirements

Is the study of business ethics purely concerned with legal requirements?

> **Test your understanding 2**
>
> **Ethical propositions**
>
> Which of the following are ethical propositions?
>
> - David is a good man.
> - Someone broke into my car last night.
> - Taxpayers should pay their taxes on time.

2 Why business ethics is important

Businesses are part of society. Society expects its individuals to behave properly, and similarly expects companies to operate to certain standards.

Business ethics is important to both the organisation and the individual.

For the organisation	For the individual
<ul><li>Good ethics should be seen as a driver of profitability rather than a burden on business.</li><li>An ethical framework is part of good corporate governance and suggests a well-run business.</li><li>Investors are reassured about the company's approach to risk management.</li><li>Employees will be motivated in the knowledge that they operate in an environment of good ethical corporate behaviour.</li></ul>	<ul><li>Consumer and employee expectations have evolved over recent years.</li><li>Consumers may choose to purchase ethical items (e.g. Fairtrade coffee and bananas), even if they are not the cheapest.</li><li>Employees will not blindly accept orders to act in a manner that they personally believe to be unethical.</li></ul>

KAPLAN PUBLISHING

Illustration 2 – Why business ethics is important

The Fairtrade mark is a label on consumer products that guarantees that disadvantaged producers in the developing world are getting a fair deal. For example, the majority of coffee around the world is grown by small farmers who sell their produce through a local co-operative. Fairtrade coffee guarantees to pay a price to producers that covers the cost of sustainable production and also an extra premium that is invested in local development projects.

Consumers in the developed world may be willing to pay a premium price for Fairtrade products, knowing that the products are grown in an ethical and sustainable fashion.

Test your understanding 3

Cost or benefit?

Is the adherence to ethical practice always a cost to business, or can it bring profits into the business?

3 How can the ethics of a business decision be judged?

Ethics goes beyond the legal requirements of a business, therefore the decision-makers in a company have to use their discretion in deciding on an ethically questionable matter. Certainly, if an action is illegal, it is almost certainly unethical.

Organisations can draft sets of criteria to be used in making difficult decisions:

- Is it legal?
- Is it contrary to our company's adopted code of ethics?
- Is it contrary to any other published official code of ethics (e.g. the ACCA Code of Ethics and Conduct)?
- Would you mind other people knowing what you have decided (e.g. if it was in tomorrow's newspapers, or you had to justify the decision to your mother)?
- Who is affected by this decision? Would they regard the decision as fair?

Expandable text

Apart from general legal requirements, there is no universal code of conduct that provides guidance on how a business should conduct itself. Companies therefore have to formulate their own value system and policies on employee conduct.

One size does not fit all. Each company must identify its own set of core values, which can be developed into a code of ethics for all employees throughout the company. Strong visible support for the code from the board of directors is essential if the code is to be effective.

Illustration 3 – How can the ethics of a business decision be

Reebok International

International companies such as Reebok have to decide where to locate their manufacturing facilities. It is cheaper to locate factories in low-wage countries but the company does not want to attract bad publicity by paying insufficient attention to human rights issues at such factories. Reebok have instituted a code of conduct to regulate working conditions in the factories of its sub-contractors, but it is still accused of not ensuring that this code is always followed.

Test your understanding 4

Ethical implications of offshoring

What are the ethical implications of a UK company deciding to outsource its customer service operations to a cheaper overseas country?

4 How is a profession distinguished from other occupations?

A profession (as opposed to other types of occupation) is characterised by the following factors:

- the mastering of specialised skills during a period of training
- governance by a professional association
- compliance with an ethical code
- a process of certification before being allowed to practise.

Examples include accounting, law, teaching and medicine. A professional accountant such as an ACCA member fulfils the above four conditions. In many countries (including the UK) it is also possible for unqualified people to call themselves accountants and set themselves up in business offering accountancy advice. Such people are not professional accountants because they belong to no professional accountancy body (such as the ACCA) and have no obligation to follow an ethical code (ACCA members have to follow the ACCA Code).

Expandable text

Some commentators stress that professionals owe an obligation to society above their duty to their client. For example, the IFAC Code of Ethics states in its Introduction that:

'A distinguishing mark of the accountancy profession is its acceptance of the responsibility to act in the public interest. Therefore a professional accountant's responsibility is not exclusively to satisfy the needs of an individual client or employer.'

In a similar way, a doctor should refuse to sell medicines to a patient if they would harm the patient, regardless of the patient's willingness to pay, or a lawyer may refuse to take on a case if he believes the case is against the public interest. Other commentators stress the role of professional bodies in ensuring that their members possess adequate insurance so that members of the public can successfully sue the professional if they are harmed by the professional's negligence. For example, ACCA members are required to take out Professional Indemnity Insurance (PII) to protect against this very risk.

Test your understanding 5

Professional football

'Professional' footballers are those paid to play football, as opposed to amateur players, but is football a profession?

Test your understanding 6

Professional and unqualified accountant

Identify three differences between a professional accountant and an unqualified accountant.

5 The accountant's role in promoting ethical behaviour

At many business meetings, or on many boards of directors, it is only the professional accountant who belongs to a profession and therefore has a duty to act in the public interest as well as in the interests of his employer and the shareholders.

The professional accountant therefore has a special role in promoting ethical behaviour throughout the business.

Expandable text

An ethical dilemma involves a situation where a decision-maker has to decide what is the 'right' or 'wrong' thing to do. Examples of ethical dilemmas can be found throughout all aspects of business operations.

Accounting issues:

- Creative accounting to boost or suppress reported profits.

- Directors' pay arrangements – should directors continue to receive large pay packets even if the company is performing poorly?

- Should bribes be paid to facilitate contracts, especially in countries where such payments are commonplace?

- Insider trading, where for example directors may be tempted to buy shares in their company knowing that a favourable announcement about to be made should boost the share price.

Production issues:

- Should the company produce certain products at all, e.g. guns, pornography, tobacco, alcoholic drinks aimed at teenagers?

- Should the company be concerned about the effects on the environment of its production processes?

- Should the company test its products on animals?

Sales and marketing issues:

- Price fixing and anti-competitive behaviour may be overt and illegal or may be more subtle.

- Is it ethical to target advertising at children, e.g. for fast food or for expensive toys at Christmas?

- Should products be advertised by junk mail or spam email?

Personnel (HRM) issues:

- Employees should not be favoured or discriminated against on the basis of gender, race, religion, age, disability, etc.

- The contract of employment must offer a fair balance of power between employee and employer.

- The workplace must be a safe and healthy place to operate in.

Illustration 4 – The accountant's role

The Guinness affair

An example of financiers behaving unethically is given by the Guinness takeover of Distillers in 1986. Guinness was bidding to take over Distillers, paying with new shares in Guinness that were to be issued. Thus it was imperative for the Guinness share price to be as high as possible, to boost the value of the new shares that were being offered.

The chairman of Guinness at the time conspired with other financiers in an illegal share support operation. They would buy shares in Guinness and would be handsomely rewarded by Guinness once the takeover went through and the shares no longer needed artificial support.

The scheme could be argued to be in the best interests of Guinness shareholders, since it contributed to the successful takeover of Distillers. However it was clearly unethical since it created a false market in Guinness shares. The scheme was judged to be illegal and the participants were all sentenced to prison terms.

Test your understanding 7

The accountant's role

An ACCA member serves on a board of directors which is discussing carrying out an illegal action. What should the accountant do in such circumstances?

6 Codes of ethics and codes of conduct

Most companies (especially large companies) have approached the business ethics issue by formulating a set of internal policies and instructing employees to follow them. Often ethics officers (also called 'compliance officers') are appointed to monitor the application of the policies and to be able to discuss ethical dilemmas with employees who approach them.

The policies can either be broad generalisations (a corporate ethics statement) or can contain specific detailed rules (a corporate ethics code).

Expandable text

Some commentators see the growth in codes of conduct as a cynical attempt by companies to escape legal liability when an employee is caught doing something wrong. The company can try to claim that it is not the company's fault when a rogue employee acts outside the stated rules.

Other commentators argue that codes of conduct are simply a marketing tool that companies can use to highlight to the public how well they behave.

In practice, a code of conduct will only work if management are seen to support it, for example by holding regular seminars at the business to promote ethical practice. The worst situation is where a code of conduct exists, but management openly deride its contents and instruct employees to disobey it.

Illustration 5 – Codes of ethics and codes of conduct

Tesco plc

Tesco states that it is committed to conducting its business in an ethical manner, treating employees, customers, suppliers and shareholders in a fair and honest manner and ensuring that there are constant and open channels of communication.

Tesco has a code of ethics for its employees, including a policy on the receipt of gifts and a grievance procedure to cover employment issues. Employees are able to ring a confidential telephone helpline to raise concerns about any failure to comply with legal obligations, health and safety issues, damage to the environment, etc.

Business code of ethics

Are all the obligations in a company's code of ethics imposed on the employee, or does the company also take on obligations to behave ethically?

7 IFAC and ACCA codes of ethics

Both the International Federation of Accountants (IFAC) and the ACCA have developed codes of ethics for their members.

The IFAC 'Code of Ethics for Professional Accountants' (issued in June 2005) lays down ethical standards to be applied by practising accountants across the world. IFAC recognise that some jurisdictions may have specific requirements and guidance that differ from its Code, in which case professional accountants should comply with the more stringent rules unless this is prohibited by local laws or regulation.

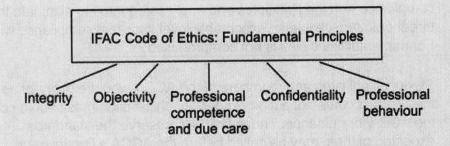

Expandable text

A professional accountant must comply with the Fundamental Principles in the Code at all times. The IFAC Code is based on a conceptual framework approach to problem resolution, rather than a rules-based approach. Professional accountants are required to identify and address threats to complying with the Fundamental Principles, rather than the Code listing a long set of rules that aim to deal with every possible eventuality.

The member bodies of IFAC are professional bodies such as the ACCA, so IFAC has no direct ability to punish an accountant who acts contrary to the Code. However IFAC would expect the transgressor's professional body to investigate the matter and punish the accountant if necessary.

The ACCA's 'Code of Ethics and Conduct' is contained in the annual Rulebook issued by the Association. All registered students, affiliates and members of the ACCA are required to comply.

The ACCA Code is based on the IFAC Code and takes a similar conceptual framework approach, listing an identical set of Fundamental Principles that must be followed.

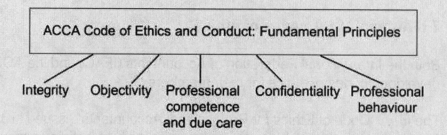

Expandable text

All ACCA members must comply with the Fundamental Principles, whether or not they are in practice. Members must identify threats to compliance with the Principles and apply safeguards to eliminate the threat or to reduce it to an acceptable level such that compliance with the Fundamental Principles is not compromised.

Students, affiliates and members of the ACCA who are in doubt as to their correct course of action in specific ethical dilemmas should contact the ACCA for guidance. Those failing to observe the standards expected of them may be called before the ACCA's Disciplinary Committee and required to explain their conduct.

Illustration 6 – IFAC and ACCA codes of ethics

ACCA Disciplinary Committee decision

An ACCA member may be called to appear before the Disciplinary Committee for breach of any of the ethical principles described above, and may be admonished, fined, suspended or excluded from membership.

For example, in January 2004 an ACCA member was convicted in a court of three counts of false accounting. This is contrary to the principles of 'integrity' and 'professional behaviour' so the Disciplinary Committee considered the matter. The member was excluded from ACCA membership and ordered to pay £750 costs.

Test your understanding 9

Scope of the ACCA Code of Ethics

Does the ACCA Code of Ethics only apply to members with a practising certificate, or to all members? Does it apply to ACCA-registered students?

Chapter summary

Definition of business ethics:
- The analysis of right and wrong in business operations, also looking at personal and corporate responsibilities in the business world

What makes an occupation into a profession?
- Training to develop skills
- Governance by a professional body
- Compliance with an ethical code
- Certification before being allowed to practise

Examples of codes of ethics
- IFAC Code of Ethics
- ACCA Code of Ethics and Conduct

Determining whether a decision is ethical:
- Is it legal?
- Is it contrary to a published code of ethics?
- Is it a fair use of power?
- Would you be embarrassed if you had to justify the decision to your mother?

Test your understanding answers

Test your understanding 1

No. Business ethics is partly concerned with legal requirements, but also with areas that are not covered by the law.

Test your understanding 2

Ethics is concerned with good/bad and with what you should/ought to do, so the first and third statements concern ethics, while the second statement concerning the break-in is a factual statement with no ethical content.

Test your understanding 3

The traditional view was always that ethical behaviour was a burden on business. If competitors were behaving unethically, then managers thought they had no choice other than to act unethically themselves. Initiatives such as Fairtrade have proved this traditional view to be false. Adherence to ethical practice can be shown to be a driver of new profit streams rather than as a cost burden.

Test your understanding 4

UK companies operate in a competitive environment, so must contain costs if they are to prosper. Outsourcing jobs offshore (e.g., to India) is a popular way of saving costs, since Indian workers are well educated and can speak good English but are paid less than UK workers. The shareholders of the company will be happy with the higher profits. The customers will be content as long as their level of service remains the same. However the UK employees will not be happy and the reduction in UK employees must be managed in compliance with UK labour laws, otherwise the move may be seen to be unethical.

Test your understanding 5

No, football is not generally considered to be a profession, since there is no formal ethical code governing footballers' behaviour. Being paid to practise your trade is not sufficient to qualify your occupation as a profession. However this matter is debatable.

Test your understanding 6

A professional accountant has passed exams in accountancy, so has a proven level of knowledge. An unqualified accountant has not passed these exams.

A professional accountant has a duty to remain up-to-date with his professional knowledge. An unqualified accountant has no such duty.

A professional accountant is a member of a professional body and must comply with all the rules of that body, including adherence to the ethical code.

Test your understanding 7

The accountant should argue against carrying out the illegal action. If he is out voted and the board decide to proceed, the accountant should take legal advice from the company's solicitors. He may discuss the matter with the ACCA to seek further advice. In the final analysis he may decide that he has no alternative but to resign from his position at the company.

Test your understanding 8

The obligations in a company's code of ethics flow in both directions, from the company to individual stakeholders, and from stakeholders to the company. For example the company agrees to act ethically towards its employees, but each employee must also act ethically towards the company.

Test your understanding 9

The ACCA Code of Ethics applies to all ACCA members, regardless of whether they have a practising certificate or not. It also applies to all students registered with the ACCA.

16

Governance and social responsibility

Chapter learning objectives

Upon completion of this chapter you will be able to:

- explain how and why in the organisation ownership and control are separated

- define the term 'corporate governance'

- define the term 'social responsibility'

- explain why being socially responsible is important for an organisation's success

- explain what role a company's management plays in maintaining appropriate standards of corporate governance

- outline how organisation decision making will be affected if the social responsibility objective is taken into account

- explain the role of NEDs

- list the advantages and disadvantages of having a remuneration committee

- explain the functions of an audit committee

- suggest the means by which the public oversight of corporate governance can take place

- explain how a stakeholder needs analysis helps an organisation to take account of its social responsibility objectives

- identify the social and environmental responsibilities of business organisations to internal, connected and external stakeholders.

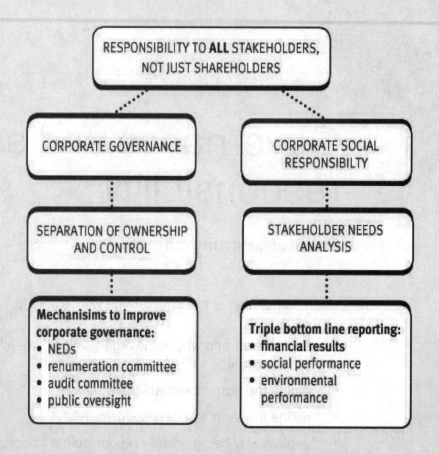

1 The separation of ownership and control

In considering the limited company as the vehicle for carrying on a business, academics point out the separation of ownership and control.

The **separation of ownership and control** refers to the situation in a company where the people who own the company (the shareholders) may not be the same people as those who control the company (the board of directors).

In a small company, the directors are also likely to own all the shares in the company, so there is no separation of ownership and control.

However in a large company there is likely to be a large number of external shareholders who play no role in the day-to-day running of the company. There is then a separation of ownership and control and the potential for a conflict of interest.

Academics might define the separation of ownership and control as the situation where decision makers do not bear a major share of the wealth effects of their decisions. You can see that this has a much wider application than occurring only in large companies. The situation also occurs in charities and other not-for-profit organisations, in financial mutuals, even in local government.

Reasons for the separation of ownership and control

- Specialist management can run the business better than those who own the business.

- The original shareholders cannot personally contribute all the capital needed to run the business, so they have to bring in external capital from people who are not interested in the day-to-day operations.

Potentially it is a win-win situation for both parties.

- Managers can get on with full-time management of the business.

- Shareholders are interested in the return from their investment and do not have the skills, time or the inclination to concern themselves with day-to-day matters.

However the shareholders will want to build in safeguards to ensure that the managers run the business in the interests of all the stakeholders fairly, not just in the managers' own interests. This is known as the 'agency problem' where managers have to be motivated to act in the best interests of the company as a whole.

Illustration 1 – The separation of ownership and control

The agency problem in a company

The directors of a large quoted company may hold a board meeting and vote themselves huge salaries, bonus shares if modest profitability targets are achieved, and contractual terms granting each of them huge compensation payments if they are sacked. These votes are in the selfish best interests of the directors, but not in the best interests of the shareholders who own the company and in whose interests the directors are meant to be working.

The problem of directors not operating in the company's best interests can be solved by aligning the interests of the directors and the interests of the company. For example, the directors could be paid a small basic salary and bonuses depending on the growth in profits achieved. Directors could be paid partly in shares to make them shareholders so that they have a direct interest in the share price and level of dividends. Adopting such procedures would reduce the agency problem of the directors acting as agents of themselves rather than as agents for the shareholders.

Test your understanding 1

Separation of ownership and control

The 'separation of ownership and control' refers to the situation where the owners of a company are always different people to the directors of the company. True or false?

2 The meaning of corporate governance

Corporate governance is the set of processes and policies by which a company is directed, administered and controlled. It includes the appropriate role of the board of directors and of the auditors of a company.

Expandable text

Consider two formal definitions of corporate governance from authoritative sources:

- 'Corporate governance is the system by which companies are directed and controlled.'

  The Cadbury Report 'The Financial Aspects of Corporate Governance', 1992

- 'Corporate governance involves a set of relationships between a company's management, its board, its shareholders and other stakeholders. Corporate governance also provides the structure through which the objectives of the company are set, and the means of attaining those objectives andmonitoring performance are determined.'

  The OECD 'Principles of Corporate Governance', 2004

Key issues in the corporate governance debate include.

- The membership of the board of directors – both executive and non-executive directors (NEDs).

- The role of the board of directors – purely to make money for the shareholders or are there wider responsibilities?

- How directors' remuneration is decided and disclosed.

- The role of both internal audit and external audit.

3 The meaning of corporate social responsibility

Corporate social responsibility (CSR) refers to the idea that a company should be sensitive to the needs and wants of all of the stakeholders in its business operations, not just the shareholders.

The **stakeholders** of a company are all those who are influenced by, or can influence, the company's decisions and actions. Examples of stakeholder groups are:

- shareholders

- directors

- other employees

- customers

- suppliers

- the government

- lenders of funds

- community organisations, especially in the local neighbourhood.

A closely linked idea is that of **sustainable development**, that companies should make decisions based not only on financial factors, but also on the social and environmental consequences of their actions.

Expandable text

A formal definition of CSR has been proposed by the World Business Council for Sustainable Development (WBCSD):

'CSR is the continuing commitment by business to behave ethically and contribute to economic development while improving the quality of life of the workforce and their families as well as of the local community and society at large.'

WBCSD meeting in The Netherlands, 1998

The WBCSD see CSR fitting into overall corporate responsibility as follows:

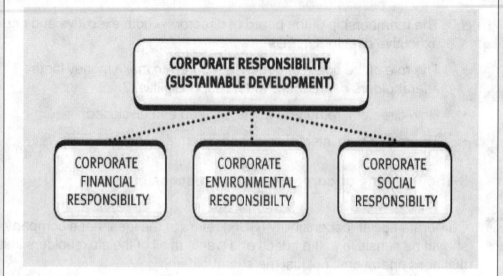

However the distinctions between each category can be blurred.

Key issues in the CSR debate include:

- employee rights, e.g. laws to prohibit ageism and other discrimination at work

- environmental protection, e.g. reducing factory emissions of poisons and pollutants

- supplier relations

- community involvement.

Illustration 2 – The meaning of corporate social responsibility

Marks and Spencer

Marks and Spencer promotes itself as a responsible business that takes the challenge of CSR seriously. It aims to listen and respond to the needs of its shareholders and build up good relationships with its employees, suppliers and society at large.

Marks and Spencer approach CSR by following three basic principles:

- products – throughout the three stages of each product's life (production, selling and usage), the aim is to encourage ethically and environmentally responsible behaviour

- people – everyone who works at the company is entitled to a mix of benefits. This approach is also encouraged amongst the company's suppliers, franchisees and other business partners

- places – the company recognises its obligations to the communities in which it trades. Successful retailing requires economically healthy and sustainable communities.

4 The importance of CSR to an organisation's success

The traditional view has been that corporate social responsibility offers no business benefits, and destroys shareholder value by diverting resources away from commercial activity. Such traditionalists argue that companies should operate solely to make money for shareholders and that it is not a company's role to worry about social responsibilities. Companies pay taxes to government, and it is governments and charities that should be responsible for social matters.

This traditional view is losing support amongst all sizes of businesses. The modern view is that a coherent CSR strategy can offer business benefits by enabling a company to:

- monitor changing social expectations
- manage operational risks
- identify new market opportunities
- retain key employees.

By aligning the company's core values with the values of society, the company can improve its reputation and ensure it has a long-term future.

The single-minded pursuit of short-term profitability will paradoxically always end in reduced profits in the longer-term, as customers drift away from the company if they no longer feel any attachment to it.

There is considerable evidence that the cost of CSR initiatives should be thought of as an investment in an intangible strategic asset rather than as an expense.

Illustration 3 – The importance of CSR to an organisation's

BAA plc

BAA owns and operates seven airports in the UK. BAA recognises that they are responsible, both directly and indirectly, for a variety of environmental, social and economic impacts from their operations.

Positive impacts: employing 12,000 people; allowing businesspeople to travel to meetings, thus supporting the global economy; allowing tourists to enrich their cultural experiences; allowing dispersed families to visit each other.

Negative impacts: large consumption of fossil fuels; emission of greenhouse gases; noise affecting people living close to airports.

BAA sees its CSR programme as managing these operational impacts in order to earn the trust of their stakeholders.

For example, local people living near airports are sensitive to the noise of aircraft approaching and taking off. If BAA did nothing about this issue, local people could complain to politicians who could pass laws to curb the number of flights which would damage the company. As part of its CSR programme, BAA will therefore offer to buy the properties of local people concerned about aircraft noise, or will offer to pay for sound-proofing of the properties.

You should consider whether such expenditure is an expense against the company's profits, or an investment in building up a strategic asset of goodwill among the local community.

Test your understanding 2

Benefits from CSR

How many of the following benefits could be realised from a successful CSR programme?

- Improvement in innovation by identifying new market opportunities.
- Improvement in the company's reputation.
- Improvement in relationships with internal and external stakeholders.
- Maintenance of strategic assets such as licences to operate.

5 The impact of corporate governance and CSR on the organisation

So far in this chapter we have described the meaning of effective corporate governance and CSR. There are mechanisms (e.g. appointment of NEDs) that can improve standards of corporate governance in a company; these are discussed in the next sections of this chapter.

Enhanced performance reporting methods including the following:

The balanced scorecard

- Financial perspective
- Customer perspective
- Internal perspective
- Innovation and learning perspective

Triple bottom line reporting

- People
- Planet
- Profit

Expandable text

CSR is a philosophy that should be implemented throughout the business from top to bottom. Traditional methods of assessing how well a company is performing have tended to look only at the recent financial results over a short period, e.g. the previous six months. CSR cannot be properly reflected in such performance statements since nearly all expenditure on CSR activities is written off as an expense as it is incurred, without any benefit or asset being recognised in the accounts. Thus expanded methods of performance reporting have been proposed.

The **balanced** scorecard approach emphasises the need to provide the user of a set of accounts with information which addresses all relevant areas of performance objectively. This information should include both financial and non-financial elements, and the usual balanced scorecard approach is to report performance from four separate perspectives:

- The **financial perspective** reports the traditional information of profits, capital employed, etc.
- The **customer perspective** reports how well customer wants have been satisfied.
- The **internal perspective** reports on the internal efficiency of the business.
- The **innovation perspective** reports on the development of new products and services.

It is argued that only by succeeding in all four of the perspectives can a company flourish in the long-term.

Triple bottom line reporting refers to expanding the reporting framework to include not just financial outcomes but also environmental and social performance. The phrase associated with triple bottom line reporting is 'People, Planet, Profit'. Academics are gradually developing workable approaches to the reporting of environmental and social performance, but there is no agreed consensus yet.

Test your understanding 3

Balanced scorecard

Identify one measure or ratio that would be appropriate to report for each of the four perspectives of the balanced scorecard approach to performance reporting.

6 Non-executive directors (NEDs)

Whilst company law refers only to 'directors' in general, two types of director have emerged.

Those who are involved in the day-to-day execution of management decisions are known as **executive directors.** Those who primarily only attend board meetings (and the meetings of board committees) are known as **NEDs.**

Current guidance is that NEDs should as far as possible be 'independent', so that their oversight role can be effectively and responsibly carried out. Being independent is similar to auditor independence, such as:

- not acting for a prolonged period of time
- having enough time to carry out the role properly
- having no links to the executives.

Typical recommendations include the following:

- At least half the board (excluding the chairman) should comprise independent NEDs. A smaller company should have at least two independent NEDs.

- One of the independent NEDs should be appointed to be the 'senior independent director'. They are available to be contacted by shareholders who wish to raise matters outside the normal executive channels of communication.

J Sainsbury plc Non-executive Directors

Sainsbury's has the following board members in its latest Annual Report:

Executive directors	NEDs
Mr Ha (chairman)	Mr D
Mr K (chief executive)	Mr Hu
Mr S (chief financial officer)	Ms M
	Mr S
	Dr McA
	Ms F

You can see that at least half the board are NEDs.

Test your understanding 4

Independent NED

Mrs X retires from the post of finance director at AB plc. The company is keen to retain her experience, so invite her to become a NED of the company. Can she qualify as an independent non-executive?

7 Remuneration committees

It is a stated principle in most codes on Corporate Governance that no director should be involved in deciding the level of their own remuneration.

The board of a listed company should therefore establish a remuneration committee of at least three (or two in the case of smaller companies) people who should all be independent NEDs.

The remuneration committee should be responsible for setting the remuneration of all the executive directors and the chairman, including pension rights and any compensation payments.

The whole board of directors should determine the remuneration of the NEDs, or the board could delegate this responsibility to a committee of the board.

Expandable text

Advantages of having a remuneration committee:

- It avoids the agency problem of directors deciding their own levels of remuneration.

- It leaves the board free to make strategic decisions about the company's future.

Disadvantages of having a remuneration committee:

- There is a danger of a 'You scratch my back, I'll scratch yours' situation in that the NEDs might recommend high remuneration for the executive directors on the understanding that the executives will recommend high remuneration for the NEDs.

- There will be a cost involved in preparing for and holding committee meetings.

Illustration 5 – Remuneration committees

J Sainsbury plc Remuneration Committee

Sainsbury's has the following board members in its latest Annual Report:

Executive directors	NEDs
Mr Ha (chairman)	Mr D
Mr K (chief executive)	Mr Hu
Mr S (chief financial officer)	Ms M
	Mr S
	Dr McA
	Ms F

The remuneration committee comprises Mr D, Ms M, Mr S and Ms F, i.e. four of the NEDs. This satisfies the rule that the committee should comprise at least three of the NEDs.

Test your understanding 5

Remuneration of NEDs

On what basis should NEDs be remunerated for their service to the company?

8 Audit committees

An **audit committee** consists of independent NEDs who are responsible for monitoring and reviewing the company's internal financial controls and the integrity of the financial statements.

The audit committee acts as an interface between the full board of directors on the one hand, and the internal and external auditors on the other hand.

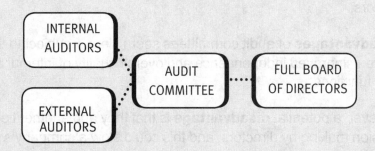

Auditors (both external and internal) have long had a problem – the people they report to and liaise with (the board) are often the people whose activities they report on.

This can cause major problems:

- External auditors become too close (familiar) to the executive directors (who run the company).

- External auditors are not comfortable reporting errors, frauds, etc. to the very people who have done them!

- Internal auditors are not comfortable reporting systems weaknesses to the very people who designed the systems!

- A board might choose to have internal auditors to give a good appearance to the outside world – but then underfund them, or give them work to do that ensures they go nowhere near areas where the directors know there are mistakes or frauds.

An audit committee is a subset of the main board. It should comprise at least three NEDs, and should act as the first point of contact for both internal and external auditors, typically doing the following.

- Being available for internal and external auditors (e.g. audit committee meetings are likely to include both sets of auditors).

- Requiring executive directors to attend as necessary.

- Reviewing accounting policies and financial statements as a whole to ensure that they are appropriate and balanced.

- Reviewing systems of internal controls.

- Agreeing agenda of work for the internal audit department.

- Receiving results of internal audit work.

- Shortlisting firms of external auditors when a change is needed.

- Reviewing independence of external audit firm.

- Considering extent to which external auditors should be allowed to tender for 'other services'.

Audit committees are not the final solution to audit problems. However, a strong committee, with knowledgeable NEDs, may strengthen the role of auditors.

The **advantages** of audit committees seem clear – subject to the points above – improved independence and overall quality of internal and external audit functions.

However, a potential **disadvantage** is that they add another tier/level to decision making by directors, and this could slow a company's activities down.

Expandable text

Recommendations on audit committees typically include the following:

- the audit committee should comprise at least three members (two for smaller companies) who should all be independent NEDs. At least one member must have recent relevant financial experience

- the company's Annual Report should describe the work of the audit committee.

KAPLAN PUBLISHING

Illustration 6 – Audit committees

J Sainsbury plc Audit Committee

Sainsbury's has the following board members in its latest Annual Report:

Executive directors	NEDs
Mr Ha (chairman)	Mr D
Mr K (chief executive)	Mr Hu
Mr S (chief financial officer)	Ms M
	Mr S
	Dr McA
	Ms F

The audit committee comprises Mr D, Mr Hu and Dr McA, i.e. three of the NEDs. This satisfies the rule that the audit committee should comprise at least three of the NEDs.

Test your understanding 6

Composition of audit committee

Why are the members of an audit committee required to be NEDs rather than executive directors?

9 Public oversight of corporate governance

Earlier in this chapter we identified the public as a legitimate stakeholder in a large company. This means that the public has a 'right to know' how such a company is being governed and a right to be involved in the governance process.

The most obvious means of public oversight of corporate governance is via the publication by companies of their Annual Report and Accounts. Companies are required by law to send a copy (or a summarised version) to each shareholder, but most companies will post a copy on their website or will provide a paper-based copy free of charge to any member of the public who requests one.

There are a number of important matters required to be disclosed in the Annual Report by law or by the Combined Code, for example the audit committee and remuneration committee must describe their role and actions during the year.

The growth in power of NEDs over recent years has added to the independent voice on company boards that might be expected to be sympathetic to the concerns of the public.

Finally, as part of their corporate responsibility activities, companies might discuss their plans with representatives of various stakeholder groups including journalists and local politicians. This gives the public a further insight into the effect that the company's activities may have upon them.

> ### Illustration 7 – Public oversight of corporate governance
>
> **J Sainsbury plc Independent NEDs**
>
> Among the independent NEDs at Sainsbury's is Anna Ford, a former BBC newsreader. She is well-known to the public and of good reputation, so the public at large might see her as 'their' representative on the board and will trust her to put forward their point of view. Anna Ford herself may have little or no experience in big business, but again the public would not see that as a disadvantage in representing them on the board.

10 Stakeholder needs analysis

We saw earlier that the corporate social responsibility (CSR) philosophy is based on the idea of being sensitive to the needs and wants of all the stakeholders in the business, not just the shareholders.

A **stakeholder needs analysis** can be carried out to bring some structure to the implementation of a CSR programme. The analysis involves doing research to determine:

- Who are the key stakeholders in the business?
- What are their needs?

Typical stakeholders and their needs have already been identified in chapter 13. However a typical list is not what is being asked for here; each company must sit down with a blank sheet of paper and identify the stakeholders of **their** business. For example, if a company has $1m in the bank earning modest interest, then the bank is probably not a key stakeholder. But if a company owes $100m to the bank and is paying large amounts of interest, then the bank probably is a key stakeholder.

In practice there is no better way of identifying stakeholder needs than asking representative stakeholders directly what they want. Possible methods are:

- questionnaires
- focus groups
- direct interviews or interviews with representatives.

Illustration 8 – Stakeholder needs analysis

Car manufacturers

As well as being sensitive to the requirements of customers with respect to factors such as price and performance, a car manufacturer should also consider the following:

- public attitudes to polution
- government policies on road tax and fuel tax

As a result it may choose to develop more environmentally-friendly vehicles as part of its long term strategy even if current demand is for larger cars, say.

Test your understanding 7

Supplier to a supermarket

A supermarket buys its goods on credit and sells them for cash, therefore it has strong cash flows at all times. What are the business needs of a supplier to such a supermarket in its relationship with the supermarket?

To some stakeholders, the company owes obligations arising from the law (e.g. to pay employees their salary each month, or to compensate them if they are made redundant). However other obligations arise voluntarily due to the company's commitment to CSR (e.g. to discuss their plans with interested pressure groups before a particular plan is adopted).

Illustration 9 – Responsibilites of businesses to stakeholders

888.com

888.com is an internet gambling site that is listed on the London Stock Exchange. It is headquartered in Gibraltar and operates under a licence granted by the Government of Gibraltar. It has responsibilities to the following stakeholders:

- **Shareholders** – since it is listed on the London Stock Exchange it must comply with the rules of that exchange, including adopting the Combined Code on Corporate Governance.

- **Employees** – to be a good employer to all its members of staff.

- **Customers** – to offer a fair, regulated and secure environment in which to gamble.

- **Government** – to comply with the terms of its licence granted in Gibraltar.

- **The public** – the company chooses to sponsor several sports teams as part of strengthening its brand. The company also tries to address public concerns about the negative aspects of gambling, e.g. by identifying compulsive gamblers on their site and taking appropriate action.

Test your understanding 8

Voluntarily turning away business

Why should a gambling company like 888.com voluntarily choose to turn away certain business, e.g. known compulsive gamblers, gamblers who may be under-age, gamblers in certain countries, etc?

Chapter summary

Definition of corporate governance:
- The systems by which companies are directed and controlled

Definition of corporate social responsibilty
- The idea that a company should be sensitive to the needs of all its stakeholders, not just shareholders

The separation of ownership and control in large companies means that rules on corporate governance are required to reduce agency problems

Codes on governance typically refer to:
- NEDS
- Renumeration committee
- Audit committee
- Public oversight

Possible expanded methods of performance reporting:
- Balanced scorecard (4 perspectives)
- Triple bottom line reporting: (People, Planet, Profit)

Test your understanding answers

Test your understanding 1

False. In a small company the directors of the company (perhaps a husband and wife) are often the sole shareholders of the company, so the agency problem does not arise. The problem is potentially most serious in a large quoted company where there is a professional board of directors and many (perhaps thousands or even millions) external shareholders.

Test your understanding 2

All of them. However these benefits will not be automatically achieved by any expenditure on CSR activities. There must be a well-managed coherent programme which is being followed.

Test your understanding 3

- Financial perspective – annual profits, earnings per share, etc.
- Customer perspective – number of complaints received per month.
- Internal perspective – percentage of units requiring reworking.
- Innovation perspective – percentage of revenues from recently-introduced products.

Test your understanding 4

It is very unlikely that Mrs X can be independent since she has been an employee of the company within the last five years. If the board believe that Mrs X is independent despite her recent employment then they must state the reasons for this determination.

Test your understanding 5

NEDs should be paid fees that reflect the time commitment and the responsibilities of the role, e.g. a fixed daily rate for when they work for the company. Share options should not be granted to NEDs since this would detract from the detached judgement that they should bring, and it would also prevent them from being identified as 'independent' NEDs.

Test your understanding 6

NEDs have no day-to-day operating responsibilities, so they are able to view the company's affairs in a detached and independent way and liaise effectively between the main board of directors and the various sets of auditors.

Test your understanding 7

The needs of a supplier to a supermarket are:

- a long-term business relationship so the supplier can plan for the future

- a large value of goods sold on regular orders

- agreed quality standards that both parties can work with

- fair prices

- prompt payments on the agreed dates.

Test your understanding 8

Either you could argue that such action was ethically correct (with the company wanting to 'do the right thing'), or you could argue that a concentration on short-term profits is likely to store up problems in the longer term. If under-age gamblers are seen to be easily gambling on a particular website, then the public reputation of that site will be damaged and its long term profitability could be in jeopardy if governments or customers turn against it.

Law and regulation governing accounting

Chapter learning objectives

Upon completion of this chapter you will be able to:

- list the authorities to which companies are accountable in financial terms

- give examples of the legislation that regulates the preparation of financial statements

- explain the criteria with which financial statements need to comply

- identify the positions of authority in the organisation which are responsible for ensuring the quality of financial records

- explain the consequences of failing to comply with the legal requirements of maintaining financial records

- list the bodies with whose regulations the accounting function should comply

- explain the role of the International Accounting Standards Committee Foundation (IASCF)

- explain the role of the International Accounting Standards Board (IASB).

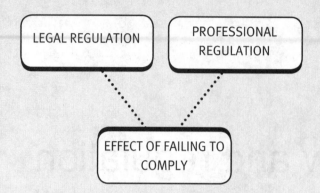

1 Authorities to whom companies are accountable

- Accountability refers to the state of being accountable, liable, or answerable for actions or conduct, of being responsible for actions or omissions.

- Companies are accountable to various bodies.

- In most countries there will be a government department set up to oversee the regulation and accounts of companies. Some examples are as follows:

Country	Name of regulatory body
UK	Companies House
Singapore	ACRA: Accounting and Regulatory Authority
Malaysia	Companies Commission of Malaysia
Hong Kong	Companies Registry
Jamaica	The Companies Office of Jamaica

- Companies are usually required to submit their financial statements to these bodies so that interested parties can inspect them.

- In addition to the financial statements, companies normally also have to retain and, if required to do so, submit documents such as a Register of Shareholders and a Register of Directors.

- Companies are accountable to the tax authorities in the countries in which they are based. They have to produce a tax return showing the amount of taxable profit and also submit returns to show the amount of sales tax (value added tax) owing.

- Companies have to retain their accounting records for a minimum period (usually seven years) in case the tax authorities or companies regulator wish to verify information.

- Companies may also be accountable to regulatory authorities, such as financial services or utilities regulators.

Expandable text

Some industries are 'regulated industries', meaning that their activities are supervised and controlled to some extent by a regulator.

The industries which are subject to regulation vary from country to country, but include industries such as financial services, utilities, charities, transport.

What these have in common is that it is seen to be in the public interest that there is some control of their activities.

For example:

- charities have access to public money, so there must be monitoring of how they spend that money

- the financial services industry invests clients' money, so there must be protection for clients against failure or poor advice

- utilities and transport needs to provide service to the whole country in a fair and efficient way, so there must be monitoring to ensure safety and fair process.

Regulated industries generally have to produce some kind of accounting information to the regulator. It could be in the form of the financial statements that are submitted to the shareholders, or might be presented in a different form.

Test your understanding 1

Companies are required to submit financial statements to Companies House, or a similar body, so that interested parties can inspect them.

Complete the following table, stating reasons why these parties would want to view the financial statements.

Party	Reason
Audit firm	
Competitor	
Supplier	
Job applicant	

Journalist	
Analyst	

Test your understanding 2

In addition to the financial statements, companies are often required to submit additional information to Companies House (or similar).

Complete the following table, showing why each type of information should be available for public inspection.

Information	Reason why made available
Register of Directors	
Register of Shareholders	
Register of Charges *	

* This shows which assets of the company have a charge over them, meaning that if the company fails to repay a loan the lender (who has 'taken' the charge) can seize the assets and sell them.

2 Legislation governing financial statements

- Most countries have a law which governs the preparation of financial statements.

- The name of this law obviously varies from country to country, as does the content.

- The companies legislation in many commonwealth countries is based on the UK Companies Acts, since those companies chose to use the existing UK legislation as a starting point when they became independent.

- Examples of the law in different countries would include:

Country	Main companies legislation
UK	Companies Act 2006
Singapore	Companies Acts 1985 and 1989
Malaysia	Companies Act (Cap 50) and various Companies (Amendment) Acts
Hong Kong	Hong Kong Companies Ordinance 1984
Jamaica	Companies Act 2004

- Companies in countries who are members of the European Union are required to follow relevant European directives and regulations. Some of these relate to accounting matters. These provisions are usually incorporated into the legislation of each member country,

Test your understanding 3

You are employed by an accounting firm in the UK.

The director of one of your firm's clients has written to your firm asking why the company needs to follow the Companies Act in producing its accounts.

Write a brief memo to the client explaining why the Companies Act came into being and why it is important that companies follow its provisions.

3 Requirements for financial statements

- The Companies Acts in the UK require that financial statements are prepared which give a 'true and fair view', although the meaning is not defined. Company law in other countries has a similar requirement.

- Research carried out by the accounting profession over the years indicates that financial statements will generally be true and fair if they:
  - follow accounting standards
  - follow generally-accepted best practice
  - have information of sufficient quantity and quality to satisfy the reasonable expectations of the users.

- **Sufficient quantity** indicates that the information must be adequately detailed. For example it would not be acceptable to list 'current assets' without showing the different categories of current asset.

- **Sufficient quality** means that the information should be reasonably accurate; it should be 'not materially misstated'.

- **Materially misstated** is a concept that you will meet again when considering the work of the auditor, but essentially it means that the financial statements may have misstatements (errors) but they should not be large enough to be important to anyone reading the accounts.

- In order to be able to prepare true and fair financial statements, companies have to maintain proper accounting records which are sufficient to show and explain the transactions.

- The content of the records is not defined but a record of transactions, assets and liabilities would be required as a minimum.

Test your understanding 4

State whether each of the following statements is true or false. If false, explain why.

- If financial statements give a true and fair view it means they are accurate.

- If financial statements give a true and fair view it means there is no fraud.

4 Responsibility for financial records

- Under companies legislation, directors are responsible for producing financial statements which give a true and fair view.

- This is delegated within the company to the finance director (FD) or chief financial officer (CFO). The financial reporting section within the accounting department will assist the FD.

- If the FD does not himself have the skills to prepare the financial statements, an accounting firm may be asked to provide assistance.

Expandable Text

- The **trial balance** will be prepared following input from all sections.

- The **sales ledger function** will estimate which debts are unlikely to be recovered.

- The **non-current assets** section will estimate depreciation rates.

- The **inventory section** will value inventory at the year end.

- Managers outside the accounting department, such as sales, may give input into estimates used. The company may also have to involve outside specialists, for example to value property.

Test your understanding 5

State whether each of the following statements is true or false.

(i)   The FD is required by the Companies Acts to prepare the financial statements.

(ii) The management accounting section is most involved in preparing the financial statements.

(iii) A firm of accountants may be hired to help with accounts preparation at the year end.

5 Consequences of compliance failure

- Failing to keep proper accounting records is a criminal offence and could lead to prosecution.

- Failing to prepare financial statements which give a true and fair view is also a criminal offence.

- In both cases, the responsibility is that of the directors, and directors can be fined for failure to comply.

- There could be problems with the tax authorities if records are found to be inaccurate; the tax authorities could investigate, and if the tax paid is too low then the company is guilty of tax evasion, which is a crime.

- If the poor accounting records mean that the financial statements do not give a true and fair view, and if this is detected by the auditor, the auditor could give a qualified audit report. This will damage the company's reputation and could make it harder to borrow money and to get shareholders to invest.

- Poor accounting records could also mean that the company has inadequate records of receivables and payables. It could therefore fail to collect money owed from customers which will damage cash flow, and pay suppliers on time which could lead to suppliers cancelling credit facilities. These issues could eventually lead to financial difficulties and the company going out of business.

Test your understanding 6

Your friend Aisha has been invited to join the board of her family's company and has come to you for advice.

Describe her legal responsibilities with respect to the financial statements.

Test your understanding 7

Explain how failure to maintain proper accounting records could lead to corporate failure.

6 Bodies governing the accounting function

- As discussed above, the accounting function has to follow the requirements of the Companies Act (or equivalent) and tax authorities in order to avoid the company facing legal action.

- The accounting profession is very keen to be 'self-regulating', meaning that the profession would prefer to issue its own regulations and deal with its own problems rather than relying on legislation.

- In many countries there is a strong accounting profession, and a history of involvement in developing national accounting standards.

- Companies have to follow the requirements not only of the law but of the standard-setting bodies.

- By the 1970s, this meant that there was a multitude of different accounting standards worldwide making it very difficult for investors to compare the financial statements of companies in different countries.

- In 1973, the International Accounting Standards Committee (IASC) was formed to try to harmonise (i.e. make more similar) accounting standards in different countries. In 2001 the IASC was replaced by the International Accounting Standards Board (IASB).

Test your understanding 8

Your friend Julia is considering investing in one of two companies.

ABC Limited is a travel company based in the UK. XYZ Limited is an aluminium company based in Jamaica.

List five problems Julia faces in comparing the financial statements of these two companies.

Test your understanding 9

The IASB, and formerly the IASC, is trying to harmonise accounting practice throughout the world.

Describe the problems such a body faces.

7 The role of the IASCF

- The International Accounting Standards Committee Foundation (IASCF) supervises the development of international standards and guidance and helps to raise money (as it is a non-profit making organisation).

- The structure is as follows:

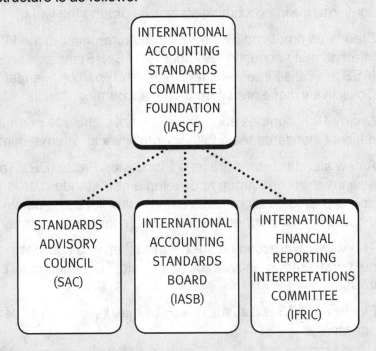

- The IASB produces international accounting standards (see below).

- The SAC consults with users of accounting standards and the accounting profession and advises the IASB as to which areas require new or amended standards and on the timetable for developing new standards.

- The IFRIC gives guidance on (often topical) issues that are not covered in an accounting standard or where the guidance is conflicting. Because the matters covered are quite narrowly defined, an interpretation can be issued relatively quickly.

Test your understanding 10

The Standards Advisory Council (SAC) consults with the users of accounts about which standards should be developed.

Suggest five user groups that would want to consult with the SAC and why.

8 The role of the IASB

- The IASB is an independent standard-setting body which is based in London. It has 14 members from nine countries.

- The IASB's aims are to develop a single set of high quality, understandable and enforceable global accounting standards and to co-operate with national accounting standard-setters to achieve convergence in accounting standards around the world.

- Standards produced by the IASC, the forerunner to the IASB, are called International Accounting Standards (IASs). Standards produced by the IASB are called International Financial Reporting Standards (IFRSs). Collectively these are international accounting standards.

- Nearly 100 countries adopt international standards or amend their national standards to bring them into line with international standards.

- A new standard starts life as a Discussion Paper (DP). The IASB assigns a working group to develop a new standard, following input from the SAC, and produces a first draft with some points for discussion. This is then made available for public comment.

- The views expressed on the DP are taken into account in producing the next draft, known as an Exposure Draft (ED). Again public comment is invited.

- Finally an IFRS is issued. The IFRS may later be amended if necessary.

Test your understanding 11

Over 100 countries have adopted international standards or have amended their national standards to comply with international standards.

Give three reasons why countries would want to do this.

Chapter summary

Legal regulation
- Tax authorities
- Legislation
- Regulatory bodies
  - IASCF
  - SAC
  - IASB
  - IFRIC

PROFESSIONAL REGULATION

Effect of failing to comply
- Criminal offence
- Fines
- Difficulty in obtaining finance

Test your understanding answers

Test your understanding 1

Party	Reason
Audit firm	To get background information on client/potential client.
Competitor	To assess market share and profitability of competitor.
Supplier	To consider likelihood of payment before allowing credit.
Job applicant	To gain background information about the company prior to interview, to consider whether company is likely fail.
Journalist	To write an article on the company's results.
Analyst	To make recommendations on purchases to investors/clients.

Test your understanding 2

Information	Reason why made available
Register of Directors	So that people know who the directors are, and what other companies they are directors of. If a director has previously been the director of an insolvent company, then a shareholder may want to reconsider a decision to invest.
Register of Shareholders	So that people can see who the shareholders are and the percentage of shares owned by each. This can help to determine which individuals/other companies will have influence over the company.
Register of Charges	Enables lenders and suppliers to establish which assets are already subject to charge and therefore cannot be sold to pay other creditors if the company fails.

Test your understanding 3

To: Vincent Squire, XYZ Limited

From: Matilda Richardson, ABC & Co

Date: 6/9/06

Subject: The Companies Act

If a business is set up as a sole trader or partnership, then people or businesses dealing with them know that if the business fails then the owners have to pay the debts of the business or become personally bankrupt.

However most businesses are set up as limited companies, which means that the shareholders do not have to contribute to the debts of the business in the event of failure. The Companies Act was brought into being in order to protect those dealing with companies in that they will be able to gain access to information about the company before becoming involved.

This offers protection to suppliers and lenders dealing with both small and large companies.

In large companies, there are many shareholders and they usually delegate the management of the company to the directors. The Companies Act requires the directors to produce financial statements to show the shareholders how well they have managed the company.

The Companies Act also lays down certain minimum levels of disclosure to ensure that a certain amount of information is available to the users. By improving financial information it will enhance the public's faith in the quality of reporting.

I hope this answers your question. If you require further information please do not hesitate to contact me.

Matilda

Test your understanding 4

- If financial statements give a true and fair view it means they are accurate

This is false.

It means that the financial statements are reasonably accurate, not materially misstated, but does not mean that the financial statements are totally accurate.

Some errors in financial statements are inevitable, so they will never be totally accurate. Numbers which are estimates, such as depreciation or allowances for bad debts, are more at risk of error.

- If financial statements give a true and fair view it means there is no fraud.

This is false.

As stated above, true and fair requires that the financial statements are reasonably rather than totally accurate. If a fraud is not material, then it will not cause a material misstatement.

Test your understanding 5

Statement	True or false?
The FD is required by the Companies Act to prepare the financial statements.	False (directors collectively).
The management accounting section is most involved in preparing the financial statements.	False (financial reporting).
A firm of accountants may be hired to help with accounts preparation at the year end.	True.

Test your understanding 6

As a director Aisha will be jointly responsible with the other directors for:

- maintaining proper accounting records, which show and explain the company's transactions
- preparing financial statements which give a true and fair view
- submitting an annual return, with details of shareholders, directors, charges.

The fact that this responsibility may be delegated to the FD or a firm of accountants does not reduce her responsibility.

Test your understanding 7

Poor accounting records could lead to the preparation of financial statements which do not give a true and fair view.

If this is detected by the auditors, they will give a qualified audit opinion.

Banks may refuse to lend money to a company which has a qualified audit opinion.

Shareholders may not wish to invest in a company which has a qualified audit opinion.

Poor accounting records may result in the company failing to 'chase' customers for payment, resulting in cash flow difficulties.

Poor accounting records may result in the company failing to pay suppliers on time, and those suppliers refusing future credit.

These factors could lead to cash flow difficulties and ultimately corporate failure.

Test your understanding 8

(1) The companies are in different industries.

(2) The companies are operating in different economic environments.

(3) The companies have prepared their accounts using different national accounting policies.

(4) The companies have probably chosen different accounting policies.

(5) The companies have prepared their accounts in different currencies.

Test your understanding 9

(1) Every national accounting profession will be convinced that its accounting method is best, making it difficult to achieve consensus.

(2) Intercountry rivalry could mean that a proposal by one country's accounting profession will be vetoed by another country with whom there is a poor international relationship.

(3) Even if the accounting profession agrees on the best treatment, standards will only be enforceable if allowed in each country or used as the basis for national accounting standards.

(4) The accounting methods will only be useful if allowed by stock exchanges.

(5) Very powerful economies can make international standards less useful by refusing to adopt them and using their own instead.

Test your understanding 10

Group	Reason
Accounting firms/profession	Need to consider whether standards are going to be too complicated to implement, and which areas present problems to their clients.
Industry (companies)	Want to consider the cost of implementing new standards, encourage cost-effective yet comprehensive solutions.
Governments	Want to ensure that proposed standards are compatible with the law.
Stock exchange regulators	Want to ensure proposed standards are likely to aid comparability between companies.
National accounting standard setters	Want to try to make the international standard compatible with their own national standards.

Test your understanding 11

(1) It is easier for multinationals, which encourages investment. A multinational will have subsidiaries in various countries, and if the subsidiaries' financial statements are prepared using international standards, or similar, it will be much simpler for the holding company to prepare the consolidated accounts for the group.

(2) It reassures investors in companies in the country. International standards are perceived as being fair and transparent, so investors will be more likely to trust the financial information given to them.

(3) It is more convenient for the national accounting standard setters, since they don't have to develop their own standards but can instead use international standards.

18

The accounting profession

Chapter learning objectives

Upon completion of this chapter you will be able to:

- outline how the accounting function has developed over time
- explain the importance of the accounting function within the overall business structure
- explain the purpose of the accounting function

1 The history of accounting

- No one really knows who 'invented' accounting; references in the Bible and the Koran indicate that some form of accounting has existed for centuries.

- Accounting records were used by ancient traders, farmers, etc. to control their assets, monitor their costs, collect payments, and calculate earnings.

- In 1494 Luca Pacioli, an Italian monk, codified existing bookkeeping practice, the 'double-entry bookkeeping system' that we know today.

- Accounting continued to develop, but increased in importance with the rise in popularity of companies as the predominant form of business entity.

- Due to the separation of ownership and management, shareholders had less detailed knowledge of business operations. Accountants were required to produce and interpret financial information to enable shareholders to make decisions.

- Accounting standards were later developed to make it easier to compare different companies, and the accounting profession grew in order to assist in the application of these sometimes complex accounting standards.

- The growth in computerisation saw a reduction in traditional bookkeeping work, and globalisation meant that many clients were large multinational companies requiring advice on many areas in addition to accounting.

- Today the accounting profession is a multimillion dollar industry, and gives clients advice on a wide range of business issues.

- Many accountants are also employed directly by companies, to produce information that is used in making decisions.

Expandable text

Since the introduction of joint stock companies around 400 years ago, limited liability companies have become the predominant form of business entity. The coming of the industrial age meant that companies needed lots of capital, and partnerships and sole proprietors could rarely contribute enough. Since limited companies can have an unlimited number of shareholders, raising large amounts of money is easier.

This means, however, that it is unlikely that this large number of shareholders will be closely involved in the management of the company. The directors have to produce financial statements to show the shareholders how well they've managed the company. Accountants are required to ensure that the financial statements show the true position (although cynics might suggest they are required to distort the truth and merely to show the company in the best possible light).

This separation of ownership and management also explains why companies are audited. The shareholders need to know if the information produced by the directors is 'true and fair', and so auditors are hired to check the information and give an opinion.

Accountants nowadays could be public accountants who work for an accounting firm and serve a variety of clients, or could work in industry and be employed directly by a company or organisation.

Public accountants perform accounting and audit work, but they also provide a variety of other services, including tax, insolvency, assurance, business advisory and corporate finance.

There are firms of all sizes, but the largest multinational firms, known as the 'Big 4', are PricewaterhouseCoopers, KPMG, Ernst & Young, and Deloitte Touche Tohmatsu. Have a look at their websites to get more insight into the services they offer.

Test your understanding 1

Complete the following table. For each business, give three examples of accounting information that would be required, and state why.

Business	Accounting information	Why required
Sheep farmer		
Nursery school		
Oil company		

2 The role of accounting within the business

- The accounting function is often thought of as a 'stand-alone' function, but there is a great deal of interaction with other departments, and it is one of the central functions of business.

- In the next section we'll look in more detail at the specific work performed by accountants, but let us consider for a moment how accounting information is used by other parts of the business.

- These are examples of financial information that would be required. Businesses would require additional information sometimes, and not all businesses would require all of this information.

- The key thing to notice is that financial information is a fundamental requirement in decision making. Without accurate information, decisions are more likely to be unsatisfactory.

Function	Financial information required
Business development	Past setup costs, expenses, revenues, in order to estimate for new project. Mix of fixed/variable costs, in order to determine breakeven point.
Sales	Credit history of, and types of, customers to establish whether a new customer is creditworthy. Prices charged in the past and impact on quantity sold.
Production	Cost of labour, materials and overheads. Cost of buying rather than making components.
Marketing	Prices charged in past and by competitors. Available budget. Costs of production (so that a profitable price can be determined).
Human resources	Salaries, pay rises, training budget.
Strategy	Cash flow forecasts, budgets, past information, profitability by product, trends in sales and profits.

Test your understanding 2

You have recently been appointed as general manager of ABC Tuition Limited which provides ACCA training courses. The company is making a loss, and you have decided to look at the number of classes being provided for each ACCA paper to see if you can restructure the business to make a profit.

List the financial information you would require and state what you would do with the information.

3 The purpose of the accounting function

- The accounting function in a company produces financial information that will be used to make decisions.

- Some information is produced for users outside the company and some for users within the company. Some examples are as follows:

Information	External/ internal users	Users	Used for
Sales invoices	Both	Accounting department	Recording in ledgers.
		Customers	Recording in customers' ledgers, paying for goods.
Ledgers	Internal	Accounting department	Preparing financial statements at the year end.
Financial statements	External	Shareholders	Deciding whether to buy/sell/hold shares.
		Lenders	Deciding whether to lend.
		Employees	Assessing likelihood of redundancy, considering whether pay rise is reasonable.
Cost information	Internal	Accounting department	Calculating production costs, making decisions as to whether to make or buy components, determining prices.

- This is not an exhaustive list; there are many other items of information that could be produced, and there are other users of the information.

Test your understanding 3

Fill in the following table showing information produced, users and purpose.

Information	External/ internal users	Users	Used for
Purchase orders			
Bank reconciliation			
Non-current assets register			
Financial statements	External	Suppliers	
		Government	

Chapter summary

Test your understanding answers

Business	Accounting information	Why required
Sheep farmer	Number of sheep (inventory)	To ensure that the farmer does not 'lose' any sheep; to ensure that sufficient food is bought.
	Cost of feed	To establish total cost of production, so that the farmer can decide what price to charge.
	Market price of wool	To establish the likely price to be realised on sale, and consider whether it is worth carrying out the activity.
Nursery school	Number of enrolled pupils (customers)	To ensure that the school has sufficient staff and equipment.
	Useful life of play equipment	To calculate depreciation, and to plan ahead for replacement.
	Fees charged by other schools	To establish the level of fee that can be charged.
Oil company	Oil price	To determine the sales price, and the viability of exploring different oilfields.
	Remaining useful lives of oilfields	So that new exploration can be planned to ensure new sources of oil when existing fields expire.
	Forecasts of demand, and other economic information	To establish how much oil will be required for petrol, plastics and other downstream products.

Test your understanding 2

Information

- Number of students attending each class.

- Cost of providing lecture notes, books, etc. to each student.

- Fee paid to freelance lecturer to teach classes.

- Salary of lecturer who teaches classes, and whether the lecturer is under-utilised (i.e. can teach more classes without additional cost) or over-utilised (being paid overtime to teach classes).

- Details of other lecturers who can teach classes and are under-utilised.

- Rental cost of each classroom and whether the cost is a fixed cost (i.e. will be paid even if the room is not used) or incremental cost (will not be paid if room is not used).

- Fee charged per student.

- Number of lectures in course.

Reason

- The manager can work out how many students are needed in each class to cover the costs and make a profit.

- If the lecturer is under-utilised and the room cost will be incurred even if the class does not run, that will affect the decision.

- The manager can also change the allocation of lecturers by switching an under-allocated lecturer to a class rather than an over-allocated one (who will be paid overtime).

Test your understanding 3

Information	External/internal users	Users	Used for
Purchase orders	Both	Accounting department	Checking that correct prices are charged by suppliers.
		Suppliers	Despatching and charging for goods ordered
Bank reconciliation	Internal	Accounting department	Checking that the cash book has been recorded accurately.
Non-current assets register	Internal	Accounting department	Recording details of individual assets
Financial statements	External	Suppliers	Assessing the likelihood of payments for goods/ services supplied.
		Government	Determining taxation and other policies.

Accounting and finance functions

Chapter learning objectives

Upon completion of this chapter you will be able to:

- identify the ways in which the accounting function influences the formulation and implementation of policy

- outline how control over organisational performance is exercised through the accounting function

- explain how financial transactions are recorded

- outline the steps involved in preparing financial statements

- distinguish between the roles of management accountants and financial accountants

- describe the processes involved in recording and analysing costs and revenues

- identify the types of information necessary to aid organisational decision making

- outline how the accounting function can assist organisational decision making

- describe the ways in which budgetary control could be exercised

- explain the main functions of the treasury

- describe the role of the finance function in calculating and mitigating business tax liabilities

- identify the roles in the organisation that are responsible for choosing the best financial option and obtaining the funds

- describe how the finance function aids in managing the company's working capital requirement

- describe the role that the treasury plays in managing risk.

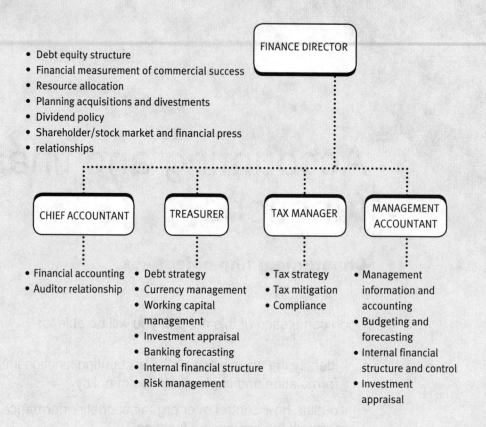

- Debt equity structure
- Financial measurement of commercial success
- Resource allocation
- Planning acquisitions and divestments
- Dividend policy
- Shareholder/stock market and financial press
- relationships

FINANCE DIRECTOR

CHIEF ACCOUNTANT

TREASURER

TAX MANAGER

MANAGEMENT ACCOUNTANT

- Financial accounting
- Auditor relationship

- Debt strategy
- Currency management
- Working capital management
- Investment appraisal
- Banking forecasting
- Internal financial structure
- Risk management

- Tax strategy
- Tax mitigation
- Compliance

- Management information and accounting
- Budgeting and forecasting
- Internal financial structure and control
- Investment appraisal

Typical structure of a head office accounting function

1 The formulation, implementation and control of policy and performance

The accounting function has an important role to play in helping management to:

- formulate policy

- implement policy by establishing procedures to be followed

- control performance.

Policy formulation is designed to achieve the organisation's objectives, so the starting point must be to identify the objectives, e.g. to maximise the reported profits after tax, subject to treating each stakeholder group properly.

 Planning is the establishment of objectives, and the formulation, evaluation and selection of the policies, strategies, tactics and action required to achieve them.

Once a plan has been adopted, it is then possible to control the activities of the business to seek to achieve the plan's outcomes. Planning and control are thus interrelated terms.

Expandable text

The planning process is conventionally split up into three timescales:

- **Strategic planning** is concerned with long-term problems external to the current business, in particular with deciding which products or services to produce for which markets.

- **Tactical planning** is concerned with ensuring that the company's resources are adequate for carrying out the strategic plans in order to achieve the desired objectives.

- **Operational planning** is concerned with the way in which the company is to be run from day to day in order to optimise performance.

You should be able to appreciate how the accounting function can contribute to the establishment of these plans. Since the achievement of plans is usually measured in terms of money, accountants are needed to help formulate the plans in the first place, to measure how well they are being achieved, and to recommend actions to take to bring current performance more closely in line with the plans.

Control over organisational performance can be achieved by:

- budgetary control, and
- the establishment of standards.

A **budget** is a plan expressed in quantitative (normally financial) terms for either the whole of a business or for the various parts of a business for a specified period of time in the future.

Budgetary control is the establishment of budgets relating the responsibilities of managers to the requirements of a policy, and the continuous comparison of actual with budgeted results.

For example, a company's sales budget may be drawn up for each quarter of the next calendar year, either in units sold or in money amounts. As the year goes by, the actual sales will be compared with the budgeted sales, and the sales director will be asked to explain any large differences between the two (budget variances).

Whereas budgets are set as the totals of amounts of costs or revenues, **standards** can be set for individual costs or revenues. For example, a **standard** cost would be the planned unit cost of the products produced or components used in a period. If a particular product is planned to require 2 kg of raw material A that is expected to cost $10 per kg, then the standard cost of raw material A in each product is $20. Again, actual costs for a period can be compared with standard costs, and the differences (cost variances) can be investigated.

It is the management accounting section in the accounting function which has particular responsibility for budgeting and standard costing matters (see later section).

Test your understanding 1

Planning and control

You have seen how business information can be divided into strategic matters, tactical matters and operational matters. Another classification would be between planning information and control information. For each of strategic, tactical and operational information, what is the emphasis between planning and control?

---

2 The accounting and reporting functions in business

This section describes:

- how financial transactions are recorded by the accounting function

- how financial information is codified and processed, and

- the steps involved in preparing financial statements.

The sequence of steps taken is shown below.

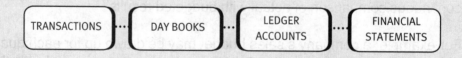

| TRANSACTIONS | ···· | DAY BOOKS | ···· | LEDGER ACCOUNTS | ···· | FINANCIAL STATEMENTS |

Whenever a business transaction takes place (a sale or a purchase, or payment of wages, etc.), there is a need to record the transaction in the accounting records. The transaction is first entered in the **books of prime entry** (or 'books of original entry').

The main books of prime entry are:

- the purchases day book
- the sales day book
- the cash book
- the petty cash book
- the journal.

The **purchases day book** is used to record the purchases made by a business, listing the invoices received from suppliers.

The **sales day book** is used to record the sales made by a business, listing the invoices issued to customers.

The **cash book** is used to record the receipts into and payments out of the organisation's bank account.

The **petty cash book** is used to record sundry small payments of cash made by a business, e.g. purchasing tea and biscuits for staff refreshments, or reimbursing the travel expenses of job interviewees.

The **journal** is used to keep a proper record of non-routine accounting adjustments made by senior accounts staff.

On a regular basis (e.g. monthly), the day books are totalled and the totals for the period are entered into the ledger accounts. For example, if the sales day book is totalled at the end of each month, the total sales for the month are posted into the ledger accounts of the business.

At the accounting year end of the business, the balance is calculated on each ledger account, and these balances are taken, with any necessary adjustments as recorded in the journal, to become the financial statements of the organisation for the period.

The main financial statements produced each year are:

- a **statement of financial position (balance sheet)** at the year end, showing the assets owned and the liabilities owed, and how these net assets are financed

- a **statement of comprehensive income (income statement)** for the year, showing the revenues earned and the costs incurred, leading to the net profit or loss arising for the year

- a **cash flow statement,** statement of cash flow summarising the cash receipts for the year and the cash payments paid out, to help readers of the accounts to understand the liquidity of the business.

Companies must send a copy of their financial statements to each of their shareholders each year. Large companies and publicly-quoted companies must appoint external auditors each year to give their independent opinion on whether the published financial statements have been drawn up properly and whether they give a true and fair view.

Test your understanding 2

Sales day book

The sales day book for X Limited listing the sales made on credit for the month of January 20X1 was as follows:

SALES DAY BOOK

Date	Customer	Invoice total $	Sales $	VAT $
3.1.X1	A Ltd	1,100	1,000	100
5.1.X1	B Ltd	3,300	3,000	300
7.1.X1	C Ltd	2,200	2,000	200
14.1.X1	D Ltd	3,300	3,000	300

What numbers would be posted to the ledger accounts at the end of January 20X1?

3 The management accounting and performance management functions

Both financial accountants and management accountants will be employed within the accounting function of a large company.

	Management accounting	Financial accounting
Why information is mainly produced	For internal use, e.g. managers and employees	For external use, e.g. shareholders, creditors, banks, government.
Purpose of information	To aid planning, controlling and decision making	To record the financial performance in a period and the financial position at the end of the period.
Legal requirements	None	Limited companies must produce financial accounts.
Formats	Management decide on the information that they require and the most useful way of presenting it.	Format and content of financial accounts must follow accounting standards and company law.
Nature of information	Financial and non-financial	Mostly financial.
Time period	Historical and forward-looking	Mainly a historical record.

Expandable text

Financial accounting is concerned with producing annual financial statements in accordance with accounting standards and the law. It covers the recording of the monetary transactions of the company, their classification and their presentation (by means of a balance sheet, income statement and cash flow statement) at the end of each accounting period in accordance with established concepts, principles, accounting standards and legal requirements.

Management accounting is carried out to assist management in discharging their duties to plan, direct and control the operations of their business. It is concerned with the process of measuring, analysing, interpreting and communicating information to management to assure appropriate use of and accountability for the company's resources.

Management accountants will use the financial accounting records as the main source of data for their work. For example, costs will already be analysed in the financial accounting records by type of expense (e.g. purchases, wages and salaries, electricity, stationery, etc.). However the management accountant may wish to use any other data sources to provide relevant information to management.

Examples of decision making that management accountants can help management with are:

- **Breakeven analysis** – what products or customer segments are currently profit-making or loss-making? Should a marketing campaign be undertaken to boost the sales of poorly-performing products, or should they be immediately discontinued?

- **Key factor analysis** – should products be made in-house with available resources or should their manufacture be outsourced to somewhere cheaper?

- **Pricing decisions** – should the prices of strongly-selling items be increased to try and increase overall profit?

- **Investment appraisal** – should a new machine be bought for the factory to replace an old machine near the end of its useful life?

You should appreciate that simply preparing an income statement for the year, as a financial accountant does, is a valuable exercise in itself, but is of no immediate help in answering all the above sorts of questions. Management accountants are needed to address these issues.

The **budgetary control** process was introduced in an earlier section, which explained that two distinct elements are involved, planning and control, as in the diagram below.

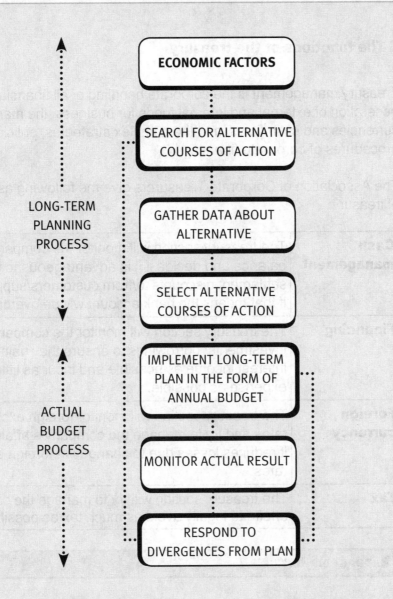

ECONOMIC FACTORS

SEARCH FOR ALTERNATIVE
COURSES OF ACTION

LONG-TERM
PLANNING
PROCESS

GATHER DATA ABOUT
ALTERNATIVE

SELECT ALTERNATIVE
COURSES OF ACTION

IMPLEMENT LONG-TERM
PLAN IN THE FORM OF
ANNUAL BUDGET

ACTUAL
BUDGET
PROCESS

MONITOR ACTUAL RESULT

RESPOND TO
DIVERGENCES FROM PLAN

Planning involves the setting of the various budgets (sales budget, manpower budget, etc.) for the appropriate future period. All the budgets of the various parts of the business need to be co-ordinated to ensure that they are complementary and in line with the overall company objectives and policies.

Once the budgets have been set and agreed for the future period, the control element of budgetary control is ready to start. This control involves comparison of the plan in the form of the budget with the actual results achieved for the budget period. Any significant divergences between the budgeted and the actual figures should be reported to the appropriate manager so that any necessary action can be taken.

4 The functions of the treasury

Treasury management is the corporate handling of all financial matters, the generation of external and internal funds for business, the management of currencies and cash flows, and the complex strategies, policies and procedures of corporate finance.

The Association of Corporate Treasurers give the following as key functions of treasury:

Cash management	The treasury section will monitor the company's cash balance and decide if it is advantageous to give/take settlement discounts to/from customers/suppliers even if that means the bank account will be overdrawn.
Financing	The treasury section will monitor the company's investments/ borrowings to ensure they gain as much interest income as possible and incur as little interest expense as possible.
Foreign currency	The treasury section will monitor foreign exchange rates and try to manage the company's affairs so that it reduces losses due to changes in foreign exchange rates.
Tax	The treasury section will try to manage the company's affairs to legally avoid as much tax as possible.

Expandable text

Cash management

Suppliers may offer the company a settlement discount, meaning that if the company chooses to pay the debt more quickly then a reduced amount can be paid. This has obvious cash flow advantages, but if paying the debt early would cause the company to become overdrawn (or the existing overdraft to increase) then the company would incur interest and other costs relating to the overdraft. Even if the company's cash balance is positive, the company would lose interest by reducing the cash balance to settle a debt early.

Similarly, the company may offer its customers a settlement discount to pay their balances early. The company benefits in that it receives money more quickly, which reduces interest charges on overdrafts and increases interest earned on positive cash balances, but means that the company receives a smaller amount.

The treasury section will calculate the effect on cash flow of each of these issues, weigh up all the possibilities, and make a recommendation as to what the company should do to maximise cash flow and profit.

Foreign currency

Companies may have borrowings in foreign currencies, or may have customers/suppliers who will pay/expect payment in a foreign currency. The treasury department will try to manage affairs to minimise the company's exposure to foreign exchange losses, i.e. minimise losses.

For example, assume a UK company buys goods costing US$1m from a US company on 1 January 20X1. The goods are due to be paid for on 31 March 20X1. The exchange rate at 1 January is £1:US$1.5, so the goods will cost £666,667 ($1m/1.5). However if the exchange rate changes to, say, £1:US$1.3, then the payment to be made will be £769,231 ($1m/1.3).

The company can manage this risk by entering into a 'forward exchange contract' at 1 January to fix the rate of exchange at which it can buy $1m at 31 March. The rate in the forward exchange contract will depend on what the market thinks will happen to exchange rates. Let us say, for example, that the company can enter into a contract to purchase $1m at the rate of £1:S1.48. The company's cost, in sterling, is then fixed at £675,676 ($1m/1.48).

Test your understanding 3

Centralised or decentralised?

In a large international group of companies, should the treasury function be centralised (i.e. one central treasury department at head office is sent all cash proceeds and carries out the group treasury policy) or should it be decentralised (i.e. each group company appoints an officer who is responsible for that company's own treasury activities)?

5 The role of the finance function in determining business tax liabilities

One of the roles of the finance function is to calculate the business tax liability and to mitigate that liability as far as possible within the law.

Tax avoidance is the legal use of the rules of the tax regime to one's own advantage, in order to reduce the amount of tax payable by means that are within the law.

Tax evasion is the use of illegal means to reduce one's tax liability, for example by deliberately misrepresenting the true state of your affairs to the tax authorities.

The directors of a company have a duty to their shareholders to maximise the post-tax profits that are available for distribution as dividends to the shareholders, thus they have a duty to arrange the company's affairs to avoid taxes as far as possible. However, dishonest reporting to the tax authorities (e.g. declaring less income than actually earned) would be tax evasion and a criminal offence.

While the traditional distinction between tax avoidance and tax evasion is fairly clear, recent authorities have introduced the idea of tax **mitigation** to mean conduct that reduces tax liabilities without frustrating the intentions of Parliament, while **tax avoidance** is used to describe schemes which, while they are legal, are designed to defeat the intentions of Parliament. Thus, once a tax avoidance scheme becomes public knowledge, Parliament will nearly always step in to change the law in order to stop the scheme from working.

Expandable text

The traditional view of neutrality towards tax avoidance can be shown by judges' comments in the past, for example Lord Clyde in 1929:

'No man in this country is under the smallest obligation, moral or other, so to arrange his legal relations to his business or to his property as to enable the Inland Revenue to put the largest possible shovel into his stores.'

More recently, even tax avoidance can be regarded with hostility. Some countries such as Australia have a General Anti-Avoidance Rule. Other countries such as the UK have used retrospective legislation to counteract the purpose of some tax avoidance schemes. In general it is safer now to stick with tax mitigation measures.

Responsibilities of the finance function

The finance function of any company is responsible by law for:

- maintaining proper accounting records that contain an accurate account of the income and expenses incurred, and the assets and liabilities pertaining to the company

- calculating the tax liability arising from the profits earned each year, and paying amounts due to the tax authorities on a timely basis. In practice, most companies (particularly small companies) will seek the advice of external tax specialists to help them calculate their annual tax liability.

The finance function should arrange the company's affairs to mitigate its annual tax liability, for example by investing in new plant and machinery that attract tax allowances, or by making gifts to charities. The managers of the finance function are then acting in the best interests of the company's shareholders, in whose interests the company should primarily be run.

> **Test your understanding 4**
>
> **Tax avoidance and tax mitigation**
>
> What is the difference between tax avoidance and tax mitigation?

6 Investment appraisal and financing viable investments

Investment appraisal is concerned with long-term investment decisions, such as whether to build a new factory, buy a new machine for the factory, buy a rival company, etc. Typically money is paid out now, with an expectation of receiving cash inflows over a number of years in the future.

There are two questions to be addressed:

(1) Is the possible investment opportunity worthwhile?

(2) If so, then how is it to be financed?

For example, if a company is offered an investment opportunity that requires paying out $1m now, and will lead to cash inflows of $2m in one year's time and $2m in two years' time, during a period when interest rates are 5%, you can see that this investment is worthwhile in real terms. If the $1m was invested to earn interest, it would be worth $1.05m in one year's time. However the investment will give you $2m in one year's time and another $2m in two years' time. So the investment is worthwhile.

The second question is how this $1m required now should be financed. Perhaps there is a surplus $1m sitting unused in a bank account. It is more likely that fresh funds will be required, possibly by issuing new shares, or possibly by raising a loan (e.g. from the bank). There are advantages and disadvantages of each possibility.

Advantages of issuing new ordinary shares:

*   Dividends can be suspended if profits are low, whereas interest payments have to be paid each year.

*   The bank will typically require security on the company's assets before it will advance a loan. Perhaps there are no suitable assets available.

Advantages of raising loan finance:

- Interest payments are allowable against tax, whereas dividend payments are not an allowable deduction against tax.

- No change is required in the ownership of the company, which is governed by who owns the shares of the company.

Generally the finance function and the treasury function will work together in appraising possible investment opportunities and deciding on how they should be financed.

Test your understanding 5

Duration of investment finance

A large company is deciding how to finance the purchase of a new machine that will cost $50,000 and have a life of five years. Is new equity finance (i.e. an issue of new ordinary shares) an appropriate method of financing the purchase?

7 Management of working capital

The previous section looked at long-term investment decisions. A company must also decide on the appropriate level of investment in short-term net assets, i.e. the levels of:

- inventory
- trade receivables (amounts due from debtors for sales on credit)
- cash balances
- trade payables (amounts due to creditors for purchases on credit).

Working capital is the capital available for conducting the day-to-day operations of an organisation, calculated as the excess of current assets over current liabilities. Thus:

Inventory	X
Trade receivables	X
Cash	X
	───
Total current assets	X
Less: Trade payables	(X)
	───
Working capital balance	X
	───

There are advantages in holding large balances of each component of working capital, and advantages in holding small balances, as below.

	Advantage of large balance	Advantage of small balance
Inventory	Customers are happy since they can be immediately provided with good.	Low holding costs. Less risk of obsolescence costs.
Trade receivables	Customers are happy since they like credit.	Less risk of bad debts. Good for cash flow.
Cash	Creditors are happy since bills can be paid promptly.	More can be invested elsewhere to earn profits.
Trade payables	Preserves your own cash.	Suppliers are happy and may offer discounts

Management must decide on the appropriate balance to be struck for each component.

Test your understanding 6

Conservative and aggressive management

A conservative management will have a policy of holding a large working capital balance, while an aggressive management will hold a low working capital balance. Describe the risks faced by the aggressive management of working capital.

Chapter summary

The financial accounting system produces annual financial statements from the transactions undertaken in the year:

The treasury function raises funds which are then deployed in the business:

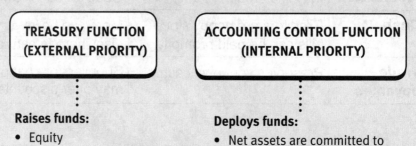

TREASURY FUNCTION (EXTERNAL PRIORITY)

ACCOUNTING CONTROL FUNCTION (INTERNAL PRIORITY)

Raises funds:
- Equity
- Loans
- Government grants

Deploys funds:
- Net assets are committed to the various product markets in the pursuit of profit

Test your understanding answers

Test your understanding 1

Strategic information consists primarily of planning matters and not so much control. Operational information consists primarily of control matters and not so much planning. Tactical information contains a mix of planning and control matters.

Test your understanding 2

Total invoice total = $14,300 would be posted to Accounts receivable.

Total sales = $13,000 would be posted to the Sales account.

Total VAT on sales = $1,300 would be posted to the VAT account.

Test your understanding 3

There is no specific correct answer to this question. It is up to the directors of the parent company of the group to decide on the best policy for the group, weighing up the pros and cons of each alternative.

Advantages of centralisation

- No need for treasury skills to be duplicated across the group. One highly-skilled team can operate at head office.
- The group's funds can be managed more efficiently, so that for example one group company would not borrow at high interest rates while another company has surplus cash earning only modest interest.

Advantages of decentralisation

- Greater autonomy should lead to greater motivation.
- Local managers can respond more quickly to local developments affecting their company.

Test your understanding 4

The modern view is that tax avoidance is action to reduce one's tax liability that complies with the letter of the law although it conflicts with the evident intentions of Parliament. Tax mitigation reduces one's tax liability while being consistent with the intentions of Parliament.

Once a tax avoidance scheme becomes public knowledge, Parliament will normally act swiftly to change the law and stop its effectiveness. On the other hand, Parliament is normally happy for tax mitigation to occur, for example to encourage new investments in plant and machinery, or gifts to charities.

Although they are legal, tax avoidance schemes are seen by many to be attempts to cheat the tax authorities, while tax mitigation is perfectly acceptable.

Test your understanding 5

No. Equity finance is most suited to large purchases (e.g. buying new companies) where the investment itself has a long life. If the amount of funds required is only modest and the underlying asset has a short lifespan, then a new loan would be more appropriate. Generally the duration of the finance should match the life of the investment it is financing. Thus a five-year loan would be suitable to finance the purchase of a machine with a five-year life.

Test your understanding 6

By holding low inventories, there is the risk of not being able to satisfy customers from inventories held, so customers may go elsewhere.

By insisting on low receivables (and therefore not offering long credit terms), customers may take their business elsewhere to suppliers who are willing to offer long credit.

By holding low cash balances, there is the risk of an unexpected bill arising (e.g. the factory roof needs replacing) but it cannot be paid.

By holding large trade payables, there is the risk that suppliers may refuse to do any further work for you.

20

Financial systems and procedures

Chapter learning objectives

Upon completion of this chapter you will be able to:

- explain what is meant by the terms 'system', 'policy', 'procedure' and 'guideline'
- identify the advantages of having a formal procedure for carrying out a task
- describe what steps need to be taken to put together a financial procedure
- describe the content of a procedures manual
- explain the main stages involved in the purchasing cycle
- explain the main stages in the sales system
- explain the main stages in processing wages
- explain the main stages involved in the cash system
- explain the main stages involved in the inventory system
- explain the purpose of organisational control
- give reasons why having appropriate control in relation to business systems and procedures is important
- describe the features of an automated financial system
- compare manual and automated financial systems, clearly stating their benefits and limitations.

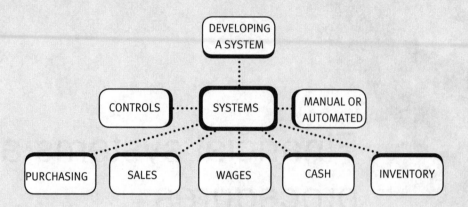

1 Terminology

* Accounting systems lay down procedures and guidelines that reflect the company's policies. These terms are explained below.

Term	Meaning
System	(1) A group of independent but interrelated elements comprising a unified whole.
	(2) A process for obtaining an objective.
Policy	A guiding principle.
Procedure	(1) A series of acts.
	(2) A set sequence of steps.
Guideline	A recommended approach for conducting a task.

Illustration 1 – Terminology

XYZ Limited has developed a new sales system.

Its policy is to process orders from customers efficiently, and to despatch goods within two days.

The system contains procedures for the ordering, despatching, invoicing, and receipt of payment for goods to ensure the policy is followed.

It also has guidelines on assessing the creditworthiness of new customers.

Give an example of each of these terms within the context of enrolling for an ACCA course: system, policy, procedure and guideline.

2 Advantages of having a formal procedure

- All transactions will be recorded in the same way, and the required information will be recorded in the correct places.

- The 'best' practice, the most efficient way of recording transactions, can be adopted by everyone.

- Staff can refer to the written procedures if they are in doubt as to what to do.

- New staff can be trained more quickly.

- The auditors can follow transactions more easily if they are recorded in the same way.

- Transactions which have not followed the procedure, which could be errors or frauds, may be identified more easily.

3 Designing financial procedures

- Each system is made up of a series of procedures. The system designer will need to first consider the objectives of the system, the required outputs, and the likely inputs.

- Taking a sales system as an example:

Objectives	To record the value of sales to each customer and the amount outstanding to be collected.
Outputs	An analysis of sales by date and product type. A report showing amounts owing from receivables and how long outstanding.
Inputs	Customers place orders by fax and by telephone.

- The designer then needs to consider the most likely sequence of events from input to outputs. For example:

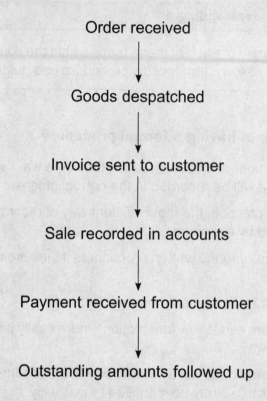

Order received

↓

Goods despatched

↓

Invoice sent to customer

↓

Sale recorded in accounts

↓

Payment received from customer

↓

Outstanding amounts followed up

- For each step in the system, a procedure is then designed, using the same format as for the system. The designer should also consider what could go wrong, and incorporate controls into the system to try to prevent such errors.

- Let us consider this for the ordering stage of the system:

Objectives	• To receive and process orders quickly and accurately. • To ensure that goods are only despatched where the amount charged will be collectable.
Outputs	• Instruction to despatch department to despatch goods. • Instruction to accounting department to invoice (charge for) goods.
Inputs	• Note of telephone call. • Fax.
What could go wrong	• Details of orders may be lost. • Details of orders may not be passed on to despatch and/or invoicing. • Order may be processed from customer who is unwilling/unable to pay.

- A procedure will then be designed to receive, record and process the order, which achieves the above objective and has controls to prevent things going wrong.

Test your understanding 2

Fill in the table, using the example of a student enrolling for an ACCA course.

Objectives	
Outputs	
Inputs	
What could go wrong	

---

4 Procedures manuals

- Companies will collate the formal procedures within each system into a procedures manual.

- A good procedures manual will contain sufficient detail to enable staff to understand the procedures they should carry out with minimal supervision and verbal instruction.

- The manual will normally contain a flowchart of each system. This is a diagram showing the stages of the system, the documents produced and the document flow. This enables an overview of the system to be easily gained.

- The diagram will be accompanied by detailed narrative notes, explaining in words the document flows and the checks to be performed at each stage.

- The procedures manual should be very specific as to who should perform each task (which position within the company), when and how frequently. This helps to ensure that staff fulfil their tasks on a timely basis and that controls are performed by the appropriate people.

Test your understanding 3

List four advantages of producing a procedures manual.

Test your understanding 4

Fill in the following table (one example for each).

Advantages of flowcharts	
Disadvantages of flowcharts	
Advantages of narrative notes	
Disadvantages of narrative notes	

5 The purchasing cycle

- The main stages in the purchasing cycle and the issues to be considered are as follows:

Requisition	• Staff decide what goods/services they wish to purchase and produce a purchase requisition.
	• This is authorised by department supervisor and passed to purchasing/ordering department.
Ordering	• Purchase department places order with suppliers.
	• Obtain several quotations to get the most competitive price.
	• Order may be authorised, especially if for a large amount.
Goods received	• Goods should be inspected to ensure that they are in good condition and the quality is correct.
	• A record should be kept of all goods received.
Invoice received	• Supplier bills company for goods/services.
	• Before recording in the accounts, checks are made to ensure goods were received and that the price is correct (i.e. same as order).
Invoice recorded	• Recorded in company's accounting system, manual or computerised.

| Payment made | • A cheque is produced for the amount owing. |
| | • This will be approved for payment by a senior manager who will first check that the details on the cheque agree with the invoices. |

Expandable Text

The purchasing cycle

XYZ Limited is a company manufacturing handbags.

Describe what will happen when the company purchases some leather to produce a handbag.

Requisition	• The production department plans what items will be produced and consults with the inventory department to see if sufficient quantities of the required raw materials are available.
	• The inventory clerk realises that there is an insufficient quantity of leather, and so prepares a requisition to order more.
	• (In a computerised system, the inventory system may be linked with the purchasing system and automatically reorders when the inventory quantity falls to a certain level.)
Ordering	• The purchasing clerk checks the price charged by three regular, reliable suppliers, and places an order with the one who charges the best price.
	• A copy of the order is sent to the goods inwards clerk, so that he/she knows to expect these goods, and to the accounting department.
Goods received	• The goods are received at the goods inwards area. The clerk inspects the goods to ensure they are as ordered, and the quantity and quality are acceptable.
	• The clerk produces a goods received note detailing the goods received, and sends copies to the inventory department and the accounts department.

Invoice received	• The invoice is received by the accounting department. The clerk checks that the price charged agrees with the price on the order and that the goods have been received.
	• The invoice is then passed to the requisitioning department for approval, and is coded* according to purchase type.
Invoice recorded	• The invoice is entered into the accounting system (manual or computerised) to the coded account.
Payment made	• At the end of the following month (suppliers normally give a month's credit) a cheque is produced for the amount outstanding. This is submitted to the managing director to be signed, together with the invoice to prove it is a valid business expense.

* Information on revenue or expenses is more useful if it can be analysed by type and department. Each specific expense type is given a unique code number, and invoices relating to that expense type are coded with that number. The accounting department then knows what expense heading to allocate it to. In this case, the inventory was purchased by the production department (say, department 03). It is an inventory purchase (e.g. expense type 01) and is to be used to manufacture a particular handbag type (say 06). The invoice would be coded 030106.

Test your understanding 5

Jane, a manager at XYZ Limited wishes to have her office repainted.

Describe the stages in the purchasing cycle for this purchase.

6 The sales cycle

- The main stages in the sales cycle and the issues to be considered are as follows:

Order received	• Depending on the business, orders may be received by post, by fax, telephone, in person or electronically. • A record should be made of incoming orders so that a check can be made that they have all been processed.
Order processed	• A check should be made to ensure that the customer has a valid credit account, or has already paid in cash. • A check should be made that the goods are in stock. • An order confirmation may be sent to the customer detailing when the goods will be despatched.
Goods despatched	• The goods are sent to the customer. • A document called a goods despatch note is produced, which will be signed by the customer confirming that the goods were received in good condition.
Invoicing	• An invoice is sent to the customer, detailing the amount charged for the goods.
Recorded in the accounts	• The invoice is coded and entered into the accounts.
Payment received	• Payment is received by cheque or credit transfer from customers. Controls should be in place to ensure that the staff are not in a position to misappropriate the payment. • The credit controller contacts those customers who are late in paying.

Expandable text

It is important that a company only sells goods to those who are able and willing to pay for them. For some businesses, such as a fast food outlet, customers pay in cash or by credit card so the company is assured of payment.

For most businesses, companies buy and sell on credit, meaning that they pay for goods purchased and receive payments themselves for sales some time after the goods/services are delivered. It is vital that a company only gives a credit account after careful consideration of the likelihood of receiving payment.

The credit controller will ask companies who wish to obtain credit to complete an application form and sometimes to give a reference from the bank and an existing supplier. The credit controller then sets a credit limit, which will normally be quite low initially.

The credit controller also monitors which companies are late in paying and 'chases' late payers when necessary.

Expandable Text

The sales cycle

XYZ Limited is a company manufacturing handbags.

Describe what will happen when the company receives an order from a department store for some handbags.

Order received	• Order received by post/fax (say). It will be given a unique number by XYZ Limited so that it can be tracked through the system.
Order processed	• A check is made to ensure that the customer's credit account is still active, and that this order will not put the customer over the credit limit. • An order confirmation is sent to the customer detailing the date of despatch.
Goods despatched	• The handbags are sent to the customer, and the goods despatch note signed.
Invoicing	• An invoice is sent for the value of the handbags plus sales tax.
Recorded in the accounts	• The invoice is coded according to handbag type and recorded in the accounts.
Payment received	• The customer pays by credit transfer, and the payment is allocated to the customer account.

Describe what happens at each stage of the sales cycle for a customer purchasing food at a fast food outlet.

7 The wages cycle

- The main stages in the wages cycle and the issues to be considered are as follows:

Hours worked recorded	• Hourly-paid employees will record details of hours worked. This is usually done using clockcards/timecards/punchcards on which a machine records starting and finishing times of work. • Hours worked are usually authorised by a supervisor.
Overtime recorded	• Salaried employees (who are not paid an hourly rate) may receive additional pay for overtime hours. If so, they will submit a timesheet with details of the hours worked.
Pay rates obtained	• Per hour or per month. • If it is a manual system, the pay clerk will manually look these up. If it is a computerised system the computer will do so. • When pay rates are changed, this must be authorised by a senior manager.
Pay calculated	• Hours x rate, or a set monthly pay. • If calculated manually someone else should check a few of the transactions.
Deductions calculated	• Depending on the country, this could be tax, social security, etc. This will be deducted from the gross pay.
Net pay paid to employee	• Nowadays usually be transfer from company's bank account to employee's bank account. • Occasionally in cash. Supervision is required to prevent theft, and employees should sign to acknowledge receipt of money.

Illustration 2 – The wages cycle

XYZ Limited is a company manufacturing handbags.

Describe what will happen when the company prepares the payroll for September 20X6.

Hours worked recorded	• The clockcards from the factory (production) workers are authorised by the factory supervisor and sent to the wages clerk.
Overtime recorded	• Salaried employees who have worked overtime submit a timesheet to their supervisors for approval, and these are then passed to the wages clerk.
Pay rates obtained	• The wages clerk looks up the pay rates.
Pay calculated	• The wages clerk calculates the gross pay. • The accountant selects five employees and checks the calculation.
Deductions calculated	• The wages clerk calculates the deductions. • For the five employees already selected, the accountant checks the calculation of deductions.
Net pay paid to employee	• The wages clerk produces a list showing the net pay to be paid to each employee. • This is approved by a senior manager and details sent to the bank for transfer.

8 The cash system

• When we refer to the cash system, we are sometimes referring to the banking system, and payments into and from the bank account. This overlaps with our consideration of the sales, purchases and wages systems above. We also need to consider the petty cash system.

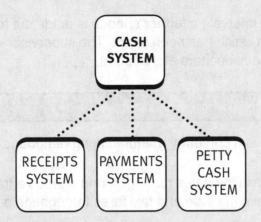

8.1 The receipts system

- Cheques are received from credit customers. These are recorded in the cash book and in the customer's personal account. The cashier then pays the cheques into the company's bank account.

- Controls must be in place to ensure that the cheque cannot be misappropriated before it is paid into the bank. Typical controls would include having two employees open the mail and listing the cheques received, and a supervisor checking that all cheques received were banked.

- Some customers may pay money directly into the company's bank account. The cashier should go through the bank statement carefully, enter details into the cash book, and ensure that details are passed to the sales ledger section to deduct the amount from the customer's balance.

8.2 The payments system

- Companies pay their suppliers, usually monthly and by cheque.

- A cheque requisition is prepared for each payment. This is a form which details the reason why a cheque is required. A cheque will be prepared and the cheque, the cheque requisition and the invoices to be paid will be submitted to a senior manager for approval and to have the cheque signed.

- Cheques for a large amount of money will usually require two signatories.

8.3 The petty cash system

- Companies will need to keep a certain amount of cash on hand to pay for small expenses such as postage stamps, biscuits, taxi fares, etc.

- A cheque will be made out to cash, to generate the initial cash for the system.

- As staff claim against the petty cash system, they complete vouchers stating what the payment is for, and attach a receipt to prove the amount.

- At regular intervals a further cheque is made out to cash to replenish the petty cash which has been spent. The supervisor will inspect the receipts and vouchers at that point.

Illustration 3 – The cash system

XYZ Limited is a company manufacturing handbags.

Paul Hewson is the sales manager, and attends a trade exhibition. He wishes to claim the train and taxi fares through the petty cash system.

Describe the process by which he does this.

(1) He fills out a petty cash voucher, detailing the purpose of the claim. He should also record his department and the purpose of the visit so that it can be coded to the correct expense heading.

(2) He staples the receipts to the back.

(3) If the expenditure is over a certain amount, which will vary according to the company, he will need to get authorisation from his supervisor.

(4) The cashier gives him the money.

(5) The cashier records the payment in the petty cash book and codes it as 'sales-travel'.

9 The inventory system

- The inventory system is really several systems, which can be summarised as follows:

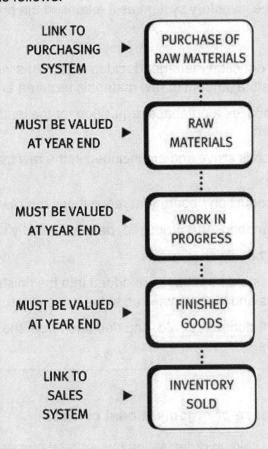

LINK TO PURCHASING SYSTEM ▶	**PURCHASE OF RAW MATERIALS**
MUST BE VALUED AT YEAR END ▶	**RAW MATERIALS**
MUST BE VALUED AT YEAR END ▶	**WORK IN PROGRESS**
MUST BE VALUED AT YEAR END ▶	**FINISHED GOODS**
LINK TO SALES SYSTEM ▶	**INVENTORY SOLD**

- The production manager will decide on the required inventory purchases bearing in mind the items to be produced and the inventory balance on hand. In some (automated) systems raw materials will be ordered automatically when the balance falls to a certain level.

- The goods are received and are stored in the raw materials store.

- When goods are required for production, the production manager completes a materials requisition form and gets the goods from the store.

- The goods are then made into 'work in progress' (partially complete goods) and eventually finished goods. The length of this process depends on the type of item being produced.

- When the goods are sold, a record must be made of the quantity removed from inventory.

- At the year end, all inventory will be counted and valued so that the balance sheet can be produced.

Illustration 4 – The inventory system

XYZ Limited is a company manufacturing handbags.

Describe the inventory system as it relates to the production of a handbag.

(1) The production manager decides what items will be produced and checks the amount of raw materials required and in stock.

(2) He produces a purchase requisition for the leather, zips, fastenings required.

(3) The goods arrive and are included in the raw material inventory record.

(4) The production department requisitions the raw materials needed.

(5) The handbags are produced, becoming firstly work in progress…

(6) …and then finished goods.

(7) The finished handbags are added into the finished goods inventory records and then transferred to the warehouse.

(8) The handbags are sold, and deducted from the finished goods records.

10 The purpose of organisational control

- Control within an organisation has several purposes:

Purpose	Why this is important
Safeguard company's assets	If assets are stolen or damaged the company will have to spend money to replace then.
Efficiency	Inefficient business practices are a waste of the company's money.
Prevent fraud	Fraud means the loss of valuable resources belonging to the company/shareholders.
Prevent errors	Errors can lead to losses in efficiency (time spent correcting) or a loss of assets (e.g. failing to invoice the correct amount, paying for goods which have not been received).

- This ties in with corporate governance, which is covered elsewhere in this workbook. The directors are required to introduce a good system of controls to safeguard the company's assets and protect the shareholders' investments. system of controls to safeguard the company's assets and protect the shareholders' investments.

- Most of our focus will be on financial controls. The company should introduce controls to prevent fraud and error.

Expandable Text

XYZ Limited is a company manufacturing handbags.

Complete this table, stating two controls which could be in operation to achieve each of the objectives listed for the inventory system.

Purpose	Example	Why important
Safeguard company's assets.	Regular inventory counts and investigation if quantity on hand is not as expected.	Staff could be stealing the handbags to sell privately, so controls need to be in place to protect the inventory.
Efficiency	Should get several quotations before placing a purchase order.	It is a waste of money to spend more than necessary, and it will reduce the profit margins on the bags.

Purpose	Example	Why this is important
Prevent fraud	Two people should open the post and list the contents.	There could be misappropriation of cheques/cash before they are banked.
Prevent errors	The payroll calculation for a sample of employees should be checked each month.	It is a waste of money to pay them too much in error, and demoralising for the employees to pay them too little in error.

Test your understanding 7

Complete the following table from the perspective of a fast food outlet.

Purpose	Example	Why this is important
Safeguard company's assets		
Efficiency		
Prevent fraud		
Prevent errors		

11 Why controls in systems are important

- Controls are important in all systems for the reasons given above.
- The specific issues in the systems we have mentioned are as follows:

System	Purpose	Key areas
Purchasing	Safeguard company's assets.	• Ensuring that only goods that have been received are paid for. • Ensuring goods are in good condition.
	Efficiency	• Ensuring that the best price is negotiated before buying.
	Prevent fraud	• Preventing purchasing staff accepting payments from suppliers to persuade them to purchase from that supplier.
	Prevent errors	• Ensuring that the correct amount is charged by suppliers. • Ensuring that they all purchases are recorded.
Sales	Safeguard company's assets	• Ensuring goods are only sold to customers who are likely to pay.
	Efficiency	• Ensuring orders are processed promptly so that customets do not go elsewhere.

	Prevent fraud	• Ensuring there is no theft of cash from customers.
	Prevent errors	• Ensuring the correct quantity of goods is despatched and invoiced.
Wages	Safeguard company's assets	• Ensuring that cash wages cannot be stolen.
	Efficiency	• Ensuring that people are only paid for overtime when necessary (approved).
	Prevent fraud	• Ensuring that there are no 'ghost' employees, people being paid but who do not work for the company. • Ensuring employees do not claim pay for hours they have not worked.
Cash	Safeguard company's assets	• Ensuring cash is kept safe from theft.
	Efficiency	• Ensuring cash is banked promptly, so as to gain interest.
	Prevent fraud	• Ensuring employees do not claim for expenses not incurred.
	Prevent errors	• Ensuring the entries in the cash book are correct.
Inventory	Safeguard company's assets	• Ensuring inventory is kept free from damage.
	Efficiency	• Ensuring inventory is only produced when it can be sold quickly.
	Prevent fraud	• Ensuring inventory cannot be stolen by employees.
	Prevent errors	• Ensuring costs of finished goods are calculated properly.

Illustration 5 – Why controls in systems are important

XYZ Limited is a company manufacturing handbags.
Complete this table, stating two controls which could be in operation to achieve each of the objectives listed for the inventory system.

Safeguard company's assets.	Ensuring inventory is kept free from damage.	• Store room kept tidy and clean. • Handbags put into plastic bags and boxes as soon as finished.
Efficiency	Ensuring inventory is only produced when it can be sold quickly.	• Forecasts of sales of each handbag style made by sales department. • Raw materials and production only scheduled when there is demand for bags.
Prevent fraud	Ensuring inventory cannot be stolen by employees.	• Warehouse to be kept locked and all inventory movements recorded. • Regular inventory counts and investigations of discrepancies.
Prevent errors	Ensuring costs of finished goods are calculated properly.	• Checks of calculations by another person. • Comparison against previous periods and estimates.

12 Automated systems

- Automated (computerised) systems are nowadays used by most organisations with the exception of very small firms.

- Large companies will have accounting software especially written for their needs ('bespoke systems') whereas smaller companies will purchase a standardised accounting package that has been written to suit any company ('off-the-shelf package'). will purchase a standardised accounting package that has been written to suit any company ('off-the-shelf package').

- Automated systems show the following features:

Uniform processing of transactions	Every transaction will be performed in exactly the same way.
Lack of segregation of functions	One person in the company, the IT manager has a lot of power as he/she can access all the data within the company.
Potential for data to be corrupted easily	An inexpert operator could accidentally corrupt data. Computer files can become corrupted on their own.
Potential for increased management supervision	Management can monitor the activities of subordinates easily. Exception reports can be used to highlight unusual transactions.

- The records maintained under manual and automated systems are similar, but the use of an automated system allows the data to be analysed more easily in a variety of ways. For example, it would be very time-consuming to produce a report showing how long customers have owed money under a manual system, but very quick using an automated system.

Illustration 6 – Automated systems

XYZ Limited is a company manufacturing handbags.

Describe five specific advantages to XYZ Limited of automating its financial systems.

(1) It can easily prepare an analysis of which products have sold at what quantities, and use this to determine its marketing strategy and production plans.

(2) It can easily prepare an aged inventory analysis, so as to identify slow-moving designs.

(3) It can use an aged receivables analysis to focus collection work on slow-paying customers.

(4) It can use passwords to protect confidential information.

(5) It can prepare an exception report detailing potential 'ghost' employees and then investigate. For example, an employee who has not taken holiday in the last 12 months or been sick may not actually exist.

ABC Limited is an ACCA tuition provider.

Give three examples of information that would be useful to the business and easily obtained using a computerised system.

13 A Comparision of manual and automated systems

- Manual and automated systems both have their advantages and disadvantages. Some of these are listed below:

Manual systems	
Advantages	**Disadvantages**
Low capital cost	Slower at performing calculations
No computer experience required	More likely to make calculation errors
Easy to correct errors (e.g. whitening fluid)	Analysis of information is more time-consuming
Ledgers are portable	Less easy to audit
Can review transactions for logical sense while entering/performing calculations	

Automated systems	
Advantages	**Disadvantages**
Quicker	Capital cost
Can perform more complex calculations	Training cost, especially for older staff
Fewer errors	Less easy to correct errors
More security (passwords)	Systems can crash
Easier to sort and analyse data	

Expandable Text

Explain each of these advantages and disadvantages of automating the financial systems.

Advantages	
Quicker	The computer can process transactions, e.g. add up enrolment revenue, more quickly than a person with a calculator.
Fewer errors	The computer will not make mistakes in adding up.
More security (passwords)	Only authorised personnel will be able to access data, e.g. enrolment data, payroll data.
Easier to sort and analyse data	Can produce an analysis of, for example, enrolment timing to make decisions on future strategy.
Disadvantages	
Capital cost	The setup costs will depend on the system, but the company would need as a minimum several terminals (for enrolment and other financial records) plus printers and software.
Training cost, especially for older staff	Staff would need to be trained in how to operate the system.
Less easy to correct errors	If errors are made, especially when the automated system is first introduced, it could be very complex to correct them.
Systems could crash	If the company does not back up regularly it could lose data.

Test your understanding 9

Your friend Josh is setting up a second-hand book shop. He has limited funds for investment and so has decided to maintain manual accounting records.

Explain to him the advantages of manual records.

Chapter summary

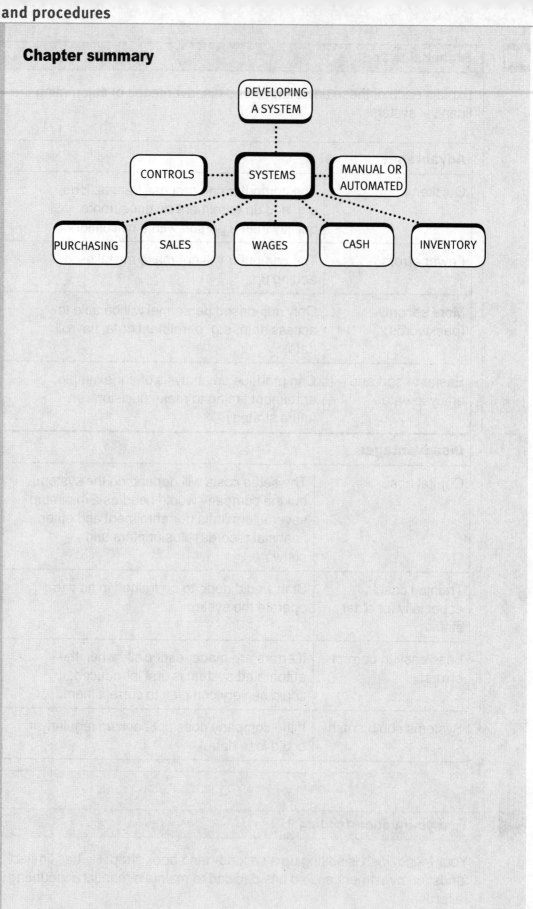

Test your understanding answers

Test your understanding 1

System	The process by which a student selects which paper he/she wants to take, enrols for the course at a tuition provider and pays.
Policy	The tuition provider has a policy that only students who have been briefed about ACCA can enrol.
Procedure	The student details are entered onto the computer and a student registration card is produced.
Guideline	Students are recommended to sit no more than three papers if in full-time employment.

Test your understanding 2

Objectives	To record accurately and efficiently which students are doing which paper and how much they have paid.
Outputs	<ul><li>A class register.</li><li>An analysis of sales revenue by paper and class.</li></ul>
Inputs	<ul><li>Personal enrolments ('walk in').</li><li>Mailed enrolment forms.</li><li>Faxed enrolment forms.</li><li>Emailed/online enrolment.</li></ul>
What could go wrong	<ul><li>The wrong amount could be charged.</li><li>Students could be enrolled for a class which is full.</li><li>Enrolling staff could misappropriate the payments made.</li><li>Faxes, mailed enrolments, etc. could be lost and not processed.</li></ul>

Test your understanding 3

(1) Staff can refer to it if they are uncertain.

(2) The process of producing it may identify flaws in the system.

(3) Auditors can refer to it.

(4) Cuts down on training cost for new staff.

Test your understanding 4

Advantages of flowcharts	Gain overview of the whole system.
Disadvantages of flowcharts	Can be hard to understand without technical knowledge.
Advantages of narrative notes	Easy to write and understand.
Disadvantages of narrative notes	Quality is dependent on the competence of the person who wrote them.

Requisition	• Jane will complete a purchase requisition detailing the work she wants to have done.
	• This will be approved by her supervisor.
Ordering	
	• The purchasing clerk will contact several painting companies and obtain quotations.
	• A purchase order will be sent to the best priced company, detailing the service contracted, the materials included, and the price.
	• This may be approved by a senior manager.
Goods received	• As this is a service, there will be no goods received and no goods received note issued.
Invoice received	• The invoice is received by the accounting department. The clerk checks that the price charged agrees with the price on the order and checks with Jane that the work was satisfactory.
	• Jane approves the invoice and codes it.
Invoice recorded	• The invoice is entered into the accounting system (manual or computerised) to the coded account.
Payment made	• At the end of the following month a cheque is produced. This is submitted to the managing director to be signed, together with the invoice to prove it is a valid business expense.

Test your understanding 6

Notice that the order of the stages is a little different, as payment is made in advance.

Order received	The customer goes to the counter and places an order.
Order processed	The server confirms the details of the order, and checks if the goods are available. If there is likely to be a delay the server tells the customer how long it will be.
Invoicing	The server tells the customer how much cash is required.
Payment received	The customer pays by cash or credit card.
Recorded in the accounts	The server records the details in the cash register. This information will be entered into the accounts automatically.
Goods despatched	The server passes the goods to the customer.

Test your understanding 7

Purpose	Example	Why this is important
Safeguard company's assets	Supervision and security cameras to ensure servers can't keep cash from customers rather than recording sale in cash register.	Cash is very susceptible to theft, since a thief can spend it immediately. Controls should therefore be in place to minimise the chances of loss of assets in this way.
Efficiency	Company should monitor demand at different times of the day, and ensure that the correct amount of food is cooked.	If too much food is cooked it may need to be thrown away if not sold in time. If too little food is cooked, customers will have to wait and will become impatient.
Prevent fraud	The cash register should be set so that when the server selects the item the customer requires from a menu the price will be selected automatically.	In a fast-moving, noisy environment the servers could charge the wrong price in error.
Prevent errors	Two people present when cashing up.	High risk environment as transactions are generally all made in cash.

Test your understanding 8

(1) Number of students in each class.

(2) The timing of enrolments, i.e. how many students enrolled early to take advantage of 'early bird' discounts.

(3) The correlation between attendance at class and exam mark.

Test your understanding 9

Low capital cost – he can spend the money saved on inventory, advertising, etc.

No computer experience required – he doesn't have to spend time learning how to use an accounting package.

Easy to correct errors (e.g. whitening fluid) – he is bound to make mistakes so it is best to make it easy to correct them.

Ledgers are portable – if he wants to take the ledgers home and do the bookkeeping from there, he can.

He can review transactions for logical sense while entering/ performing calculations – he may notice mistakes on invoices, etc. as he is entering them into the accounts, and can correct as he goes.

The relationship of accounting with other business functions

Chapter learning objectives

Upon completion of this chapter you will be able to:

- explain how the accounting department integrates andco-ordinates with the buying department

- explain how the accounting department integrates andco-ordinates with the production department

- explain how the accounting department integrates andco-ordinates with the marketing department

- define what is meant by the term marketing

- explain the components of the marketing mix

- describe how the marketing function is integrated intostrategic plans of the organisation

- explain the costs and benefits of services.

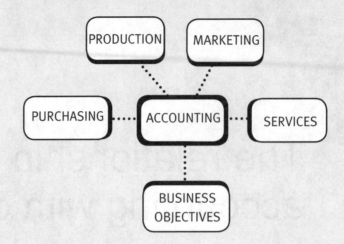

1 Purchasing

- In this chapter we consider the stages in the purchasing cycle from the perspective of the accounting function.

- The purchasing/buying function is responsible for placing and following up orders. It co-ordinates with the accounting department as follows:

Establishing credit terms	The accounting department will work with the buying department to liaise with suppliers to obtain a credit account and to negotiate credit terms which are acceptable.
Prices	The accounting department can advise the buying department on the maximum price that should be paid to maintain margins.
Payment	Payments may be approved by the buying department but are made by the accounting department.
Data capture, e.g. orders	Order details will be input by the buying department and details passed to accounting department.
Inventory	The purchasing department will consult with the inventory section of the accounting department to determine the quantity of items already in stock and therefore the quantity required.
Budgeting	The accounting department will consult with the buying department on likely costs in preparing budgets.

Expandable text

XYZ Limited is a company manufacturing handbags.

Describe how the buying department liaises with the accounting department when buying some leather to make handbags from DEF Limited, a new supplier.

Establishing credit terms	The buying department will advise the accounting department that the preferred supplier is DEF. The accounting department contacts the credit controller at DEF and provides the information required to set up a credit account.
Prices	The accounting department obtains the cost estimate for the handbag being produced. It discusses with the buying department how much can be paid for the leather in order to maintain margins.
Payment	The payment for the leather is approved by the buying department and then made by the accounting department.
Data capture, e.g. orders	Order details for the leather will be input by the buying department and details passed to the accounting department to check that the price on the invoice is correct.
Inventory	Before placing the order, the buying department will consult with the inventory section to determine how much suitable leather is already in stock.

Test your understanding 1

Complete the following table, showing how the purchase and accounting departments would liaise in the case of a company with a chain of fast-food outlets.

Establishing credit terms	
Prices	

Payment	
Data capture, e.g. orders	
Inventory	
Budgeting	

2 Production

The production department plans and oversees the production of goods. It liaises with the accounting department as follows:

Cost measurement, allocation, absorption	The production department measures quantities of materials and time used; the management accountant gives a monetary value to them. Costs are then allocated and absorbed to calculate production costs based on advice given by the production department.
Budgeting	The production department will decide how many items of what type are to be produced. The cost of producing these will be determined by the accounting and production departments together, and incorporated into the overall budget.
Cost v quality	The production and accounting departments will discuss the features that can be included in products and the raw materials that should be used. They should agree which better quality materials and features justify the extra cost, and discuss how to maximise quality and profit.
Inventory	The production department will liaise with the inventory section to ensure that there are sufficient raw materials in stock for the production that is planned.

Illustration 1 – Production

XYZ Limited is a company manufacturing handbags.

The company has commissioned a designer to design a new style of handbag and discussions are taking place about the materials to be used and the quantity to be produced.

Describe how the accounting and production departments would liase over this.

Cost measurement, allocation, absorption	The production department would estimate the quantity of raw materials required and (in conjunction with the purchase department) estimate their cost. Together with the accounting department overheads will be allocated to determine the full cost of the handbag.
Budgeting	The production department, accounting department and marketing department will discuss how many bags are likely to be sold at what price and determine how many should be produced. A budget can then be produced.
Cost v quality	The production, accounting (and marketing) departments will discuss the various grades of leather and the material that could be used, their costs, and the extra price that could be charged for better quality material. They will decide on the best combination of cost/quality/profit.
Inventory	The production department will discuss with the inventory section of the accounting department the materials required. Some existing materials may be usable for the new product or entirely new materials may need to be purchased.

3 Marketing

3.1 What is meant by 'marketing'?

Marketing is defined by the Institute of Marketing as 'the management process that identifies, anticipates and supplies customer needs efficiently and profitably.'

The key emphasis is thus on customer needs:

- Identifying and anticipating needs – market research.

- Supplying customer needs – product design and development.
- Efficiently – distribution.
- Profitably – pricing decisions and promotion (informing customers about your product so they buy it).

Marketing involves much more than just advertising!

Expandable text

Marketing orientation

The emphasis in marketing on pre-empting and meeting customers' needs gives rise to a belief system that places the customer at the centre of organisational activity. This marketing orientation is a philosophy of business that permeates all areas focusing attention towards the customer and believing, deep within corporate culture, that to meet the customers' needs better than competitors is the path to corporate success.

Product orientation

Management view is that success is achieved through producing goods and services of optimum quality. The major task is to pursue improved research and development and extensive quality control services.

While customers will generally welcome a better product, this approach has the following dangers:

- costs escalate in the pursuit of the 'perfect product' and customers are no longer willing to pay the resulting price
- the product may include features that customers do not want or value.

Test your understanding 2

Marketing is mainly concerned with which of the following?

A   Increasing sales revenue

B   Streamlining production

C   Anticipating and meeting customer needs

D   Maximising profit.

3.2 The marketing mix

The marketing mix is the set of controllable variables that a firm blends to produce desired results from its chosen target market.

There are four basic elements (the '4Ps'), which must be managed to satisfy customers' needs at a profit.

Product	This includes product features, durability, design, brand name, packaging, range, after-sales service, warranties and guarantees.
Place	Choice of distribution channels, transportation, outlet management, stocks and warehouses.
Promotion (distribution)	Advertising, personal selling, publicity, sales promotion techniques.
Price	Price levels, discounts, allowances, payment terms, credit policy.

Expandable text

According to **Kotler et al.** (1999) 'the marketing mix is a set of controllable tactical marketing tools ... that the firm blends to produce the response it wants in the target market'. Hence, in an effective marketing programme all of those elements are 'mixed' to successfully achieve the company's marketing objectives.

The marketing mix is concerned with how to influence consumer demand and is primarily the responsibility of the marketing department.

The variables are commonly grouped into four classes that Jerome McCarthy refers to as 'the four Ps' – product, price, promotion and place (or distribution):

- **Price** – an organisation may attack competitors by reducing price or increasing the size for the same money. The question of price policy in terms of competitors may be stated as Jet petrol's statement, 'We will always sell at 1-2p below the market leaders'.

- **Promotion** – advertising, money-back coupons, special prizes are all means of boosting sales without cutting price. Whereas a price cut may lead to a retaliatory war from competitors, a money-off coupon is seen as a temporary initiative and competitors may ignore it.

- **Place** – refers to the outlets, geographic areas and distribution channels. Some manufacturers have specified that only their goods can be sold in an outlet, e.g. most car manufacturers stipulate this requirement. Others choose a competition strategy involving vertical integration by which they take over distribution outlets and block a competitor's products. An example of this is the retail shoe industry.

- **Product** – refers to anything offered for attention, acquisition, use or consumption that might satisfy a want or need. Products can be physical objects, services, persons, places, organisations and ideas. An organisation may choose to lead the competition by being the best performer in those areas that it believes customers count as important and competitors can be outscored.

Beyond the 4Ps other elements of the marketing mix have come to light through the work of **Kotler** amongst others:

- **People** – this relates to both staff and the need to understand customer needs.

- **Processes** – these are the systems through which the service is delivered.

- **Physical evidence** – testimonials and references regarding proposed service.

3.3 Product issues

There are two main product issues to consider:

- Product definition – The main issue regarding product is to define exactly what the product should be. This can be done on three levels:

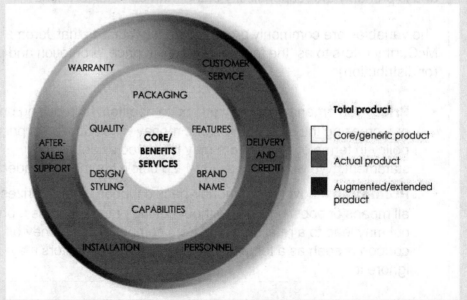

- Product positioning – With all of these factors the question of product positioning is critical – how does our product compare with the offerings of competitors? Is our product better? If so, in what way?

Illustration 2 – Marketing

A new car could be specified as follows:

- Core/generic product – personal transportation.

- Actual product – range of engine sizes, different body shapes offered, etc.

- Augmented product – manufacturer's warranty or dealer's discounted service contract.

Expandable text

The **core product** – what is the buyer really buying? The core product refers to the use, benefit or problem-solving service that the consumer is really buying when purchasing the product, i.e. the need that is being fulfilled.

The **actual product** is the tangible product or intangible service that serves as the medium for receiving core product benefits.

The **augmented product** consists of the measures taken to help the consumer put the actual product to sustained use, including installation, delivery and credit, warranties, and after-sales service.

A product, therefore, is more than a simple set of tangible features. Consumers tend to see products as complex bundles of benefits that satisfy their needs. Most important is how the customer perceives the product. They are looking at factors such as aesthetics and styling, durability, brand image, packaging, service and warranty, any of which might be enough to set the product apart from its competitors.

3.4 Pricing issues

There are four key considerations (the '4Cs') when deciding the price of a product:

- **Cost** – the price must be high enough to make a profit.
- **Customers** – what are they willing to pay?
- **Competition** – is our price higher than competitors?

- **Corporate objectives** – e.g. the price could be set low to gainmarket share.

These issues can be blended to give a range of pricing tactics, including the following:

- Cost plus pricing – the cost per unit is calculated and then a mark-up added.
- Penetration pricing – a low price is set to gain market share.
- Perceived quality pricing – a high price is set to reflect/create an image of high quality.
- Price discrimination – different prices are set for the same product in different markets, e.g. peak/off-peak rail fares.
- Going rate pricing – prices are set to match competitors.
- Price skimming – high prices are set when a new product is launched. Later the price is dropped to increase demand once the customers who are willing to pay more have been 'skimmed off.
- Loss leaders – one product may be sold at a loss with the expectation that customers will then go on and buy other more profitable products.
- Captive product pricing – this is used where customers must buy two products. The first is cheap to attract customers but the second is expensive, once they are captive.

3.5 Promotional issues

Promotion is essentially about market communication. The primary aim is to encourage customers to buy the products by moving them along the **AIDA** sequence:

Awareness ⊠ Interest ⊠ Desire ⊠ Action

Towards this firms will use a combination of different promotional techniques as part of their 'promotional mix', including:

- Advertising – e.g. placing adverts on TV, in newspapers, onbillboards, etc.
- Sales promotion techniques – e.g. 'Buy one get one free'.
- Personal selling – e.g. door-to-door salesmen.
- Personal relations (PR) – e.g. sponsoring sports events.

3.6 Place (distribution) issues

The key decision under 'place' is between:

- **Selling direct** – here the manufacturer sells directly to the ultimate consumer without using any middlemen, e.g. accountancy firms deal directly with their clients without recourse to brokers or other middlemen.

- **Selling indirect** – here the channel strategy could comprise a mixture of retailer, distributors, wholesalers and shipping agents, e.g. food distribution will often involve distributors and retailers to get the product from farmer to consumer.

Expandable text

Variations in marketing mix settings

Different companies put different emphasis on each of the four components of the marketing mix.

For example, some companies place all the focus on making a good quality product; other companies place the emphasis on making it at a cheap price or emphasise the promotion and advertising to sell it. A manufacturer of desks might wish to sell to both the consumer market and the industrial market for office furniture. The marketing mix selected for the consumer market might be low prices with attractive dealer discounts, sales largely through discount warehouses, modern design but fairly low quality and sales promotion relying on advertising by the retail outlets, together with personal selling by the manufacturing firm to the reseller. For the industrial market, the firm might develop a durable, robust product that sells at a higher price; selling may be by means of direct mail-shots, backed by personal visits from salespeople.

An interesting comparison can be made between different firms in the same industry; for example, Avon and Elizabeth Arden both sell cosmetics but, whereas Avon relies on personal selling in the consumer's own home, Elizabeth Arden relies on an extensive dealer network and heavy advertising expenditure.

Test your understanding 3

Apply the 4Ps marketing mix to the audit department of a large firm of accountants.

3.7 The strategic marketing process

The marketing process impacts the strategic planning process of an organisation as follows:

1 Strategic analysis of the firm and its business environment

Marketing analysis will include:

- analysis of brand strength, product quality, reputation, etc.
- analysis of competition
- market research to determine market attractiveness
- detailed analysis of customer expectations and power.

2 Strategic choice

Marketing decisions will include:

- decisions regarding which products to sell
- segmenting potential markets (e.g. by age) and then targeting attractive segments
- developing strategies for each of the marketing mix variables.

3 Strategy implementation

Implementing marketing strategies will include:

- setting budgets for advertising, etc.
- setting targets for sales revenue, market share, brandawareness, etc.
- monitoring and control.

Expandable text

Strategic analysis

Market research can be carried out as follows:

(a) Desk research

Here use is made of information which already exists, e.g. government statistics can provide demographic data; trade associations can provide more specialised data about market sizes and trends; the organisation's own systems should be able to provide information such as sales trends, sales per region, sales per product and stock turnover.

(b) Field research

This is normally conducted by asking people, ideally chosen at random, for their views on different products. Sometimes individuals are asked to try out products and they are then asked for detailed reactions.

(c) Test marketing

Before a new product is launched, a test marketing campaign may be mounted in an area which is relatively small, typical, with a stable population, and which possesses the required promotional facilities. This can be regarded as the refinement of the marketing mix and campaign before a full national and international launch is approved.

Strategic choice

Markets can be segmented in many different ways:

- Geographic – The EU could be split into different countries or viewed as one market. Television advertising regions.

- Demographic – Age, sex, income – e.g. Saga Holidays targets the over 50s. Family lifecycle models – e.g. 'empty nesters'.

- Psychological – Older people are more security conscious.

- Socio-economic – Class based systems e.g. A, B, C1, etc.

Attractive segments can be selected using a range of criteria including:

- Size

- Growth prospects

- Intensity of competition.

Targeting strategies can include:

- Differentiated, where each segment is approached with a different marketing mix e.g. Ford offering a range of different cars at different prices to meet varying customer needs.

- Undifferentiated, where all segments are approached with the same basic marketing mix e.g. originally Ford only offered one colour – black.

- Concentrated, where only one segment is targeted.

Test your understanding 4

Analysis of brand strength would come under which part of the strategic planning process?

A   Strategic analysis.

B   Strategic choice.

C   Strategic implementation.

3.8 Relationship with accounting

- The marketing department co-ordinates with the accounting department as follows:

Budgeting	The accounting department will discuss the likely sales volume of each product with the marketing department, in order to produce the sales budget.
Advertising	The accounting department will help the marketing department in setting a budget, and in monitoring whether it is cost effective. For example, they could help in measuring new business generated as a result of different advertising campaigns.
Pricing	The accounting department will have input into the price that is charged. Often products are priced at cost plus a percentage. Even if the marketing department determines the price based on market forces they need to consult with the accounting department to ensure that costs are covered.

Market share	The accounting department can provide the marketing department with information on sales volumes for each product, to help the marketing department in determining market share.

- In many companies there can be a great deal of antagonism between marketing and accounting, especially over pricing and cost control.

4 Service provision

- Companies very often provide services to customers, at the same time as a sale or afterwords, e.g. a computer retailer may charge an extra fee to help customers set up their system, or a car dealer may provide car servicing.

- There are several issues about which the service departments may need the input of the accounting department.

Charge-out rates	This is the hourly rate which the company charges clients. It should be higher than salary, as it should include a share of overheads, e.g. training and any profit the company wishes to make. However if the charge-out rate is too high customers will not use the service. Many accounting firms base charge-out rates for their staff on roughly three times that person's salary.
Estimating costs	Problems arise in determining the amount of overhead to be included in the charge-out rate. Also, if the service takes longer to provide than expected, the company may not be able to pass on the extra cost.
Problems measuring benefits	Market conditions may mean that the charge-out rate contains a very low profit element. The company may question whether it is worth carrying out these services. The problem is that the benefits are intangible and not easy no measure, but nevertheless real. A company with effective service provision has happier customers, and happy customers are more likely to buy from the company in future, therefore leading to lower selling costs. But it is very difficult to measure these benefits.

Illustration 3 – Service provision

GHI Limited is a retailer of computers.

GHI offers a service to customers whereby they will go to the customer's house and set up their new system.

What factors should be taken into account in determining the fee to be charged for this service?

- wages cost of the employee

- employer's social security cost

- transport costs

- other indirect employee costs, such as training

- how long the job will take

- GHI's required return on the service

- cost savings due to providing service, e.g. fewer calls to GHI's 'problem hotline'

- fee charged by competitors for the same service

- price charged for the computer (if computer price is low, charge more for this service and vice versa).

Test your understanding 5

JKL Limited is a car dealer, dealing in new and second-hand cars.

JKL also has a service department which services cars for customers and others. The fee charged to customers will include parts used and an hourly rate for the time spent by service personnel.

List the factors that should be taken into account by JKL in determining the hourly rate to be charged for such services.

Test your understanding 6

JKL Limited is a car dealer, dealing in new and second-hand cars.

JKL also has a service department which services cars for customers and others. The fee charged to customers will include parts used and an hourly rate for the time spent by service personnel.

List the benefits to JKL of providing such a service.

Chapter summary

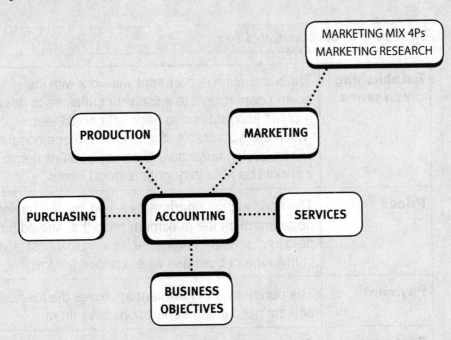

Test your understanding answers

Test your understanding 1

Establishing credit terms	The accounting department will work with the buying department to liaise with suppliers to obtain a credit account and to negotiate credit terms which are acceptable. Since the fast-food company will be buying large quantities of just a few items, it should be able to negotiate good terms.
Prices	The accounting department can advise the buying department on the maximum price that should be paid to maintain margins. Achieving low cost is vital in this type of business where prices are low.
Payment	The purchasing department approves the invoices, and the accounting department pays them.
Data capture, e.g. orders	Order details will be input by the buying department and details passed to the accounting department so that the price can be checked when the invoice comes in.
Inventory	The purchasing department will consult with the inventory section of the accounting department to determine the quantity of items already in stock and therefore the quantity required. They will also discuss likely usage of raw materials in the near future.
Budgeting	The accounting department will consult with the buying department on likely costs in preparing budgets, as the buying department will have more focus on trends in raw materials costs.

Test your understanding 2

C

The key focus of marketing is customer needs.

Test your understanding 3

Product

- When considering product definition it is usual to start with the generic product – what needs is the customer seeking tosatisfy? In the case of an audit, the client will want to satisfy Companies Act requirements and may also have theexpectation that the auditors will identify frauds and give advice as to how the company's accounting system can be improved.

- To satisfy these needs, the product should consist of the basic audit plus additional detailed work on the cash section toidentify fraud and also a 'management letter' commenting on the company's accounting system and internal controls.

- To differentiate the product offered from those of smaller firms, a large firm of accountants would probably stress the extra quality of its work, how this enhances clients' reputations, the ability to service larger clients and the greater expertise it can offer regarding systems advice.

- The basic product could be extended by offering accountancy and business consultancy, though these will probably already be provided by other divisions within the firm.

Price

- Most accountancy firms will use a cost-plus system as astarting point when pricing an audit. To enable this each employee will be assigned a charge-out rate that reflects their own salary, a contribution to cover general overheads and a profit element. To price an audit, a budget will be agreed for how long the job will take and what level of staff are used and then the charge-out rates applied.

- One problem with this approach is that most of the firm's costs are fixed – salaries, building costs, etc. – so calculating asuitable charge-out rate can be difficult.

- The price obtained in this way can then be adjusted to take into account the activities of competitors. While it may be possible to justify charging higher fees than smaller firms by emphasising the extra quality offered ('perceived quality pricing'), thisargument will not work when other large firms are involved. In this case the firm may have to match competitors' bids and rely on their own reputation ('going rate pricing') or even undercut them to win new audits ('penetration pricing').

- Firms undercutting each other has become commonplace as more and more companies put their audits out to tender.

- Another factor to be considered is the extent of fees generated from a particular client. Large clients may use the threat ofmoving elsewhere to put pressure on their existing auditors to drop their fees.

- Finally, the setting of the audit fee may be linked to thepossibility of getting other more lucrative work. Thus a firm may be willing to treat the audit as a loss-leader when profits will be made on tax compliance work, business advisory regarding takeovers, etc.

Promotion

A large firm of accountants will have the following elements in its promotional mix:

- Advertising – on the whole most firms do not use advertising to win business. This would be considered unprofessional, may contravene professional guidelines and may not be worthwhile as company directors will probably have heard of them already. If circumstances change, then advertisements could be placed in the Financial Times and professional accountancy magazines.

- Sponsorship – a large firm of accountants could improve itsprofile by sponsoring sports and arts events. It is common for firms to sponsor operas, art exhibitions, etc.

- Personal selling – this is likely to be the main method used by any firm. A manager or partner from the firm will typically take a director from the potential client out for lunch, golf, a day at the races, etc. and discuss with them their detailed requirements and try to convince them that they can offer a better/cheaper service.

- To win new business a firm may also incorporate the use of active references within personal selling. This is where existing clients are asked if they mind their names being put forward as satisfied customers.

Place

- The firm of accountants will sell direct rather than using any form of audit broker or other middleman.

- The other option to consider here is whether the audit should be carried out at the client's premises or to bring records to their own office and complete the work there. With smaller clients it may be possible to adopt the latter approach but with all others the audit will be done at the client's premises.

Test your understanding 4

A

Strategic analysis would include an assessment of the firm's strengths and weaknesses, including brand name.

Test your understanding 5

- Wages cost of the employee.

- Employer's social security cost.

- Other indirect employee costs, such as training.

- JKL's required return on the service.

- Fee charged by competitors for the same service.

- The depreciation charge on service equipment used (a share of this overhead should be included in the charge-out rate).

- Other service department overheads, e.g. service receptionists, waiting area.

Test your understanding 6

- JKL can offer customers a one-stop solution for all their motoring needs.

- Customers would think it strange/inconvenient if there were no service department.

- JKL can enhance overall customer satisfaction by providing good service.

- Customers may buy a new car when they see new models on display.

- If JKL does not offer service functions, customers will go elsewhere for servicing and may buy cars elsewhere.

Internal and external audit

Chapter learning objectives

Upon completion of this chapter you will be able to:

- define what is meant by internal and external auditing
- explain the purpose of internal and external auditing
- explain the differences between the roles of internal and external auditor.

```
                        ┌──────────────────────┐
                        │    TYPES OF AUDIT     │
                        └──────────────────────┘
```

Internal auditing
- Established by management to assist management in running the business
- Not required by law

External auditing
- An independent examination of the published financial statements, reporting on whether they give a true and fair view
- Required by law for large companies and public companies

Common characteristics
Although there are differences between the objectives and roles of internal and external auditing, both types of audit may use similar audit techniques to test the transactions undertaken by a company

1 The meaning of internal auditing and external auditing

In studying auditing, it is necessary to distinguish between internal auditing and external auditing.

Internal auditing is an independent activity, established by management to examine and evaluate the organisation's risk management processes and systems of control, and to make recommendations for the achievement of company objectives.

External auditing is the independent examination of the evidence from which the financial statements are derived, in order to give the reader of those statements confidence as to the truth and fairness of the state of affairs which they disclose.

Expandable text

Alternative definitions are as follows:

Internal auditing is an appraisal activity established within an entity as a service to the entity. Its functions include, amongst other things, examining, evaluating and monitoring the adequacy and effectiveness of internal control.

Auditing Practices Board 'Glossary of Terms'

Internal auditing is an independent, objective assurance and consulting activity designed to add value and improve an organisation's operations. It helps an organisation accomplish its objectives by bringing a systematic, disciplined approach to evaluate and improve the effectiveness of risk management, control and governance processes.

The Institute of Internal Auditors 'Official Definition'

The objective of an (external) audit of financial statements is to enable the auditor to express an opinion whether the financial statements are prepared, in all material respects, in accordance with an applicable financial reporting framework.

Auditing Practices Board 'Glossary of Terms'

An external audit is a periodic examination of the books of account and records of an entity carried out by an independent third party (the auditor) to ensure that they have been properly maintained, are accurate and comply with established concepts, principles, accounting standards, legal requirements and give a true and fair view of the financial state of the entity.

CIMA 'Official Terminology'

You should recognise the following key points from these definitions:

- internal auditing is established by the management of a company to help them manage the company, by reporting to management on the company's risks and systems of control

- external auditing is required by law in large companies and public companies. Independent auditors inspect the accounting records and systems, in order to report to the shareholders on whether the published financial statements give a true and fair view.

The differences between the two sorts of auditing will be discussed further in the next sections below.

The differences in roles can be summarised in tabular form.

Differences between internal and external audit

	Internal auditing	External auditing
Role	To advise management on whether the organisation has sound systems of internal controls to protect the organisation against loss.	To provide an opinion to the shareholders on whether the financial statements give a true and fair view.
Legal basis	Generally not a legal requirement. However the Combined Code on Corporate Governance recommends that if a listed company does not have an internal audit department, it should annually assess the need for one.	Legal requirement for large companies, public companies and many public bodies.
Scope of work	Determined by management. Covers all areas of the organisation, operational as well as financial.	Determined by the auditor in order to carry out his statutory duty to report. Financial focus.
Approach	Increasingly risk-based. Assess risks. Evaluate systems of controls. Test operations of systems. Make recommendations for improvements.	Increasingly risk-based. Test underlying transactions that form the basis of the financial statements.
Responsibility	To advise and make recommendations on internal control and corporate governance.	To form an opinion on whether the financial statements give a true and fair view.

Test your understanding 1- Internal auditing - cost or benefit?

Is internal audit a necessary cost that must be incurred by a company, or does it offer benefits?

Test your understanding 2- Bank insistence on external audit

Why might a bank insist on an external audit of a company's accounts before lending money to the company?

Expandable text

The purpose of internal and external audit

Company directors have a legal requirement to produce true and fair annual financial statements. To help ensure this is done, companies are required to have their published financial statements audited by an external team of experts (external auditors).

Directors also need assurance on other financial matters. This assurance is primarily for their own internal use, although in recent years pressure has grown for increasingly more of such work to be made publicly available.

This additional work is carried out by internal auditors, who may be company employees or outside experts from a firm of accountants.

Internal audit

Internal audit is part of the organisational control of a business; it is one of the methods used by management to ensure the efficient and orderly running of the business as a whole, and is part of the overall control environment.

Internal auditors' work has expanded in recent years, and the role of internal audit often now includes:

- helping to set corporate objectives
- helping to design and monitor performance measures for these objectives.

Corporate governance

A properly functioning internal audit department is part of good corporate governance, as recognised by all national and international corporate governance codes.

Internal audit enables management to perform proper risk assessments (another central theme of corporate governance codes) by means of properly understanding the strengths and weaknesses of all parts of the control systems in the business.

The function of internal audit in the context of corporate risk management

Internal audit has a particular interest in evaluating the company's risk management structures. Internal audit can:

- manage the basic data used by management to identify risks
- identify techniques for prioritising and managing risks
- report on the effectiveness of risk management solutions (e.g. internal controls).

The structure and operation of an internal audit function

The Combined Code on corporate governance states that companies without an internal audit function should **annually review the need for one.**

Where there is an internal audit function, the board should **annually review its scope of work**, authority and resources.

Ideally, the internal audit function should be staffed with **qualified, experienced staff**, whose work is closely monitored by an audit committee.

Scope of internal audit

Internal audit staff are typically expected to carry out a variety of tasks:

- reviewing internal controls and financial reports
- reviewing risk management systems
- carrying out special assignments (e.g. fraud investigations)
- conducting operational reviews (e.g. into efficiency of parts of the business).

Limitations of internal audit

- Internal auditors have an unavoidable independence problem. They are employed by the management of the company and yet are expected to give an objective opinion on matters for which management are responsible.
- Internal audit will only succeed if it is properly staffed and resourced.
- If internal auditors identify fraud, they may be unwilling to disclose it for fear of the repercussions (which could involve the collapse of the company and the loss of their jobs).

These limitations can be reduced if an **audit committee:**

- sets the work agenda for internal audit
- receives internal audit reports
- is able to ensure the internal audit is properly resourced
- has a 'voice' at main board level.

Expandable text

External audit

The purpose of external audit, as set out in the Auditing Practices Board (APB) definition, is for the external auditor to report his opinion on whether the financial statements give a true and fair view in accordance with an identified financial reporting framework (e.g. UK accounting standards and company law). An unqualified opinion (i.e. a reported opinion that the financial statements do give a true and fair view) makes the financial statements more reliable in the eyes of the readers of the statements.

An external audit may also have secondary objectives:

- The fact that employees of the company know that their work may be inspected by external auditors may encourage them to document their work properly and dissuade them from fraud.

- The fact that the external auditors will inspect the company's accounting system means that they may be able to suggest improvements to the system which could tighten the controls.

Advantages of an external audit

- Disputes between management may be more easily settled. For instance, a partnership which has complicated profit-sharing arrangements may require an independent examination of those accounts to ensure as far as possible an accurate assessment and division of those profits.

- Major changes in ownership may be facilitated if past accounts contain an unqualified audit report, for instance, where two sole traders merge their business to form a new partnership.

- Applications to third parties for finance may be enhanced by audited accounts. However, do remember that a bank, for instance, is likely to be far more concerned about the future of the business and available security than the past historical cost accounts, audited or otherwise.

- The audit is likely to involve an in-depth examination of the business and so may enable the auditor to give more constructive advice to management on improving the efficiency of the business.

Disadvantages of an external audit

The disadvantages are basically twofold:

- The audit fee! Clearly the services of an auditor must be paid for. It is for this reason that few partnerships and even fewer sole traders are likely to have their accounts audited. The accountant's role as the preparer of financial statements, as a tax adviser and general financial adviser, becomes much more important to such concerns.

- The audit involves the client's staff and management in giving time to providing information to the auditor. Professional auditors should therefore plan their audit carefully to minimise the disruption which their work will cause.

Expandable text

External audit

Someone **independent** from outside the company being audited is brought in to examine the annual published financial statements.

They will issue a report that:

- explains the audit process

- gives opinions as to the **truth and fairness** of the accounts, and whether they have been **properly prepared**.

The process is highly regulated so that those likely to place reliance on published accounts are protected from poor or inconsistent auditing.

- Many organisations (typically large companies) are legally required to have an external audit.

- Only certain people are legally allowed to be external auditors.

- The external audit process is regulated by law, and by audit standards to ensure consistent quality.

Internal audit

Management may wish to have other things checked. For example:

- effectiveness of accounting systems

- effectiveness of internal control systems

- value for money audit, looking at the economy, efficiency and effectiveness of operations
- whether internal policies are being upheld
- anything else!

In the past, there was no legal requirement for this - it was up to management to decide. However, it is increasingly expected, and in the future may become a requirement, for some companies (especially if listed on a stock exchange).

A company may use internal employees to do these tasks, or may hire outside specialists (e.g. a firm of accountants) to provide the services required.

Key differences

Independence

External auditors must be, and be seen to be, independent of their clients, so that their opinions can be trusted.

Internal audit opinions would also be of more benefit if they were totally independent. However, internal auditors are appointed by the directors and report to the directors (and could be employees) so it is far harder to maintain independence. One way of reducing this problem is to require internal auditors to report to an audit committee.

Legal

External audits are legally required for many companies. Internal audit is recommended, and almost expected, for many companies - but there is no legal requirement in most countries (e.g. the UK) at present.

Appointment and reporting

External auditors are usually appointed by the shareholders, and also report to the shareholders. Internal auditors are appointed by directors and report to directors.

Process/work

External audits are controlled by the law, but mostly by audit standards. Guidance for internal audit is limited to fundamental principles and a small quantity of standards, so there is greater flexibility in how the work is done.

Test your understanding 3

Who can carry out internal audit?

Internal audit may be carried out by employees of the company being audited, or may be carried out by external accountants who are paid for delivering this service. True or false?

Test your understanding 4

Reporting of audit conclusions

To whom does internal audit and external audit report?

Chapter summary

```
                          ┌─────────────────────┐
                          │        AUDIT         │
                          └─────────────────────┘
```

Internal auditors look at how organisations manage their risks.

They are appointed by management, traditionally as employees but increasingly as outsourced experts, to report to management on the company's risk management processes.

External auditors are independent accountants who report their opinion as to whether the financial statements give a true and fair view.

They can not be employees of the company being audited.

	Internal audit	External audit
Role	Internal auditors exist to assist management, by advising on the organisation's risk management process and systems of control.	External auditors are appointed to report to the shareholders whether the financial statements give a true and fair view.
Requirement	No legal requirement, but corporate governance guidelines recommend that the need for internal audit is regulary reviewed.	Legal requirement for public companies, large companies and many public bodies.
Scope of work	Determined by management. Covers both operational and financial matters.	Determined by the auditor in order to carry out his statutory duty to report. Financial focus.

Test your understanding answers

Test your understanding 1- Internal auditing - cost or benefit?

The benefits of internal audit should exceed the costs. The IIA definition stresses that internal audit is a value-adding activity by helping an organisation to manage its risks and achieve its objectives. If an organisation believes that the costs of internal audit would exceed the benefits, then it shouldn't operate that internal audit function. This is a choice to be made by the directors of a company; there is no requirement to operate an internal audit department.

Test your understanding 2- Bank insistence on external audit

Before a bank lends money to a company, it wants to be reasonably certain that it will get its money back, plus interest. The bank will look at the company's recent financial statements to ensure that the company is financially healthy. However the bank will want to be sure that the financial statements can be relied upon to give a true and fair view. Thus the bank will typically insist that the accounts are subject to an external audit.

Test your understanding 3

True. Internal auditors can either be employees of the company being audited, or may be external experts brought in. Compare this with external auditors who have to be external to the company; employees of the company are not allowed to carry out an external audit of that company.

Test your understanding 4

Internal audit reports to the management of the company. In a smaller company, internal audit is likely to report directly to the board of directors of the company being audited. In a larger company where there is an audit committee, internal audit is likely to report to the audit committee.

External audit reports to the shareholders of the company being audited.

Internal financial control

Chapter learning objectives

Upon completion of this chapter you will be able to:

- define what is meant by internal control and internal check

- outline the purpose of internal control

- explain the different types of internal control

- describe the responsibilities of management for internal financial control

- outline the features necessary to make sure the internal financial procedures in the organisation are effective.

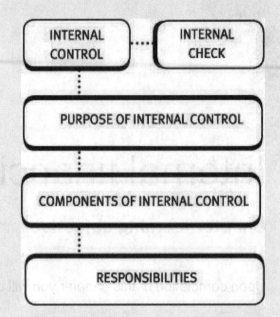

1 The meaning of internal control and internal check

 Internal control is the process designed and effected by management to provide reasonable assurance about the achievement of the entity's objectives with regard to:

*   reliability of financial reporting
*   effectiveness and efficiency of operations, and
*   compliance with applicable laws and regulations.

Definition based on the Auditing Practices Board 'Glossary of Terms'.

Expandable text

For example, an accounts department might have a policy to check the additions and multiplications on a purchase invoice received, before it is approved for payment. This control would help to ensure that the correct amounts are paid to the organisation's suppliers, and would therefore improve the reliability of the amounts reported as purchases.

 Internal check is an element of internal control, concerned with ensuring that no single task is executed from start to finish by only one person. Each individual's work is subject to an independent check by another person in the course of that other person's duties.

Expandable text

The purpose of internal checking is to reduce the likelihood of errors and fraud. Errors should be reduced since an employee will take more care over their work if they know it is going to be looked at by someone else, and any errors which are made should be spotted by the second person so that corrections can be made. Similarly an employee will be dissuaded from defrauding the company if they know that their work will be checked and that it is likely that their fraud will be discovered.

Clearly it is possible that two or more employees could collude together to defraud their company, so it is risky to rely on a single internal control at any stage of operations. However a comprehensive suite of controls should reduce the risk of material error or fraud to an acceptably low level.

Illustration 1 – The meaning of internal control and internal check

Consider a company that sells bottled drinks to supermarkets and other retailers. The company maintains its inventories in a central warehouse. Internal controls would be established by management to ensure the security of the inventories (so that they are not stolen by employees or third parties) and to ensure the accuracy of the accounting figures for inventories included in the financial statements.

Typical controls could be:

- physical controls – keeping the front door locked when not in use, and banning visitors from entering the warehouse storage area

- regular inventory counts – the inventories held could be counted every six months to check the accuracy of the continuous inventory records.

An internal check on inventory quantities could be implemented at each inventory count by ensuring that no individual counts the items that they are responsible for maintaining. In this way it would not be possible for an employee to steal items of inventory, and then to pretend at the regular count that the stolen items were still there in the warehouse. Such a theft would require collusion between employees if it is going to remain undetected.

Internal controls and risk

Can a company's internal controls be so well designed that they eliminate the risk of failing to achieve the company's objectives?

2 The purpose of internal control

The purpose of internal control is implied by the definition given earlier, to help management achieve the entity's objectives, especially in terms of ensuring:

- the orderly and efficient conduct of the business
- the safeguarding of assets
- the prevention and detection of fraud and error
- the accuracy and completeness of the accounting records, and
- the timely preparation of reliable financial information.

Why do companies need internal controls?

Internal controls are there to prevent risks occurring or to minimise the impact of risks (i.e. to help prevent things going wrong). Even when controls are in place documents may still get lost or portable assets may go missing. The level and extent of internal controls required depend on what the risks are if such controls fail. It is particularly important that stringent controls exist where there are associated legal requirements.

Expandable text

Documents are batched and prenumbered so staff can check that there are none missing. If any sales invoices go missing debts may not be collected and income may be understated; cash flow would therefore also be affected resulting in payment difficulties.

If purchase invoices go missing the company would be overstating profits and if money owing to those creditors was spent elsewhere, cash flow problems could result later.

But what if the amounts involved are small? Does one invoice really matter? Experience shows that if one invoice has gone missing it is highly likely that several more are also missing, and the larger the organisation gets, the bigger the numbers get, and the tighter the controls have to be to prevent significant errors.

Authorisation controls are another type of internal control and are particularly important. For example, suppose that a clerk routinely authorises false purchase invoices raised by a friend outside the company. The company pays the invoices and the friend and the clerk share the proceeds. This is a very common type of fraud. Controls to prevent this require payments to be authorised only with reference to purchase invoices that are attached to goods received notes, or authorisations for the receipt of services by managers completely unconnected with the accounting function.

Why internal control interests the external auditor

The principal reason why internal control interests the external auditor is that reliance on internal controls will reduce the amount of **substantive testing** of transactions and resultant balances in the ledger accounts required.

At an early stage in their work the auditors will have to decide the extent to which they believe they can place reliance on the internal controls of the enterprise. As the audit proceeds, that decision will be kept under review and, depending on the results of their examination, they may decide to place more or less reliance on these controls.

Expandable text

The operation of internal controls should ensure the completeness and accuracy of the accounting records. If the auditors are satisfied that the internal control system is functioning properly, there is therefore a reduced risk of error in the accounting records.

It is very important to the auditor to establish what internal control system exists and then to test that system to find out whether it is working properly.

Another reason that the auditor needs to consider the adequacy of the accounting system is that the auditor typically has a statutory responsibility to form an opinion as to whether proper accounting records have been kept. This implies the operation of a sound system of internal control.

By recording the accounting system and checking its operation by tests of control, the auditor can reduce the amount of detailed substantive procedures. The total amount of work is reduced as a result and a more efficient audit achieved.

Why internal control interests the internal auditor

A key objective of the internal auditor is to review the organisation's system of internal control and to provide assurance that the corporate governance requirements are being met. Therefore internal controls are fundamental to the work of the internal auditor. Like external auditors, internal auditors have to make decisions on the extent of reliance on controls to manage risks and therefore the level of testing to be carried out.

Expandable text

An objective and adequately resourced internal audit function should be in a position to provide the Board with much of the assurance it requires regarding **the effectiveness** of the **system of internal control**.

Therefore, both the internal and external auditors have a common interest in confirming the system of internal control.

To provide assurance, internal audit needs to check:

- that the controls in place are adequate to guard against the risks identified
- that the controls are operating effectively.

This requires a decision on whether the right controls are in place for the type and level of risk identified. The auditor will be interested not just in whether there are sufficient controls but in examples of over-control and inefficiencies. Traditionally, internal audit staff were seen as 'business prevention', because they were seen as adding in additional 'unnecessary' controls. However, increasingly, internal auditors need to be adding value and therefore will review the cost effectiveness as well as the adequacy of controls.

Test your understanding 2

Substantive testing or systems testing?

Would an external auditor prefer to carry out an audit using exclusively substantive testing, or would he prefer to be able to rely on the internal controls of the business having carried out tests on those controls?

3 The components of internal control

- the control environment
- the entity's risk assessment process
- the information system relevant to financial reporting
- control activities
- monitoring of controls.

The term 'internal control' can refer to any of these five components.

The **control environment** is the overall attitude of management regarding internal controls and their importance. It encompasses management's philosophy, e.g. a commitment to integrity and ethical values, a formal organisation structure and proper training of staff.

Expandable text

The control environment sets the tone of the organisation in terms of the control consciousness of its employees. It is the foundation for effective internal control, providing discipline and structure. For example, if senior management openly engage in unethical behaviour, and urge fellow employees to ignore internal rules, then the whole tone of the organisation will be damaged and internal control will be weak.

The **risk assessment process** is an entity's process for identifying and responding to business risks.

Expandable text

Business risk is the possibility that an event or transaction could occur that will adversely affect the organisation's ability to achieve its objectives and execute its strategies. It is conventionally split between internal and external factors, as below.

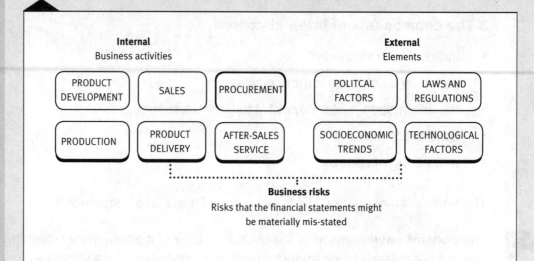

Once risks have been identified, management must investigate their significance, the likelihood of their occurrence, and how they should be managed.

The **information system** relevant to financial reporting objectives consists of the procedures and records established to process the transactions that the entity carries out, and to maintain accountability for the related assets, liabilities and equity balances. Many information systems make extensive use of information technology (IT).

Expandable text

The information system must be able to:

- identify and record all valid transactions

- describe the transactions in sufficient detail to permit proper classification for financial reporting

- measure the transactions to permit the recording of their proper monetary value in the financial statements

- determine the correct accounting period in which transactions should be recognised

- present properly the transactions and related disclosures in the financial statements.

Control activities are the policies and procedures that help ensure that management directives are carried out, for example that necessary actions are taken to address risks that threaten the achievement of the entity's objectives. Control activities, whether within IT or manual systems, have various objectives and are applied at various organisational and functional levels.

Different books identify different categories of control activities. One possibility is:

- **A**uthorisation
- **C**omparison
- **C**omputer controls
- **A**rithmetical controls
- **M**aintaining a trial balance and control accounts
- **A**ccounting reconciliations
- **P**hysical controls.

(Use the mnemonic **ACCA MAP** to remember these categories.)

> ### Expandable text
>
> Control activities can take a number of forms.
>
> **Performance reviews** involve looking at reports and analyses to identify management or control issues from past performance. For example, a comparison of actual and budgeted figures might highlight business risks if implementation of the budget is slipping or bookkeeping problems if the variance is due to errors in the recorded figures.
>
> **Information processing** encompasses the controls that are performed to check accuracy, completeness and authorisation of transactions. For example, a computer printout of every new name added to the company payroll might help prevent the fraudulent addition of bogus employees.
>
> **Physical controls** are often overlooked, but they are just as important as administrative or accounting procedures. For example, there is no point in having an efficient inventory tracking system if there is inadequate security to prevent staff or third parties from simply stealing high value items.
>
> **Segregation of duties** splits any given transaction into three elements: authorisation, recording and maintaining custody of assets. This is a potentially effective means of preventing fraud because it will require collusion between at least two members of staff. For example, ordering goods for personal use will be impossible because one member of staff must place the order and another will receive (have custody of) the goods. It would require both staff members to work together to defraud the system.

Monitoring of controls is a process to assess the quality of internal control performance over time. It involves assessing the design and operation of controls on a timely basis and taking necessary corrective actions.

Management must decide whether existing control procedures are adequate. This could change over time. For example, a system might become overwhelmed if the entity grows too rapidly.

The operation of controls must also be checked. Compliance failures may arise because of lack of staff motivation or through poor training and supervision.

Expandable text

In practice, the choice of controls may reflect a comparison of the cost of operating individual controls against the benefits expected to be derived from them.

Many of the internal controls which would be relevant to larger enterprises are not practical, appropriate or necessary in small enterprises. Managements of small enterprises have less need to depend on formal internal controls for the reliability of the records and other information, because of their personal contact with, or involvement in, the operation of the enterprise itself.

In many larger companies, internal audit will contribute to the monitoring of control activities, however the extent of internal audit's involvement is up to management to decide.

Alternative analysis of internal controls

There are three key types of control that can be considered.

Preventive controls

These are controls that prevent risks occurring. For example, authorisation controls should prevent fraudulent or erroneous transactions taking place. Other preventive controls include segregation of duties, recruiting and training the right staff and having an effective control culture.

Detective controls

These are controls that detect if any problems have occurred. They are designed to pick up errors that have not been prevented. These could be exception reports that reveal that controls have been circumvented (for example, large amounts paid without being authorised). Other examples could include reconciliations, supervision and internal checks.

Corrective controls

These are controls that address any problems that have occurred. So where problems are identified, the controls ensure that they are properly rectified. Examples of corrective controls include follow-up procedures and management action.

Clearly the most powerful type of control is **preventative**. It is more effective to have a control that stops problems occurring rather than to detect or correct them once they have occurred. There is always a possibility that it is too late to sort out the problem.

Illustration 2 – Examples of specific control activities

Management in an organisation are responsible for weighing up the costs and benefits of possible controls and establishing an appropriate internal control system. Below are listed a number of possible controls – try to decide which of the 'ACCA MAP' categories each control belongs to.

- Approval and control of **documents and transactions of importance** – in a purchases system, for example, there should be pre-set authority limits. An order up to the value of $1,000 could be approved by a department head, up to $5,000 by any one director, and beyond this by the board as a whole.

- Controls over **computerised applications** and the IT environment.

- Checking the **arithmetical accuracy** of the records – such controls include checking the casts on a purchase invoice, and recalculating the sales tax on sales invoices.

- Maintaining and reviewing **control accounts** and **trial balances** – control accounts include sales and purchase ledger control accounts, bank reconciliations and non-current asset registers.

- Comparing the results of **cash**, **security** and **inventory counts** with the accounting records.

- Comparing **internal data** with **external sources** of information – this might include supplier statement reconciliations.

- Comparing and analysing the financial results with budgeted amounts.

- Producing and reviewing **exception reports**, e.g. lists of purchasing transactions above certain limits or payments made without a purchase order.

- **Limiting direct physical access** to assets and records – an important general principle with respect to assets and records is that of **segregation of duties**. In particular there should be a division of responsibilities for:

  - **authorising** or initiating the transaction

  - the physical **custody** and control of assets involved

  - **recording** the transaction.

No one person should be in a position both to misappropriate an asset and to conceal the act by falsifying the records. For example, in a sales system the duties of receiving money from debtors and writing up the sales ledger should be separated. If not, money could be misappropriated and the records falsified to cover this.

Test your understanding 3

Components of internal control

For each of the five components of internal control identified in ISA 315, give one specific example of an internal control that you might find in a well-controlled company:

- Control environment

- Risk assessment process

- Information system

- Control activities

- Monitoring of controls

4 Management responsibility

It is management's responsibility to establish proper internal control arrangements within their company. This responsibility may derive from statutory requirements or from general corporate governance arrangements.

Expandable text

Company law varies from country to country, but typically the directors of a company are required by law to keep proper accounting records, to safeguard the assets of the company, and hence to take reasonable steps to prevent and detect fraud and other irregularities. Such requirements imply the necessity for proper internal control.

This requirement is set out more clearly in the Combined Code on Corporate Governance. Principle C2 of the Code states that:

'The board should maintain a sound system of internal control to safeguard shareholders' investment and the company's assets.'

Provision C2.1 of the Code goes on to explain that the board should, at least annually, conduct a review of the effectiveness of the system of internal controls and should report to shareholders that they have done so. This review must cover all material controls, including financial, operational and compliance controls and risk management systems.

Expandable text

The Turnbull Report was issued in 1999 to give guidance to directors on how to comply with these sections of the Combined Code. This Report again emphasises that:

'The board of directors is responsible for the company's system of internal control.'

Furthermore it is the role of management to implement board policies on risk and control, and all employees have some responsibility for internal control as part of their accountability for achieving objectives.

Management should report regularly to the board on the risks faced and the effectiveness of the system of internal control in managing those risks.

In its annual assessment of internal control, the board should consider:

- The changes in the nature and extent of significant risks since the last annual assessment.

- The scope of management's ongoing monitoring of risks, including the reports management has made to the board and any relevant work by internal audit.

- The incidence of any significant control failings or weaknesses that have been identified during the year.

Internal financial control is part of overall internal control. Although the auditors, for example, will be particularly interested in testing and reporting on the financial controls, the board is responsible for all the controls in the company: financial, operational and compliance controls.

Principles and provisions

What is the difference in reporting requirements between the principles in the Combined Code in respect of internal control and the provisions of the Combined Code?

5 Ensuring the effectiveness of internal financial procedures

Effectiveness is a measure of the extent to which organisational objectives are being achieved. Management's objectives for internal financial procedures will be as described earlier, namely as ensuring:

- the orderly and efficient conduct of the business
- the safeguarding of assets
- the prevention and detection of fraud and error
- the accuracy and completeness of the accounting records and
- the timely preparation of reliable financial information.

The best way for management to set about achieving these objectives will be to establish a strong set of internal financial controls within the organisation, i.e. to implement all five components of internal control in the financial reporting function.

Internal auditors can be used to recommend improvements in internal financial control. As an incidental by-product of their work, external auditors may also recommend improvements in control.

Expandable text

By implementing a high quality corporate governance regime and a strong internal control system, management can be confident that financial objectives will be met as far as practicable.

Corporate Governance

The board	Employees	Internal audit	External audit
• balance of executive and non-executive directors (NEDs)	• proper training	• operational internal audit assignments will investigate standards of internal control	• will report weaknesses in internal control discovered during the course of their audit work
• supplied with information to enable it to carry out its duties	• awareness of need for ethical behaviour		
• overall responsibility for the internal control system			

Internal Control

Good control environment	Regular risk assessment process	Good information system and communication of information	Appropriate control activities	Monitoring of controls

---

Test your understanding 5

External audit and internal control

Is the reporting of internal control weaknesses to management the primary objective of external audit?

Chapter summary

> **Internal control** is the process designed and effected by management to provide reasonable assurance that the entity's objectives will be achieved.

> **Internal check** ensures that no single task is executed from start to finish by only one person

> The **purpose of internal control** is to help management achieve the entity's objectives, by ensuring:
> - the orderly conduct of business
> - the safeguarding of assets
> - the prevention and detection of fraud and error
> - the accuracy of the accounting records, and
> - the timely preparation of reliable financial information.

> The **five components of internal control** are:
>
> | The control environment | The entity's risk-assessment process | The information system relevant to financial reporting | Control activities | Monitoring of controls |
> |---|---|---|---|---|

> It is the **responsibility** of management to establish a system of internal control

Test your understanding answers

Test your understanding 1

No. There will always be a residual risk of not achieving the company's objectives, however well the internal controls are designed. Internal controls will always have inherent limitations, such as the possibility that they will be circumvented by employees colluding together, or the possibility that they fail due to human error. It is for this reason that one must talk of internal controls providing **reasonable assurance** about achieving the organisation's financial reporting objectives, not absolute assurance.

Test your understanding 2

The appropriate audit strategy must be tailored to the characteristics of the organisation being audited. In the audit of a small business, the most appropriate audit approach will usually be exclusively substantive testing, i.e. direct testing of the balances appearing in the financial statements. In the audit of a large business, this would not be efficient. The external auditor would then prefer to test the internal controls in the accounting system and, provided that the controls are proved to be working properly, he can then rely on those controls and carry out a reduced amount of substantive testing, and still be in a position where he has gathered sufficient audit evidence to form an opinion on whether the financial statements give a true and fair view.

Test your understanding 3

Control environment – communication of ethical values to personnel through policy statements and codes of conduct.

Risk assessment process – management monitors changes in the operating environment to plan for the future.

Information system – quarterly management accounts are presented to the board of directors for their consideration.

Control activities – an annual inventory count is held to confirm the quantities of inventories physically held.

Monitoring of controls – internal audit conduct a regular review of sales personnel's compliance with the company's terms of sales contracts.

Of course, your examples may be very different, but you should have identified one control for each of the five components.

Test your understanding 4

You should remember from an earlier chapter that in their Annual Report and Accounts a listed company must include a narrative statement of how it has applied the principles of the Code, and whether or not it has complied throughout the period with the provisions of the Code. There is no prescribed form for the statement setting out how the principles have been applied. Companies have a free hand in explaining their governance policies, including any special circumstances which have led them to adopt a particular approach.

A listed company must therefore explain in its Annual Report how it has maintained a sound system of internal control, and whether or not the board has conducted a review of internal control effectiveness.

Test your understanding 5

No. The primary objective of external audit is to report to the shareholders on whether the financial statements give a true and fair view. However external auditors will examine the internal financial controls as part of their audit work, and if they discover weaknesses in those controls, they will communicate those weaknesses to management (normally to the audit committee if one exists) together with their recommendations as to how those weaknesses can be addressed.

Fraud

Chapter learning objectives

Upon completion of this chapter you will be able to:

- explain the meaning of fraud

- identify and describe the prerequisites of fraud

- describe examples of fraud in a business organisation

- explain what is meant by 'window dressing' and 'cooking the books'

- explain the possible implications of fraud to the company

- explain what measures might be taken by an organisation to prevent and discover fraud

- describe the duties and responsibilities of management for the prevention and discovery of fraud.

```
┌─────────────────────────────────────┐
│                Fraud                 │
│  'an intentional act ... involving   │
│   the use of deception to obtain an  │
│   unjust or illegal advantage'       │
└─────────────────────────────────────┘
                  ⋮
┌─────────────────────────────────────┐
│  The primary responsibility for the  │
│  prevention and detection of fraud    │
│  rests with the directors of a        │
│  company.                             │
└─────────────────────────────────────┘
                  ⋮
┌─────────────────────────────────────┐
│  The best way for the directors to    │
│  discourage fraud is to promote a     │
│  strong control environment and       │
│  establish an effective internal      │
│  control system within the company.   │
└─────────────────────────────────────┘
```

1 The meaning of fraud

Fraud is an intentional act by one or more individuals among management, those charged with governance, employees or third parties, involving the use of deception to obtain an unjust or illegal advantage.

Auditing Practices Board 'Glossary of Terms'

- **Fraud** is an intentional act involving the use of deception to obtain an unjust or illegal advantage. It may help you to think of fraud as 'theft by deception'. Fraud is a criminal offence, punishable by fine or by imprisonment.

- **Error** is an unintentional mistake. Error is an inevitable part of human nature, so systems of internal check are essential in order to prevent or detect ant possible errors.

- **Irregularity** is something contrary to a particular rule or standard.

- **Misstatement** is something stated wrongly. Misstatement can arise due to fraud, other irregularity or error.

Expandable text

Fraud should be contrasted with **error**. While fraud is an intentional act, error is unintentional. For example, if a purchase ledger clerk deliberately enters a false invoice from a friend into the purchase ledger, hoping that it will be paid so that the clerk and the friend can split the proceeds, this is a fraud. However if the clerk accidentally enters an invoice twice into the ledger, this is an error.

An **irregularity** would occur if a petty cash system designed to limit individual vouchers to less than $50, but allowed a single voucher of $70 to be processed.

An example of **misstatement** may be when a balance sheet shows a building at cost $1m, whereas the actual cost was $1.3m.

As far as the financial statements are concerned, fraud comprises both the use of deception to obtain an unjust or illegal financial advantage and intentional misrepresentations affecting the financial statements. It is ultimately up to the courts to decide in each instance whether fraud has occurred, for example:

- deliberate falsification of documents/records

- deliberate ignoring of errors requiring correction

- deliberate suppression of relevant information.

Expandable text

Note that fraud may be carried out by management, employees or third parties. For example:

- Managers may deliberately select inappropriate accounting policies.

- Employees may steal the proceeds of cash sales and omit to enter the sale into the accounting records.

- Third parties may send bogus invoices to the company, hoping that they will be paid in error.

Test your understanding 1

A rogue has sent your company a bogus invoice for advertising in a non-existent publication. The rogue spoke to a purchase ledger clerk at your company and convinced her that the company had placed several previous advertisements in the publication in the past, so that this repeat advertisement was genuine. The clerk was innocently fooled into passing the invoice for payment.

(a) Has the rogue committed a fraud?

(b) Has the clerk committed a fraud?

(c) Will the rogue be paid?

2 The prerequisites of fraud

There are three prerequisites for fraud to occur: dishonesty, opportunity and motive. All three are usually required – for example an honest employee is unlikely to commit fraud even if given the opportunity and motive.

Fraud is more likely to occur in a business environment with poor or no controls. If the control environment is lax and management has implemented few specific control activities, then the potential for fraud is high.

Factors that might increase the risk of fraud and error:

- management domination by one person, or a small group of people

- unnecessarily complex corporate structure

- high turnover rate of key accounting personnel

- personnel who do not take leave/holidays

- understaffed accounting department

- volatile business environment

- inadequate working capital

- deteriorating quality of earnings

- inadequate segregation of duties

- lack of monitoring of control systems

- unusual transactions – in cash, or direct to numbered bank accounts

- payments for services disproportionate to effort

- significant transactions with related parties

- inadequate IT systems.

If management has established a strong system of internal control (remember the five components of internal control studied in an earlier chapter), then the potential for fraud is greatly reduced.

> ### Expandable text
>
> For example, the following controls should prevent a false billing fraud from being successful:
>
> - A purchase order must be filled in for each item of goods and services required. No invoice can be paid unless there is a corresponding purchase order (and goods received note for goods received).
>
> - All the supporting documentation should be presented to the cheque signatory when cheques are being signed, so that the signatory can confirm that everything is in order. Once paid, this supporting documentation should be stamped 'Paid' to prevent it from being submitted again in the future.
>
> - Operate a list of approved suppliers. Nothing is to be paid to non-approved suppliers without specific senior management approval.
>
> - Reduce to the minimum practical number, the number of people authorised to order goods or to authorise invoices for payment.
>
> - Company policy should be never to agree to any business proposition verbally at a meeting or on the telephone. The offer and agreement must be made in writing, by email/letter/fax, etc. That way the terms of any contract cannot be disputed later.
>
> If a bogus invoice is received, inform the authorities, e.g. local trading standards officers or the police. They may wish to investigate the matter and bring the sender to justice.

> ### Test your understanding 2
>
> **Role of internal audit**
>
> What is the role of internal audit, if any, in preventing and detecting fraud in a company?

3 Examples of fraud in a business organisation

'Forewarned is forearmed', so the saying goes. By studying examples of fraud seen previously in businesses, you should be better able to assess the risk that such frauds may occur in your business, so that you will be able to respond properly to the threat.

Frauds can be carried out by managers, employees or by third parties of the organisation in question.

Example frauds by management

- financial statement fraud, e.g. 'window dressing' and 'cooking the books'
- misappropriation of assets
- false insurance claims
- using the company's assets for personal use.

Example frauds by employees

- sales ledger fraud – 'teeming and lading', stealing cash sales and cheques received
- purchase ledger fraud
- skimming schemes
- payroll fraud.

Example frauds by third parties

- false billing fraud
- bank account fraud
- advance fee fraud
- Ponzi schemes.

Expandable text

The frauds listed above are briefly described below.

Misappropriation of assets

Although all employees of a company may steal assets to a minor degree (e.g. taking pads of paper or blank recordable CDs home with them), management are able to conceal more major thefts by amending the accounting records. For example:

- They may steal physical assets (e.g. inventory or non-current assets) and adjust the accounts to show that these items were written off.

- They may sell intellectual property (e.g. plans of a new product) to a competitor for cash.

Such frauds are usually hard to detect, because the accounting records look to be in order.

False insurance claims

A manager may steal a high value asset (e.g. a notebook computer) and claim that it was stolen from him while on company business. The company then lodges an insurance claim to remedy its loss. The insurance company is defrauded.

Using the company's assets for personal use

Some instances are minor (e.g. sending personal emails from company computers), but management are in a position to take matters further (e.g. using the company's assets as collateral for a personal loan in favour of the manager).

Sales ledger frauds

There are several possibilities:

- Stealing receipts from debtors (e.g. cheques received in the post) and then writing off the sales ledger balance as a bad debt.

- Pocketing the proceeds of cash sales and never entering them in the accounting records.

- 'Teeming and lading' frauds in which the receipts from one debtor are pocketed by the fraudster, with this sales ledger balance being cleared by a subsequent receipt from another debtor. (See the illustration below for an example.)

Purchase ledger frauds

A dummy purchase invoice can be entered into the purchase ledger records, with the cash being paid to a bank account set up for the purpose by the fraudulent purchase ledger clerk. Alternatively a purchase ledger clerk can collude with a third party to inflate the amount of an invoice, with the surplus amount being shared between the protagonists.

Skimming schemes

In a skimming scheme the fraudster diverts small amounts from a large number of transactions, believing that no one will bother to investigate the small differences individually, although in aggregate they can total to a worthwhile sum.

Payroll fraud

A typical example is to add a bogus employee to the payroll and to pay their monthly 'salary' into a bank account set up for the purpose by the fraudster.

False billing fraud

This has been described earlier. Typically a fraudster will send a bogus invoice to a company, claiming that it is in respect of the company's inclusion in a non-existent trade directory, or similar.

Bank account fraud

Some companies print their bank account details on their invoices, inviting debtors to pay money directly into the account. Alternatively they may pay their bills by cheques that show both the bank account numbers and what the required signature looks like. Unfortunately this gives fraudsters the information they need, for example to set up standing orders and direct debits out of the account and into a bank account under their control. This situation is avoided by designating the account 'deposit only' so that no one can set up a standing order, etc. on the account.

Advance fee fraud

This is a confidence trick where a company is invited to pay a modest fee up front in the promise of being paid a large amount in the future. The typical form is an email from Nigeria claiming that they want to transfer a large sum of money out of the country but need some money immediately to pay the necessary fees to get the money released. Of course, if any fees are paid, the promised large sum never materialises. Such emails have become so common that they are known as '419 frauds' after the section of the Nigerian criminal code that they violate. Indeed many companies now routinely filter out all emails from Nigeria in their anti-spam settings, which has upset legitimate Nigerian businesses.

Since the Nigerian email has become so notorious, new variations on the theme have been developed, such as being told that you have won a large sum in a lottery or have been left money in a will, but you must pay an administrative fee before the money can be paid. An astonishingly large number of people in the west still seem to fall foul of these bogus offers, and the offers will continue to be sent while people are still taken in by them.

Ponzi schemes

A Ponzi scheme is a fraudulent investment offer that involves paying abnormally high returns to early investors out of the new money paid in by subsequent investors, rather than from any genuine underlying business. Charles Ponzi emigrated to America in 1903 and set up his savings scheme in Boston offering 50% interest in 45 days, or 'double your money' in 90 days. About 40,000 people sent him a total of $15m for the scheme. When it inevitably collapsed, only about $5m was returned to the investors. The lesson to learn is that if a scheme looks 'too good to be true' then it probably is too good to be true. You should only invest in schemes where you understand the underlying business rationale of the investment. Modern Ponzi schemes use financial jargon to confuse potential investors, claiming to earn their huge profits by 'hedge futures trading' or 'global currency arbitrage' or similar. Often there is no underlying business at all, and the scheme will always collapse in the end, usually with the initial promoters vanishing with all the assets of the scheme.

Illustration 1 – Teeming and lading

'Teeming and lading' is a 'juggling' fraud normally on the sales ledger whereby the receipts of later debtors are allocated to pay off earlier debtors. For example Company X might invoice customers for $100 per day who, for the sake of simplicity, all pay their bills after one week. On day 8 the company will receive $100 from the sales of day 1. The accounts clerk steals this money. On day 9 the company receives $100 from the sales of day 2, but the clerk pretends that this money is in respect of the sales of day 1, and so on each day. In practice, as the fraudster grows in confidence, he often steals larger and larger sums, which increase the amount of earlier invoices that he is settling through later receipts.

As long as the organisation regularly issues invoices for similar amounts and the fraudster takes no holidays to allow someone else to see what is happening, such a fraud can continue for some time. Each debtor balance is settled in due course, so no one realises anything is wrong. Usually, one day the fraudster fails to turn up for work, and is never seen again while he keeps the proceeds of the fraud.

Methods to discourage teeming and lading frauds include:

- rotating duties within the accounts department
- insisting that everyone takes their annual holidays
- sending regular statements to debtors
- internal audit could carry out a circularisation of debtors, asking them to confirm the balances that they are recorded as owing to the company
- employing honest employees in the first place, e.g. checking references given by job applicants when they apply to work at the company.

Test your understanding 4

Teeming and lading

Can a teeming and lading fraud be carried out on the purchase ledger system?

4 Fraudulent financial reporting

Fraudulent financial reporting involves intentional misstatements (including omissions of amounts or disclosures) in financial statements in order to deceive financial statement users.

Examples of fraudulent financial reporting include:

- recording fictitious entries in the accounting records, particularly those close to the accounting year end (see 'Window dressing' below)

- inappropriately adjusting assumptions or judgements used to estimate account balances

- omitting, advancing or delaying recognition in the financial statements of transactions that have occurred during the year

- concealing facts that could affect the amounts recorded in the financial statements

- altering records related to significant and unusual transactions.

In daily language, such schemes can be referred to as 'cooking the books'. Other descriptions are 'creative accounting' and 'earnings management'. One category of such schemes is 'window dressing'. All these schemes may or may not comply with the letter of standard accounting rules, but they are usually contrary to the spirit of these rules. Ultimately it is up to the courts to decide whether a particular scheme is fraudulent, but hopefully the external auditors will have persuaded the directors of a company against a fraudulent scheme long before it gets to court.

Examples of creative accounting include:

- window dressing

- delaying or accelerating a company's expenses

- manipulation of revenue recognition

- off-balance sheet accounting.

Expandable text

Window dressing

Window dressing is the entering into of transactions before the year end that are often reversed out after the year end, the substance of which was primarily to improve the appearance of the company's financial statements.

For example, a company might have promised its shareholders that it would achieve $10m sales during the year. In December it becomes clear that sales of only $9.5m are going to be achieved. One possibility would be to enter a sale for $0.5m in the December accounts, and then to issue a credit note to the customer for $0.5m in January. The customer doesn't mind, and the shareholders are happy because $10m of sales were recorded for the year. However the entering of the $0.5m sale in the records was arguably fraudulent. A more subtle approach would be to get in touch with a regular customer in December, and offer them a special discount if they will bring forward $0.5m of their intended January purchases to December. Again, everybody is happy, and the question of whether a fraud has occurred is less clear-cut.

Delaying or accelerating a company's expenses

Showing an expense as an asset on the balance sheet rather than writing it off immediately against profits is a quick way to improve your reported profits, as practised spectacularly by WorldCom before its collapse. This is contrary to acceptable accounting practices.

Accelerating a company's expenses may appear a strange objective. However if a new bonus scheme is being introduced that will pay you a bonus if next year's profits are high, you might be tempted to charge as many expenses as you can to this year, thus improving next year's reported profit figure.

Manipulation of revenue recognition

If a company is engaged on a long-term contract, they are supposed to recognise the revenues from the contract on a reasonable basis as the contract is fulfilled. It would be fraudulent to recognise all the revenue in the first year of the contract and none in subsequent years.

A similar problem arises when sales are recorded as soon as goods are ordered by customers, rather than when they are shipped to the customer. This practice has been tried by several internet retail sites, but again is contrary to acceptable accounting practice.

Off-balance sheet accounting

A balance sheet is supposed to include all the assets and liabilities of the organisation. Off-balance sheet accounting is the deliberate exclusion of certain assets and liabilities from the published balance sheet.

One example is a short-term lease. If you lease a building for, say, two years then under current accounting practices you do not have to show the asset or the related obligation to pay the rental amounts on the balance sheet. You have the use of the asset and you have a contractual obligation to pay the rentals, but neither the asset nor the liability are shown on your balance sheet.

Test your understanding 5

Reasons for fraudulent financial reporting

Suggest four reasons why the management of a company might want to cook the books.

5 The possible implications of fraud to the company

There is a spectrum of implications of fraud, from the immaterial to the critical. Including

- Misuse of assets
- Loss of assets
- Financial difficulties
- Collapse of the company.

Expandable text

When a material sum of money has been lost, companies will often look around for someone external to blame, regardless of the fact that it is management who have failed in their responsibility to prevent fraud from occurring. In particular the external auditors are known to carry insurance against being sued, so they are often a first target to be sued for negligence by a company that has lost money through fraud. If the external auditors had given an audit opinion that the accounts showed a true and fair view for the period while a material fraud was occurring, then there may possibly be a legal case for negligence that the company could bring against the auditors.

If an employee has been caught red-handed while attempting a fraud, many companies seem to believe that instant dismissal is the best policy, hoping that the problem will then disappear. In practice the fraudulent employee is likely to get a new job and to defraud his new employer. Thus it is best for society if a defrauded company risks some adverse publicity by reporting the fraudulent employee to the police so that the employee can be punished by law, rather than repeating their fraudulent behaviour again and again in the belief that they will never be punished.

Once a fraud has been identified, internal audit should be sent to the department to investigate the circumstances and to make recommendations to improve the controls in the area to deter future fraud. Internal audit should report their findings to the audit committee who can monitor whether the recommendations are swiftly implemented by management.

6 Measures to prevent and detect fraud

The principal strategy of any organisation to prevent and detect fraud is to establish an effective internal control system. You should recall from an earlier chapter that internal control comprises five components:

- the control environment
- the risk assessment process
- the information system
- control activities, and
- monitoring of controls.

The first step of any fraud prevention system is therefore to ensure that each of the five components above is set up and working properly, for example as in the table below.

Component	Example in practice
Control environment	A formal organisation structure assigns authority and responsibility throughout the company.
Risk assessment process	The company employs IT experts who can advise on incorporating new technologies into the production process.
Information system	Monthly management accounts are submitted to senior management so that they can monitor the company's performance on a timely basis.

Control activities	Segregation of duties is enforced in the accounts department.
Monitoring of controls	Internal audit are charged with reviewing the effectiveness of internal controls throughout the business.

Effective internal controls help ensure that the company is not unnecessarily exposed to avoidable risks.

Effective financial controls, including the maintenance of proper accounting records, are an important element of internal control. But the internal control system must go beyond financial controls to cover the control environment and culture of control established by management.

All internal controls play a role in helping to manage the risks that are significant to the achievement of a company's objectives. Since a company's objectives and the environment within which it operates are constantly evolving, the risks it faces are continually changing. An effective system of internal control therefore requires a regular evaluation of the risks to which the company is exposed. Since profits can be viewed in economic terms as the reward for successful risk taking, the objective of internal controls must be to manage risk properly rather than to eliminate it.

Test your understanding 6

Internal controls over payroll

Consider the internal controls that you would expect to find in a well-run payroll department in a manufacturing company. The first column of the table below identifies certain of the key tasks that the department is responsible for. The second column identifies some of the risks that must be countered by control procedures. Fill in the control procedures that you might see, in the third column of the table below.

Payroll department task	Risks/objectives	Procedures
Salary Information collected from clock cards, timesheets, etc.	• Staff punch clock cards for friends. • Timesheets claim false hours. • Overtime is claimed that was never worked.	

Adjustments made for: • **starters** • **leavers** • **pay rises** • **overtime**	• Start/leaving dates wrong. • Staff who leave continue to get paid. • Payroll details changed to redirect money. • Fake pay rises put through. • New employees do not exist.	
Gross wages calculated	• Inaccurate calculations.	
Taxes (and other items) deducted	• Calculations could be wrong. • Failure to update system for tax changes.	
Pay list produced for bank	• Incomplete set of pay slip. • Pay list incorrect.	
Employees and tax authorities paid	• Wrong amounts paid to tax authorities. • Taxes paid late. • Employees paid late. • Where staff are paid in cash, the cash is stolen.	

7 The duties of management in preventing and detecting fraud

The duties of 'management' can be split between:

• the duties of the board of directors

• the duties of the audit committee

• the duties of employees generally (including senior employees below board level).

Expandable text

The board of directors is required by the Combined Code to maintain a sound system of internal control. At least annually, the board should conduct a review of the effectiveness of the internal control system and should report to shareholders that they have done so. A sound internal control system is the first line of defence in the prevention and detection of fraud.

The audit committee is required by the Combined Code to monitor and review the company's internal control and risk management systems. This should ensure the continuing effectiveness of the controls in preventing and detecting fraud.

The specific duties of employees are set out in their contract of employment and in what they are told to do by their supervisors, but there will always be an implied duty to act honestly and to report suspected or actual frauds encountered to supervisors. Fraud prevention and detection is the responsibility of every employee in a company, not just the board of directors.

Test your understanding 7

Fraud prevention in a small company

A small company may have informal working arrangements and few specific control policies and procedures. How can the directors still ensure that fraudulent behaviour is prevented and detected?

Chapter summary

Meaning of fraud
Fraud is an intentional act involving the use of deception to obtain an unjust or illegal advantage

Examples of fraud
- financial statement fraud, e.g. window dressing, or delaying recognition of expenses
- Teeming and lading by sales ledger clerks
- False billing by external parties

The primary responsibility for the prevention and detection of fraud rests with the directors of a company.

The best way for the directors to discourage fraud is to maintain a strong internal control system, e.g. promote a high quality control environment and implement effective control procedures.

The work of internal and external audit may help to detect fraud after it has occurred.

Test your understanding answers

Test your understanding 1

(a) Yes. He is deliberately deceiving the company, hoping to be paid an amount of money.

(b) No. She has no dishonest intent, but has made a mistake in believing the rogue.

(c) It depends on the other controls in force. If the company has no other controls over payments apart from the clerk's authorisation, then the rogue will be paid. Hopefully there are other controls (e.g. supervisory controls) that will prevent any payment being made in such an instance.

Test your understanding 2

It is up to the directors to decide what internal audit should do, but normally, where there is an effective internal audit department, the internal auditors will be given the responsibility to test the internal control system and to recommend improvements. The better the control system, the less likely it is that fraud will be attempted, or will succeed if it is attempted.

The directors may also ask the internal auditors to carry out a specific investigation into situations where fraud has been discovered, to learn lessons for the future and ensure that such a fraud cannot be repeated.

Test your understanding 3

The precise role of the audit committee will vary from company to company, but the Combined Code on Corporate Governance recommends that the audit committee should keep under review the company's internal control and risk management systems. They should implement improvements where weaknesses are found, in order to reduce the probability of fraud being carried out.

The audit committee should also ensure that there are arrangements in place whereby employees of the company can, in confidence, raise concerns about possible improprieties that they are concerned about ('whistle-blowing' arrangements). Employees may wish to report their suspicions about the behaviour of fellow employees through this channel of communication to those in authority.

Test your understanding 4

Although teeming and lading frauds normally occur in the sales system, they may also be carried out in the purchases system. It is a matter of pocketing money now and juggling the records to make it appear that everything is normal.

For example, if an organisation receives an invoice for $100 daily, and pays these invoices after seven days, then a fraudulent clerk can pocket the payment on day 8 (i.e. pay the cheque/bank transfer into an account that he controls) which should have been used to pay the purchase from day 1. He then uses the payment on day 9 to pay the creditor from day 1, and so on. Once again, the creditors will be happy that they are being paid, so nothing looks amiss. It is only when the clerk fails to turn up for work, and the creditors dispute the balance that they owe, that the fraud is discovered.

Test your understanding 5

(1) Management bonuses might depend on achieving a stated profit level.

(2) Management may wish to boost the share price to please shareholders, by reporting high profits.

(3) Management may fear that their company will face a takeover threat and they will lose their jobs unless high profits are reported.

(4) There may be conditions attached to loans that have been taken out (e.g. minimum acceptable accounting ratios) and the company is in danger of breaching these conditions.

Test your understanding 6

Payroll department task	Risks/objectives	Procedures
Salary Information collected from clock cards, timesheets, etc.	• Staff punch clock cards for friends. • Timesheets claim false hours. • Overtime is claimed that was never worked.	• All timesheets signed off as correct by line managers. • Clock card machine in open view. • Clocking in/out supervised. • Clock cards kept somewhere secure when not in use. • Clock cards sequenced, and sequence checked each day. • Clock cards checked to personnel records, to ensure no fake employees. • All overtime authorised in advance, and reviewed when claimed.

Adjustments made for:	• Start/leaving dates wrong.	• Take up references, and check qualifications, of new staff.
• **starters** • **leavers** • **pay rises** • **overtime**	• Staff who leave continue to get paid. • Payroll details changed to redirect money. • Fake pay rises put through. • New employees do not exist.	• New staff sign personnel form, with photo. • Random headcounts. • Leaver's form, signed by leaver and manager. • Personnel records kept secure. • All pay data on computer password protected. • Regular check of pay data to personnel files.
Gross wages calculated	• Inaccurate calculations.	• Random check of calculations by manager. • Use computerised payroll package. • Use outside payroll bureau.
Taxes (and other items) deducted	• Calculations could be wrong. • Failure to update system for tax changes.	• Random checks of calculations by manager. • Any amendments to tax data authorised by manager. • Regular check of tax rates to law.

Pay list produced for bank	• Incomplete set of pay slip. • Pay list incorrect.	• Payslips numbered, and checked back to calculations and personnel files. • Pay list reviewed by managers to ensure figures look reasonable. • Pay list authorised before sending to bank.
Employees and tax authorities paid	• Wrong amounts paid to tax authorities. • Taxes paid late. • Employees paid late. • Where staff are paid in cash, the cash is stolen.	• Use payroll control account, and follow up on differences. • Have set system of payment to ensure deadlines not missed. • Avoid paying in cash. • Where cash wages exist, use sealed envelopes. • Employee counts wages, and signs for them. • Only actual employee can receive and sign for wages. • Uncollected wages kept in safe until collection.

Test your understanding 7

If there are few control activities, then the other components of internal control become more important. In particular, the directors of a small company should promote a strong control environment, recruiting employees of the highest calibre in the first place and keeping them happy with decent pay and conditions. A commitment to ethical values, integrity and competence should be communicated throughout the company.

A small company is unlikely to have an internal audit department, but members of the accounts department may have a roving brief to recommend improvements in control.

While the external audit of a small company's accounts is not mandatory in most jurisdictions, a company may choose voluntarily to have an external audit. This would both help to prevent fraud (since employees know that their work may be inspected by auditors at a later date) and should have a reasonable chance of detecting any material fraud that has occurred.

Recruitment and selection, managing diversity and equal opportunity

Chapter learning objectives

Upon completion of this chapter you will be able to:

- explain the importance of effective recruitment and selection to the organisation

- describe the recruitment and selection processes and explain the stages in these processes

- describe the roles of those involved in the recruitment and selection processes

- describe the methods through which organisations seek to meet their recruitment needs

- explain the advantages and disadvantages of different recruitment and selection methods

- outline the main features of employment legislation

- explain the purposes of a diversity policy within the human resources plan

- explain the purpose and benefits of an equal opportunities policy within human resource planning

- explain the practical steps that an organisation may take to ensure the effectiveness of its diversity and equal opportunities policy.

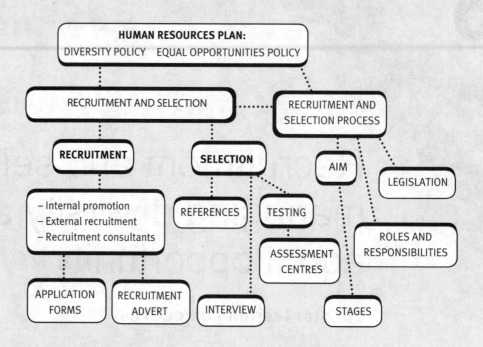

1 Recruitment and selection

Recruitment and selection are part of the same process and some people often refer to both as the recruitment process. This is not entirely accurate:

- The process of recruitment as distinct from selection involves the attraction of a field of suitable candidates for the job.

- The selection processes are aimed at selecting the best person for the job from that field of candidates.

The overall aim of the recruitment and selection process is to obtain the quantity and quality of employees required to fulfil the objectives of the organisation.

Expandable text

The process can be broken down into three main stages:

- defining requirements – preparing job descriptions, job specifications and personnel specifications

- attracting potential employees – use and evaluation of various methods of reaching sources of applicants

- selecting the appropriate person for the job or the appropriate job for the person.

1.1 Recruitment

Recruitment is the process of generating a supply of possible candidates for positions within an enterprise.

- It is concerned with attracting candidates to fill positions in the organisation.
- It is the process of contacting the labour market (internal and external), communicating opportunities and information and generating interest.

The best recruitment campaign will encourage a small number of highly suitable applicants, be cost effective, be speedy and show courtesy to all candidates.

The recruitment plan includes:

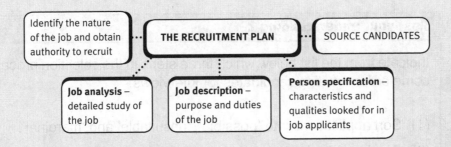

Test your understanding 1

Why might the economic situation in a country (or specific area of a country) have a marked effect on ability to attract the right candidates?

1.2 Selection

Selection is the choosing from a number of candidates the most suitable for a specified position.

The aim of selection is to identify, from those coming forward, the individuals most likely to fulfil the requirements of the organisation.

The methods of selection should be tailor-made for a particular organisation and job. The selection process can involve:

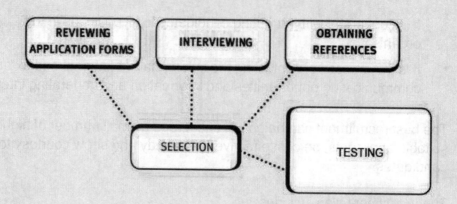

Test your understanding 2

Indicate from the list below which three steps in the selection process will come before inviting candidates for interviews.

(1) Sort applications into 'possible', 'unsuitable' and 'marginal'.

(2) Send standard letters to unsuccessful applicants.

(3) Assess each application against key criteria in the advertisement and specification.

(4) Deal with responses to job advertisements.

(5) Take up all references.

1.3 The importance of recruitment and selection

Recruiting people who are wrong for the organisation means they are likely to be discontented, unlikely to give of their best, and end up leaving voluntarily or involuntarily when their unsuitability becomes evident.

Consequences of effective recruitment and selection	Consequences of poor recruitment and selection
The person appointed will: • have the technical competence and ability to perform certain tasks • have the potential for training, development and future promotion • be flexible and adaptable to possible new methods, procedures or working conditions • be sociable, work harmoniously and fit within the cultural and social structure of the organisation • comply fully with all the legal requirements relating to employment and equal opportunities.	• high staff turnover • the cost of advertising • the management time involved in selection and training • the expense of dismissal • the effects of high turnover on the morale, motivation and job satisfaction of staff • reduced business opportunities • reduced quality of product or service.

Test your understanding 3

Why is it important to make recruitment activity systematic and consistent throughout the organisation?

Test your understanding 4

One of the many adverse consequences of poor recruitment and selection is the possibility of a high level of staff turnover. Outline the direct financial costs and the intangible costs associated with constantly recruiting and training new staff.

2 The recruitment and selection process

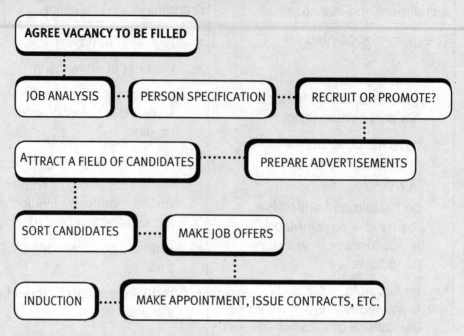

2.1 Agree vacancy to be filled

A vacancy presents an opportunity to either reassess the requirements of the job or to consider restructuring. A number of questions should always be asked prior to recruiting to the vacancy:

- Why replace at all? Alternatives to recruitment include retraining, promotion and job rotation

- What is the purpose of the post?

- Has the function changed?

- Can workloads be adjusted?

- Can the job be carried out on a part-time rather than a full time basis? Alternatives to full-time employment include home working (or teleworking), job-sharing, flexi-time or fixed-term contracts.

2.2 Job analysis

The process of job analysis starts with a detailed study and description of the tasks that make up the job and the kind of person required to do the job.

A job description is a broad statement of the purpose, scope, duties and responsibilities of the job.

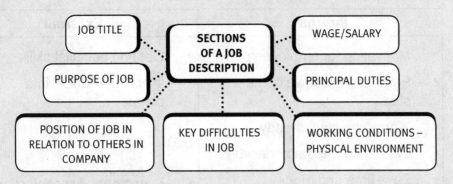

2.3 Person specification

A person specification defines the attributes of the ideal candidate – it is a blueprint of the qualities required of the jobholder. There are two main theories relating to the content of a person specification – **those put forward by Alec Rodger and John Munro Fraser**.

Rodger – 7 point plan	Fraser – 5 point plan
S Special aptitudes C Circumstances I Interests P Physical makeup D Disposition A Attainments G General intelligence	F Flexibility and adjustment I Impact on other people R Required qualifications M Motivation I Innate abilities

2.4 Recruit or promote?

There are many alternatives to external recruitment, e.g.

- promotion of existing staff (upwards or laterally)

- secondment (temporary transfers to another department, office, plant or country) of existing staff, which may or may not become permanent

- closing the job down, by sharing out duties and responsibilities among existing staff

- rotating jobs among staff, so that the vacant job is covered by different staff, on a systematic basis over several months.

Internal	External
• Motivating for employees	• Obtain specialist skills
• Part of career development plan	• Inject 'new blood' into company
• 'Know' the staff already	BUT
• Candidate understands work	
• Save time and money	• May create dissatisfaction in existing employees
• No induction necessary	• May cost more (higher wage)

2.5 Attracting a field of candidates

It is important to know where suitable applicants are likely to be found, how to make contact with them and to secure their application.

Potential sources to consider are:

- employment service job centres and agencies
- private employment agencies
- career advisory offices
- universities, colleges and schools
- professional and executive appointments registers
- executive search or headhunting
- advertising.

2.6 Recruitment consultants

Any organisation which is considering the use of external recruitment consultants would make its decision upon the following:

- the availability, level and appropriateness of expertise available within the organisation and its likely effectiveness
- the cost of using consultants against the cost involved in using the organisation's own staff, recognising the level of the vacancy or vacancies against the consultant's fee
- the particular expertise of the consultants and the appropriate experience with any particular specialised aspect of the recruitment process
- the level of expertise required of potential employees and therefore the appropriate knowledge required of the consultants.

Test your understanding 5

Recruitment consultants can assist in selecting the best staff to fill particular vacancies but what factors should the organisation consider before deciding to use them?

2.7 Preparing recruitment advertisements

The object of recruitment advertising is to home in on the target market of labour and to attract interest in the organisation and the job.

The method of advertising will depend on:

- the type of organisation
- the type of job
- whether the advertisement will be for internal or external recruitment or both
- the choice of medium.

The content of the advertisement should be:

- concise, but comprehensive enough to be an accurate description of the job, its rewards and requirements
- attractive to the maximum number of the right people
- positive and honest about the organisation. Disappointed expectations will be a prime source of dissatisfaction when an applicant actually comes into contact with the organisation

Test your understanding 6

If you were looking for a job in an accounting department what information would you expect to find in the advertisement?

2.8 Choosing advertising media

The selection of the right medium depends on several factors:

- Type of organisation.
- Type of job.
- Geographic coverage of the medium.
- Readership and circulation.
- Cost of medium

- Frequency and duration.

Issues to take into account:

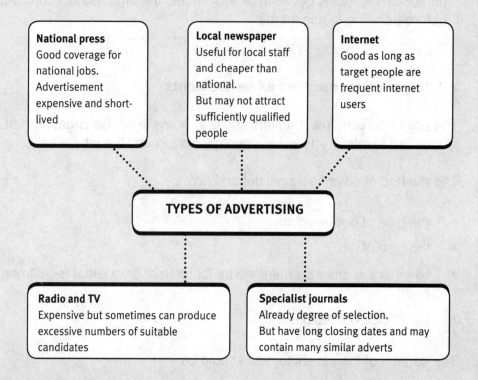

National press
Good coverage for national jobs. Advertisement expensive and short-lived

Local newspaper
Useful for local staff and cheaper than national.
But may not attract sufficiently qualified people

Internet
Good as long as target people are frequent internet users

TYPES OF ADVERTISING

Radio and TV
Expensive but sometimes can produce excessive numbers of suitable candidates

Specialist journals
Already degree of selection.
But have long closing dates and may contain many similar adverts

2.9 Sorting candidates

Methods of selection generally start with the shortlisting of applicants. The potential candidates then face a variety of other methods used in the selection process. These include:

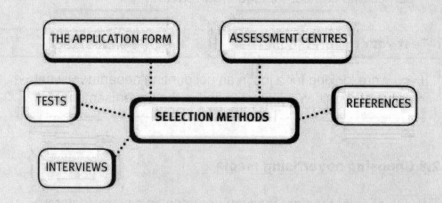

THE APPLICATION FORM

ASSESSMENT CENTRES

TESTS

SELECTION METHODS

REFERENCES

INTERVIEWS

These are discussed in more detail below.

Test your understanding 7

Why is there a need for a planned and systematic approach to recruitment and selection?

3 Selection methods

3.1 Application forms

Application forms are used to obtain relevant information about the applicant and allow for comparison with the person specification of the job. They should also give the applicants some ability to express themselves beyond the limited factual remit of the form. Their usefulness includes:

- eliminating unsatisfactory candidates
- saving interview time
- forming initial personal record for employee.

3.2 Selection interviews

Interviews are by far the most widely used selection technique. Their purpose is to:

- find the best person for the job
- ensure the candidate understands what the job is and what the career prospects are
- make the candidate feel that they have been given fair treatment in the interview.

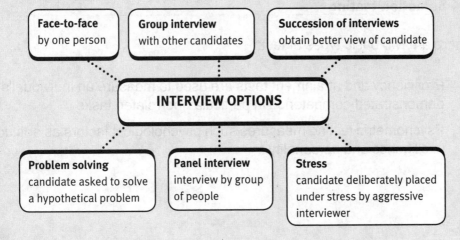

Face-to-face by one person

Group interview with other candidates

Succession of interviews obtain better view of candidate

INTERVIEW OPTIONS

Problem solving candidate asked to solve a hypothetical problem

Panel interview interview by group of people

Stress candidate deliberately placed under stress by aggressive interviewer

3.3 Interview technique

Advantages of the interview technique	Disadvantages of the interview technique
• places candidate at ease • highly interactive, allowing flexible question and answers • opportunities to use non-verbal communication • opportunities to assess appearance, interpersonal and communication skills • opportunities to evaluate rapport between the candidate and the potential colleagues/bosses.	• too brief to 'get to know' candidates • interview is an artificial situation • halo effect from initial impression • qualitative factors such as motivation, honesty or integrity are difficult to assess • prejudice – stereotyping groups of people • lack of interviewer preparation, skill, training and practice • subjectivity and bias.

Test your understanding 8

The validity of a face-to-face interview as a means of gauging a person's ability, character and ambition is regularly challenged. Briefly outline the main shortcomings of the interview technique.

3.4 Selection testing

There are two basic types of test:

- Proficiency and attainment tests are used to measure an individual's demonstrated competence in particular job-related tasks.

- Psychometric testing measures such psychological factors as aptitude, intelligence and personality.

Testing is often used to supplement interviews. The range includes:

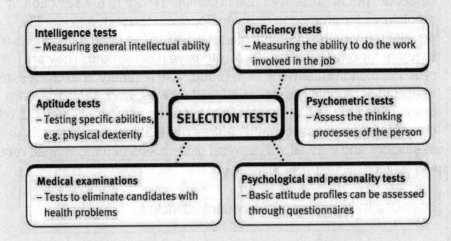

3.5 Assessment centre

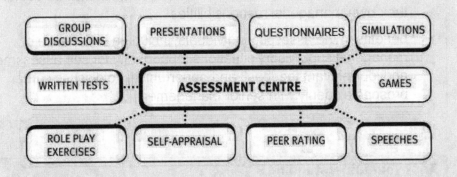

Trained assessors observe and evaluate individuals through a selection of pre-programmed exercises or trials.

Typical criteria used for assessment during the process are:

• planning and leadership	• communication
• analytical skills and problem solving	• assertiveness
• decision-making ability	• energy
• sensitivity and creativity	• initiative
• social skills.	• stress tolerance.

Expandable text

The assessment centre is really a combination of many forms of selection, but at present its use is confined more to the selection of employees for promotion or as an appraisal technique to identify development needs. Groups of around six to ten candidates are brought together for one to three days of intensive assessment. They are presented, individually and as a group, with a variety of exercises, tests of ability, personality assessments, interviews, work samples, team problem solving and written tasks. As well as being multi-method, other characteristics of assessment centres are that they use several assessors and they assess several dimensions of performance required in the higher-level positions.

The advantages of assessment centres include:

- a high degree of acceptability and user confidence

- avoidance of a single-assessor bias

- reliability in predicting potential success (if the system is well conducted)

- the development of skills in the assessors, which may be useful in their own managerial responsibilities

- benefits to the assessed individuals, including experience of managerial/supervisory situations, opportunity for self-assessment and job-relevant feedback and opportunities to discuss career prospects openly with senior management.

Test your understanding 9

Why are assessment centres part of a competency-based selection process used by many major employers when recruiting staff for their graduate training scheme?

3.6 Limitations of selection testing

Testing has its limitations:

- There is not always a direct relationship between ability in the test and ability in the job.

- They are subject to coaching and practice effects.

- The interpretation of test results is a skilled task, for which training and experience is essential.

- It is highly subjective (particularly in the case of personality tests).

- It is difficult to exclude bias from tests.

- A test measuring arithmetical ability would need to be constantly revised or its content might become known to later applicants.

- Personality tests can often give misleading results because applicants seem able to guess which answers will be looked at most favourably.

> **Test your understanding 10**
>
> List the advantages and limitations of selection testing.

3.7 References

The purpose of references is to confirm facts about the employee and increase the degree of confidence felt about information given during interviews and from application forms and CVs.

References should contain two types of information:

- Straightforward factual information. This confirms the nature of the applicant's previous job(s), period of employment, pay, and circumstances of leaving.

- Opinions about the applicant's personality and other attributes.

A standard form to be completed by the referee might pose a set of simple questions about:

- job title
- main duties and responsibilities
- period of employment
- pay/salary
- attendance record.

3.8 Problems with references

Main problem – lack of criticism especially where referee is a friend of the candidate.

Opinions should obviously be treated with some caution. Allowances should be made for:

- prejudice (favourable or unfavourable)
- charity (withholding detrimental remarks)
- fear of being actionable for libel (although references are privileged, as long as they are factually correct and devoid of malice).

4 Responsibility for staffing

4.1 Who is involved in recruitment and selection?

Expandable text

Most managers are likely to be involved in the recruitment and selection of staff, although it is a central part of human resource management and a personnel function.

- Senior managers/directors will be responsible for identifying the overall needs of the organisation – human resources planning – and involved in recruiting people – from within or outside the organisation – for senior positions.

- The full extent of the involvement of the HR (personnel) department will vary according to the circumstances of the organisation.

- In many cases the recruit's prospective boss – the line manager will be involved in the recruitment. In a small business he/she might have sole responsibility.

- For some organisations, help from recruitment consultants or agencies is sought.

Test your understanding 11

What might happen if the organisation failed to keep internal applications for vacancies a secret from the applicant's line manager?

4.2 Roles and responsibilities

The contribution of those involved in the recruitment and selection process is outlined below:

Senior managers/directors
- clarifying corporate objectives
- designing an effective structure
- providing a system for HR planning

Line managers in large companies
- requesting more human resources
- advising on requirements
- having a final say on the selection

ROLES AND RESPONSIBILITIES

HR department
- assessing needs for staff
- maintaining records of employees
- advertising for new employees
- designing application forms
- ensuring compliance with legislation
- liaising with recruitment consultants
- interviewing and selection testing

Recruitment consultants
- analysing the demands of the job
- advising on or helping with job analysis
- designing job advertisements
- screening applications
- helping with short-listing for interview
- offering a list of suitable candidates
- advising on interview procedures

Test your understanding 12

An organisation is undertaking a programme of recruitment, and the human resources department has decided that it may be appropriate to use recruitment consultants.

Describe any five tasks that recruitment consultants would undertake on behalf of the organisation.

5 Equal opportunities and the management of diversity

5.1 What is diversity?

People are not alike. Everyone is different. The concept of diversity embodies the belief that people should be valued for their difference and variety.

Diversity can be defined as recognising, appreciating, valuing, and utilising the unique talents and contributions of all individuals regardless of age, career experience, colour, communication style, culture, disability, educational level or background, employee status, ethnicity, family status, function, gender, language, management style, marital status, national origin, organisational level, parental status, physical appearance, race, regional origin, religion, sexual orientation, thinking style, speed of learning and comprehension, etc.

5.2 The benefits of a diverse workforce

Diversity is perceived to enrich an organisation's human capital. Besides their ability to do the job a diverse workforce brings additional benefits including:

- increased competitive advantage.

- improved effectiveness and efficiency by maximising the human resource potential

- increased creativity and innovation

- broader range of skills

- better customer relations and service to diverse customers

- ability to recruit best talent from entire labour pool

- improved working relationships in an atmosphere of inclusion.

Test your understanding 13

What additional benefits might organisations experience by including disabled people in their workforce?

5.3 Representative workforce

An organisation's workforce should be 'representative' of the composition of the operational environment.

- Some organisations set themselves goals on the representation of certain groups to address the problem of under-representation.

- The HR plan is a useful device to help the organisation recruit a diverse workforce and be representative of the external community.

- Included in the plan are numerical goals with time frames for achievement and specific activities to achieve them, with the aims of improving recruitment, training and promotion of under-represented groups. Non-numerical goals are activities associated with actions to improve access to facilities, targeted recruitment and advertising, or modification of employment policies and procedures.

- The monitoring activity is a crucial component of the planning cycle. It is here that an employer can determine whether goals are being attained and problems resolved.

Monitoring implies the need to be proactive in managing the needs of a diverse workforce in areas such as:

- tolerance of individual differences
- communicating effectively with (and motivating) ethnically diverse work forces
- managing workers with increasingly diverse family structures and responsibilities
- managing the adjustments to be made by an increasingly aged work force
- managing increasingly diverse career aspirations/patterns and ways of organising working life (including flexible working)
- confronting issues of literacy, numeracy and differences in qualifications in an international work force.

Expandable text

In general, managers expect employees to work with others and be willing to obey, whilst at the same time expecting to see evidence of personality, creativity and independence. Selecting employees that conform to the goals of the enterprise, yet offer valuable individuality, is the key to an organisation's health and effectiveness.

As the workforce becomes more diverse in terms of gender, race, culture, age, religion, disability, sexual orientation and ethnicity, organisations need to create cultures in which all employees can develop their potential and flourish. Not only is this the 'right' thing to do, but also how an organisation manages diversity will have a measurable impact on productivity, retention and its profitability.

From the employer's point of view, an organisation's work force is representative when it reflects or exceeds the demographic composition of the external work force. A representative work force reflects or exceeds the current proportions of women, visible minorities and persons with disabilities in each occupation as are known to be available in the external work force and from which the employer may reasonably be expected to draw.

A representative work force is a good indication that an employer is not limiting access to the skills and talents of workers by discriminating on the basis of sex, race, colour or disability. A non-representative work force signals the need for evaluation and action, so that whatever is blocking or discouraging certain groups from employment and advancement may be corrected.

Test your understanding 14

How can management achieve a fair representation of designated groups in an organisation?

5.4 Diversity assessment

A diversity assessment is a formal review of the structure of the work force and its management, to check whether or not there is an appropriate mixture of people from different backgrounds and with different cultural and religious views.

Illustration 1 – Equal opportunities and the management of

For example, a diversity assessment might find that there are very few women or very few men from a particular racial or religious background in senior management positions. Measures for correcting this imbalance can then be considered – for example by asking why the imbalance has arisen and then taking steps to deal with the problem.

It is a structured process to gather information about the experience of current employees and, if desired, former employees using:

- focus groups of current employees
- personal interviews with senior managers
- telephone interviews of employees who have left the organisation.

A diversity assessment provides information about what helps and hinders:

- the creation of an inclusive work environment where all employees can flourish
- career advancement
- teamwork

- high morale, commitment and productivity
- retention of diverse employees
- recruitment and hiring of diverse individuals.

Test your understanding 15

What is a representative workforce?

5.5 Equal opportunities

'Equal opportunities' is a generic term describing the belief that there should be an equal chance for all workers to apply and be selected for jobs, to be trained and promoted in employment and to have that employment terminated fairly.

- Employers should only discriminate according to ability, experience and potential.
- All employment decisions should be based solely on a person's ability to do the job in question; no consideration should be taken of a person's sex, age, racial origin, disability or marital status.

Two main reasons for adopting an equal opportunities policy:

- It is morally wrong to treat parts of the population as inferior or inadequate.
- Organisations do not benefit from excluding any potential source of talent.

Test your understanding 16

It is very noticeable in some organisations that there is opposition by employers to recruit older staff. What arguments might they put forward for adopting such a policy?

- Equal opportunities has been promoted as a key component of good management as well as being legally required, socially desirable and morally right.
- Managing diversity offers an opportunity for organisations to develop a workforce to meet their business goals and to improve approaches to customer care.

The main differences between diversity and equal opportunities are:

Diversity	Equal opportunities
• voluntary	• government initiated
• productivity driven	• legally driven
• qualitative	• quantitative
• opportunity-focused	• problem-focused
• inclusive	• targeted
• proactive.	• reactive.

Test your understanding 17

What practices might an organisation with anti-discrimination policies apply to the recruitment and selection process?

5.6 The legal position

While employment legislation can vary considerably from country to country, it typically refers to the following:

Area	Typical Terms
Rights	Gives employees certain rights, such as: • a right not to be unfairly dismissed • a right to a redundancy payment if made redundant and • a right to a minimum period of notice to terminate the contract.

Contracts	Requires an employer to provide employees with a written statement of certain particulars of their employment. The statement typically includes details of: • pay • job title • place of work • length of notice and • details of disciplinary or grievance procedures.
Working hours	Limits the hours of work to an average of 48 a week, say. It also gives the right to: • four weeks paid leave a year and • one day off each week, say.
Rights of parents	Gives parents of children under five the right to request flexible working arrangements. Gives rights for maternity and paternity leave.

Legislation relating to discrimination typically includes the following:

Legislation	Typical terms
Pay	Implies an equality clause into all contracts of employment if workers of the opposite sex do the same job or a different job of equal value. Deals not only with pay, but other terms, e.g. holiday and sick leave.
Sex Discrimination	Discrimination in employment affairs because of marital status or sex is illegal. This applies especially to the selection process as it offers protection to both sexes against unfair treatment on appointment.

Racial Discrimination	Prohibits discrimination on grounds of: • race • nationality or • colour unless there is a genuine occupational qualification, e.g. for reasons of authenticity.
Disability Discrimination	Prohibits discrimination on the grounds of disability.

Illustration 2 – How the law protects employees

The question of whether two jobs are of equal value involves a weighing and balancing between the features of the claimant's and comparator's jobs. This is evaluated by reference to:

- skill and knowledge demands
- responsibility demands
- planning & decision making demands
- physical demands
- environmental demands.

It thus allows comparisons between quite different types of jobs. Examples of claims between very different jobs, which have been successful at tribunal or settled in favour of the claimant(s) include:

- cook – shipboard painter
- nursing home sewing room assistant – plumber
- canteen workers = surface mineworkers – clerical staff.

Chapter summary

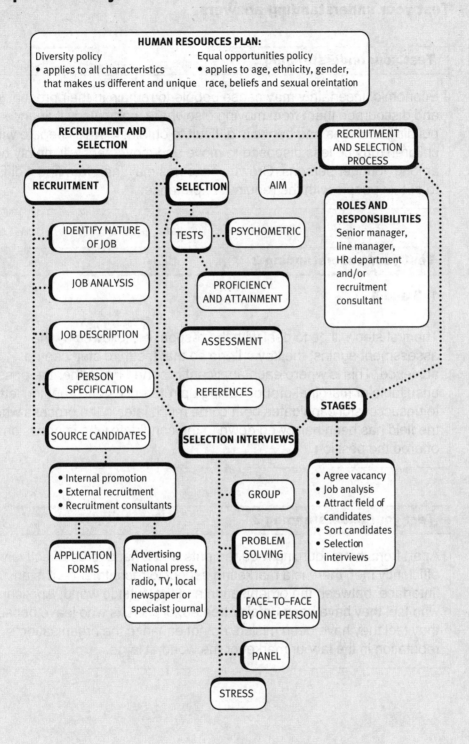

HUMAN RESOURCES PLAN:

Diversity policy
- applies to all characteristics that makes us different and unique

Equal opportunities policy
- applies to age, ethnicity, gender, race, beliefs and sexual oreintation

RECRUITMENT AND SELECTION

RECRUITMENT AND SELECTION PROCESS

RECRUITMENT

SELECTION

AIM

ROLES AND RESPONSIBILITIES
Senior manager, line manager, HR department and/or recruitment consultant

IDENTIFY NATURE OF JOB

TESTS

PSYCHOMETRIC

JOB ANALYSIS

PROFICIENCY AND ATTAINMENT

JOB DESCRIPTION

ASSESSMENT

PERSON SPECIFICATION

REFERENCES

STAGES

SOURCE CANDIDATES

SELECTION INTERVIEWS

- Internal promotion
- External recruitment
- Recruitment consultants

GROUP

- Agree vacancy
- Job analysis
- Attract field of candidates
- Sort candidates
- Selection interviews

PROBLEM SOLVING

APPLICATION FORMS

Advertising National press, radio, TV, local newspaper or speciaist journal

FACE–TO–FACE BY ONE PERSON

PANEL

STRESS

Test your understanding answers

Test your understanding 1

Economic uncertainty may cause people to remain in their present job and discourage them from moving elsewhere, particularly if finance from building societies and banks is difficult to obtain. Married people with children may be less disposed to move and movement will mainly be among younger persons. Growth industries may therefore find it difficult to obtain people with the required experience.

Test your understanding 2

1, 3 and 4

The first step will be to deal with the responses, followed by the assessment against the key criteria so that the third step can be achieved. This is where each applicant is sorted into either the possible, unsuitable or marginal group. Taking up references and sending letters to unsuccessful candidates both come much later in the process when the field has been narrowed down to the candidate who is provisionally offered the position.

Test your understanding 3

Apart from the resourcing requirements which need to be effectively and efficiently met, there is a marketing aspect to recruitment – it is an 'interface' between the organisation and the outside world. Applicants who feel they have been unfairly treated, or recruits who leave because they feel they have been misled, do not enhance the organisation's reputation in the labour market or the world at large.

Test your understanding 4

The costs of high staff turnover can be substantial. They include:

- Termination costs – the costs associated with severance packages, administrative functions related to the termination, etc.

- Replacement costs – the costs associated with advertising, interviewing candidates, pre-employment administrative expenses, travel/moving costs, etc.

- Vacancy costs – the costs associated with overtime expenses, temporary help, etc.

- Learning curve costs – the costs associated with training staff, the new recruit's lack of productivity for the first 6-12 months, etc.

- Intangible costs – costs such as the impact to staff morale, customer service disruption, overwork/absenteeism among remaining employees, and the loss of organisational knowledge

So not only are there the direct financial costs of replacing staff but also other repercussions such as the potential loss of key skills, knowledge and experience, disruption to operations and the negative effect on workforce morale. In addition, high turnover represents a considerable burden both on HR and line managers as they are constantly recruiting and training new staff.

Test your understanding 5

A company considering the use of recruitment consultants should include the following six factors in its decision:

- the cost effectiveness of the use of outside consultants bearing in mind the level of the vacancy and the consultant's fee

- any internal problems such as lack of impartiality which may make the use of an outside consultant necessary

- any problems which are likely to arise with internal staff if an outside consultant is used for the work

- the availability of in-house expertise and its likely effectiveness

- the availability of a consultant with adequate experience of any specialised aspects of the recruitment problem

- the need to develop its own expertise in recruitment, which may override the immediate benefits arising from the use of a consultant for this specific vacancy.

Test your understanding 6

You would expect it to include information about:

- the organisation: its main business and location, at least
- the job: title, main duties and responsibilities, and special features
- conditions: special factors affecting the job
- qualifications and experience (required, and preferred); other attributes, aptitudes and/or knowledge required
- rewards: salary, benefits, opportunities for training, career development, and so on
- application process: how to apply, to whom, and by what date.

Test your understanding 7

A planned and systematic approach will address the 'need to know' questions.

Managers need to know about the job to be filled – is it really necessary or can it be covered adequately by re-allocating or re-organising other jobs? If it is necessary what does it entail in terms of duties and responsibilities?

They also need to know what qualities and attributes a person would need to perform the job effectively. Once this is decided they need to know the best way to attract a range of applicants and then how to assess their suitability for the job. This means knowing about the best sources of labour and methods of recruitment and planning the most appropriate methods of selection.

KAPLAN PUBLISHING

Test your understanding 8

The main shortcomings of the interview technique stem from faults on the part of the interviewer. Typical faults are:

- 'cloning' – a tendency by an interviewer to seek to appoint a similar type of person on every occasion

- forming an initial impression in the first stages of the interview and then being coloured by that impression for the remainder of the interview ('halo or horns effect')

- failing to distinguish between verbal skills, education and natural intelligence – frequently, applicants who can express their ideas clearly and persuasively are automatically deemed to be intelligent; this may not be the case

- prejudice where an interviewer may inherently believe that women, or people of a certain age group, or candidates who wear brown shoes to an interview are unsuitable for a certain type of position

- lack of preparation – far too often, an interviewer will not analyse the job profile and the application form in advance. Thus many important questions that could yield important insights are unasked, or phrased in a clumsy manner

- not enough time allowed after the interview to evaluate the facts and to put them together with evidence from other sources, e.g. application forms, tests, etc.

Test your understanding 9

The graduate training schemes that some major employers offer are intended as a fast track to senior management and assessment centres are designed to evaluate whether the candidate possesses the core competencies that are needed to be successful at a senior level in the business. The idea is that the job description and person specification as traditionally written do not illustrate the actual skills (mental competencies) required in the job. Also, if there is mass recruitment, or recruitment of people without previous work experience (e.g. graduates, police cadets, nurses) there is little to go on. Exercises might include technical tests (of dexterity or problem identification), aptitude tests (of mechanical ability, spatial awareness, computer literacy), psychometric tests (intelligence, verbal/mathematical reasoning, personality) in-tray exercises, group discussions, presentations, etc. They are intended to allow selectors to gain an insight into personal qualities, such as management skills, leadership skills and team membership suitability.

Test your understanding 10

The advantages of selection testing include that it is:

- standardised
- objective
- accurate when well validated and assessed by qualified examiners
- precise
- generally can be administered in groups.

The limitations of testing include that:

- it measures what candidates can do rather than will do
- it is time consuming if many attributes must be assessed
- what is being measured is not always apparent to candidates
- it may provide more precision than is usually necessary
- it can frustrate the candidates.

Test your understanding 11

If the organisation failed to keep internal applications for vacancies a secret from the applicant's line manager, it could result in the line manager blocking attempts by staff to move into another job, especially if it is a post outside their department. Alternatively, and worse, such employees may be 'blacklisted' by their line manager, who may see their request to move jobs as a personal slight against them.

Test your understanding 12

Choose any five of the following tasks undertaken by recruitment consultants:

- understand the practices, procedures and relevance of job descriptions, person specifications and selection criteria, help in their construction and advise on their uses

- advise on the appropriateness of recruitment criteria and develop measures by which applicant might be assessed

- design the vacancy advertisements, ensuring that the advertisement is properly constructed and contains the correct information so as to attract interest from appropriate candidates

- assist with or undertake the screening of applications following the advertisements, ensuring that the procedure for application has been followed

- assist with or undertake the screening of applicants, ensuring that unsuitable applicants are removed and suitable applicants noted

- assist management by listing potential candidates and supporting the list with brief personal illustrations, notes and, if required, recommendations

- ensure that advice is given on the conduct and procedures of the interview, the structure of the interviewing panel and ensure that all candidates provide satisfactory information

- advise on the appropriateness or otherwise of the means of testing applicants, or undertake other screening such as psychometric tests as required by management

- select the team to undertake the interviews, ensuring that the team consists of individuals with appropriate skills and who have an interest in and knowledge of, the vacancy

- alternatively, the consultants themselves might conduct the interview and selection process, but only upon the direct instruction of the management within definite prescribed guidelines.

Test your understanding 13

Additional benefits might include:

- diverse perspectives – disabled people have considerable life experience, solving challenging problems on a regular basis. Creative problem-solving skills can help companies find new solutions and lead to more satisfied customers

- larger pool of potential employees – disabled people make up a large percentage of the working-age population in Britain. By including them in their workforce companies will not be missing out on a large pool of talent, skills and expertise

- representative workforce – if a company's workforce mirrors the diversity of its operational environment, companies will be more representative of their customers and potential customers. A diverse workforce enables companies to connect with all sectors of the community increasing their customer base and creating a positive image of the company

- universal access – employing disabled people promotes universal access, which in turn benefits everyone. For example, automatic doors also are not only accessible to disabled people but also improve access for other employees and customers with heavy loads, or children, in tow. Larger print, larger computer monitors and improved lighting reduce eyestrain. Ergonomic chairs and workstations cut down on health complaints, and flexible work arrangements increase the job satisfaction of all employees.

Test your understanding 14

HR plans are drawn up to help achieve a fair representation of designated groups in an organisation. They must contain:

- numerical goals
- activities to achieve the goals
- a monitoring and evaluation procedure to follow the implementation.

Numerical goals must be realistic, related to the workforce analysis and project opportunities for hiring, training and promotion.

Non-numerical goals are activities associated with creating a supportive environment.

Test your understanding 15

An organisation's workforce is representative when it reflects or exceeds the demographic composition of the external workforce. Some organisations set themselves goals on the representation of certain groups, e.g. there is an under-representation of certain ethnic groups within the police force. To address this type of problem, a diversity assessment will show how an organisation's systems and culture may provide supports or may act as barriers to diversity.

Test your understanding 16

They may use the following excuses:

* the organisation has a 'young' culture or image

* the older worker is less skilled or has less experience with new technology or IT-based work

* older workers are prone to sickness more than younger employees

* age-based pay systems mean paying more for older staff (even though most organisations operate performance-based pay systems)

* the organisation has a young customer base that older staff would not relate to

* the payback period on training will be too short.

Test your understanding 17

An organisation with anti-discrimination policies might apply some of the following practices:

* recruitment – job advertisements should not discriminate on the grounds of sex, e.g. it would be appropriate to advertise a vacancy for a 'sales person' rather than for a 'salesman'

* selection – interviewers at selection interviews should avoid questions such as: 'Do you intend to get married and have children soon' (sex discrimination), or 'Are you able to work on religious holidays' (discrimination on the grounds of religious belief)

* selection, training and promotion – applying policies based strictly on the ability, experience and potential of employees

* pay – applying an equal pay policy.

Review and appraisal of individual performance

Chapter learning objectives

Upon completion of this chapter you will be able to:

- explain the purpose of performance appraisal

- know what criteria could be used to assess staff performance

- know what is meant by performance appraisal

- describe the objectives of performance appraisal from the point of view of the individual and the organisation

- identify and explain the stages in performance appraisal

- identify the skills needed to carry out the appraisal effectively

- explain the benefits of effective appraisal for the organisation and the individual

- describe the barriers to effective appraisal

- outline the ways in which those barriers could be overcome

- know what methods could be used to evaluate the effectiveness of performance appraisal.

1 Performance appraisal

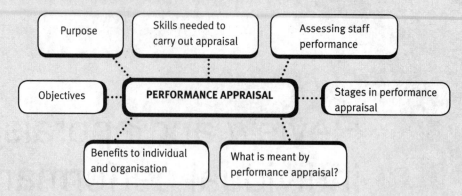

Performance appraisal may be defined as 'the regular and systematic review of performance and the assessment of potential with the aim of producing action programmes to develop both work and individuals'.

1.1 Purpose of performance appraisal

Performance appraisal aims to improve the efficiency of the organisation by ensuring that the individual employees are performing to the best of their ability and developing their potential for improvement.

1.2 Criteria to assess staff performance

An effective appraisal system can be used to assess attitudes, behaviour and performance but must have a balance of both measures of results and measures of activities. They may be a combination of:

- quantitative measures using some form of rating scale

- qualitative measures involving an unstructured narrative report on specific factors and overall levels of behaviour and work performance.

A key issue in performance appraisal is determining what constitute valid criteria or measures of effective performance. The problem is made more difficult because almost all jobs have many dimensions so that performance appraisal must employ multiple criteria or measures of effectiveness in order to accurately reflect the actual performance of the employee.

Appraisal criteria may include the following:

Volume of work produced:	Knowledge of work:	Quality of work:	Management skills:	Personal qualities:
• within time period • evidence of work planning • personal time management • effectiveness of work under pressure	• gained through experience • gained through training courses • gained prior to employment	• level of analytical ability • level of technical knowledge accuracy • judgement exercised • cost effectiveness	• communication skills • motivation skills • training and development skills • delegation skills	• decisionmaking capabilities • flexibility • adaptability • assertiveness • team involvement • motivation • commitment to organisational goals

Beer et al. (1984) suggest four criteria for assessing performance:

- **high commitment** – the workforce is motivated and understanding, and are willing to interact with management about changes within the organisation. Improved commitment may lead to more loyalty and better performance for the business. It can also benefit the individual through enhanced self-worth, dignity, psychological involvement, and identity

- **high competence** – the capacity of employees to learn new tasks and roles if the circumstances require it and the organisation's ability to attract, keep, or develop employees who have valuable skills and knowledge

- **cost effectiveness** – can be evaluated in terms of wages, benefits, turnover, absenteeism, strikes, etc.

- **higher congruence** – the internal organisation, the reward system, and the 'input, throughput, and output' of personnel, which need to be structured in the interests of all stakeholders.

Illustration 1 – Criteria to assess staff performance

A key issue that has to do with the criteria of effectiveness is the question of whether they should focus on the activities (tasks) of the job-holder or the results (objectives) achieved. For example, a salesperson might be assessed in terms of activities, i.e. number of cold calls or speed of dealing with complaints or in terms of results, e.g. total sales volume or number of new customers. Measures of results do not reflect how those outcomes were achieved.

There are advantages and disadvantages of using either results or activities as criteria. Appraisal based on results has the advantage of encouraging and rewarding the outcomes desired by the organisation. However, it has the disadvantage that it might encourage people to break rules or go against company policy to achieve what is desired. It may lead to frustration if the failure to achieve results is due to factors beyond the control of the individual. Assessment in terms of results does not generate information about how the person is doing the job and hence has limited value in suggesting ways of improving performance.

A major advantage of appraising in terms of activities is that it helps generate information that can help in the training and development of poor performers. However, it may only encourage people to concentrate on their activities at the expense of results achieved. This can lead to excessive bureaucratic emphasis on the means and procedures employed rather than on the accomplishments and results. There are then problems in incorporating the successful nonconformist into the appraisal system.

Test your understanding 1

Although it is impossible to identify any universal measures of performance that are applicable to all jobs, it is possible to specify a number of characteristics that a criterion of job performance should possess if it is to be useful for performance appraisal. In terms of your quality of work, if you were being assessed on your accuracy, what characteristics would you expect the measurement criterion to have?

1.3 What is meant by performance appraisal?

An appraisal is a process by which the progress, performance, results and sometimes personality of an employee are reviewed and assessed by his or her immediate superior.

For this to happen, employees must know not only what is expected of them, but also the reason for doing the job the way they do it, and how good/bad they are at their work. Each person will be appraised individually on:

- the progress they have been making in their job
- their strengths and weaknesses
- their future needs as regards training and development
- their potential for promotion.

The other side of this is that management are fully aware of what the staff are supposed to be doing and how they are actually doing it. This can be achieved if performance criteria are established jointly, appropriate on-the-job behaviour is mutually understood and the review is a continual process focused on growth and development. The organisation's appraisal scheme is inextricably linked to its control structure:

- it clarifies specific jobs relating them to the objectives of the organisation
- it develops realistic and appropriate performance standards
- it assesses competencies
- it uses feedback and reward to improve performance
- it links performance to organisational goals.

It aims to make the behaviour of employees predictable and, hence, controllable.

The diagram below shows performance management as a control system.

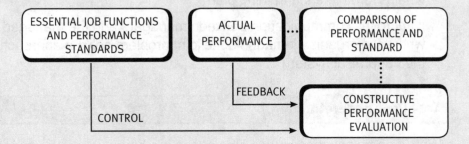

1.4 The objectives of appraisals

The objectives of an appraisal from the individual's point of view include the following:

- it compares the individual's performance against a set and established standard
- it identifies work of particular merit done during the review period
- it provides a basis for remuneration
- it establishes what the individual has to do regarding the objectives of the organisation
- it determines the future employment of the individual, e.g. to remain in the same job, be transferred, promoted or retired early

- it determines whether the individual is in a job where proper use is being made of his or her skills and talents

- it establishes key results which the individual needs to achieve in work within a set period of time

- it identifies training and development needs.

An appraisal system is used by the organisation to review and change, to inform and monitor and to examine and evaluate employees.

The objectives from the organisation's point of view include the following:

- it monitors human resource selection processes against results

- it identifies candidates for promotion, early retirement, etc.

- it helps to identify and provide a record of any special difficulties/hazards surrounding the job, perhaps not previously realised

- it identifies areas for improvement

- it provides a basis for human resource planning

- it helps formulate the training plan

- it improves communication between managers and the managed where the organisation adopts the joint problem-solving approach in their appraisal system

Test your understanding 2

Why is appraisal necessary if employees are being given day-to-day feedback on their performance?

2 The process of performance appraisal

2.1 The stages of performance appraisal

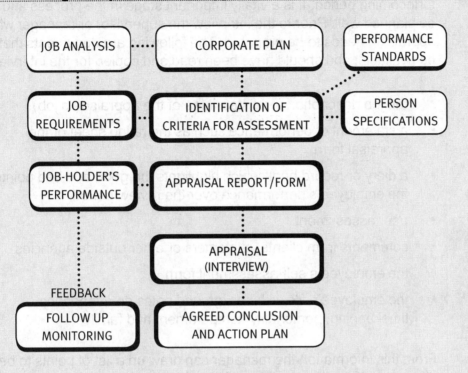

The process of performance appraisal usually entails:

- identifying the criteria for assessment – perhaps based on job analysis, job requirements, performance standards and person specification

- assessing competence

- manager preparing an appraisal report – sometimes both appraiser and appraisee prepare a report and they are then compared. Assessments must be related to meaningful performance criteria and a common standard so that comparisons can be made between individuals

- manager interviewing the job-holder for an exchange of views about the appraisal report

- identifying and agreeing future goals and targets for improvement, solutions to problems

- manager's own superior reviewing the assessment to establish the fairness of the procedure

- agreeing, preparing and implementing action points, plans to achieve improvements, e.g. training needs

- following up – giving the results of the appraisal, monitoring the progress of the action plan, carrying out agreed actions on training, promotion and so on and giving regular feedback.

Expandable text

The appraisal interview is the point at which the employee and manager meet formally to discuss performance and agree targets for the forthcoming period. It is a vitally important stage in the process and must be planned well. Prior to the interview the supervisor or manager who is appraising needs to be prepared. The following are documents that may be available, and should have been read and copied for the interview:

- the job description (or a clear idea of the appraisee's job)
- a statement of performance such as the rating sheet or the appraisal form
- a diary or record book which highlights the good and bad points of the employee's performance over the review period
- peer assessment
- comments from clients, customers or other outside agencies
- the employee's self-assessment form
- the employee's file with background notes on attendance, timekeeping, personality, temperament and family.

From this information the manager can draw up a list of points to be discussed during the interview. Other documentation includes the appraisal form for both parties to complete at interview, including an assessment of past performance from the last appraisal, a set of objectives for the forthcoming review period, a development and action plan and a section for signatures and comments.

Once you have done your homework and have the information you need to hand, there are a few points to bear in mind about appraisal interviews:

The environment and atmosphere are important. Planning too many interviews in one day is not a good idea, nor is holding them at an inconvenient time. The interviewee should not be intimidated by the physical setting of the interview; sitting on a huge chair behind a large desk may be appropriate for a disciplinary interview but is not appropriate for an appraisal interview. Constant interruptions during the interview should be avoided because it is discourteous, disruptive and shows a lack of professionalism.

Your approach should be sketched out, with the main points you wish to make, prior to the interview. It also helps if the interviewee has an understanding of what is going to happen. A highly-structured interview plan with a rigid order of items goes against the spirit of the more freewheeling joint appraisal/problem-solving interview. Note taking during the interview should only happen if the appraisee has agreed.

Conducting the interview

The first steps are to put the employee at ease, explain the purpose of the interview and then discuss the employee's progress. During the discussion there are many social communicating skills at play. The following list of skills is a guide of 'must do's' while conducting the interview:

- Ask open questions requiring more than a yes or no answer.
- Ask closed questions only when clarification is needed.
- Allow time for the appraisee to ask questions.
- Refrain from asking multiple or confusing questions.
- Encourage conversation with body language and appropriate cues.
- Periodically summarise, reflect and check your understanding.
- Build upon answers.
- Refrain from talking too much.
- Handle difficult or sensitive areas carefully.
- Be tolerant of pauses and silences.
- Listen carefully, making sure that the interviewee knows you are listening.
- Keep the conversation from wandering off into irrelevant areas.

The present approach in staff appraisals is to encourage the manager to act as a counsellor rather than a judge or a critic. The emphasis is on helping the subordinate to overcome any shortcomings and become more effective in the future. This requires open appraisals which are frequently held, often in an informal atmosphere, at pre-set dates. Much of the success or failure of such schemes is determined by the face-to-face attitude generated by the manager at the counselling sessions.

At the end of the interview, the manager should sum up the whole discussion, and restate any decisions, commitments, agreements or recommendations that have been made. This ensures that there is a full understanding about the future actions or plans of both parties. Agree on alternative courses of action in case the first is not possible. Note that the action plan should include:

- training and development needs
- recommended action along with the key dates by which the action is to take place
- the resources needed for support.

After the interview the manager or supervisor should inform the appraisee of the results of the appraisal and write up on the following:

- agreed action plans on training, promotion, etc.
- the shortcomings and weaknesses that were discussed and the results
- any help or assistance the employee needs and what was promised at the interview.

The follow-up procedures will include taking the steps to help the employee attain the agreed objectives by:

- providing feedback
- training
- rescheduling work
- altering work methods
- upgrading equipment.

Illustration 2 – The process of performance appraisal

Whichever type of appraisal method is used the criteria must be clearly stated, understood and agreed by the subordinate. Subordinates must also be clear about the objectives and results required.

While many people view the performance appraisal process as beginning after six or 12 months of employment and view it as a review of how the employee has performed for the previous period, a successful performance management process begins during the hiring process. It continues as an ongoing cycle from recruitment, through selection, induction/orientation, and goal setting and on to performance appraisal and evaluation. This process occurs in three stages with the following components:

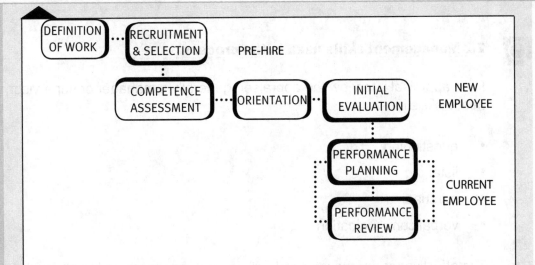

There are a few types of staff appraisal processes in use:

- Review and comparison – consists of the individual being assessed and analysed in terms of objectives, tasks, workflows and results achieved. These are then compared with previously agreed statements of required results and performance levels.

- Management by objectives – managers agree certain objectives with their subordinates and then review the results achieved. It is based on the idea that if subordinates know their objectives they are more likely to reach them.

- The task-centred method – relates to what the subordinate is doing and how they do it. It avoids the more formal approach to staff appraisal and adopts a continual assessment approach.

Test your understanding 3

What would happen without follow up?

2.2 Management skills used in the process

In an appraisal interview the appraiser, generally a manager or supervisor, needs skills in:

- questioning
- listening
- persuading
- verbal communication.

The effectiveness of the interview will depend very much on the skill of the superior conducting the interview.

- **'Tell and sell'** – the appraiser adopts the strategy of a salesperson, trying to persuade and convince the subordinate that the appraisal is fair and that they can and must change in certain ways, and that they should agree to the training, retraining or transfer plans being recommended. It is a one-way communication system.

- **'Tell and listen'** – the appraiser listens to the job-holder's perception of the job and their problems, expectations and aims and does not dominate the interview. Because it is important to listen to the subordinate and be prepared to change an evaluation in the light of new evidence, this method is likely to be more effective.

- **Joint 'problem solving'** – represents a shift in emphasis from the first two methods. Here, the appraiser uses many social skills to encourage the interviewee to do a self-assessment, admit their own problems and suggest solutions to them. The skills are of a counsellor using two-way face-to-face communication.

2.3 The benefits of appraisal

Effective appraisal is grounded in the belief that feedback on past performance influences future performance, and that the process of isolating and rewarding good performance is likely to repeat it.

Agreement on challenging but achievable targets for performance motivates employees by clarifying goals and setting the value of incentives offered.

Staff appraisal can have benefits for both the employer (the organisation) and the employee:

Benefits for the employer	Benefits for the employee
• It provides a formal system for assessing the performance and potential of employees, with a view to identifying candidates for promotion. • It provides a system for identifying ways of improving the competence of employees, in order to raise the general level of efficiency and effectiveness of the work force. • It is a valuable system for human resource planning, and ensuring that employees are ready for promotion, to fill management job vacancies that arise. • If it is well managed, communications can be improved between managers and staff and so improve working relationships.	• The employee gets feedback about performance at work, and an assessment of competence. • A formal appraisal system offers the employee an opportunity to discuss future prospects and ambitions. • An appraisal interview may be used as a basis for considering pay and rewards. • Appraisal can be used to identify and agree measures for further training and development, to improve the employee's competence.

Test your understanding 4

Are appraisals good for motivation?

2.4 The barriers to effective staff appraisal

There have been studies on the effects of appraisal, which show some negative effects, e.g.:

- criticism had a negative effect on goal achievement

- subordinates generally reacted defensively to criticism during appraisal interviews

- inferior performance resulted from defensive reactions to criticism

- repeated criticism had the worst effect on subsequent performance of individuals who had little self-confidence.

J Lockett suggests that appraisal barriers can be identified as follows:

Appraisal as confrontation	• Differing views regarding performance. • Feedback is subjective – the manager is biased, allowing personality differences to get in the way of actual performance. • Feedback is badly delivered. • Assessment is based on yesterday's performance not on the whole year. • Disagreement over prospects and solutions.
Appraisal as judgement	• Appraisal is seen as a one-sided process – the manager is judge, jury and counsel for the prosecution. • Appraisal is imposed.
Appraisal as chat	• Lack of will from either party. • An unproductive conversation. • No outcomes set.
Appraisal as bureaucracy	• A traditional ceremony. • No purpose or worth.
Appraisal as an annual event	• A traditional ceremony. • No purpose or worth.
Appraisal as unfinished business	• Frustration at limited appraisal time. • No belief that issues will be followed up.

Test your understanding 5

List six areas which can impact upon a successful appraisal system if not addressed.

2.5 Overcoming the barriers to effective appraisal

One of the barriers to effective appraisal was the view of employees that the annual appraisal was not treated as something important, and that nothing was done after an appraisal interview had finished.

- There must be a system of follow-up and feedback.

- There may be agreement between the interviewer and the employee in the appraisal interview about further training that the employee needs, or ways in which the employee can be developed. These agreements should be recorded as part of the official record of the appraisal interview.

- The action plan that has been agreed with the employee should be reported to senior management and the HR department.

- The interviewer is normally the manager of the employee. He or she should follow up the appraisal report and should arrange the training or development that has been agreed.

- At the next appraisal interview, the interviewer and the employee should discuss whether the agreed training or development was provided, and what has been its effect.

The appraisal system itself should be assessed and the claims made by **Lockett** will need to be addressed to ensure:

- **Relevance** – does the system have a useful purpose and is it relevant to the needs of both the organisation and the individual?

- **Fairness** – is there reasonable objectivity and standardisation of criteria throughout the organisation?

- **Serious intent** – is the management committed to the system or has it been thrust on them by the HR department? Do the appraisers have training in interviewing and assessment techniques? Is there a demonstrable link between performance and reward?

- **Co-operation** – is the appraisal a participative, problem-solving activity with the appraisee given time and encouragement to prepare for it to be able to make a constructive contribution? What type of conclusion emerges from the process?

- **Efficiency** – is it costly and difficult to administer and does it seem too time consuming compared with the value of its outcome?

Another way of ensuring effective appraisals is to apply the 4Fs:

- **Firm** – managers should be willing to discuss negative as well as favourable aspects of performance.

- **Factual** – subjective aspects should be avoided.

- **Fair** – all employees should be treated the same.

- **Frequent** – appraisals should be held on a regular basis rather than when a problem arises.

2.6 Evaluating the effectiveness of the appraisal system

Evaluating the appraisal scheme can involve the following:

- calculating the costs and benefits of the appraisal process

- investigating if there have been any improvements in performance by the individual and the organisation

- asking appraisers and appraisees their opinions on the process

- monitoring performance results

- watching take up of training and development opportunities

- checking succession and promotion processes/results

- reviewing other factors such as staff turnover – a figure that is too high or too low is an indication that something is wrong in an organisation. Also, the appraisal scheme ought to identify individuals who are ready for promotion and if many talented people leave on the grounds that there are no job opportunities then the overall development system may be at fault.

The process of assessment and staff appraisal should highlight some of the causes of dissatisfaction, find solutions and remedy them before the employee becomes disillusioned, looks for another job and resigns.

The causes of staff leaving fall into three categories:

- Discharge – as a result of an employee's unsuitability, disciplinary action or redundancy.

- Unavoidable – because of marriage, moving house, illness or death.

- Avoidable – due to pay, working conditions, relationships with work colleagues.

From records, the staff turnover can be calculated by dividing either the total separations (those leaving the organisation) or the total replacements by the average number in the workforce, and expressing the result as a percentage. Examination of this figure may highlight vital information, e.g. poor selection techniques or poor working conditions.

Test your understanding 6

Should a firm with 2% staff turnover be congratulated or shown the warning signal?

Chapter summary

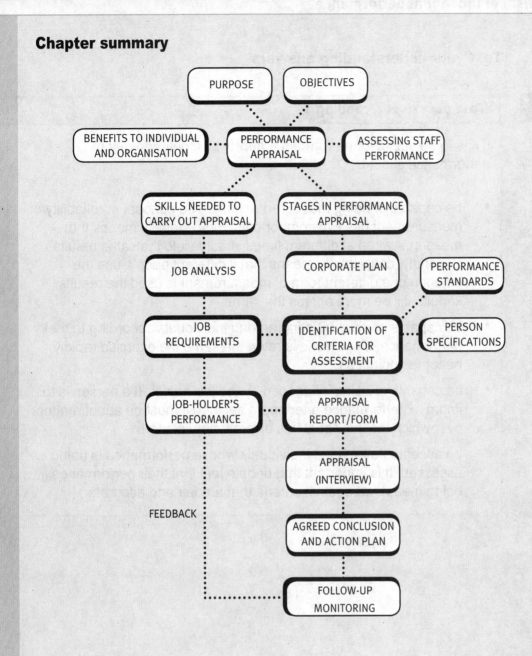

Test your understanding answers

Test your understanding 1

If it is to be useful for performance appraisal a criterion of job performance should:

- be capable of being measured reliably. The concept of reliability of measurement has two components. First, stability means that measures taken at different times should yield the same results. Secondly, consistency means that if different people use the criterion or a different form of measurement is used the results should still be more or less the same

- be capable of differentiating among individuals according to their performance. If everyone is rated the same the exercise rapidly becomes pointless

- be capable of being influenced by the job-holder. If a person is to improve performance after appraisal then it must be about matters over which the individual has discretionary control

- be acceptable to those individuals whose performance is being assessed. It is important that people feel that their performance is being measured against criteria that are fair and accurate.

Test your understanding 2

Although managers are constantly making judgements about their subordinates and giving them feedback:

- they may notice the successes and failures but rarely form a complete and objective picture
- they may be aware of the shortcomings but may not have devoted any time to thinking about improvement and development
- judgements are not so easy to justify in detail to the employee's face
- they rarely give adequate critical feedback unless required to do so.

Appraisals are necessary for:

- getting the manager and subordinate together so that both can contribute to the assessment and plans for improvement
- forming and agreeing the traits and standards against which individuals can be assessed objectively and consistently
- recording assessments.

Test your understanding 3

People naturally want to know how well they have done on a particular task and need the reassurance that they are on the right track and have achieved what was expected of them.

It is difficult to maintain or improve work performance in the absence of feedback on how well one is doing. Without follow up the appraisal would just be seen as a friendly chat, with little effect on future performance as circumstances change. The individual might also feel cheated.

Test your understanding 4

Good for motivation	Bad for motivation
• Feedback on performance is regarded as essential in motivation because it gives people a chance to evaluate their achievement and make future calculations about the amount of effort required to achieve objectives and rewards • Agreement of challenging but attainable targets for performance motivates people by clarifying goals and by the value of incentives offered • A positive approach to appraisals allows people to solve their work problems and apply creative thinking.	• People do not react well to criticism, especially at work • If people have a favourable self-image, they may be impervious to criticism but if these people are not criticised but are given an 'easy' appraisal they will continue as they are – confirmed in their behaviour and sense of self-worth – even doing a bad job • Where people have a poor self-image, they may be encouraged by low level criticism.

Test your understanding 5

There are a number of areas which can impact upon a successful appraisal system if not addressed, these include:

- low priority given to appraisal by the organisation
- inconsistencies in how appraisal meetings are conducted and how meetings are recorded
- difficulties in remembering events from earlier in the year can result in concentrating on more recent areas of work
- focusing on some areas of work to the exclusion of others
- interruptions
- inadequate preparation
- poor recording
- lack of training
- diversity issues are not addressed
- lack of time or suitable meeting place.

A badly designed appraisal system introduced by untrained staff will damage relationships and provide no benefits to individual employees, the organisation or service users.

Test your understanding 6

This statistic reveals that the labour force would turn over once in 50 years. It is to be congratulated for having a stable and secure workforce but it could be in trouble if there is no young blood to bridge the generation gap and cover any retirements.

27

Training, development and learning

Chapter learning objectives

Upon completion of this chapter you will be able to:

- explain what is meant by learning
- give reasons why learning in the workplace is important
- explain **Kolb's** experiential learning theory
- describe the learning styles identified by **Honey and Mumford**
- explain the implication of **Kolb** and **Honey** and **Mumford's** theories
- define the terms training, 'development' and 'education'
- identify the distinguishing characteristics of each of the above
- identify the benefits of training for an individual and the organisation
- describe the stages in the training and development process
- what methods could be used to identify training needs?
- how can the effectiveness of the training programme be evaluated?
- what roles does the HR department play in encouraging the organisation and its staff to learn?

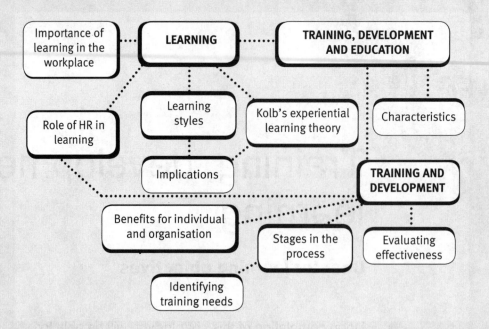

1 Learning

1.1 What is meant by learning?

Learning can be defined as 'the process of acquiring knowledge through experience, which leads to a change in behaviour'. It includes the acquisition of a new skill, new knowledge, a modified attitude or a combination of all three.

Learning can be formal, informal or incidental:

- Formal learning is undertaken deliberately when individuals consciously 'learn' and 'study'. It is typically institutionally sponsored, classroom-based, and highly structured.

- Informal learning is usually intentional but not highly structured. Examples include self-directed learning, networking, coaching and mentoring.

- Incidental learning is defined as a by-product of some other activity, such as task accomplishment, interpersonal interaction, trial and error experimentation, learning from mistakes or even formal learning. When people learn incidentally, their learning may be taken for granted, tacit, or unconscious.

The pace of learning or progress changes with familiarity – this is known as the learning curve. The shape of the learning curve depends on the type of work or task and the individual.

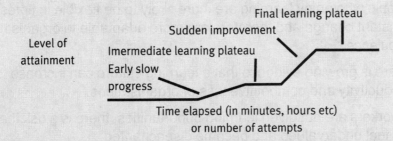

Expandable text

A fictitious curve for learning from a study guide is shown below:

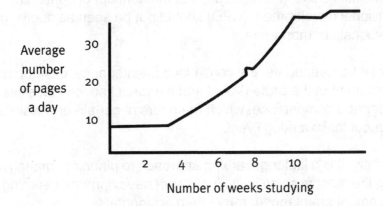

Experience has shown that learning does not take place at a steady rate:

- Initially progress may be slow with sudden improvement followed by further progress for some time.

- There will be a final levelling off when, without enormous effort, little further progress will be achieved.

1.2 Learning in the workplace

Many employers, mostly of small businesses, perceive investment in work-related learning to be a drain on their business. However, studies have shown that organisations that deliberately foster a culture of learning are those that are on the leading edge of development and change.

Learning in the workplace is important for the following reasons:

- It can lead to increased competence, understanding, self-esteem and morale.

- People who enjoy learning are more likely to be flexible in times of constant change and therefore are more adaptable to organisational turbulence.

- There is growing evidence that a learning culture can increase the productivity and competitiveness of organisations.

- If workers are not given learning opportunities, there is a risk that they will feel undervalued and become disenchanted.

As is so often said by management writers – if you want to develop an organisation, then develop its people and they will develop the organisation.

Lifelong learning should be the concern of all employees in the organisation and, despite its title, it is arguable that the concept of continuing professional development (CPD) should not be seen as applying only to professionals or managers.

 CPD can be defined as 'the continuous maintenance, development and enhancement of the professional and personal knowledge, skills and ability, often termed competence, which members of certain professions require throughout their working lives'.

Put simply, it is a lifelong learning approach to planning, managing and getting the most from an individual's own development. Learning and development are planned, rather than accidental.

 The learning organisation is one that facilitates the learning of all its members and continuously transforms itself.

- They generate and transfer knowledge.

- They learn from others and from past experience.

- They tolerate risk and failure as learning opportunities.

- They have a systematic, ongoing, collective and scientific approach to problem solving.

Test your understanding 1

Define informal learning in the workplace. How does it differ from formal learning?

Give one example of each type of learning – formal, informal and incidental.

KAPLAN PUBLISHING

1.3 Kolb's experiential learning theory

'Experiential learning' can apply to any kind of learning through experience.

David Kolb suggests that learning is a series of steps based on learning from experience. He suggested that classroom learning is false and that actual learning comes from real life experiences.

- Experiential learning comes from DOING and this ensures that learners actually solve problems.

- To learn effectively from experience (which includes work placements and practical activities within taught courses) usually involves completing a cycle of activities.

- All four stages of the learning cycle (shown below) have to be addressed.

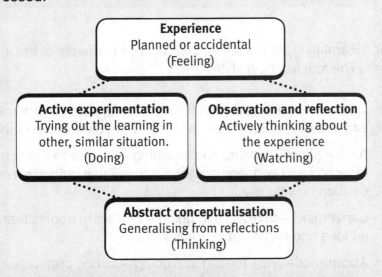

Experience
Planned or accidental
(Feeling)

Active experimentation
Trying out the learning in other, similar situation.
(Doing)

Observation and reflection
Actively thinking about the experience
(Watching)

Abstract conceptualisation
Generalising from reflections
(Thinking)

Illustration 1 – Learning

It doesn't matter where you start on the cycle:

- if you start with the activity, and work round to the abstract conceptualisation stage, you would be learning inductively

- if you start with theory, and then plan and carry out some activity, you are working deductively

- if you observe someone else's activity, draw conclusions then plan and carry out your own, then you would be starting at the reflection stage.

Applying his learning cycle to the study of individual differences, **Kolb** identified four learning styles.

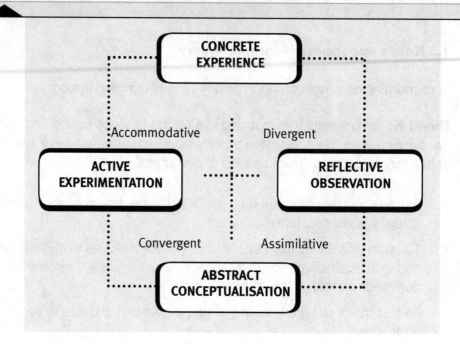

Each learning style is a combination of two elements of the learning cycle. The four learning styles are:

*   Divergent – feeling and watching – preference for concrete experiences, but to reflect on these from different perspectives.

*   Assimilative – thinking and watching – prefers to swing between reflection and conceptualisation and will use inductive reasoning to develop new theory.

*   Convergent – thinking and doing – prefers to apply ideas, will take an idea and test it out in practice.

*   Accommodative – feeling and doing – strong preference for concrete experiences and active experimentation (hands on).

Expandable text

Here are brief descriptions of the four **Kolb** learning styles:

- Divergent (feeling and watching) – These people are able to look at things from different perspectives. They are sensitive. They prefer to watch rather than do, tending to gather information and use imagination to solve problems. They are best at viewing concrete situations from several different viewpoints. **Kolb** called this style 'diverging' because these people perform better in situations that require ideas-generation, for example, brainstorming. People with a diverging learning style have broad cultural interests and like to gather information. They are interested in people, tend to be imaginative and emotional, and tend to be strong in the arts. They prefer to work in groups, to listen with an open mind and to receive personal feedback.

- Assimilative (watching and thinking) – The assimilating learning preference is for a concise, logical approach. Ideas and concepts are more important than people. These people require good clear explanation rather than practical opportunity. They excel at understanding wide-ranging information and organising it in a clear logical format. People with an assimilating learning style are less focused on people and more interested in ideas and abstract concepts. People with this style are more attracted to logically sound theories than approaches based on practical value. They are important for effectiveness in information and science careers. In formal learning situations, people with this style prefer reading, lectures, exploring analytical models, and having time to think things through.

- Convergent (doing and thinking) – People with a converging learning style can solve problems and will use their learning to find solutions to practical issues. They prefer technical tasks, and are less concerned with people and interpersonal aspects. They are best at finding practical uses for ideas and theories and can solve problems and make decisions by finding solutions to questions and problems. They are more attracted to technical tasks and problems than social or interpersonal issues and like to experiment with new ideas, to simulate, and to work with practical applications. A converging learning style enables specialist and technology abilities.

- Accommodative (doing and feeling) – The accommodating learning style is 'hands-on', and relies on intuition rather than logic. These people use other people's analysis, and prefer to take a practical, experiential approach. They are attracted to new challenges and experiences, and to carrying out plans. They commonly act on 'gut' instinct rather than logical analysis. People with an accommodating learning style will tend to rely on others for information than carry out their own analysis. They prefer to work in teams to complete tasks. They set targets and actively work in the field trying different ways to achieve an objective. This learning style is prevalent and useful in roles requiring action and initiative.

Test your understanding 2

Describe the stages in **David Kolb's** experiential learning cycle.

1.4 Learning styles – Honey and Mumford

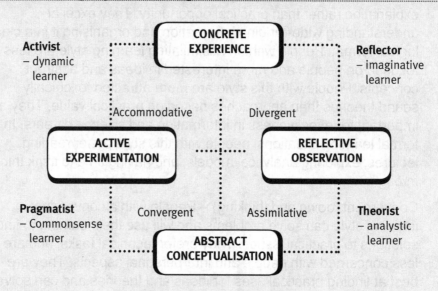

There are different ways of learning and people learn more effectively if they are aware of their own learning style preferences. **Honey and Mumford** have drawn up a classification of four basic learning styles around **Kolb's** sequence, identifying individual preferences for each stage:

KAPLAN PUBLISHING

	Activists – involve themselves fully without bias to new experiences. They are open-minded, enthusiastic, constantly searching for new challenges but are bored with implementation and long-term consolidation. They enjoy learning through games, competitive teamwork tasks and role-plays.
	**Reflectors** – prefer to step back to ponder and observe others before taking action. They are in general cautious, may be perceived as indecisive and tend to adopt a low profile. The reflector prefers learning activities that are observational (like carrying out an investigation).
	Theorists – adapt and integrate information in a step-by-step logical way. They prefer to maximise certainty and feel uncomfortable with subjective judgements, lateral thinking and anything flippant. The theorist prefers activities that explore the interrelationship between ideas and principles.
	Pragmatists – are keen to try out ideas, theories and techniques to see if they work in practice. They are essentially practical, down-to-earth people, like making practical decisions, act quickly on ideas that attract them and tend to be impatient with open-ended discussions. The pragmatist prefers learning activities that are as close as possible to direct work experience.

Expandable text

Individual preferences mean that:

- Dynamic learners – activists – are primarily interested in self-discovery; they ask 'What if?' questions. In terms of learning they need a variety of new and challenging activities where they can have a lot of the limelight – business games, competitive tasks, role-playing exercises. This learner wants to touch everything. Problem solving, small group discussions or games, peer feedback, and self-directed work assignments all help this learner, who likes to see everything and determine their own criteria for the relevance of the materials.

- Imaginative learners – reflectors – are primarily interested in personal meaning. They question, Why? To instruct imaginative learners teachers need to motivate and provide expert interpretation. Their preferred method of teaching is simulation or discussion. They need time to think over, assimilate and prepare for activities, or review what has happened and reach decisions without pressures and tight deadlines. Lectures are helpful to this learner. They look for an instructor who is both a taskmaster and a guide.

- Analytic learners – theorists – are primarily interested in facts as they lead to conceptual understanding. They question, What? Teachers need to give them the facts that deepen understanding. These learners need opportunities to question, probe and explore methodically the assumptions and logic, and the interrelationships between ideas and events, using case studies, theoretical readings and reflective thinking exercises.

- Common sense learners – pragmatists – are primarily interested in how things work. To instruct this type of learner teachers need to act as coach. Students need to practise techniques with coaching/feedback from a credible expert, and they must see a link between the subject matter and a problem or opportunity on the job. Group work and peer feedback often leads to success.

Illustration 2 – Learning

It is generally agreed that a combination of different types of learners will make an effective team in an organisation. In discussing an issue, the most likely question the Reflector will pursue is Why it is important; the Theorist, in contrast, will be interested in What it is all about; the Pragmatist will be concerned with How it can be applied in the real world; and the Activist will be keen to know What if we were to apply it here and now.

Test your understanding 3

Briefly describe the four learning styles in the **Honey and Mumford** model.

1.5 Implication of Kolb and Honey and Mumford's theories

Most people exhibit clear strong preferences for a given learning style. We should not assume that the ability to use or 'switch between' different styles comes easily or naturally to many people.

People who have a clear learning style preference, for whatever reason, will tend to learn more effectively if learning is geared to their preference. For instance – according to **Kolb:**

- people who prefer the 'assimilating' learning style will not be comfortable being thrown in at the deep end without notes and instructions

- people who prefer to use an 'accommodating' learning style are likely to become frustrated if they are forced to read lots of instructions and rules, and are unable to get hands-on experience as soon as possible.

Honey and Mumford designed a self-description questionnaire so that people can discover their preferred learning style. The scoring reveals the person's strength of preference for each of the four learning styles.

- Those who like active learning tick statements such as 'I often act without considering the possible consequences' and 'I am often one of the people who puts life into a party'.

- Reflectors agree with statements such as 'I like the sort of work where I have time for thorough preparation' and 'I am always interested to find out what people think'.

- Theorists tick statements such as 'I tend to solve problems using a step-by-step approach'.

- Pragmatists agree with 'What matters most is whether something works in practice'.

A feature of **Honey and Mumford's** model is that it provides suggestions about the best ways for individuals to learn. The most effective learning methods are different for each learning style.

- **Activists** – have a practical approach to training, are flexible and optimistic. They prefer practical problems, enjoy participation and challenge, are easily bored and have a dislike of theory. They must have hands-on training.

- **Theorists** – require their learning to be programmed and structured; designed to allow time for analysis; and provided by people who share the same preference for ideas and analysis.

- **Reflectors** – need an observational approach to training. They need to work at their own pace – slow, cautious and non-participative – where conclusions are carefully thought out. They do not find learning easy especially if rushed.

- **Pragmatists** – need to see a direct value and link between training and real problems and aim to do things better. They enjoy learning new techniques and tasks and are good at finding improved ways of doing things.

Test your understanding 4

(a) What style of learner will:

Learn best from:	Be less likely to learn from:
• activities where they can observe other people first	• situations where they are 'thrown in' without adequate time to plan or think
• being given time to think things over	• role play in front of others
• the opportunity to discuss ideas with others	• activities where they are told what to do
• having time to prepare?	• having to make shortcuts for the sake of expediency?

(b) Draw up a similar chart for one other style.

2 Training and development and education

2.1 Definitions of training, development and education

A common confusion that exists is the distinction between education, training and development.

Expandable text

A typical dictionary definition of 'education' includes the words: 'systematic instruction, schooling or training' and conversely, in defining 'training' includes 'to educate, rear, bring up'.

When trying to draw a distinction between the two, we often find that:

- education is used to describe what goes on in schools and colleges of a formal, theoretical or academic nature, or where the learning is directed to wider aspects of study than the work of the organisation to which the employee belongs

- training is used to describe the imparting of specific, practical skills to employees, which will be relevant to their present or next immediate job.

Training is defined as learning that is provided in order to improve performance on the present job.

According to **Michael Armstrong** (not examinable by name):

- **Education** is defined as 'the activities which aim at developing the knowledge skills, moral values and understanding required in all aspects of life rather than a knowledge skill related to only a limited field of activity'.

- **Training** is 'the planned and systematic modification of behaviour through learning events, programmes and instruction which enable individuals to achieve the level of knowledge, skills and competence to carry out their work effectively'.

- **Development** is 'the growth or realisation of a person's ability and potential through conscious or unconscious learning and educational experiences'.

2.2 The characteristics of training, development and education

Within organisations, human resources development (HRD) programmes are divided into three main categories:

- training for the present
- educating for the future
- developing to lead.

The main characteristics of each include:

- **Training** usually implies a planned process to modify attitude, knowledge, skill or behaviour to achieve effective performance in an activity or range of activities. It is job-orientated rather than personal.
- **Education** is usually intended to mean basic instruction in knowledge and skills designed to enable people to make the most of life in general. It is personal and broadly based.
- **Development** suggests a broader view of knowledge and skills acquisition than training, concerned more with changes in attitudes, behaviour and potential than with immediate skill. It relates more to career development than job development – learning for growth of the individual, but not related to a specific present or future job.

Generally it is argued that development is more general, more future orientated and more individually orientated than training.

The survival of the organisation requires development throughout the ranks in order to survive, while training makes the organisation more effective and efficient in its day-to-day operations.

Unlike training and education, which can be completely evaluated, development cannot always be fully assessed.

- Training can be fully evaluated immediately upon the learners returning to work.

- Education can only be completely evaluated when the learners move on to their future jobs or tasks.

Whether it is training, development or education, they all involve learning and the emphasis is on how the activity is organised, i.e. is it systematic – a planned and deliberate approach.

3 Training and development

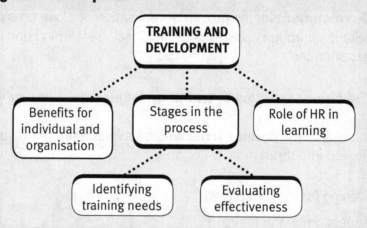

3.1 Benefits of training

Organisations should view training as an investment. The benefits of training and development for an individual and the organisation include:

For the individual:

- improved skills and (perhaps) qualifications
- increased confidence and job satisfaction.

For the organisation:

- motivated employees
- increased competence and confidence
- higher productivity
- skilled workforce
- low staff turnover

- improved health and safety
- higher quality performance
- a more flexible workforce.

> **Test your understanding 5**
>
> List some more of the benefits of training for an organisation.

3.2 The stages in the training and development process

A systematic approach to training and development should be adopted. It will involve:

- Identifying training needs
- Defining the learning required
- Setting training objectives
- Planning the training
- Delivering/implementing the training
- Evaluating training

Expandable text

- **Identifying training needs** – this could include an investigation into the organisation's current performance as well as mapping the corporate skills base. It should drill down to the level of the individual to target specific needs.

- **Defining the learning required** – specify the knowledge, skills or competencies that have to be acquired.

- **Setting training objectives** – as with all objectives these should have clear, specific, measurable targets in relation to the behaviour and standard of behaviour required in order to achieve a given level of performance.

- **Planning the training** – this covers who provides the training, where the training takes place and divisions of responsibilities between trainers, line managers or team leaders and the individual personally.

- **Delivering/implementing the training** – a combination of formal and on-the-job training programmes will be used.

- **Evaluating training** – a cost-benefit analysis with feedback to improve selection of method and delivery.

Expandable text

There has been a massive increase in training effort during the last 20 years. The fact remains, however, that far too many organisations devote insufficient resources to training and may have a serious training problem. The managers at Professional Publishing have included training in their corporate plan and want to see a systematic training programme in place over the next two years.

The training process that might be designed by Professional Publishing begins with the identification of training needs in relation to the organisational objectives. The process moves on to the identification of appropriate target groups for training and the design of suitable training experiences, and goes through the application of this design to the evaluation of the outcome of the training.

This process is more complex than the description might suggest and the figure below gives a more complete account of what is involved.

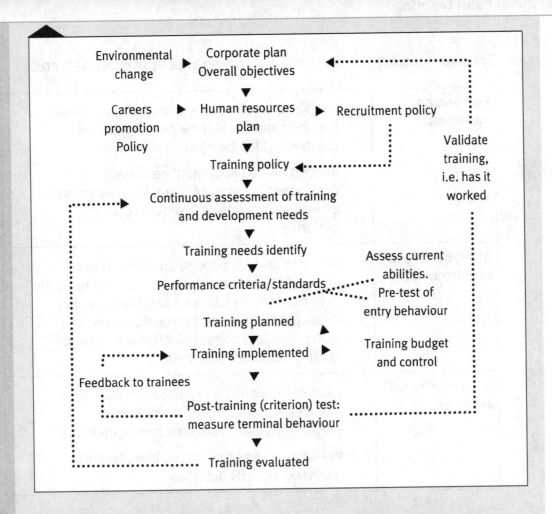

What steps would be included in a training strategy?

3.3 Methods used to identify the training needs

The training needs will be indicated by a job training analysis. However, it is vital that the line manager begins with an understanding of the organisational strategy and departmental goals and objectives before he or she carries out the training needs analysis.

A job training analysis is the process of identifying the purpose of the job and its component parts, and specifying what must be learnt in order for there to be effective performance.

A training 'gap' or need is any shortfall in terms of employee knowledge, understanding, skill or attitudes against what is required by the job or the demands of organisational change.

The main methods for determining the training needs of individuals are:

Performance appraisal	• each employee's work is measured against the performance standards or objectives established for their job • training and development needs are considered in terms of future job performance as well as in terms of improving current performance.
Analysis of job requirements	• the skills and knowledge specified in the appropriate job description are compared with data concerning jobs and activities, e.g. job descriptions, personnel specifications, and leadership and communication activities to identify candidates for training.
Organisational analysis	• uses data about the organisation as a whole, e.g. its structure, markets, products or services, human resources requirements, etc. • the key success factors are identified and analysed into HR activities.

Other approaches include information gained from records of employee performance, feedback from customers or simply from observation of employees.

- Other methods available include surveys of staff with questionnaires or interviews of superiors and subordinates and customer surveys covering their satisfaction and dissatisfaction.

Illustration 3 – Training and development

There are various indicators of organisational health, which may well suggest that training is necessary. Such indicators might include labour turnover, absenteeism or the level of grievances. For example, several studies have shown that inadequate training often leads to workers failing to achieve production targets, which affects their chances of gaining financial incentives. Many such employees experience frustration, which manifests itself in grievances and labour turnover.

Expandable text

Identifying the training and development needs

(i) Organisational strategy

Training and development must be a part of the personnel or manpower strategy linked to the overall business strategy and, as part of this wider strategy, should promote organisational and individual learning. It is vital that the line manager has an understanding of the organisational strategy and departmental goals and objectives before he or she carries out the training needs analysis.

(ii) Training needs analysis

The training needs analysis (TNA) is an essential part of the process to determine the knowledge, skills and experience required to do a particular job. The results of the TNA will identify the training and development needs which will contribute to the business objectives outlined in the organisational strategy. By emphasising the 'needs' rather than the 'wants', the approach taken will be more cost effective in terms of financial resources.

(iii) Individual past performance

Identifying training needs and achieving departmental plans means the supervisor or line manager must have a knowledge of each individual in terms of their past experience, level of qualification and job performance. Some organisations have details of the training and development history of each employee on a computer database which can be accessed easily and used to determine the stage of development for each employee and also to identify whether they are ready to take on challenging roles and responsibilities.

(iv) The appraisal interview

Most line managers appraise their staff or carry out a performance review annually. If the management style is participative the appraisal will involve a discussion in which the individual employee will be encouraged to assume ownership of the training and development plan. The aim of an appraisal will be:

- to review past performance and achievement of objectives;
- to discuss individual aspirations and
- to identify opportunities for training and development in the future.

This is the first stage of the TNA, where the present performance levels of the individual are matched and compared with the key competencies required in the future role to identify the 'learning gap'. This information will form the basis of the training and development plan.

(v) Observation

Part of the job of the supervisor or line manager will be to observe individual performance levels. Although it is subjective, it still provides a valuable source of information for the identification of training and development needs.

Test your understanding 7

When training staff conduct a comprehensive training needs analysis in their organisation. What basic data would they need for this process at the organisational, the job and the individual level?

3.4 Methods of training and development

The training manager is responsible for determining, organising, managing and directing training activities as well as acting in an advisory capacity. Responsibility for training is usually shared between personnel training specialists and departmental supervisors.

Training and development methods for individuals include:

- Training courses, both external and in-house
- Mentoring
- Coaching
- Computerised interactive learning
- Planned experiences
- Self managed learning.

Training and development methods for groups include:

- Lectures
- Discussions
- Case studies and role playing
- Business games
- T-group exercises (Here trainers leave the group to its own devices).

Outdoor training equates the skills of outdoor pursuits – planning, organising team building and dealing with uncertainty – with management qualities of leadership, communication, co-ordination, motivation and creativity.

Implementation of training can be either in-house or external.

- External sources of training include: college, universities, training organisation and consultants.

- For in-house provisions, infrastructure and staffing must be carefully considered.

3.5 Evaluating the training programme

Hamblin (not examinable by name) defines evaluation as 'any attempt to obtain information (feedback) on the effect of a training programme and to assess the value of the training in the light of that information'.

Training-centred evaluation aims to assess the inputs to training, i.e. whether we are using the right tools for training. Hamblin suggests that there are five levels at which evaluation can take place:

Levels of evaluation	Achieved by:
Reactions – of the trainees to the training, their feelings about how enjoyable and useful it has been, etc.	• End-of-course questionnaires – obtain immediate feedback on the perceived value of the training but may not be the best way of evaluating the effectiveness of the programme.
Learning – what new skills and knowledge have been acquired or what changes in attitude have taken place as a result of the training.	• Attainment tests – limited to the immediate knowledge and skills improvement and may not indicate whether the learning will be transferred to the workplace or job. • Interviews – appraisal or performance reviews provide an opportunity to discuss the individual's progress during and after a training and development programme.

Job behaviour – at this level evaluation tries to measure the extent to which trainees have applied their training on the job.	• Observation – the end results of the learning and development can be assessed by observation of improvements in job performance levels. • Career development – the speed of promotion of an individual may be used as an indication of the effectiveness of the training and development and also the level of support given to the development plan by the organisation.
Organisation – training may be assessed in terms of the ways in which changes in job behaviour affect the functioning of the organisation.	• At the departmental level the effective training and development of staff can mean the achievement of targets, goals and objectives measured in terms of output, productivity, quality, etc.
Ultimate value – this is a measure of the training in terms of how the organisation as a whole has benefited	• Measured in terms of greater profitability, survival or growth.

Whatever evaluation method is used it should be done before, during and after the event.

- Before the event will clarify the existing skills, knowledge and attitudes to help the trainer plan the event and provide a yardstick by which to measure them.

- During the event will determine the rate of learning, allowing the trainer to pace the learning to suit the trainee and offer remedial help where needed.

- After the event can be immediately after the training or over a long time.

Test your understanding 8

Outline **Hamblin's** general approach to the assessment of training.

4 Role of management in a learning organisation

The role of the management in a learning organisation is to encourage continuous learning and acquisition of new knowledge and skills and to transform these into actual behaviour, products and processes within the organisation.

Expandable text

To enable learning to take place within the organisation, management should adopt the following apporch:

- The process of strategy formulation should be designed with learning in mind, and should incorporate experimentation and feedback.

- All members of the organisation should be encouraged, and given the opportunity, to contribute to policy making as part of the learning process.

- Information should be seen as a resource to be exploited by all members of the organisation, not as a 'power tool' reserved for a chosen few.

- Accounting systems should be designed in such a way that members of the organisation can learn how the cash resource is used.

- Employees should be encouraged to see internal users of their outputs as 'customers'.

- Employees should be encouraged to see the diversity of rewards they enjoy (not just cash), and there should be openness about why some people are paid more than others.

- The structures of the organisation – everything from office layout to managerial hierarchy – should be regarded as temporary arrangements that can be altered in response to changing conditions.

- Employees who have contacts outside the organisation – salesmen, customer service staff, purchasing staff, etc. – should impart the knowledge they determine from such contacts to improve the organisation's knowledge base.

- Management must foster a climate in which workers understand that part of their task is to improve their own knowledge, and to share knowledge with other members of the organisation.

- A priority for management should be the provision of opportunities for structured learning – courses, seminars, etc.

Chapter summary

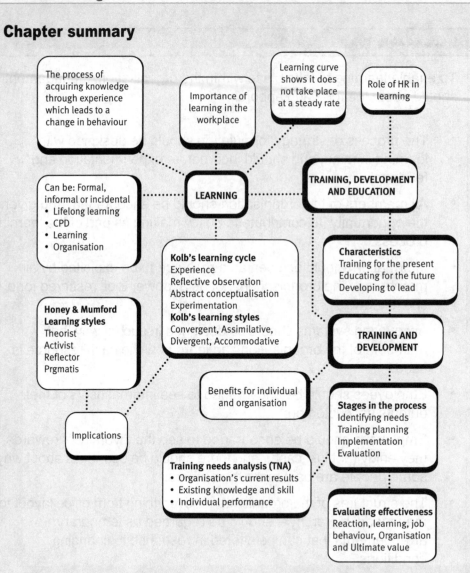

The process of acquiring knowledge through experience which leads to a change in behaviour

Importance of learning in the workplace

Learning curve shows it does not take place at a steady rate

Role of HR in learning

LEARNING

TRAINING, DEVELOPMENT AND EDUCATION

Can be: Formal, informal or incidental
• Lifelong learning
• CPD
• Learning
• Organisation

Kolb's learning cycle
Experience
Reflective observation
Abstract conceptualisation
Experimentation
Kolb's learning styles
Convergent, Assimilative, Divergent, Accommodative

Characteristics
Training for the present
Educating for the future
Developing to lead

Honey & Mumford Learning styles
Theorist
Activist
Reflector
Prgmatis

TRAINING AND DEVELOPMENT

Benefits for individual and organisation

Stages in the process
Identifying needs
Training planning
Implementation
Evaluation

Implications

Training needs analysis (TNA)
• Organisation's current results
• Existing knowledge and skill
• Individual performance

Evaluating effectiveness
Reaction, learning, job behaviour, Organisation and Ultimate value

Test your understanding answers

Test your understanding 1

Informal learning can be defined as 'any learning that occurs in which the learning process is not determined or designed by the organisation'. For example, getting help from a co-worker is informal learning.

Formal learning is different because it includes both an expressed organisation goal and a defined process. Going to a two-hour class on first aid is formal learning.

Incidental learning is the by-product or unintended outcome of a learning experience, e.g. watching and overhearing two colleagues discussing how to do something.

Test your understanding 2

Experiential learning theory **(Kolb)** – learning involves a cycle with four stages

EXPERIENCE

EXPERIMENTATION

REFLECTIVE OBSERVATION

ABSTRACT CONCEPTS AND GENERALISATION

- Experience, which may be either planned or accidental
- Reflective observation, which is looking back at the experience and introspectively reviewing the general issues raised and their significance
- Abstract conceptualisation, which can be viewed as generalising from reflection and analysing to develop a body of ideas, theories or principles, which can then be applied to other similar problems or situations; hypotheses are developed, based on experience and knowledge
- Active experimentation, which is consciously trying out the learning in similar situations; it involves creativity, decision making and problem solving.

The experiential learning method proposes putting learners in active problem solving roles and using a form of self-learning which encourages them to be committed to the chosen learning objectives.

Test your understanding 3

The four learning styles in the **Honey and Mumford** model are:

- **Theorist**: this individual likes to understand the theory that supports the practice. Theorists learn with facts, concepts and models.

- **Reflector**: this individual learns by observing and thinking about what he has seen. Reflectors prefer to avoid 'jumping in' to a task, and would rather watch from the sidelines.

- **Activist**: this individual learns by doing and acting. Activists like to 'get their hands dirty'.

- **Pragmatist:** this individual likes to see how theory is put into practice in the 'real world'. Pragmatists find abstract theories and concepts of no use unless they can see their relevance to practical action.

Test your understanding 4

(a) Reflector

(b) Other learning styles (only one of the following was required).

Activists are less likely to learn from:	**Activists are less likely to learn from:**
• new experiences and activities • exercises where they become involved • role play, business games and short-term tasks • excitement and drama • being 'thrown in at the deep end'.	• lectures, explanations, reading and observing • theoretical sessions • activities involving analysing data • activities where they are told precisely what to do • repeat activities (such as practising a skill).
Theorists learn best from:	**Theorists** are less likely to learn from:
• new experiences and activities • exercises where they become involved • role play, business games and short-term tasks • excitement and drama • being 'thrown in at the deep end'	• shallow unclear situations • unstructured situations, especially with no clear point • being asked to make a decision without a policy • situations with emotional overtones • being rushed into any exercise without its relevance being explained.

Pragmatists learn best from:	Pragmatists are less likely to learn from:
• exercises where the link to the job is explained or obvious • practical relevant activities • situations where implementation is important (as well as learning) • drawing up action plans to use back at work • the opportunity to learn from a coach or copy a role model.	• activities with no clear relevance to their job • no clear practical aspects or guidelines on how to do things • situations where people seem to lack a goal • situations where there is no relevant reward to the exercise • situations where the trainer is perceived to be 'out of touch' with their world.

Test your understanding 5

The benefits of training for an organisation include:

- developing a workforce with the skills the organisation requires

- improving the skills of employees so that they can do their work better

- providing a means of testing the skills of employees (post-training reviews)

- enhancing the job satisfaction of staff and their commitment to the organisation

- attracting good-quality individuals to work in the organisation with the prospects of suitable training

- improving the efficiency and effectiveness of the workforce generally, and so improving profitability

- reducing the requirement for detailed supervision.

Test your understanding 6

There should be a systematic approach to creating a training strategy.

- It should begin with an analysis of the organisation's skills requirements. This involves deciding what skills the workforce should have if the organisation is to achieve its objectives, and comparing this with the skills that the workforce currently has, and is likely to have in the future unless a training programme is established. The difference between the skills the workforce needs and the skills available is called the skills gap.

- The next step is to decide on the extent to which training should be used to close the skills gap. There should be a training needs analysis, to establish the scale of the training requirements, and what the objectives of a training programme for the organisation should be. This establishes objectives for training.

- Next, decisions should be made about what training is needed to meet the training objectives. A detailed set of training programmes for different categories of staff should be prepared. These plans should include decisions about the type of training required (face-to-face training, in-house or external training, computer-based training and so on), the subject matter for each programme, the numbers of individuals to be trained in each programme. There should also be a training budget for the resources required and the expected cost.

- When the detailed plan is approved, each training programme should be planned in detail. Courses should be scheduled, and in the case of in-house programmes, training providers should be asked to prepare the courses for delivery.

- The next step is for the training programme to be implemented and the courses delivered.

- There should be a post-training evaluation of the programmes and their effectiveness. Individual employees might be required to take tests. The effectiveness of training for individuals who have taken external examinations, for example trainee accountants, can be judged by whether they pass the examinations. From the organisational perspective, there should also be a post-implementation review to establish whether the training strategy has been successful in achieving the training objectives and closing the skills gap.

Test your understanding 7

The data for the three levels is as follows:

- Organisational level – data about the organisation as a whole, e.g. its structure, markets, products or services, human resource requirements, etc.

- Job level – data concerning jobs and activities, e.g. job descriptions, personnel specifications and leadership and communication activities.

- Individual level – data about individuals, e.g. appraisal records, personal training records, test results, notes made at counselling interviews and results of attitude surveys.

Test your understanding 8

Hamblin's general approach to the assessment of training can be shown as:

RESULTS OF TRAINING	EVALUATION STRATEGY
Training ▼	Training-centred – assess inputs and methods
Reactions ▼	Reactions-centered – trainee reaction
Learning ▼	Learning-centred – measures lerning achieved, e.g. tests, examinations
Changes in job behaviour ▼	Job-related – measure of learning applied in workplace
Changes in organisation ▼	Organisational development – measures organisational changes resultaing from training
Impact on organisational goals	Cost benefit – what has training done for profitability ?

28

Improving personal effectiveness at work

Chapter learning objectives

Upon completion of this chapter you will be able to:

- explain the purposes of personal development plans

- identify the stages in putting together a personal development plan

- give reasons why continuous monitoring and feedback is important

- explain the purpose of time management

- describe the time management techniques that one might employ to improve one's use of time

- describe the barriers to effective time management and how they may be overcome

- outline how information technology could be used to improve personal effectiveness

- explain the terms mentoring, coaching and counselling.

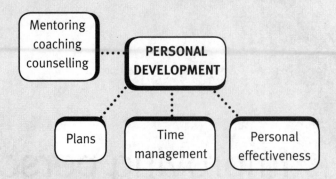

1 Personal development plans

A personal development plan is a 'clear developmental action plan for an individual that incorporates a wide set of developmental opportunities including formal training'.

During their career, employees are increasingly encouraged to manage their own development. In consultation with management, they might be asked to set up personal development plans whereby they set targets and propose actions/activities to achieve them.

Development is more general than training, is more forward-looking and orientated towards the individual, and is concerned with enabling the individual to fulfil his or her potential.

Training	Development
• Immediately practical • Connected to job performance	• No immediate practical application • Over time it enables a person to deal with wider problems

1.1 Purposes of personal development plans

The purpose of personal development is to ensure 'growth' during the person's career.

- The growth should be triggered by a job that provides challenging, stretching goals.

- The clearer and more challenging the goals, the more effort will be exerted, and the more likely it is that good performance will result.

- If the person does a good job and receives positive feedback, he or she will feel successful (psychological success). These feelings will increase the feelings of confidence and self-esteem and lead to involvement in the work, which in turn leads to the setting of future stretching goals.

This career-growth cycle is outlined below:

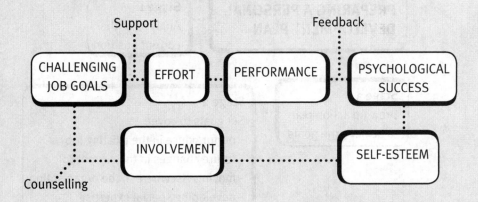

The purpose of the plan will be aimed at:

- improved performance in the current job
- developing skills (manual, intellectual, mental, perceptual or social) for future career moves within and outside the organisation
- developing specialist expertise.

Illustration 1 – Personal development plans

There are usually mechanisms and programmes in an organisation to help the individual with development planning. To assess job requirements and current competence and training requirements information can be gleaned from their job analysis, job description, role definition, personnel specifications and competence definitions (generally used for recruitment purposes), training needs analysis, self appraisal and performance appraisal and informal feedback from friends and colleagues.

Test your understanding 1

What methods will the manager/supervisor use to support employee development?

1.2 Preparing a personal development plan

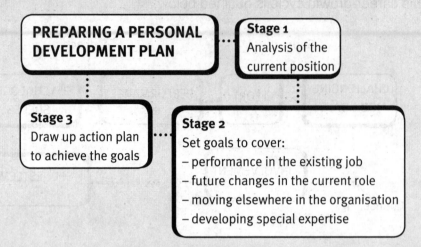

Stage 1 Analysis of current position – requires the individual, with their manager, to carry out a personal SWOT (strengths, weaknesses, opportunities, threats) analysis.

- This can be as simple as assessing what an individual does by referring to the job description, evaluating which aspects of a job an individual likes and dislikes on the one hand, and those aspects that an individual does well and not so well in on the other.

Tasks the person likes and does well	Tasks the person likes but doesn't do well
Tasks the person dislikes but does well	Tasks the person dislikes and does not do well

Stage 2 Set goals – following the above analysis, personal goals should be set for the individual.

- The tasks the person does not do well are examined and reasons are established.

- This can take the form of an alternative and more traditional type of SWOT analysis by examining the person's strengths and weaknesses.

- Particular weaknesses should be identified as being the cause of failure to carry out certain tasks well. This should then inform a personal set of objectives in order to overcome these weaknesses.

Illustration 2 – SWOT

Strengths	Weaknesses
What advantages do you have?	What could you improve?
What do you do well?	What do you do badly?
What resources do you have access to?	What should you avoid?
What do other people see as your strengths?	
Opportunities	**Threats**
Where are the good opportunities facing you?	What obstacles do you face?
What are the interesting trends you are aware of?	Are the required specifications for your job or products changing?
	Is changing technology threatening your position?
	Could any of your weaknesses seriously threaten your job/business?

Goals should have the characteristic of SMART objectives:

- Specific
- Measurable
- Attainable
- Realisitic
- Time bounded.

Stage 3 Draw up action plan – an action plan and training programme should be based on addressing the identified weaknesses and trying to move more of the tasks of the current role into the 'do well' side of the matrix on the left-hand side. It is easier to improve the performance of individuals in tasks that they like performing than in those that they don't.

When drawing up and implementing an action plan, some degree of control is necessary to monitor the extent to which the programme is achieving the goals and stated objectives.

Control processes give people structure, define methods and indicate how their performance will be measured. It is reassuring to know what you are required to do and how the outcome will be measured.

Test your understanding 2

How do you use the SMART acronym to ensure your goals are achievable?

Test your understanding 3

To assess the extent to which a goal has been met we need to be able to measure it. How might the performance expectations be described?

1.3 The importance of continuous monitoring and feedback

Once the goals and personal ambitions have been defined and the person has begun the development plan, the monitoring must begin. Monitoring in simple terms means watching over something that is happening.

Control processes give people timely, relevant feedback on their performance – this is information about how they did in the light of some goal and that can be used to improve performance. Feedback will usually be provided by the manager or supervisor, and should be concurrent – or certainly not long delayed. People naturally want to know how well they are doing on a particular task and need the reassurance that they are on the right track and are achieving what is expected of them.

- Feedback should be clear and frequent and this can only be achieved if there is continuous monitoring of the task.

- Feedback can also have a motivating effect by providing recognition of work done which in turn provides the incentive to sustain and improve performance levels.

- Recognition, praise and encouragement create feelings of confidence, competence, development and progress that enhance the motivation to learn.

Illustration 3 – Personal development plans

How am I doing? Just imagine being completely denied any feedback whatsoever – no guidance, no praise, and no constructive criticism for the things you do. If you received no input at all, how much initiative would you demonstrate? Would your productivity be high, or low? What would your morale be like as time went on? And if you experienced this kind of treatment in the workplace, how likely would you be to look for a job somewhere else?

The sad fact is that most of us take feedback for granted. But interpersonal feedback is a critical nutrient for everyone – it is the psychological equivalent of food and water. Without strong, clear feedback to use as a reference point, people are incapable of functioning fully and productively.

Test your understanding 4

Why should feedback be concurrent?

2 Time management

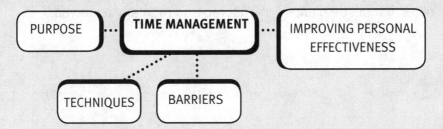

Whatever the qualities or attributes of a successful manager, or the qualities of the people working for him or her, one essential underlying criterion is the effective use of time.

Time is a unique resource – you cannot hire, rent or buy more time. The supply is totally irreplaceable and everything requires time.

2.1 The purpose of time management

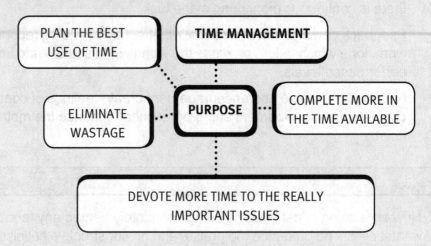

The purpose of time management (TM) is to:

- plan the best use of time
- cut down on time wasted
- devote more time to the really important issues, or jobs on hand
- complete more in the time available.

This will allow you to:

- eliminate wastage
- refuse excessive workloads
- monitor project progress
- allocate resource (time) appropriate to a task's importance
- plan each day/week efficiently.

Since Personal Time Management is a management process just like any other, it must be planned, monitored and regularly reviewed.

2.2 Time management techniques

Time management techniques include the following:

- **Spend time planning and organising** – using time to think and plan is time well spent. In fact, if you fail to take time for planning, you are, in effect, planning to fail.

- **Produce an activity log** – a breakdown of your time spent in a typical week, divided between activities at work, home, study, leisure and travel. Consider what proportion of your time was important to you, important to others and could easily be delegated to others.

- **Cost your time** – every occasion when you 'save' an hour, or put it to better use, you become more cost-effective.

Costing your time	Conserving time means:	The rest of the time may be wasted and lost due to:
- What is your total cost? - How much productive time do you achieve? - What utilisation do you obtain? - How much would a temp or subcontractor charge?	- communicating effectively - organising meetings effectively - reducing paperwork - controlling interruptions - setting time objectives for tasks	- lack of focus on task - failure to delegate - interruptions - fatigue – loss of attention - failure to communicate - failure to anticipate.

- **Make lists** – plan the whole of the coming week in advance, then make a list every day before you start work. Refuse to do anything that is not on the list for the day.

- **Prioritise** – look at the list and assess tasks for relative importance, amount of time required, and any deadlines – sorting out what you must do, from what you could do, and from what you would like to do.

| TASKS, DUTIES, ACTIVITIES WITH APPROXIMATE TIME ASSESSMENT |

| **Must (Ms)**
– Has to be done
in whole or part
today – probably
by a certain time | **Ought (Os)**
– Should be done
during today but
as a last resort
could be delayed | **Prefer (Ps)**
– Would like to do but
must not spend too
much time to the
detriment of Ms & Os |

- **Schedule the work:** use a monthly calendar or planning notebook to schedule important activities, due dates, deadlines, and appointments. Highlight important dates with a marker.

- **Concentrate and control:** work on one thing at a time avoiding, where possible, disruption by the unexpected.

Illustration 4 – Time management

Time management can also be improved by developing appropriate skills (faster reading, report writing, handling meetings and assertiveness skills), target setting, negotiating and delegating.

Which category are you in?

Stephen Covey outlines what he sees as the four generations of time management approaches:

First generation: Reminders	Followers limit their time management efforts to keeping lists and notes. They see these papers as reminders. Items that are not done by the end of the day are transferred to the next day's list in the evening.
Second generation: Planning and preparation	These people use calendars and appointment books. They will note where meetings are held and identify deadlines; this is sometimes even done on a computer. This generation plans and prepares, schedules future appointments and sets goals.
Third generation: Planning, prioritising, and controlling	Third generation time managers prioritise their activities on a daily basis. They tend to use detailed forms of daily planning on a computer or on a paper-based organiser. This approach implies spending some time in clarifying values and priorities.

Fourth generation: Being efficient and proactive	Fourth generation people understand the difference between urgency and importance, e.g. some people may go their entire lives completely missing out on important things (like spending time with their children before they have grown up) because it was never 'urgent'. The point is not to ignore urgent things, but to embrace important things without waiting for them to become urgent.

Test your understanding 5

We will assume you earn $50,000 per annum basic pay. On top of this the direct and indirect costs of your employment are $25,000. You work 37.5 hours per week for 44 weeks of the year.

What is the cost of your time per hour?

2.3 Barriers to effective time management

The main influences on a person's use of time are outlined in the diagram below:

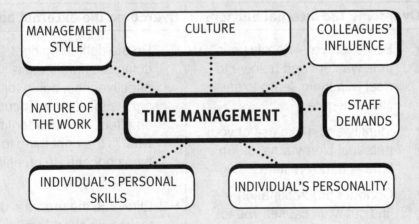

Influences include:

- Established jobs with routine and predictable work have fewer barriers than new or developing work.

- Jobs involving contact with others are more prone to interruptions than those with no near contacts.

- People with offices of their own can operate an 'open door' policy for staff communications but a 'closed door' policy when a physical barrier is needed.

- The location of colleagues, customers and suppliers can contribute to time wasted in travelling.

- Some organisation's cultures favour strict adherence to protocol and procedures, discouraging informal contacts. Others encourage an open access communications policy that can be stimulating but time wasting.

- An individual's personal work standards are going to be influenced by the type of decision making (slow and deliberate or quick) in the firm.

- The attributes and style of the job-holder depend on personality and preferences, e.g. some are more assertive and find it easier to deal with colleagues who waste their time.

Barriers to effective time management may be internal or external.

```
┌─────────────────────────────────────────────┐
│      BARRIERS TO EFFECTIVE TIME MANAGEMENT   │
└─────────────────────────────────────────────┘
```

Internal
Discipline
Procrastination
Lack of motivation

External
Workload issues
Available resources

Overcome the internal barriers	Overcome the external barriers
• Be assertive – identify your time wasters and resolve to deal with them, learn to say NO, delegate.	• Do the right thing right – doing the right thing is effectiveness; doing things right is efficiency. Focus first on effectiveness (identifying what is the right thing to do), then concentrate on efficiency (doing it right).
• Identify and make use of your personal biorhythms, or 'up' time and 'down' time.	
• Conquer procrastination – find out what causes you to put off doing something and remedy it, e.g. a feeling of inadequacy could be due to lack of information, lack of a particular skill or lack of training.	• Eliminate the urgent – urgent tasks with short-term consequences often get done to the detriment of the important tasks – those with long-term, goal-related implications.
• Promise yourself a reward.	• Break big jobs into little steps.
	• Use negotiation to improve the use of time.

Illustration 5 – Time management

What task are you doing on a regular basis that you should shift to a different time? Personal biorhythms are such that we are not at our peak of productivity or energy all day every day. For whatever reason, there are some times of the day when we have more energy, or are more creative, or are more willing to do unpleasant tasks. At other times of the day, we might be more inclined toward slowing down, being restful, letting our minds drift, or staying away from anything that looks like work.

Daily patterns can be discovered. You can simply keep a journal for a week. Make a note every hour or so that records how you feel, how much energy you have, how creative you feel, or if you are in a sour mood. At the end of the week you might find that there is a pattern. The important thing is that you are looking for your very own pattern, not somebody else's.

Once you see a bit of a pattern, then you can work on shifting things around.

Check your own personal biorhythms, and find the best time during the week for doing a specific regular task. Make a decision to perform this task at the ideal time for you.

Keep this going for a few weeks, and then decide whether this shift was right for you.

Test your understanding 6

How can the differences in attributes and style of the job-holder influence their use of time?

3 Improving personal effectiveness

Effectiveness means setting the right goals and objectives and then making sure they are accomplished. Being effective means getting the result that you want.

Using a planning aid

You may well have gathered by now that you will need a planning aid of some sort (a time/appointments diary, a work-planner or daily schedule form) to assist in planning the day's activities and managing your time.

Information technology available to support and improve personal productivity includes:

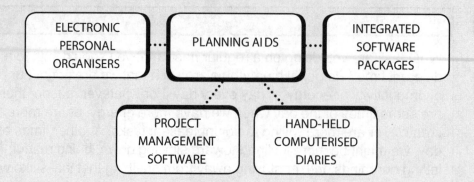

Integrated software packages like MS Outlook® or GoalPro 6® have the following features for personal productivity management:

- A **calendar** allows users to timetable their activities for the day and plan meetings with others. It will also be able to generate reminders, for example when a deadline is approaching, or the date of a meeting.

- An **address book.**

- **To do** lists.

- A **journal.** This can automatically record interactions with people involved in a project, such as email messages and record and time actions such as creating and working on files. The journal will keep track of all of this and is useful both as a record of work done and as a quick way of finding relevant files and messages without having to remember where each one is saved.

- A **jotter** for jotting down notes as quick reminders of questions, ideas, and so on.

Hand-held computers like the Palm does not attempt to do the work of a complete computer. It tracks appointments and contacts, synchronises them with a desktop computer, and takes the occasional note. The features include date book, address book, To Do list, calculator, Expense Tracking, and memo-pad.

Illustration 6 – Improving personal effectiveness

Check out the activity log from the following website http://www.deskdemon.com/pages/uk/advice/7dayprimer. Without modifying your behaviour any further than you have to, note down the things you do as you do them and their degree of importance and urgency. Every time you change activities, whether answering the phone, working, in a meeting, making coffee, gossiping with colleagues or whatever, note down the time of the change. As well as keeping track of activities, you could also write down how you feel – are you wide awake, concentrating, tired, full of energy? Do this at various points throughout the day.

4 Mentoring, coaching and counselling

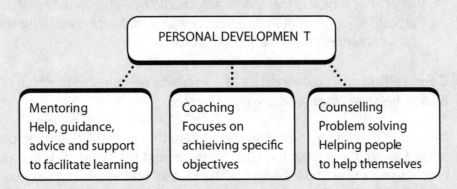

Mentoring is a process where one person offers help, guidance, advice and support to facilitate the learning or development of another. It follows an open and evolving agenda and deals with a range of issues.

The mentoring process consists of three core activities, which set it apart from other developmental activities:

- exchange of knowledge that is unique to a business, industry, profession or organisation

- a sustained partnering relationship

- measurable, beneficial outcomes for the individual parties involved and for the larger organisation.

A mentor is a guide, counsellor, tutor or trainer who:

- can give practical study support and advice

- can give technical, ethical and general business guidance

- can help with development of interpersonal and work skills

- is an impartial sounding board – no direct reporting responsibility

- is a role model who can help improve career goals.

Coaching: focuses on achieving specific objectives, usually within a preferred time period. It is more about improving the performance of someone who is already competent rather than establishing competency in the first place, or focusing on the task and ensuring that the learner gains competence.

- It is usually on a one-to-one basis, is set in the everyday working situation and is a continuing activity.

- It involves gently nudging people to improve their performance, to develop their skills and to increase their self-confidence so that they can take more responsibility for their own work and develop their career prospects.

- Most coaching is carried out by a more senior person, or manager. What is essential is that the coach should have the qualities of expertise, judgement and experience that make it possible for the person coached to follow the guidance.

Counselling can be defined as 'a purposeful relationship in which one person helps another to help himself/herself'.

It is a way of relating and responding to another person so that the person is helped to explore his/her thoughts, feelings and behaviour with the aim of reaching a clearer understanding. The clearer understanding may be of himself/herself or of a problem, or of the one in relation to the other.

The counsellor needs to be:

- **Observant.** There is a need to note behaviour, which may be symptomatic of a problem.
- **Sensitive.** There is a need to acknowledge and understand that another person's beliefs and values may be different from their own (for example religious beliefs).
- **Empathetic.** There is a need to appreciate that the problem may seem overwhelming to the individual.
- **Impartial.** There is a need to remain impartial and refrain from giving advice.
- **Discreet.** There will be situations when an employee cannot be completely open unless they are sure that the comments they make will be treated with confidentiality.

Through active listening, the use of open questions and clarifications, the counsellor encourages reflection and help the client identify issues and solutions. Counselling does not involve giving advice or making suggestions.

Test your understanding 7
How can a mentor assist a new recruit?

Chapter summary

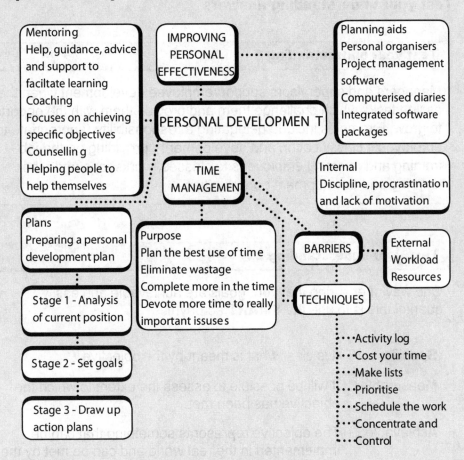

Mentoring
Help, guidance, advice and support to faciltate learning
Coaching
Focuses on achieving specific objectives
Counselling
Helping people to help themselves

IMPROVING PERSONAL EFFECTIVENESS

Planning aids
Personal organisers
Project management software
Computerised diaries
Integrated software packages

PERSONAL DEVELOPMENT

TIME MANAGEMENT

Internal
Discipline, procrastination and lack of motivation

Plans
Preparing a personal development plan

Purpose
Plan the best use of time
Eliminate wastage
Complete more in the time
Devote more time to really important issuses

BARRIERS

External
Workload
Resources

Stage 1 - Analysis of current position

Stage 2 - Set goals

Stage 3 - Draw up action plans

TECHNIQUES

···Activity log
···Cost your time
···Make lists
···Prioritise
···Schedule the work
···Concentrate and
···Control

Test your understanding answers

Test your understanding 1

Managers and supervisors support employee development when they assign tasks which challenge them and provide them with the opportunity to grow. Examples include delegating a responsibility (appropriate to the employee's classification and development), providing on-the-job training and referring employees to classes, workshops and other learning and development opportunities.

Test your understanding 2

One way of ensuring that your goals are achievable and easily quantifiable is to use the **SMART** acronym.

Specific: It is clear what is meant by the objective.

Measurable: It will be possible to assess the extent to which the objective has been met.

Achievable: The objective represents something that can be implemented in the real world and can be met by the resources available.

Relevant: It will contribute to your overall work outcomes.

Timely: Delivery of the objective is linked to a specific date.

Test your understanding 3

Standards should be written in clear language, describing the specific behaviours and actions required for work performance to meet, exceed or fail expectations.

The performance expectations should be described in terms of:

- timeliness – deadlines and dates
- cost – budget constraints and limits
- quality – subjective and objective measures of satisfaction
- quantity – how many
- customer satisfaction
- independent initiative demonstrated and
- any other relevant verifiable measure.

The acceptable margin for error should be specified as should any specific conditions under which the performance is expected to be accomplished or the performance assessed, e.g. assuming the required information is received on time from IT department, using job aids provided by Mr X, assuming this task is performed 50% of the day.

Test your understanding 4

Feedback is information about what has happened, the result or effect of our actions. The environment or other people 'feed back' to us the impact of our behaviour, be that upshot intended or unintended. Concurrent feedback is information that is 'fed back' to us as we perform; so it serves as the basis for learning and intelligent self-adjustment en route. Delayed feedback comes after the task is completed and can only be used to affect future performance.

Test your understanding 5

You work 37.5 hours per week for 44 weeks of the year = 1,650 hours.

$75,000 ÷ 1,650 = $45.45 per hour.

Test your understanding 6

The differences in attributes and style are due to the fact that some people:

- are more assertive and find it easier to deal with colleagues who waste their time
- have more skills and experience than others
- work best in the morning, whilst others work best later in the day
- are untidy and disorganised whilst others are neat and methodical
- like to concentrate their efforts into short, intensive periods, whilst others pace their work
- can deal with several tasks simultaneously, whereas others can only cope with one issue at a time
- are task-oriented as opposed to people-orientated
- like to delegate while others prefer to keep the work to themselves.

Test your understanding 7

Mentoring is the use of specially-trained individuals to provide guidance and advice that will help develop the careers of those allocated to them. They can assist by:

- drawing up personal development plans
- giving advice on administrative problems facing the new recruit
- helping to tackle projects by pointing the recruit in the right direction.

Effective communications and interpersonal skills

Chapter learning objectives

Upon completion of this chapter you will be able to:

- define the term 'communication'
- explain the stages of the communication process
- identify the factors that need to be taken into consideration to ensure that information will be received and understood
- distinguish between formal and informal methods of communication
- explain the main communication flows that might be found in an organisation
- explain the role of the grapevine in spreading information
- identify the consequences of ineffective communication
- explain the importance of good communication to employees and managers
- describe the attributes of effective communication
- identify and describe the barriers to effective communication
- describe how these barriers might be overcome
- explain the characteristics and effectiveness of the following communication patterns: Circle, Y, Wheel, Chain, All channels.

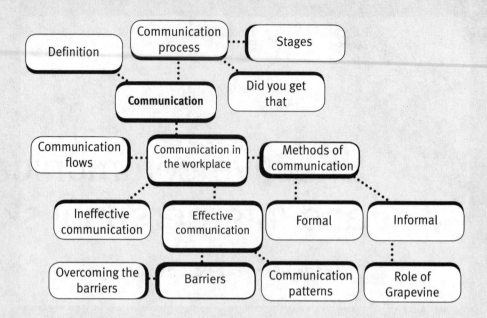

1 Communication

Communication is the interchange of information, ideas, facts and emotions by two or more persons. It establishes relationships and makes organising possible.

Expandable text

A great deal of communication can take place without any words at all. The raised eyebrow, the curled lip, the frown and the glare all say a great deal; so also can more obvious physical gestures, e.g. the pat on the back or arm around the shoulders and posture changes. Body language is about:

- eye contact – looking people in the eye with a relaxed and friendly gaze

- facial expressions

- posture and distance.

In the organisation communication may take the form of:

- giving or receiving information and instructions

- exchanging ideas

- announcing plans and strategies

- laying down rules or procedures

- comparing actual results against a plan

- manuals, organisation charts and job descriptions (communication about the structure of the organisation and individual roles).

2 Communication process

2.1 The stages of the communications process

The process of communication can be modelled as shown in the following diagram:

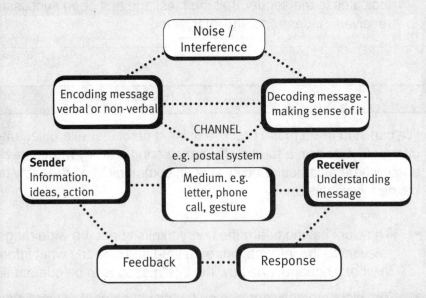

Expandable text

The communication process involves the following stages/elements:

- Sender (encoder) – initiates the communication process. To encode is to put the message into words or images.

- Message – the information that the sender wants to transmit

- Channel (the words channel and medium are often used interchangeably) – is the means of communication. It can be thought of as a sense, e.g. smelling, tasting, feeling, hearing and seeing. Sometimes it is preferable to think of the channel as the method over which the message will be transmitted: telecommunications, newspaper, radio, letter, poster or other media.

- Receiver (decoder) – the person or group for whom the communication effort is intended. The receiver decodes or interprets the message. Thus, in the feedback loop, the receiver becomes the sender and the sender becomes the receiver.

- Noise – anything that interferes with the communication or makes it difficult to understand. Noise can arise from many sources, e.g. factors as diverse as loud machinery, technical noise (a poor telephone connection), smudges on a printed page, status differentials between sender and receiver, distractions of pressure at work or emotional upsets.

- Feedback – ensures that mutual understanding has taken place in a communication and makes the communication a two-way process. It indicates to the sender that the message has been successfully received, understood and interpreted.

Illustration 1 – Communication process

We can step through the process using a particular example. Imagine an information clerk in a tourist office answering a query from a traveller about where a particular building is. In communicating the reply there will be the following steps:

- The clerk having heard the query thinks about the wide range of data relevant to the information requested and decides what information, in what language, and how the information is to be communicated.

- The clerk mentally decides on the actual content or wording of verbal and other messages to be given and any other forms of communication to be used.

- The message is transmitted by speech and perhaps also by gesture. The clerk may reinforce the verbal message by giving the inquirer some written information, a street plan in this case. The route to be taken may be shown on a map.

- The traveller receives the message by listening and perhaps looking.

- The message is decoded. The language, pronunciation and words used may be difficult to understand.

- The decoding should lead to the complete understanding of the reply given to the original query, or the reply may not be fully understood.

- The understanding of the reply may lead to action. The traveller may be satisfied with the answer to the query and exit the office. There may, however, be only partial understanding and the query may be restated.

2.2 Ensuring information will be received and understood

Various steps may be taken in order to ensure effective communication. These include:

- Selecting the appropriate channel
- Adopting feedback
- Using more than one communication network
- Restricting the number of communication 'links in the chain'
- Ensuring clarity

Expandable text

- **Selecting the appropriate channel** – the choice of medium used depends on factors such as urgency, permanency, complexity, sensitivity and cost.

- **Adopting feedback** – the 'two-way' nature of communication is ensured, so that the receiver seeks clarity and the sender seeks acknowledgement.

- **Using more than one communication network** – sometimes it is possible to use the informal communication network to reinforce the message sent, e.g. the friendship network.

- **Restricting the number of communication 'links in the chain'** – the shorter the distance between sender and recipient of a message, the fewer the 'breakdown' points in the communication process; allowing messages to be conveyed more directly to the recipients encourages this aspect.

- **Ensuring clarity** – sensitivity to the needs of the recipient of the message (relating to experience, awareness, intelligence, perception, etc.) reinforces the intention to produce a clear message.

Test your understanding 1

Give four examples of what you would interpret as either negative or positive feedback.

3 Communication in the workplace

3.1 Formal and informal methods of communication

The effectiveness of an organisation depends to a large extent on the effectiveness of communication by its managers and employees.

Information is exchanged in two ways, formally and informally.

- Formal communications help to provide management structure, so that individuals know what is expected of them and know how they have actually performed. For example, an organisation needs plans, procedures, policies and performance reports, official planning documents and the formal communication of management decisions.

- Information is communicated informally by means of face-to-face conversations, telephone conversations, emails and text messages. Informal communications are a feature of co-operation between individuals. People need to communicate in a way that promotes constructive working relationships.

Illustration 2 – Communications in the workplace

Both types of communication are essential in an efficient and effective business organisation.

The management of S&J makes a formal announcement to the press about a possible acquisition on Thursday. However, most people had already heard about it, because the news had been 'leaked' on Tuesday and passed from person to person within the company and the media.

3.2 Formal communication flows

Work-flow is an important factor that shapes the formal pathway or channel for the sending and receiving of communications.

Communication through the formal channels in an organisation may be:

- **Vertical** – downwards, from superior to subordinate or upwards from subordinate to superior.

- **Horizontal or lateral** is communication between people at a similar level in the organisation's management hierarchy. It is communication between individuals in the same work or peer group, and also between individuals in different work groups.

- **Diagonal** – interdepartmental communication by people of different ranks.

Information also flows into and out of the organisation. Managers communicate with sources such as suppliers and customers.

- Inflow, e.g. research and surveillance. Organisations receive information necessary to identify and respond appropriately to environmental change, threat, opportunity or challenge.

- Outflow, e.g. advertising, marketing, and public relations refer to activities that involve the transmission of messages into the environment with the aim of informing and systematically influencing these people.

Expandable text

Formal communication channels

In organisations formal communication channels are normally established as part of the organisation's structure. Work-flow is an important factor that shapes the formal pathway or channel for the sending and receiving of communications. Communication flow may be downwards, from superior to subordinate, upwards from subordinate to superior, or lateral between equals.

- **Downward communication** provides a basis for giving specific job instructions, policy decisions, guidance and resolution of queries. Such information can help clarify operational goals, provide a sense of direction and give subordinates data related to their performance. It also helps link levels of the hierarchy by providing a basis for co-ordinated activity. Too much emphasis on downward communication can create problems. People will become reluctant to come forward with their suggestions and problems and may be averse to taking on new responsibilities. There is also a risk of management getting out of touch with their subordinates. For these reasons it is important to stress upward communication.

- **Upward communication** provides management with feedback from employees on results achieved and problems encountered. It creates a channel from which management can gauge organisational climate and deal with problem areas, such as grievances or low productivity, before they become major issues.

- **Lateral or horizontal communication** channels refer to communication between people or groups at the same level in the organisation. Four of the most important reasons for lateral communication are:

(1) Task co-ordination – department heads may meet periodically to discuss how each department is contributing to organisational objectives.

(2) Problem solving – members of a department may meet to discuss how they will handle a threatened budget cut.

(3) Information sharing – members of one department may meet with the members of another department to explain some new information or study.

(4) Conflict resolution – members of one department may meet to discuss a problem, e.g. duplication of activities in the department and some other department.

Co-ordination between departments depends on this form of contact, e.g. line and staff positions rely heavily on advice passing laterally. Managers also communicate with sources outside the organisation, e.g. suppliers and customers.

Test your understanding 2

Explain the difference between vertical and lateral (or horizontal) communication. In what circumstances or situations would you expect to find very little horizontal communication?

3.3 Informal communication channels

While the organisational structure will have a designated, formal communications network, it is inevitable and not necessarily bad that in almost all organisations there will be a number of informal communication channels.

Informal communication:

- can move in any direction

- skips authority levels

- is as likely to satisfy social needs as it is to facilitate task accomplishments.

A grapevine is the network of social relations that arises spontaneously as people associate with one another.

Grapevine activity, or 'bush telegraph' as it is sometimes known, is likely to flourish in many common situations such as when:

- there is a lack of information about a situation and people try to fill in the gaps as best they can

- there is insecurity in the situation

- there is a personal interest in a situation, e.g. when a friend is disciplined by a supervisor people may well gossip about it

- there is personal animosity in a situation and people seek to gain advantage by the spreading of rumours

- there is new information which people wish to spread quickly.

The grapevine is sometimes used deliberately by management to give out information that it would not wish to transmit formally. It may wish to prepare staff for the formal announcement of some bad news.

Rumour is another type of informal communication. This is a message transmitted over the grapevine and is not based on official information. As a rumour it may be true or false or have elements of both.

Gossip, together with rumour, is often communicated by the grapevine: gossip is idle talk, often of little consequence, but it can be hurtful if malicious and about particular people. However, it can be a morale booster, a socialising force which spells out group norms, and it can be beneficial to the individual as a means of sharing employment worries.

Test your understanding 3

Evaluate the following recommendations:

(1) Informal communications in the workplace should not exist.

(2) Over-reliance on informal communication networks can arise from the failure of formal communication systems.

(3) Informal communications can be used by management to its advantage.

(4) Gossip can have a positive side in that it is a morale booster and can be beneficial to the individual in the workplace.

3.4 Ineffective communication

Ineffective communication includes poor, or inadequate control, as well as faulty co-ordination.

Lack of downward communication is likely to result in:

- poor awareness of corporate objectives at lower management levels

- poor understanding of working instructions and responsibilities

- poor morale of junior managers because they are not consulted about changes which affect them or their working conditions.

Lack of upward communication, including 'feedback', has the following undesirable consequences for management:

- early warning of troubled areas is not received

- benefit of creative ability in subordinates is lost

- participation of subordinates is limited

- need for change is not appreciated because management is isolated from the operation areas

- control becomes difficult

- introduction of change is difficult.

Lack of lateral communication often leads to:

- divisions in management teams
- lack of co-ordination
- rivalry between sections and departments
- lack of advice and involvement by staff specialists.

Illustration 3 – Communications in the workplace

Perhaps the best way to think about the way in which communication can go wrong is to consider what good communication would be like:

- It would use appropriate language (e.g. no jargon; written so that the intended recipient can understand it).
- It would go only to who should receive it – not to everyone.
- It would use the right medium to communicate the information.
- The information would get to the recipient in good time for it to be used.

Taking the above list, it is easy to produce a list of how communications go wrong:

- Information is omitted or distorted by the sender.
- Information is misunderstood due to the use of inappropriate jargon or lack of clarity.
- Information is presented using an inappropriate medium (e.g. via email rather than in a proper report, or via telephone when face-to-face is better).
- Information arrives too late, or is incomplete.

3.5 The importance of good communication to employees and managers

Communication is a process that links various parts of the systems. Without a formal communication system, managers would not be able to fulfil their role.

Effective communication is essential so that:

- Instructions and guidelines are properly understood.

- Individuals know what they are expected to do.

- There is better co-ordination between people and groups in the organisation – all the systems for administration, purchasing, production and marketing can be synchronised to perform the right actions at the right times and co-operate in accomplishing the organisation's goals.

- Managers are able to plan and control operations more effectively.

- Individuals are more willing to work together in teams or groups, because they are being told what is happening and where their contribution fits in.

- Forming, swapping and testing of ideas is encouraged.

- Secrecy, misunderstanding and mistrust are eliminated. Open communication increases trust.

- Interpersonal relations can be developed and maintained between subordinates, supervisors, peers, customers and suppliers.

- Arguments and conflicts in the work place are reduced.

Test your understanding 4

Explain the importance of clear communication.

3.6 The attributes of effective communication

The ultimate test of the effectiveness of communication – for whatever purpose, however it is delivered or whatever its nature – is that those who need the information receive it in a comprehensible form, in the right format, on time and in a state where it can be acted on.

Effective communication will ensure that the right person receives the right information at the right time. This means it must be:

- Timely

- Accurate, complete and to the point

- Directed to the right people

- Understandable

- **Timely** – when the communication is intended to result in action, then the speed of communication will be related to the urgency of that action. A report that a machine is out of action is of little value if it is delayed while several hours or days of production are lost.

- **Accurate, complete and to the point** – any information contained in a communication should be factually correct and all the facts should be stated; otherwise wrong conclusions may be drawn or wrong decisions taken. It is also generally accepted that a brief message will generally be more acceptable than a long-winded one.

- **Directed to the right people** – most companies can produce examples of instructions, data sheets or control reports which are distributed in accordance with predetermined lists or recipients, often on the basis of seniority or status. Very often some of the recipients have no use for the information and may indeed be led to investigate matters which have no relevance to the job they have to do.

- **Understandable** – Communication always needs care in its presentation. Not everyone has the capability of logical analysis, and this is why well-designed formal presentations are often more effective than informal oral communications. In upwards and lateral communication, however, a disordered emotional outburst will sometimes give a clearer general impression, to be clarified in further discussion, than a simple recital of facts.

3.7 Barriers to effective communication

Poor communication can be the result of barriers to and breakdowns in communication, which should always be analysed to prevent continuing occurrence.

A barrier to communication is anything that stops information from:

- getting to its intended recipient(s)
- being understood by the recipients and
- being acted on in the way intended.

Barriers to communication may be due to:

- the personal background of the individuals communicating, e.g. natural reserve and status barriers can result in reluctance to pass information upwards for fear of incurring criticism
- language differences or the use of technical or professional jargon

- difference in education levels

- noise, i.e. the message is confused by extraneous matters

- conflict within the organisation and between individuals

- overload, i.e. too much information being communicated

- distance between communicators

- simple misunderstanding as to content or context

- distortion of information by the receiver.

Test your understanding 5

X is a junior manager in his early 40s who joined his company at the age of 16. He sticks to a strict routine, arriving and leaving work punctually. He is married with two children at school. He has always worked in the functional section that he now manages and is the most experienced employee in his particular field. However, he is not familiar with latest developments in information technology and feels swamped by an excess of useless information. He claims that he is, in any case, aware of the information he needs, but his subordinates worry because they notice that he ignores information that does not agree with his opinions.

D is a young accounting graduate who works in the management information department. She has been promoted quickly to supervisor level, having joined the company a few years ago straight from university. She is single and lives close to the office and often works late because she loves computers and is fascinated by their potential. She frequently and fluently tells anyone willing to listen that the company is old-fashioned and needs to be dragged into the twentieth century. X hears this, disapproves but does not comment, and carries on in his usual way.

Although D and X are located in different buildings on the same site, their work requires them to co-operate regularly. Their relations are getting more and more strained and their work is suffering.

Required

Identify and describe the barriers to communication between the two colleagues.

3.8 Overcoming barriers to communication

When there are significant barriers to communication, it is important to:

- identify what those barriers are, and

- consider ways of dealing with the problem.

Some general rules to ensure communication is effective are:

- avoid communication overload

- ensure the right information gets to the right person at the right time

- agree and confirm priorities and deadlines for receipt of information

- keep communication simple

- develop empathy with 'listeners'

- confirm, by repeating back, what has been said

- confirm that the information you have given has been understood

- avoid inconsistent verbal/non-verbal communication.

Illustration 4 – Communications in the workplace

A manager is frequently accused of upsetting his staff by the tone of his memos. How can this situation be resolved?

The manager concerned could spend time reading memos sent by other managers then compare and contrast both the content and tone with that of his own memos. He can call more meetings or speak to staff individually rather than sending memos all the time. He can ask staff, informally, what they dislike about his memos. He can make it clear to staff that the memos are not intended to cause offence. He can ask to, be asked to, or arrange to, attend a short course on communication skills.

Although anticipating is preferable to reacting to problems when they occur, this is not always possible. Unexpected difficulties will invariably arise. Example of these include:

- Unexpected breakdowns of equipment may occur.

- A communication method may be inappropriate for a particular message.

- Receiver(s) may not be in the correct frame of mind to accept a message.

- Messages may be delayed causing mistrust and suspicion.

- An official message may be received before a manager has the opportunity to discuss an issue informally with his staff.

- People may not be available to receive important messages.

Ultimately, successful communication depends on continuous feedback and monitoring of existing communication systems. Information received from monitoring should be evaluated and findings acted on swiftly. If difficulties are identified these need to be corrected before further damage can occur.

> ### Test your understanding 6
>
> Five possible barriers to communication are as follows.
>
> (a) The persons communicating might come from very different backgrounds, in terms of work experience and expertise, or socially. Substantial age differences, and lifestyles, can also create barriers to communication.
>
> (b) The message might be distorted in transmission, e.g. if it has to be transmitted to several people before it reaches the end user.
>
> (c) In a multi-national organisation employees might have to overcome a language barrier to communicate with each other.
>
> (d) If there is information overload, an individual might be given too much information, and be unable to understand the message.
>
> (e) Where there is conflict within the organisation, and two individuals or departments are hostile towards each other, communications from one to the other will be treated with suspicion or disbelief.
>
> ### Required
>
> Describe how those five barriers could be overcome.

4 Communication patterns

When we look beyond two-person communication to the linkages among work groups, departmental or organisational members, we are concerned with communication networks, which are systems of communication lines linking various senders and receivers.

The flow of information is regulated by several factors:

- the proximity of workers to one another
- the rules governing who communicates with whom
- the status hierarchy
- other elements such as job assignments and duties.

Five major types have been studied in depth: wheel, circle, all-channels, chain and 'Y'.

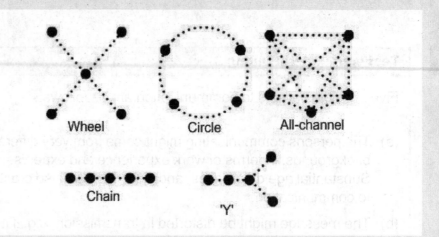

There has been extensive research on communication networks. The results of these studies indicate that each of the different networks has different strengths and weaknesses:

- In the centralised networks (chain, wheel and 'Y'), group members have to go through a person located in the central position in the network in order to communicate with others. This leads to unequal access to information in the group.

- In decentralised networks (circle and all-channels) information can flow freely between members without having to go through a central person.

The main conclusions of the experiment were:

- The wheel is always the quickest way to reach a conclusion, and the circle the slowest.

- For complex problems, the all-channel is the most likely process to reach the best decision.

- The level of satisfaction for individuals is lowest in the circle, fairly high in the all-channel, mixed in the wheel, with the central figures usually expressing greater satisfaction, and the rest feeling isolated.

- Under time pressure the all-channels system either restructures, to become a wheel, or disintegrates.

Test your understanding 7

What is the difference between a wheel and a circle pattern of communication?

Give an example of each.

Chapter summary

Communication process

Sender ···▶ Encoding ···▶ Message Media ···▶ Decoding ···▶ Receiver

◀ Noise ▶

Feedback ◀···· ◀···· Response ◀····

Definition
Communication is the interchange of information, ideas, fact and emotions by two or more persons

COMMUNICATION

Stages, Sender, Receiver, Message, Feedback and Noise

COMMUNICATION IN THE WORK PLACE

Communication flow
Vertical, Horizontal, Diagronal

Methods of communication

Effective communication
Timely, Accurate, Complete Understandable, Directed

Ineffective communication

Formal, e.g. plants, reports, Procedures

Informal, e.g. phone call, email

Barriers and overcoming the barriers

Communication patterns
Centralised networks: all-channels, circle
Decentralised networks: Y, chain, wheel

Grapevine
Bush telegraph, rumour and gossip

Test your understanding answers

Test your understanding 1

Negative feedback, i.e. a sign that your message was not having its desired effect could include:

- no action being taken
- wrong action being taken
- silence or blank look
- request for clarification
- incorrect reading back of the message.

Positive feedback, i.e. a sign that the message was received and understood could include:

- action taken as requested
- accurate reading back of message
- smile, nod
- affirmative statement, e.g. 'Yes I've got that'.

Test your understanding 2

Vertical and lateral (horizontal) communication flows are associated with hierarchical organisations. Vertical communication flows up and down the scalar chain, from boss to subordinate and from subordinate to boss. Lateral communication flows between colleagues or between different sections and departments.

Very little formal horizontal communication may occur in an organisation that is managed in an authoritarian style. This is because the manager 'at the top' wants to know everything that is happening, and wants to be involved in all decision making. Information must therefore be passed up to the top manager so that decisions can be passed back down to someone else.

Test your understanding 3

(1) Informal communications in the workplace are inevitable and management should recognise it and use it to their advantage.

(2) True, in the absence of a formal communication system, rumour and gossip will receive too much employee attention and belief.

(3) True, there are circumstances when management can effectively harness the informal system.

(4) True.

Test your understanding 4

Clear communication is important because it:

- ensures that individuals need to know what is expected of them
- provides co-ordination within the organisation
- ensures control of the organisation's plans, procedures and staff
- ensures that the instructions of management are understood
- assists with group and team cohesiveness
- assists with the reduction of stress
- removes bias, distortion and omission
- removes secrecy and provides openness
- ensures that the right information is received by the appropriate person
- reduces conflict between individuals and departments.

Test your understanding 5

Analysis of the case reveals that there are a variety of reasons for the barriers in communication that exist between X and D. The major reasons are:

Differences in social background; for instance, age, education, marital status, etc. These might result in:

- failure to understand each others' point of view, values and priorities

- failure to listen to the information the other person is giving

- lack of shared 'vocabulary', which might lead to lack of understanding of the message

- stereotyping each other into specific classes with similar traits and characteristics, e.g. 'stick-in-the mud'.

X and D are located in different departments and buildings which may mean they do not share the same departmental objectives and may not have the opportunity to meet and discuss their differences face-to-face. Communication which is limited to telephone calls prevents access to non-verbal messages, which could provide additional information about each other.

Personal barriers may exist which will hinder effective communication. These may be due to:

- Distrust and feeling threatened by and fearing the computerised systems, which can result in any information provided by the system being viewed with scepticism.

- D seeing X as an older person who has failed to advance his career, having reached only junior manager, which may result in her talking down to him. On the other hand X may resent D being promoted to supervisor at a relatively young age.

- D resenting X working 9 to 5, and exhibiting a reluctance to become familiar with the computerised system. X may feel that his family commitments do not allow him to give the extra time required to the organisation, in order that he may learn more about the new computer system.

- D's attitude leading her to make comments which imply criticism of people like X and this could lead to a degree of resentment on the part of X which may also restrict communication.

If the situation described in the question causes personal conflict or antagonism between X and D, then further communication problems can occur:

- emotions (anger, fear, frustration) will creep into communications and further hinder the transmission of clear information

- the receiver of the information will tend to hear what they want to hear in any message and ignore anything they do not want to accept.

Test your understanding 6

(a) When individuals communicating with each other come from different backgrounds, they should be encouraged by management to show consideration for the other person. When an engineer communicates with an accountant, the engineer must be wary of using engineering jargon without explaining it, just as accountants must be careful of using accounting and finance terms that non-accountants are unlikely to know. A highly-educated person, when communicating with someone less educated, should choose his words carefully, so that his message is clear and understandable.

(b) Communication flows should be organised so that there are as few links in the communication chain as possible between the sender of the message and its eventual recipient. Lateral communications should replace unnecessary upward and downward communication flows. Electronic communication systems should contribute towards this aim.

(c) Language difficulties can be reduced in two ways. First, employees should be given language training as appropriate in another language. Secondly, the organisation should select an official language for all its meetings at a certain level of management and above. In many global corporations, English is the official language.

(d) Information overload can be reduced by improvements in reporting systems. For long reports, there should be a much briefer summary containing all the essential points and recommendations. Control reports should use reporting by exception, and draw attention to performance of an unusual or unexpected nature (such as large variances). Narrative can be summarised into tables and diagrams.

(e) Attempts to resolve conflict between individuals or departments should be made by the management in charge of them both. A solution to the problem of conflict is partly an improvement in communications. Management should arrange for more direct contact between individuals in different departments, and should use their interpersonal skills to try to overcome misunderstandings and disagreements.

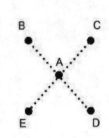	In a wheel pattern of communication, one person at the centre communicates directly with everyone else in the group, and the other group members communicate only with the individual at the centre and not with each other. A wheel pattern might occur when there is a dominant or authoritarian leader who retains all decision-making powers.
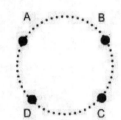	In a circle pattern of communication, each individual communicates with two other people, and eventually the communication links come back to the point at which they started. For example, if four people communicate with each other: A might communicate with B and D B might communicate with A and C C might communicate with B and D D might communicate with C and A This type of communication pattern might be typical of some informal communication links, so that information gets passed on from one person to another, and eventually arrives back at the original source.

30

MULTIPLE CHOICE
QUESTIONS

Chapter 1: The Business Organisation

(1) **Which one of the following does not fall within the definition of an organisation given by Buchanan and Huczynski:**

A   service companies

B   factories

C   retail companies

D   political parties

E   shareholders in a quoted company

F   charities

G   local councils

H   the army, navy and air force

I   schools.

(2 marks)

(2) **Which one of the following is not a recognised means of achieving coordination:**

A   Standardised work processes

B   Standardised outputs

C   Standardised payment systems

D   Standardised skills and knowledge

E   Direct supervision

F   Mutual adjustment

(1 mark)

(3) **A hospital manager is considering the use of temporary nursing staff to fill shortages due to sickness. Which level of planning is involved here?**

A   Strategic

B   Tactical

C   Operational

(1 mark)

(4) The three steps in strategic planning are strategic analysis, strategic choice and strategy into action (strategy implementation). Which of the following is part of strategic choice?

A   SWOT analysis, to provide a comprehensive picture of strengths and weaknesses

B   Stakeholder analysis - to understand stakeholder expectations/influence in order to clarify objectives.

C   What is our objective in terms of industry positioning - are we seeking No1 spot?

D   How do we want to get there? Organic growth, acquisition or some joint arrangement such as franchising?

(2 marks)

Chapter 2: Organisational structure

(5) Conflic\ting demands over allocation of resources is most likely to be a disadvantage from which type of organisational structure?

A   Entrepreneurial

B   Matrix

C   Divisional

D   Geographical

(2 marks)

(6) The line of authority relates to _____. Which phrase completes the sentence?

A   Scalar chain

B   Span of control

C   Number of managerial levels

D   Ownership vs control

(2 marks)

(7) A narrow span of control is likely to lead to a tall management structure – true or false?

A   True

B   False

(1 mark)

(8) **Which of the following does not affect the amount of decentralisation that occurs in a firm?**

A   Management style

B   Nature of the work

C   Location of employees

D   Size of the organisation

(2 marks)

(9) **An informal organisational structure can arise in an organisation due to _____. Which one of the following does not complete the sentence?**

A   Friendships

B   Personal relationships

C   The grapevine effect

D   Common interests

(2 marks)

Chapter 3: Organisational culture

(10) **Which of the following is not an element of organisational culture?**

A   Norms of behaviour

B   Symbols

C   Shared values

D   Size of the organisation

(2 marks)

(11) **According to Schein, there is a strong link between culture and _____. Which word best fills the blank?**

A   Management style

B   Leadership

C   Influence

D   Size of the organisation

(2 marks)

(12) **According to Charles Handy's four cultural types, which of the following organisations is least likely to adopt a person culture?**

A Barristers chambers

B Advertising company

C University research department

D Firm of solicitors

(2 marks)

(13) **Which of the following is one of Hofstede's five traits?**

A Power distance

B Power measure

C Power range

D Power length

(2 marks)

Chapter 4: Leadership, management and supervision

(14) **A supervisor is a person given _____ for planning and controlling the work of their group. Which word correctly completes this sentence?**

A Authority

B Autonomy

C Autocracy

(2 marks)

(15) **Which of the following is not one of the elements of management as identified by Fayol?**

A Control

B Co-ordination

C Commitment

D Command

(2 marks)

(16) **Which of the following can be delegated?**

    A   Responsibility

    B   Authority

    C   Obligation

    D   Liability

(2 marks)

(17) **Which of the following statements is correct in relation to Bennis's thinking on leadership?**

    A   He focuses on the need to inspire.

    B   He focuses on the need to impose.

    C   He focuses on the need to insult.

    D   He focuses on the need to instruct.

(2 marks)

(18) **A manager has been assessed on the Blake and Mouton grid as in the (1,9) position. Which of the following best describes this manager?**

    A   He has a high concern for people and task.

    B   He has a high concern for people and a low concern for task.

    C   He has a low concern for people and a high concern for task.

    D   He has a low concern for people and a low concern for task.

(2 marks)

Chapter 5: Individual and group behaviour in business organisations

(19) **One advantage associated with a cohesive group is satisfaction of the _____ needs of the members. Which word correctly completes the sentence?**

    A   Creative

    B   Social

    C   Teamwork

    D   Communication

(2 marks)

(20) **Which of the following types of behaviour is more likely to defuse conflict when dealing with other people?**

   A   Assertive

   B   Aggressive

   C   Passive

(2 marks)

(21) **Which of the following is not a factor required to make a cohesive group?**

   A   Team solidarity

   B   Leadership

   C   Team solidity

   D   Team identity

(2 marks)

(22) **Behaviour can be caused, _____ and is goal directed. Which of the following completes the sentence?**

   A   Forced

   B   Induced

   C   Influenced

   D   Motivated

(2 marks)

Chapter 6: Team formation, development and management

(23) **A team has been formed to plan the Christmas social event for the company. One of the members of the team, John, is heard to comment negatively on other people's ideas. Which of Belbin's roles does he fulfil?**

   A   The finisher

   B   Monitor evaluator

   C   Shaper

   D   Team worker

(2 marks)

(24) **ABC Limited is a small marketing agency. A group has been formed, chaired by Nicholas, to work on an advertisement for a new client. Progress on the advertisement is slow – many ideas are being put forward, but there is a lot of criticism within the group of other people's ideas. Which of Tuckman's group stages applies in this case?**

A   Forming.

B   Storming.

C   Norming.

D   Performing.

(2 marks)

(25) **Which of the following is not a criterion for a successful team as per Peters and Waterman?**

A   Voluntary membership.

B   Structured communication.

C   Action orientated.

D   Small number.

(2 marks)

(26) **Which of the following is more likely to occur in the behaviour within a group rather than a team?**

A   People accommodate each other.

B   Feelings are expressed freely.

C   Commitment can be very high.

D   Decisions are made by consensus.

(2 marks)

Chapter 7: Motivating individuals and groups

(27) **Which of the following is due to a worker being motivated rather than satisfied?**

A   Less waste generated.

B   Low staff turnover.

C   Good morale.

D   Better attendance.

(2 marks)

(28) **Bob is a caretaker at a school where his wife is a teacher. They have three young children and have just moved from a terrace house into a semi-detached. Which of Maslow's hierarchy of need is motivating Bob?**

A   Basic

B   Safety

C   Social

D   Ego

(2 marks)

(29) **Parallels can be drawn between Maslow's hierarchy of needs and Herzberg's two-factor theory. For example, Maslow's ego need can be linked to the motivating factor of acknowledgement.**

Which hygiene factor from the following would best match with Maslow's social need?

A   Sports facilities

B   Pay

C   Pension

D   Working conditions

(2 marks)

(30) **Vroom's theory states that people's motivation is the product of anticipated worth that an individual places on a goal and the _____ of achieving that goal. Which word correctly completes this sentence?**

A   Probability

B   Liability

C   Plausibility

D   Vulnerability

(2 marks)

Chapter 8: Information technology and information systems in business

(31) **Many large organisations have established a computer intranet for the purpose of:**

    A   providing quick, effective and improved communication amongst staff using chat rooms

    B   providing quick, effective and improved communication to staff

    C   providing quick, effective and improved communication to customers

    D   providing quick, effective and improved ordering procedures in real time

(2 marks)

32 **A company uses a computer system for its middle management that can be used to assist with working out possible solutions to management problems. The system includes modelling and forecasting facilities, such as linear regression analysis and statistical analysis.**

This type of system is:

    A   a management information system (MIS)

    B   an expert system

    C   an executive information system (EIS)

    D   a decision support system (DSS).

(2 marks)

(33) **An Extranet is:**

    A   a system that enables the computer systems of two different organisations to communicate with each other

    B   an Intranet system that also provides access to certain selected external users

    C   the provision of IT services for a computer network by an external organisation

    D   a computer network that uses dedicated communications links for security purposes.

(2 marks)

(34) **Would a time sheet be considered data or information?**

A   Data

B   Information

(1 mark)

Chapter 9: Political and legal factors

35   **This same categorisation of environmental factors is sometimes referred to as SLEPT analysis.**

Which of the following categories is not represented within this acronym?

A   Social/cultural

B   Legal

C   Environmental

D   Political

E   Technological

(2 marks)

(36) **The process of backing up data and keeping copies off-site in a fire-proof box is an example of data protection.**

Is the above statement

A   True

B   False?

(1 mark)

(37) **Peter Wong was dancing on his desk one lunchtime and tripped, injuring himself. Who is responsible for the accident?**

A   Peter

B   Peter's employer

C   Both Peter and his employer

(1 mark)

Chapter 10: Macroeconomic factors

(38) **Which of the following is not one of the four macroeconomic policy objectives of governments?**

A   Economic Growth

B   Inflation

C   Unemployment

D   Balance of trade

(2 marks)

(39) **Which one of the following would cause a fall in the level of aggregate demand in an economy?**

A   A decrease in the level of imports.

B   A fall in the propensity to save.

C   A decrease in government expenditure.

D   A decrease in the level of income tax

(2 marks)

(40) **Which of the following policies for correcting a balance of payments deficit is an expenditure-reducing policy?**

A   Cutting the level of public expenditure.

B   Devaluation of the currency.

C   The imposition of an import tax.

D   The use of import quotas.

(2 marks)

(41) **Which of the following would not correct a Balance of Payments deficit?**

A   Re-valuing the currency.

B   Raising domestic interest rates.

C   Deflating the economy.

D   Imposing import controls.

(2 marks)

Chapter 11: Social and technological factors

(42) **Downsizing is the process of removing layers of management.**

    A   True

    B   False

(1 mark)

(43) **Outsourcing means contracting-out aspects of the work of the organisation, previously done in-house, to specialist providers.**

    A   True

    B   False

(1 mark)

Chapter 12: Competitive factors

(44) **Which of the following is not a Generic Strategy as described by Michael Porter:**

    A   Cost focus

    B   Differentiation

    C   Diversification

    D   Differentiation focus

(2 marks)

(45) **Which of the following is not one of the "Five Forces" as depicted in Michael Porters model of the Industry.**

    A   Competitive rivairy

    B   Power of Suppliers

    C   Power of Buyers

    D   Threat of substitutes

    E   Barriers to Entry

(2 marks)

(46) **Which of the following are not examples of "Support Activities" as described in Michael Porters Value Chain.**

A   Technology Development

B   Human Resource Management

C   Procurement

D   Firm Structure

(2 marks)

(47) **Inbound logistics is the storing, distributing and delivering finished goods to customers.**

Is the above statement

A   True

B   False?

(1 mark)

Chapter 13: Stakeholders

(48) **Which of the following would not be described as a connected stakeholder?**

A   Shareholders

B   Customers

C   Suppliers

D   Managers

(2 marks)

(49) **Stakeholders can move from quadrant to quadrant within Mendelow's matrix. True or False?**

A   True

B   False

(1 mark)

(50) **If a stakeholder has low interest but high power, then according to Mendelow's matrix the strategy management should follow in relation to that stakeholder is:**

A   Minimal effort

B   Keep satisfied

C   Keep informed

D   Fully consider the stakeholder i.e. a key player

(2 marks)

(51) **Which of the following would be described as an external stakeholder?**

A   Customer

B   Supplier

C   Trade Union

D   Competitor

(2 marks)

Chapter 14: Committees

(52) **You are convening a meeting. Which one of the following would you be doing?**

A   Deciding on the individuals who will be attending the meeting.

B   Drawing up an agenda for the meeting.

C   Issuing a notice of the meeting.

D   Writing up the record of the meeting.

(2 marks)

(53) **Since joining the project team, your friend has learned quite a lot about formal meetings, but she has never come across the term 'motion'. One of the following is your explanation of what a 'motion' is when referring to a meeting.**

A   It is an objection to the chair about an alleged irregularity in the convening, constitution or conduct of the meeting.

B   It is a stand-in for an absent member, who has the right to be present but not to speak.

C   It is an interruption of the proceedings of a meeting before they have been completed.

D   It is a proposal put to a meeting.

(2 marks)

(54) **There are a number of recognised qualities of a good chair. Which one from the following list would not be acknowledged as such?**

A A sound knowledge of the relevant regulations.

B The ability to be decisive.

C Skill in communicating rulings clearly but tactfully.

D A thorough understanding of the motion in question.

(2 marks)

Chapter 15: Business ethics and ethical behaviour

(55) **Your supervisor at work instructs you to carry out an activity that you believe is illegal. This is an example of an ethical dilemma.**

A True

B False

(1 mark)

(56) **Investigation into the nature of ethical concepts and propositions is called:**

A Meta-ethics

B Normative ethics

C Applied ethics

D Environmental ethics

(2 marks)

(57) **An ethical framework is part of good corporate governance.**

A True

B False

(1 mark)

(58) **Business ethics concerns which group of people in a company?**

A Directors only

B Sales and marketing employees only

C Qualified accountant employees only

D All employees

(2 marks)

(59) **Which of the following is not an indication that a proposed action is unethical?**

A   Lack of transparency

B   Contrary to the law

C   Use of superior power to dominate a weaker party

D   Not specifically dealt with in the company's code of conduct

(2 marks)

(60) **All companies throughout the world should follow an identical ethical code of conduct.**

A   True

B   False

(1 mark)

(61) **Which of the following occupations is not a profession?**

A   Accountancy

B   The army

C   Nursing

D   Musician

(2 marks)

(62) **What is the purpose of professional indemnity insurance (PII)?**

A   To protect accountants from non-payment of fees by clients

B   To protect clients from accountants' negligence

C   To protect accountants from being liable for misdeeds by their employees

D   To protect accountants if partners become personally bankrupt

(2 marks)

(63) **It is ethically acceptable to pay bribes to foreign government officials in order to secure contracts for one's employer.**

A   True

B   False

(1 mark)

(64) **Which of the following conditions would be unacceptable in a job advertisement?**

A   Must be a qualified accountant

B   Must be a non-smoker

C   Must be at least 5' 6" tall

D   Must be punctual and self-motivated

(2 marks)

(65) **Which of the following would be unacceptable in a company's code of conduct for its employees?**

A   Maximum number of days off for sickness each year

B   No smoking of cigarettes inside the building

C   Employees who meet the public must be smartly dressed

D   No personal use of company photocopying machines without prior permission from a manager

(2 marks)

(66) **A company can escape legal liability for an employee's misdeed as long as the company's code of conduct for employees prohibits the action.**

A   True

B   False

(1 mark)

(67) **The IFAC Code of Ethics and the ACCA Code of Ethics and Conduct identify the same Fundamental Principles to be observed by professional accountants.**

A   True

B   False

(1 mark)

(68) **A professional accountant is working in a South American country that has its own code of conduct for accountants that is not as strict as the IFAC Code in certain areas.**

A The accountant must comply with both the local code and the IFAC Code in all areas, whichever is stricter.

B The accountant need only comply with the local code.

C The accountant can choose, for each area, which code to follow.

D The accountant must comply with all statutory requirements in the country, but otherwise is free to take whatever action he chooses, since codes of conduct are non-statutory.

(2 marks)

(69) **Which of the following is not a fundamental ethical principle identified by the ACCA?**

A Integrity

B Objectivity

C Confidentiality

D Independence

(2 marks)

(70) **Which of the Fundamental Principles in the IFAC Code of Ethics requires that 'a professional accountant should be straightforward and honest in all professional and business relationships'?**

A Integrity

B Objectivity

C Professional competence

D Professional behaviour

(2 marks)

Chapter 16: Governance and social responsibility

(71) **The separation between ownership and control is only relevant in the context of limited companies.**

A True

B False

(1 mark)

(72) **Which of the following would reduce the agency problem in a large quoted company?**

A   Pay the directors a fixed amount of cash each year.

B   Pay the directors a bonus in shares based on the reported profit.

C   Employ the directors on a rolling five-year contract.

D   Offer the directors large contractual parachute payments (compensation payments if they are removed from office).

(2 marks)

(73) **According to the Cadbury Report, corporate governance is the system by which companies are:**

A   Run in the interests of all stakeholders.

B   Run in the interests of the shareholders.

C   Directed and controlled.

D   Administered within the law.

(2 marks)

(74) **Corporate social responsibility is solely concerned with a company's obligations to its external stakeholders.**

A   True

B   False

(1 mark)

(75) **Which of the following are legitimate stakeholders in a company?**

(i)   Shareholders

(ii) Past employees now receiving a pension

(iii) Local government

(iv) Investors in debentures issued by the company

A   (i) and (iii) only

B   (i), (ii) and (iii) only

C   (i), (iii) and (iv) only

D   (i), (ii), (iii) and (iv)

(2 marks)

(76) The modern view is that an exclusive focus on short-term shareholder value is self-defeating; long-term success depends on managing multiple priorities and stakeholder interests.

A   True

B   False

(1 mark)

(77) Traditional profit and loss financial reporting struggles to recognise the benefits of Corporate Social Responsibility.

A   True

B   False

(1 mark)

(78) A visible CSR programme can assist the Human Resources department in recruiting and retaining employees.

A   True

B   False

(1 mark)

(79) What proportion of the board members of a large UK-listed company should comprise independent NEDs?

A   At least one quarter.

B   At least one third.

C   At least one half.

D   At least two thirds.

(2 marks)

(80) Mr X owns 20% of the shares of AB plc and is paid £20,000 pa as a fee to act as a NED of the company. Can Mr X qualify as an independent NED?

A   Yes

B   No

(1 mark)

(81) **Which one of the following is not a responsibility of the remuneration committee?**

A   Setting the remuneration of an executive chairman.

B   Setting the remuneration of the senior NED.

C   Monitoring the level of remuneration of senior management below board level.

D   Appointing consultants to advise on executive directors' remuneration.

(2 marks)

(82) **What is the minimum acceptable number of NEDs to serve on the remuneration committee of a small UK-listed company?**

A   1

B   2

C   3

D   4

(2 marks)

(83) **Which of the following is not a responsibility of the audit committee?**

A   Appoint the external auditors each year.

B   Review the external auditors' independence.

C   Monitor the integrity of the financial statements.

D   Review the company's internal financial controls.

(2 marks)

(84) **The audit committee of a UK-listed company should comprise at least three NEDs (or two in the case of smaller companies).**

A   True

B   False

(1 mark)

(85) **The public at large are a legitimate stakeholder of a large listed company.**

A   True

B   False

(1 mark)

(86) **Audit committee meetings of companies quoted on the London Stock Exchange are open to the public if individuals book a place in the audience in advance.**

A   True

B   False

(1 mark)

(87) **Which of the following are the needs of the public at large in their role as a stakeholder group to a company?**

(i)   Ethical behaviour

(ii) Care for the environment

(iii) Acceptance of social responsibility

(iv) High dividend payments

A   (i) and (ii) only

B   (i) and (iii) only

C   (i), (ii) and (iii) only

D   (i), (ii), (iii) and (iv)

(2 marks)

(88) **Focus groups are a useful tool in stakeholder needs analysis, but they must be closely managed to ensure that a small group of individuals do not dominate the proceedings.**

A   True

B   False

(1 mark)

(89) **Which of the following is a connected stakeholder of a company?**

A   Shareholders

B   Employees

C   Directors

D   The government

(2 marks)

(90) **Statement I: The cost of training employees is an expense that must be written off in the accounts.**

Statement II: This means that the company received no benefit from the expenditure involved.

Which of these statements are true or false?

	Statement I	Statement II
A	True	True
B	True	False
C	False	True
D	False	False

(2 marks)

Chapter 17: Law and regulation governing accounting

(91) **Which of the following bodies oversees company registration in the UK?**

A   Companies Act

B   Companies House

C   Companies Home

D   Companies officer

(2 marks)

(92) **To which of the following bodies are companies not generally accountable in terms of submitting annual returns?**

A   Tax authorities

B   Central government departments

C   Competition authorities

(1 mark)

(93) **Which of the following are advantages of having legislation which governs the preparation of financial statements?**

   A   Guaranteed minimum levels of disclosure of financial matters.

   B   Helps to keep governments busy.

   C   Means that accounts prepared in different countries are more comparable.

   D   Means that accounts will comply with accounting standards.

(2 marks)

(94) **Which of the following are disadvantages of having legislation which governs the preparation of financial statements?**

   A   Guaranteed minimum levels of disclosure of financial matters.

   B   Makes accounts more comparable.

   C   Increased regulatory requirements lead to increased costs.

   D   Investors have more faith in financial statements.

(2 marks)

(95) **Which of the following statements is true?**

   A   Companies legislation is identical in all countries.

   B   Companies legislation in similar in all countries.

   C   Companies legislation is identical in commonwealth countries.

   D   Companies legislation is similar in commonwealth countries.

(2 marks)

(96) **Which of the following statements is false?**

   A   Companies legislation is intended to protect investors.

   B   Companies legislation is intended to protect lenders.

   C   Companies legislation is identical to the requirements of accounting standards.

   D   Companies legislation is similar in commonwealth countries.

(2 marks)

(97) **Which of the following must be true for financial statements to give a true and fair view?**

A   They must be accurate.

B   They must show a correct valuation of the company.

C   They must not be materially misstated.

D   They must be filed at Companies House.

(2 marks)

(98) **Which of the following is not necessary in order for financial statements to give a true and fair view.**

A   They must not be materially misstated.

B   They must follow accounting standards.

C   They must have reasonable detail.

D   There must be no fraud.

(2 marks)

(99) **Which of the following is necessary for a company to have proper accounting records?**

A   There should be a computerised system.

B   The finance director should be a qualified accountant.

C   There should be control accounts.

D   They should show and explain the transactions.

(2 marks)

(100) **Which of the following is not necessary in order for a company to have proper accounting records?**

A   They should show and explain the transactions.

B   There should be a computerised general ledger.

C   There should be a record of income and expenses.

D   There should be a record of assets and liabilities.

(2 marks)

(101)**Which section of the accounting department has most involvement in preparing the financial statements?**

A   Financial reporting.

B   Taxation.

C   Management accounting.

D   Treasury.

(2 marks)

(102)**Which section of the accounting department is unlikely to be involved in the preparation of the financial statements?**

A   Inventory

B   Sales ledger

C   Treasury

D   Non-current assets

(2 marks)

(103)**What are the potential consequences of financial statements failing to give a true and fair view?**

A   The company will be 'struck off' the register of companies.

B   The company will be forced to place a statement to that effect on its website.

C   The directors will be forced to resign.

D   The auditors will give a qualified audit report.

(2 marks)

(104)**Which of the following is not a potential consequence of failing to keep proper accounting records?**

A   The directors will be asked to resign.

B   The directors will be prosecuted and fined.

C   True and fair accounts will not be able to be produced.

D   Customers may not be chased for payment.

(2 marks)

(105) **Which of the following is not a potential consequence of failing to prepare true and fair accounts?**

A   The auditors will give a qualified report.

B   Investors will be unwilling to buy shares.

C   Banks will be unwilling to lend money.

D   The Registrar of Companies will force the company to prepare them again.

(2 marks)

(106) **Who is responsible if the financial statements do not give a true and fair view?**

A   The directors.

B   The chief executive officer.

C   The finance director.

D   The auditor.

(2 marks)

(107) **Who produces international accounting standards?**

A   International Accounting Standards Committee.

B   International Accounting Standards Board.

C   Companies House.

D   Accounting firms.

(2 marks)

(108) **Which of the following is an advantage of harmonising accounting standards worldwide?**

A   All financial statements will be identical.

B   Users will be able to compare financial statements more easily.

C   Financial statements will be in accordance with the law.

D   Laws around the world will be harmonised.

(2 marks)

(109) **Which of the following is not an advantage of harmonising accounting standards worldwide?**

A   Financial statements will be shorter.

B   Users will be able to compare financial statements more easily.

C   Multinationals will be able to produce their financial statements more quickly.

D   Developing countries will have a basis for developing their own standards.

(2 marks)

(110) **Why does the accounting profession want to develop accounting standards?**

A   It wants to have influence over their content.

B   Members of Parliament are too busy.

C   It wants to make sure they are very easy.

D   The Companies Act is out of date.

(2 marks)

(111) **Which of the following produces accounting standards?**

A   IASB

B   SAC

C   IASCF

D   IFRIC

(2 marks)

(112) **Which of the following produces interpretations?**

A   IASB

B   SAC

C   IASCF

D   IFRIC

(2 marks)

(113) **Which of the following consults with the users of accounts?**

   A   IASB

   B   SAC

   C   IASCF

   D   IFRIC

(2 marks)

(114) **Which of the following raises money?**

   A   IASB

   B   SAC

   C   IASCF

   D   IFRIC

(2 marks)

(115) **Which of the following are produced as part of the process of preparing international accounting standards (IASs)?**

   A   Interpretation

   B   Exposure draft

   C   Directive

   D   Regulation

(2 marks)

(116) **Which of the following are not produced as part of the process of preparing IASs?**

   A   Interpretation

   B   Exposure draft

   C   Discussion paper

   D   IFRS

(2 marks)

(117)**Which of the following are produced as part of the process of preparing IASs?**

A   Discussion paper

B   Legislation

C   Recommendation

D   Pronouncement

(2 marks)

(118)**Which of the following are not produced as part of the process of preparing IASs?**

A   Exposure draft

B   Recommendation

C   Discussion paper

D   Standard

(2 marks)

Chapter 18: The accounting profession

(119)**Professional services in which of the following business areas is not normally found within a 'Big 4' accounting firm?**

A   Business advisory

B   Assurance

C   Conference organisation

D   Insolvency

(2 marks)

(120)**Which of the following best explains why accounting standards have been developed?**

A   To ensure that accounts prepared by different accounting firms are the same.

B   To ensure that accounts prepared in different countries are the same.

C   To ensure that accounts are prepared accurately.

D   To make it easier for users to compare the accounts of different companies.

(2 marks)

(121) **The accounting department has produced some information on the quantity of goods sold at different prices. For which other department would this information be most useful?**

A   Production

B   Marketing

C   Purchasing

D   Human resources

(2 marks)

(122) **The accounting department has produced some information on the number of staff in each department and the distribution of their salaries. For which other department would this information be most useful?**

A   Production

B   Marketing

C   Purchasing

D   Human resources

(2 marks)

(123) **The purpose of accounting is to produce financial information that is useful to a wide range of users. Which of the following information will be of most interest to shareholders?**

A   Proportion of fixed and variable costs

B   Profits

C   Interest rates

D   Depreciation rates

(2 marks)

(124) **The purpose of accounting is to produce financial information that is useful to a wide range of users. Which of the following information will be of most interest to banks?**

A   Proportion of fixed and variable costs

B   Profits

C   Borrowings

D   Depreciation rates

(2 marks)

(125)**Anna works in the accounting department of ABC Limited. She tells you that she has spent the day reconciling suppliers' statements. In which section does Anna work?**

A   Cashier

B   Management accounting

C   Payroll

D   Purchase ledger

(2 marks)

(126)**Boris works in the accounting department of DEF Limited. He tells you that he has spent the day vetting potential credit customers. In which section does Boris work?**

A   Cashier

B   Management accounting

C   Sales ledger

D   Purchase ledger

(2 marks)

(127)**Celeste works in the accounting department of GHI Limited. She tells you that she has spent the day preparing a cash flow forecast. In which section does Celeste work?**

A   Cashier

B   Management accounting

C   Sales ledger

D   Purchase ledger

(2 marks)

(128)**Desmond works in the accounting department of JKL Limited. He tells you that he has spent the day researching interest rates at different banks. In which section does Desmond work?**

A   Cashier

B   Management accounting

C   Treasury

D   Purchase ledger

(2 marks)

Chapter 19: Accounting and finance functions

(129) **What is a plan expressed in quantitative terms for a specified future period of time?**

A   A standard

B   A policy

C   A control limit

D   A budget

(2 marks)

(130) **What sort of information will management be interested in for the purposes of controlling their business?**

A   Financial information only

B   Non-financial information only

C   Both financial and non-financial information

(1 mark)

(131) **In a manual accounting system, the first record of transactions such as sales or purchases, from which details are transferred into the accounting ledgers, is made in the books of prime entry.**

A   True

B   False

(1 mark)

(132) **Which of the following is not required in the financial statements of a small company prepared in accordance with International Accounting Standards?**

A   Balance sheet

B   Income statement

C   Cash flow statement

D   Auditors' report

(2 marks)

(133) **The treasury department of a company can be run as a profit centre that is expected to generate profits for the company.**

A   True

B   False

(2 marks)

(134) **Which of the following responsibilities would not be given to a typical treasury department?**

A   Preparing the annual report and accounts for publication

B   Advising whether new funds should be raised by a share issue or by a loan

C   Managing the banking relationship

D   Preparing regular cash flow forecasts

(2 marks)

(135) **Which of the following is legal?**

A   Tax avoidance

B   Tax evasion

C   Overstating deductions in a tax computation to reduce the tax liability

D   Understating income in a tax computation to reduce the tax liability

(2 marks)

(136) **The legal duty for a company to pay the correct amount of tax rests with the tax advisers to the company.**

A   True

B   False

(1 mark)

(137) **The annual cost of debt finance is usually lower than the annual cost of equity finance, particularly since interest payments are allowable against tax, while dividend payments are not allowable against tax.**

A   True

B   False

(1 mark)

(138) **Which of the following sources of finance is most appropriate to finance the building of a new factory?**

    A   Bank overdraft

    B   Five-year loan

    C   Thirty-year loan

    D   Hire purchase

(2 marks)

Chapter 20: Financial systems and procedures

(139) **You are given the following extract from a systems manual: '... the purchase officer gives a copy of the purchase order to the goods inwards department and another to the accounts department. When the invoice is received the accounts clerk matches it with the order to ensure that the price charged is correct. The invoice is passed to the requisitioning department for approval, and then entered into the accounts...'.**

What does this extract describe?

    A   A system

    B   A policy

    C   A procedure

    D   A guideline

(2 marks)

(140) **You are given the following extract: '...the clerk multiplies the hours worked by the hourly rate to determine the gross pay...'.**

What does this extract describe?

    A   A system

    B   A policy

    C   A procedure

    D   A guideline

(2 marks)

(141) **Which of these is an advantage of having a formal procedure for carrying out a task?**

    A   All transactions should be recorded in an identical way.

    B   Staff are allowed to be creative.

    C   Staff are allowed to use their judgement more.

    D   It can be rather inflexible.

        (2 marks)

(142) **Which of these is not an advantage of having a formal procedure for carrying out a task?**

    A   Transactions can normally be recorded more quickly as the learning effect is reduced.

    B   Transactions should be recorded uniformly.

    C   Best practice can be adopted by all staff.

    D   It reduces flexibility.

        (2 marks)

(143) **Tony is trying to design a procedure for the processing of orders from customers.**

Which of the following is not an objective of that procedure?

    A   To ensure that orders are processed promptly.

    B   To ensure that goods are only despatched to customers who are likely to pay.

    C   To ensure that all orders are recorded.

    D   To ensure that customers sign to accept the goods.

        (2 marks)

(144) **Jacob is trying to design a procedure for the calculation of cash wages to employees.**

Which of the following is not an objective of that procedure?

A   To ensure that gross wages are calculated correctly.

B   To ensure that deductions are calculated correctly.

C   To ensure that wages are paid only to employees entitled to them.

D   To ensure that staff are only paid for hours worked.

(2 marks)

(145) **Which of the following is an advantage of using flow charts to describe a system?**

A   It is easy to get an overall picture of the system.

B   It is easy for everyone to understand.

C   The system will contain more controls.

D   The system will be better.

(2 marks)

(146) **Which of the following is a disadvantage of using narrative notes to describe a system?**

A   It is easy to get an overall picture of the system.

B   The quality of the notes is likely to be variable, as determined by the capability of the writer.

C   They are easy for anyone to understand.

D   They are quick to write.

(2 marks)

(147) **Which of the following is not a stage in the purchasing cycle?**

A   Receipt of goods.

B   Receipt of cash.

C   Placing of order.

D   Matching of invoices with orders and goods received notes.

(2 marks)

(148)Which of the following documents would not appear in the purchasing cycle?

A   Order

B   Invoice

C   Time sheet

D   Goods received note

(2 marks)

(149)Which of the following would be earliest in the sales cycle for a company selling goods on credit to wholesalers?

A   Receipt of payment

B   Dispatch of goods

C   Receipt of order

D   Dispatch of invoice

(2 marks)

(150)Which of the following would be earliest in the sales cycle for a fast food outlet selling fried chicken?

A   Receipt of payment

B   Dispatch of goods

C   Receipt of order

D   Demand for payment

(2 marks)

(151)Which of the following is not a stage in the wages system?

A   Entering details from timesheets.

B   Authorising of clockcards.

C   Transfer from the company's bank account.

D   Payment of invoice.

(2 marks)

(152)Which of the following is not the name of a document used to record hours worked?

A   Clockcard

B   Punchcard

C   Watchcard

D   Timesheet

(2 marks)

(153)Which of the following is a term used in the petty cash system?

A   Timesheet

B   Goods received note

C   Requisition

D   Voucher

(2 marks)

(154)Which of the following is not a category of inventory?

A   Accrual

B   Raw materials

C   Work-in-progress

D   Finished goods

(2 marks)

(155)Which of these comes earliest in the inventory system?

A   Transfer to warehouse.

B   Requisition of raw materials.

C   Purchase of raw materials.

D   Sale of finished goods.

(2 marks)

(156) **Which of the following is not a purpose of organisational control?**

A Safeguarding assets

B Preventing fraud

C Avoiding foreign exchange risk

D Efficiency

(2 marks)

(157) **Safeguarding the company's assets is a purpose of organisational control. Which of the following controls is not designed to achieve this?**

A Locking cash in the safe.

B Checking the payroll has been calculated correctly.

C Reconciliation of cheques received in the post to the amount banked.

D Reconciliation of the amount recorded in the cash register with the physical cash.

(2 marks)

(158) **Which of these controls relates to the purchasing system?**

A Agreeing invoices to goods received notes.

B Checking creditworthiness.

C Authorising timesheets.

D Keeping the finished goods warehouse locked.

(2 marks)

(159) **Which of these controls relates to the sales system?**

A Agreeing invoices to goods received notes.

B Checking creditworthiness.

C Authorising timesheets.

D Keeping the finished goods warehouse locked.

(2 marks)

(160) **Which of the following is not a feature of an automated system?**

A   Uniform processing of transactions.

B   Lack of segregation of functions.

C   Simple to correct errors.

D   Potential for increased management supervision.

(2 marks)

(161) **Which of the following is a feature of an automated system?**

A   Uniform processing of transactions.

B   Low capital cost.

C   No computer training required.

D   System will not crash.

(2 marks)

(162) **Which of the following is not a disadvantage of a manual system?**

A   Slower at performing calculations.

B   More likely to make calculation errors.

C   Analysis of information is more time consuming.

D   Cheaper to set up.

(2 marks)

(163) **Which of the following is not an advantage of a manual system?**

A   Information which is easy to analyse.

B   Simple correction of errors (e.g. whitening fluid).

C   Ledgers are portable.

D   Can review transactions for logical sense while entering/ performing calculations.

(2 marks)

(164)**Which of the following is not a disadvantage of an automated system?**

A   Capital cost.

B   Training cost, especially for older staff.

C   Information easy to analyse.

D   Systems can crash.

(2 marks)

(165)**Which of the following is not an advantage of an automated system?**

A   Lower capital cost

B   Can perform more complex calculations

C   More security (passwords)

D   Easier to sort and analyse data

(2 marks)

Chapter 21: The relationship of accounting with other business functions

(166)**Which of the following is an example of co-ordination between the purchasing and accounting departments?**

A   Establishing credit terms.

B   Determining sales price.

C   Allocating costs.

D   Deciding on pay rises.

(2 marks)

(167)**Which of the following is not an example of co-ordination between the purchasing and accounting departments?**

A   Approving payments.

B   Determining quantity required for inventory.

C   Budgeting.

D   Allocating costs.

(2 marks)

(168) **Which of the following is an example of co-ordination between the production and accounting departments?**

A   Establishing credit terms.

B   Determining sales price.

C   Allocating costs.

D   Deciding on pay rises.

(2 marks)

(169) **Which of the following is not an example of co-ordination between the production and accounting departments?**

A   Allocating costs.

B   Budgeting.

C   Balancing cost and quality.

D   Approving orders.

(2 marks)

(170) **Which of the following is not an example of co-ordination between the marketing and accounting departments?**

A   Reviewing advertising cost/benefit.

B   Pricing.

C   Assessing market share.

D   Assessing creditworthiness.

(2 marks)

(171) **Which of the following should be taken into account in determining charge-out rates to be used by a service department?**

A   Wages cost.

B   Number of hours taken.

C   Foreign exchange rates.

D   Interest rates.

(2 marks)

(172)**Which of the following should not be taken into account in determining charge-out rates to be used by a service department?**

A Employer's contribution to staff pensions

B Actual number of hours taken on a specific job.

C Rates charged by competitors.

D Overheads of service department.

(2 marks)

(173)**Which of the following is an advantage of providing good service?**

A Greater customer satisfaction.

B Higher payroll costs.

C Higher inventory turnover.

D Economies of scale.

(2 marks)

(174)**Which of the following is not an advantage of providing good service?**

A Reduced marketing costs, so more likely to sell to existing customers.

B Customers less likely to buy elsewhere.

C Provides a one-stop shop.

D Economies of scale.

(2 marks)

Chapter 22: Internal and external audit

(175) **Who gains benefit from the external audit of a company's financial statements?**

A The directors only.

B The shareholders only.

C Only the lenders of funds to a company.

D All readers of the financial statements.

(2 marks)

(176)**An internal audit function is normally required by law in a large quoted company.**

   A   True

   B   False

(1 mark)

(177)**To whom is an external audit report addressed?**

   A   The directors.

   B   The audit committee.

   C   The shareholders.

   D   All readers of the financial statements.

(2 marks)

(178)**The primary purpose of an internal audit is to report on whether the financial statements give a true and fair view.**

   A   True

   B   False

(1 mark)

(179)**Internal auditors look at the management of all risks faced by a company (operational risks, strategic risks, etc.) whereas external auditors concentrate on financial risks only.**

   A   True

   B   False

(1 mark)

(180)**Which categories of audit are typically required by law for all companies?**

   A   Neither internal audit nor external audit.

   B   Internal audit only.

   C   External audit only.

   D   Both internal audit and external audit.

(2 marks)

Chapter 23: Internal financial control

(181) **All of an organisation's internal controls would be of interest to the external auditor.**

A   True

B   False

(1 mark)

(182) **Who is responsible for there being satisfactory internal controls within a company?**

A   The board of directors.

B   The audit committee.

C   The internal auditors.

D   The external auditors.

(2 marks)

(183) **Which type of audit is concerned with the evaluation of the internal controls of an organisation?**

A   Substantive audit.

B   Systems audit.

C   Operational audit.

D   Value for money audit.

(2 marks)

(184) **Which of the following is not one of the components of internal control?**

A   The entity's risk assessment.

B   The documentation of control procedures.

C   The monitoring of controls.

D   The control environment.

(2 marks)

(185) **A formal organisation structure is part of which of the five components of internal control?**

A   The entity's risk assessment process.

B   The documentation of control procedures.

C   The monitoring of controls.

D   The control environment.

(2 marks)

(186) **One categorisation of control activities is between preventative controls, detective controls and corrective controls. Into which category would the proper segregation of duties be allocated?**

A   Preventative

B   Detective

C   Corrective

(1 mark)

(187) **Comparing the actual performance of a business with the budgeted performance for the period is an example of a control activity carried out by management.**

A   True

B   False

(1 mark)

(188) **How often, as a minimum, does the Combined Code on Corporate Governance state that the boards of listed companies should conduct a review of the effectiveness of the system of internal control?**

A   Every six months.

B   Every 12 months.

C   Every two years.

D   Every three years.

(2 marks)

(189) **The audit committee of a listed company is responsible for the company's system of internal controls.**

A   True

B   False

(1 mark)

(190) **The external auditors of Company X, a publicly-quoted company with an audit committee, have discovered a serious weakness in internal financial control during their audit, but management is undecided whether improvements in control should be introduced.**

To whom should the auditors communicate the details of this weakness in control?

A   The audit committee

B   The non-executive directors

C   The shareholders

D   The police authorities

(2 marks)

(191) **Segregation of duties ensures that the same person is responsible for authorising a transaction, recording a transaction, and maintaining custody of the asset.**

A   True

B   False

(1 mark)

Chapter 24: Fraud

(192) **A fraud is always committed by a person inside the organisation, such as an employee or manager, and cannot be committed by a third party external to the organisation.**

A   True

B   False

(1 mark)

(193)**Which of the following is not a necessary ingredient of a fraud?**

A   A deliberate act.

B   Collusion between two or more persons.

C   Deception.

D   An objective of unfair advantage.

(2 marks)

(194)**Which of the following factors suggests an increased risk of fraud and error in a company's recording of its transactions?**

A   Simple corporate structure.

B   Well-resourced internal audit department.

C   Stable business environment.

D   Employees paid bonuses depending on sales achieved.

(2 marks)

(195)**An ineffective control environment can create an opportunity to commit fraud.**

A   True

B   False

(1 mark)

(196)**Segregation of duties in the accounts department is an effective control to discourage fraud.**

A   True

B   False

(1 mark)

(197)**Which of the following types of fraud is not carried out by a third party to the business?**

A   '419' fraud.

B   Ponzi scheme.

C   False billing fraud.

D   Teeming and lading fraud.

(2 marks)

(198) **Why would auditors be interested in examining large credit notes issued at the start of the financial year?**

A   Credit notes suggest non-current assets may be being stolen.

B   Credit notes suggest window-dressing of sales.

C   Credit notes suggest cash may be being stolen.

D   Credit notes suggest purchases may be misstated.

(2 marks)

(199) **During which type of economic situation do financial statement frauds normally come to light?**

A   Economic boom.

B   Economic recession.

(1 mark)

(200) **Who is primarily responsible for the prevention and detection of fraud in a company?**

A   The executive directors.

B   The non-executive directors.

C   The board of directors as a whole.

D   The internal auditors.

(2 marks)

(201) **An internal control which is required by law can be excluded from implementation in a company if the expected costs of operating the control exceed the expected benefits of the control.**

A   True

B   False

(1 mark)

(202) **Which of the following controls should discourage a teeming and lading fraud from being carried out in the payments received department?**

A   Two people should be present at the opening of the mail.

B   A list should be prepared at the mail-opening of all monies received.

C   Regular rotation of duties in the department.

D   Control account reconciliations should be carried out each month.

(2 marks)

(203) **The effectiveness of controls cannot rise above the integrity of the people who administer them.**

A   True

B   False

(1 mark)

(204) **The directors of a company are required by law to publish financial statements that give a true and fair view of the company's financial performance and position. Thus it follows that any accounts given a qualified audit report by the external auditors must have been prepared fraudulently by the directors.**

A   True

B   False

(1 mark)

(205) **The Combined Code on Corporate Governance requires all companies to establish whistleblowing arrangements whereby employees who suspect that fraud is occurring in their department can confidentially raise their concerns with senior management.**

A   True

B   False

(1 mark)

Chapter 25: Recruitment and selection, managing diversity and equal opportunity

(206)**'Equal opportunities' is a generic term describing the belief that there should be an equal chance for all workers to apply and be selected for jobs, to be trained and promoted in employment and to have that employment terminated fairly.**

    A   True

    B   False

(1 mark)

(207)**Which of the following is not part of Rodger's 7 point plan for person specification?**

    A   Special aptitudes

    B   Impact on other people

    C   Disposition

    D   General intelligence

(2 marks)

(208)**The ability to demonstrate the skills necessary to perform a particular task could be tested using psychometric testing.**

A: True
B: False

(1 mark)

Chapter 26: Review and appraisal of individual performance

(209)**During the appraisal interview the appraiser needs to demonstrate the following skills**

    A   questioning

    B   listening

    C   persuading

    D   verbal communication

    E   coercion

Which of the above is incorrect?

(2 marks)

(210)Which of the following are not considered to be causes of staff leaving

A   Discharge

B   Unavoidable

C   Avoidable

D   Appraisal

(2 marks)

(211)An "avoidable" reason for staff leaving is due to

A   pay

B   working conditions,

C   relationships with work mates

D   unsatisfactory promotion prospects

(2 marks)

Chapter 27: Training, development and learning

(212)Which of the following is not one of the learning styles postulated by Honey and Mumford?:

A   Theorist.

B   Reflector.

C   Assimilator

D   Activist.

E   Pragmatist.

(2 marks)

(213)Development is 'the planned and systematic modification of behaviour through learning events, programmes and instruction which enable individuals to achieve the level of knowledge, skills and competence to carry out their work effectively'

A   True

B   False

(1 mark)

(214) **Job analysis is the process of identifying the purpose of the job and its component parts, and specifying what must be learnt in order for there to be effective performance.**

    A   True

    B   False

                                                           (1 mark)

Chapter 28: Improving personal effectiveness at work

(215) **Which of the following is not a characteristics of objectives:**

    A   specific

    B   motivational

    C   attainable

    D   realistic

    E   time bounded

                                                          (2 marks)

(216) **Which of the following skills is not one of the skills that the counsellor needs to demonstrate?**

    A   Observant.

    B   Sensitive.

    C   Empathetic.

    D   Advisory.

    E   Discreet.

                                                          (2 marks)

Chapter 29: Effective communications and interpersonal skills

(217) **Which of the following is not part of the communication process?**

    A   Sender.

    B   Message

    C   Receiver.

    D   Distortion

    E   Feedback

                                                          (2 marks)

(218) **Which of the following is not one of the four of the most important reasons for lateral communication:**

A   task co-ordination

B   problem-solving

C   information sharing

D   conflict resolution

E   specifiying job instructions

(2 marks)

(219) **Horizontal communication may occur in an organisation that is managed in an authoritarian style.**

A   True

B   False

(1 mark)

MULTIPLE CHOICE ANSWERS

Chapter 1: The Business Organisation

(1) **E**

All the others fall within Buchanan and Huczynski's definition:

"Organisations are social arrangements for the controlled performance of collective goals."

(a) "Social arrangements" - organisations have structure to enable people to work together towards the common goals. Larger organisations tend to have more formal structures in place but even small organisations will divide up responsibilities between the people concerned. Shareholders in a quoted company may meet at the company's annual general meeting but do not usually work together within any form of structure.

(b) "Controlled performance" - organisations have systems and procedures to ensure that goals are achieved. These could vary from ad-hoc informal reviews to complex weekly targets and performance review. Shareholders may have individual targets for their shares but will not have any shared systems or procedures to ensure that goals are achieved.

(c) "Collective goals" - organisations are defined primarily by their goals. A school has the main goal of educating pupils and will be organised differently from a company where the main objective is to make profits. Shareholders may have very different goals e.g. income V capital growth.

(2) **C**

Standardised work processes, outputs, and skills and knowledge all contribute to co-ordination - but care must be taken to avoid the risk of stultifying initiative.

Standardised payment systems however, whilst administratively convenient, are not a recognised means of facilitating coordination.

(3) **C**

The example given concerns short term control and is thus operational.

(4) **D**

Strategic choice has three key angles to consider:

- What is the basis of our strategy? In particular how are we going to compete - high quality, low costs?
- Where do we want to compete? Which markets, countries, products?
- How do we want to get there? Organic growth, acquisition or some joint arrangement such as franchising?

Chapter 2: Organisational structure

(5) **B**

The main difficulty in matrix organisations is conflicts over the lines of control which can lead to conflicting demands over allocation of resources.

(6) **A**

The scalar chain can be defined as the line of authority which can be traced up or down the chain of command.

(7) **A** by definition.

A narrow span of control, means that one manager has direct authority over only a few subordinates, leading to many layers of management and a tall management structure.

(8) **B**.

This affects the span of control, not the amount of decentralisation that occurs in a firm.

(9) **C**.

This is a disadvantage of the informal structure, not a reason for the informal organisation to arise.

Chapter 3: Organisational culture

(10) **D**

This is an influence on the culture of the organisation, not an element of culture.

(11) **B**

Schein argues that the culture is set by the first leaders, and the attributes of future leaders are set by the culture.

(12) **B**

This is likely to adopt a task culture, due to the commitment needed by the team to get the job done on time.

(13) **A**

The five traits are individualism vs collectivism, uncertainty, power distance, masculinity vs femininity and confuscianism vs dynamism.

Chapter 4: Leadership, management and supervision

(14) **A** by definition.

(15) **C**

The five elements are forecasting and planning, control, organisation, command and co-ordination.

(16) **B**

Responsibility can not be delegated because it is an 'obligation owed'. Obligation to complete a task and liability for a task can not be delegated.

(17) **A**.

Bennis focuses on the need to inspire change, not to impose change.

(18) **B**.

The other options relate to the other corners of the grid.

Chapter 5: Individual and group behaviour in business organisations

(19) **B**.

The other options are advantages of cohesive groups, e.g. greater creativity, but do not relate to the needs of the members.

(20) **A.**

Aggressive behaviour is more likely to lead to conflict and passive behaviour ignores the conflict.

(21) **C.**

The factors required for a cohesive group are leadership, right mix of skills, clear objectives, commitments to shared goals, team identity and team solidarity.

(22) **D.**

Behaviour is always affected by an individual's needs, and the individual's motivation to meet those needs.

Chapter 6: Team formation, development and management

(23) **B.**

The finisher ensures that timetables are met. The monitor evaluator criticises other people's ideas. The shaper promotes activity. The team worker is supportive and tries to diffuse any conflict.

(24) **B.**

Forming is the initial stage when the group is just a collection of individuals. Storming is the conflict stage (this is where the group is now). The norming stage will establish behaviour patterns, individuals roles, etc. Performing is the stage when the group acts efficiently and performs the task set (the group is not yet at this stage as progress is slow on the advertisement).

(25) **B.**

For a successful team, communication should be unstructured. The other options are criteria as per **Peters** and **Waterman**.

(26) **A.**

The other options are more likely to be seen in a team than a group.

Chapter 7: Motivating individuals and groups

(27) **A**.

Satisfaction relates to a worker being content with their job, hence leading to answers **B**, **C** and **D**. If a worker is motivated, they will make fewer mistakes and therefore generate less waste.

(28) **B**.

Bob's basic needs are great, but are probably satisfied by his and his wife's income. Security for himself and his family is the highest motivational force. Higher order needs are unlikely to provide motivation.

(29) **A**.

Social needs can be met to some extent by the provision of sports facilities.

(30) **A** by definition.

Chapter 8: Information technology and information systems in business

(31) **B**

An intranet is an internal network within an organisation that makes use of the internet. It can be used for communications to employees and also between employees. However, e-mail is used for communications between employees within an intranet, not chat rooms.

(32) **D**

Decision support systems are used to assist managers in developing forecasts or solutions to problems. They are generally used at middle management level, whereas executive information systems are used by senior managers to obtain information from both internal and external sources. A MIS is a system providing information for management, in the form of reports or file interrogation facilities, but do not offer any decision-making support (such as forecasting and modelling facilities).

(33) **B**

An Extranet is similar to an Intranet, with the exception that access to the system is provided to some external users as well as to employees of the organisation. Answer A describes electronic data interchange (EDI) and answer C describes outsourcing.

(34) **A**

Data as the information has not yet been processed.

Chapter 9: Political and legal factors

(35) **C**

Environmental. This E within the acronym SLEPT represents Economic

(36) **B**

False, the definition applies to data security

(37) **A**

Under most health and safety legislation employees are supposed to take responsibility for their own safety. There is nothing to suggest that the employer had failed to provide a safe working environment or that Peter was expected to dance as part of his contract of employment.

Chapter 10: Macroeconomic factors

(38) **D**

Balance of trade should be Balance of payments

(39) **C**

AD = C + I + G + (X - M)

Reducing government expenditure will decrease aggregate demand.

Reducing imports, savings and tax will all act to increase aggregate demand.

(40) **A**

The other three are expenditure switching policies which will make imported goods either more expensive or hard to obtain.

(41) **A**

Revaluing the currency would worsen the balance of payments deficit by making exports more expensive and imports cheaper.

Chapter 11: Social and technological factors

(42) **B**

False – the expression relates to delayering.

(43) **A**

True

Chapter 12: Competitive factors

(44) **C**

Diversification

(45) **E**

Porter talked about the threat of new entrants as one of his five forces. Discussing barriers to entry is a factor to consider when assessing the force but is not a force itself.

(46) **D**

Firm Structure should be Firm Infrastructure

(47) **B**

False, this describes the Outbound logistics section of the primary activities in Porter's value chain.

Chapter 13: Stakeholders

(48) **D**

Managers are an internal stakeholder.

(49) **A**

Stakeholders can move from quadrant to quadrant as a result of specific events/differing strategies e.g. workers may have low interest in a financing decision, but will have a significant interest in any decision which could affect job security.

(50) **B**

The other options relate to the other quadrants in Mendelow's matrix.

(51) **C**

The other stakeholders are examples of connected stakeholders.

Chapter 14: Committees

(52) **C**

Convening a meeting means making arrangements for people to attend. There are two ways of convening a meeting. As noted above, a notice can be issued and, if the meeting is one of a series or cycle of similar gatherings it may be convened automatically, e.g. on the first Monday of each month at 10am. Deciding on the individuals who will be attending the meeting is part of the process of convening a meeting, as is drawing up an agenda. The record of the meeting will be written down in the minutes.

(53) **D**

The motion is a proposal put to a meeting. The original motion is sometimes amended in the course of debate and may then be carried in altered form as a 'substantive motion'. The other explanations in the list above refer to a point of order, an adjournment and a proxy. A point of order is an objection to the chair about an alleged irregularity in the convening, constitution or conduct of the meeting. An adjournment is an interruption of the proceedings of a meeting before they have been completed and a proxy is a stand-in for an absent member, who has the right to be present but not to speak.

(54) **D**

It is not necessary for anyone at the meeting to have a thorough understanding of the motion in question. To have been invited, each person will have a contribution to make and some will know more than others. A chairperson would, however, need a sound knowledge of the relevant regulations on convening, constituting and conducting a meeting. He or she would need the ability to be decisive and also be skilled in communicating rulings clearly but tactfully.

Chapter 15: Business ethics and ethical behaviour

(55) **A**

In an ethical dilemma you have a morally difficult decision to take involving judgement of what is the right or wrong thing to do in the circumstances.

(56) **A**

Meta-ethics concerns the study of what is ethical behaviour, and whether such behaviour is ethical in all circumstances or whether it is only relative to its society or cultural background.

(57) **A**

Corporate governance is concerned with how boards of directors run and control their business. Adopting a strong ethical framework throughout the company will assist the directors in discharging their responsibilities.

(58) **D**

Business ethics concerns everyone in a company.

(59) **D**

The fact that an action is not dealt with in the code of conduct has no bearing on whether it is ethical or unethical.

(60) **B**

Different companies have different core values, which should be developed into the company's code of conduct.

(61) D

There is no certification process before a musician is allowed on stage, and no ethical code that musicians have to follow.

(62) B

PII ensures that funds are available to recompense clients who are harmed by the accountant's negligence.

(63) B

The payment of such bribes is never ethical, even if they are commonplace in that particular country or culture.

(64) C

Since men are on average taller than women, a minimum height restriction is discrimination on the grounds of gender and therefore unacceptable.

(65) A

It is not the employee's fault if they pick up a long-term sickness. As long as the sickness is genuine and confirmed by a doctor's certificate, it is inappropriate to state a maximum number of sick days per year.

(66) B

The company may still be liable in law.

(67) A

Both the IFAC Code and the ACCA Code identify the same five Fundamental Principles to be followed.

(68) A

A professional accountant must always comply with the IFAC Code unless this would be contrary to local laws or regulations.

(69) A

Independence (though closely linked with objectivity) is not in itself a fundamental principle.

(70) **A**

This is the meaning of 'integrity'.

Chapter 16: Governance and social responsibility

(71) **B**

The concept of separation between ownership and control is relevant in any scenario where the decision makers do not bear a major share of the wealth effects of their decisions, e.g. in a charity, local government, financial mutual, etc., as well as in a large company.

(72) **B**

Reducing the agency problem implies motivating directors to act in the interests of all stakeholders, particularly the shareholders. Paying a bonus in shares would grant shares to the directors so would give them a direct motivation to maximise shareholder wealth.

(73) **C**

The Cadbury Report defines corporate governance as the system by which companies are directed and controlled.

(74) **B**

Corporate social responsibility is concerned with a company's obligations to all its stakeholders, external (such as the government and the public) and internal (particularly employees).

(75) **D**

Stakeholders are those who are influenced by, or can influence, the company's decisions. Each of the listed parties qualifies as a legitimate stakeholder. For example, pensioners will be keen that the company does not collapse since this might endanger the payment of their pensions each month.

(76) **A**

An exclusive focus on short-term profitability will drive away the very customers on whom the company depends in the longer-term.

(77)**A**

Traditional profit and loss financial reporting would write off most CSR expenditure in full as an expense as it is incurred, while modern commentators might argue that an investment in a strategic asset is being made.

(78)**A**

An increasing number of potential employees are asking about a company's CSR activities in job interviews. In a competitive job market (especially among new graduates) it helps interviewers to attract the best applicants if they can point to an effective CSR programme. This can also help to retain staff by generating a 'feel-good' factor amongst the workforce.

(79)**C**

The Higgs Report recommendations, now contained in the Combined Code, require that at least half the board (excluding the chairman) should comprise independent NEDs.

(80)**B**

A significant shareholder cannot be independent of the company, so Mr X cannot be an independent NED. The fact that he is paid a reasonable fee to serve as a NED is irrelevant.

(81)**B**

The remuneration committee is made up of NEDs, so should not advise on the remuneration of NEDs. This responsibility should be given to the board as a whole, who could delegate it to a committee of the board.

(82)**B**

A small listed company may establish a remuneration committee of only two independent NEDs. (The normal requirement is a minimum of three for listed companies that are not small.)

(83)**A**

The audit committee can make recommendations in relation to the appointment, but it is the shareholders at each annual general meeting who appoint the external auditors.

(84) **A**

UK-listed companies must comply with the Combined Code on Corporate Governance which requires that audit committees should comprise at least three NEDs, or two in the case of smaller companies.

(85) **A**

The stakeholders in a company are all those parties who are influenced by, or can influence, the company's decisions and actions. A large listed company will often be of such a size that the public in general can be seen as a stakeholder of the company.

(86) **B**

Meetings of audit committees are closed to the public.

(87) **C**

High dividend payments are a need of the shareholder group, not the public at large.

(88) **A**

Focus groups are useful in gathering ideas from larger numbers of stakeholders (e.g. employees) but they must be managed carefully if they are to generate useful results.

(89) **A**

Shareholders have a financial relationship with the company. Employees and directors are internal stakeholders. The government is an external stakeholder.

(90) **B**

Although the cost is written off as incurred, the company is likely to receive benefits in the form of a more competent or motivated employee, who should generate higher profits for the company in the future.

Chapter 17: Law and regulation governing accounting

(91) **B**

A and **D** are not bodies; **A** is legislation, **D** is a role. **C** is untrue.

(92) **C**

Companies have to submit tax returns (A) and annual accounts (B). However, they will only have dealings with competition authorities if requested to do so.

(93) **A**

Governments are probably busy enough. **C** requires international accounting standards, not legislation. **D** is untrue as legislation and accounting standards are different.

(94) **C**

Others are advantages

(95) **D**
(96) **C**
(97) **C**

A and **B** are not necessary for a true and fair view. D is irrelevant.

(98) **D**

Others are required.

(99) **D**

Others are not required.

(100) **B**

Others are required.

(101) **A**
(102) **C**

Others are likely to be involved.

(103) **D**
(104) **A**

The others are potential consequences.

(105)**D**

The others are potential consequences.

(106)**A**

(107)**B**

It used to be **A**.

(108)**B**

(109)**A**

(110)**A**

(111)**A**

(112)**D**

(113)**B**

(114)**C**

(115)**B**

(116)**A**

(117)**A**

(118)**B**

Chapter 18: The accounting profession

(119)**C**

The 'Big 4' typically provide business advisory, assurance and insolvency services, but not conference organisation as it requires administrative rather than accounting skills.

(120)**D**

Accounting standards make accounts more comparable, but different accounting policies and different business specifics means they will never be 'the same'. Accounting standards help to ensure that financial statements give a true and fair view, but not that they are 'accurate'.

(121)**B**

This information would be used by the marketing department in setting price.

(122)**D**

This information would be used by the Human Resources department in determining salary structures and policies.

(123)**B**

The other information will also be of some use, but shareholders will be more concerned with profits as this generally determines the value of their shares.

(124)**C**

Although banks will be interested in profits (as a means of generating cash) they will be most interested in the likelihood of their being repaid, and so will want to know what other borrowings there are.

(125)**D**

(126)**C**

(127)**B**

(128)**C**

Chapter 19: Accounting and finance functions

(129)**D**

This is the definition of a budget. It is drawn up and approved prior to the budget period, and is normally expressed in terms of money.

(130)**C**

Managers will be interested in both financial information (e.g. the profit earned in the previous quarter) and non-financial information (e.g. the number of units produced or the number of hours worked in the previous quarter).

(131)**A**

Transactions are first entered into the books of prime entry, such as the sales day book or purchases day book. On a regular basis, such as monthly, the entries in the day books are totalled up, and the totals are posted to the ledger accounts.

(132)D

Auditors' reports are only required for the financial statements of large companies and publicly-quoted companies.

(133)A

Some companies do decide to run their treasury as a profit centre. Operating units are charged the market rate for the services that the treasury provides to them, especially for risk management tools such as SWAPS. Some treasury departments also sell these services externally.

(134)A

The chief accountant (or financial controller, or whatever the job title is for the accountant in charge of financial accounting matters) would draft the annual report and accounts.

(135)A

Tax avoidance is legal (though sometimes ethically questionable), while tax evasion is illegal. Overstating deductions or understating income are examples of tax evasion.

(136)B

The company itself is responsible for paying the correct amount of tax each year. It may employ external advisers to help it with its tax computation, but the legal responsibility remains with the company.

(137)A

The cost of debt finance is lower than the cost of equity finance, since interest is tax-allowable as stated in the question, and also since the providers of debt are taking a lower risk by lending money (because their debt ranks ahead of equity in the event of a winding up) and so they are happy to be paid a lower return.

(138)C

The duration of the funding method should match the life of the asset being acquired. The factory could reasonably be expected to have a thirty-year life, so a thirty-year loan is the most appropriate.

Chapter 20: Financial systems and procedures

(139)A

Not **C**, as this description includes a collection of procedures, making it a system.

(140)C

Not a system, since a single procedure rather than a collection.

(141)A

D is a disadvantage. **B** and **C** are not true.

(142)D

Others are advantages,

(143)D
(144)C
(145)A

It's usually more difficult for people to understand **B**, **C** and **D** are untrue

(146)B

C and **D** are advantages. **A** is untrue.

(147)B

Others are stages in the purchasing cycle.

(148)C

Others are documents in purchasing cycle.

(149)C

Normally order, despatch of goods, despatch of invoice, receipt of payment.

(150)**C**

Normally order, demand payment, receive payment, despatch goods.

(151)**D**

Others are stages in the wages system.

(152)**C**
(153)**D**
(154)**A**
(155)**C**

Order will be: **C**, **B**, **A**, **D**.

(156)**C**
(157)**B**
(158)**A**
(159)**B**
(160)**C**
(161)**A**
(162)**D**
(163)**A**
(164)**C**
(165)**A**

Chapter 21: The relationship of accounting with other business functions

(166)**A**

B would be discussed with marketing, **C** with production, **D** with personnel.

(167)**D**

D would be discussed with production.

(168)**C**

A is purchasing, **B** is marketing, **D** is personnel / human resources.

(169)**D**

(170)**D**

(171)**A**

B is not appropriate since asks for 'rate'. **C** and **D** are not relevant.

(172)**B**

The rate will be calculated by reference to budgeted total hours. This rate is then applied to actual hours to calculate the charge to individual jobs / departments.

(173)**A**

(174)**D**

Chapter 22: Internal and external audit

(175)**D**

Financial statements that have been audited are more reliable than unaudited statements. Therefore all the readers of the financial statements will benefit by being able to rely on the truth and fairness of the statements.

(176)**B**

In most countries there is no legal requirement to have an internal audit department. The Combined Code requires listed companies that do not have an internal audit function to review the need for one annually, but there is no requirement to have an internal audit department.

(177)**C**

An external audit report is addressed to the shareholders of the company being audited.

(178)**B**

The primary purpose of an external audit is to report on whether the financial statements give a true and fair view. The purpose of an internal audit is whatever management want it to be; management choose the purpose of each individual internal audit assignment.

(179)**A**

Internal auditors carry out the work given to them by management, which may include investigating all the risks facing a company and reporting on how well these risks are being managed. External auditors carry out work to decide whether the financial statements give a true and fair view; they therefore focus on financial risks only.

(180)**A**

Internal audit is not required by law for any sorts of company. It is up to the management of every company to decide whether to establish an internal audit department. External audit is typically only required for large companies and public companies, not for all companies.

Chapter 23: Internal financial control

(181)**B**

The external auditor is only interested in whether the financial statements give a true and fair view, within the limits of materiality. Some internal controls may be exercised over immaterial areas (e.g. different controls exercised over petty cash balances at different locations) or over areas that have no audit relevance (e.g. controls over operational scheduling matters within the factory). Such controls are of no interest to the external auditor.

(182)**A**

The board of directors is responsible for ensuring that there are satisfactory internal controls. The audit committee, internal auditors and external auditors will all be interested in the quality of internal controls, but it is the directors who are responsible.

(183)**B**

A systems audit looks at the effectiveness of the internal control system. A substantive audit is designed to check the balances in the financial statements. Operational audit looks at an operational area, e.g. procurement or marketing. A valuefor- money audit looks at the economy, effectiveness and efficiency of a particular function.

(184)**B**

The five components of internal control are identified in ISA 315 to be the control environment, the risk assessment process, the information system, control activities and the monitoring of controls.

(185)**D**

The control environment comprises the attitudes and actions of management towards internal control generally and its importance within the entity. By establishing a formal organisation structure for the business, management are setting a tone of discipline and structure which should improve control throughout the entity.

(186)**A**

Preventative controls are designed to prevent risks from occurring. By ensuring the proper segregation of duties, one individual is not able to process a transaction entirely on their own, thus errors should be picked up and fraud should only be possible if there is collusion between staff.

(187)**A**

Comparing actual and budgeted performance is an example of a 'Comparison control' from the 'ACCA MAP' mnemonic of types of control activities.

(188)**B**

The Combined Code requires that, at least annually, the board should conduct a review of the effectiveness of the system of internal controls.

(189)**B**

The board of directors as a whole is responsible for the company's system of internal control. It may delegate aspects of monitoring the system to the audit committee, but it cannot escape ultimate responsibility for the system.

(190)**A**

Best practice (as set out in International tandards on Auditing) requires the external auditor to communicate weaknesses discovered in internal control to those charged with governance, which in this case is the audit committee.

(191)B

Segregation of duties ensures that the same person is not responsible for authorising a transaction, recording a transaction, and maintaining custody of the asset.

Chapter 24: Fraud

(192)B

Frauds can be committed by persons both internal to and external to the organisation. For example, a false billing fraud is an attempt by an external third party to be paid by submitting a bogus invoice.

(193)B

Collusion is not necessary for a fraud. One person can carry out a fraud alone, for example the petty cashier can steal money for themselves and draw up a bogus petty cash voucher for the stolen cash.

(194)D

If employees are paid bonuses which depend in size on the level of sales achieved, they may be tempted to 'invent' nonexistent sales in order to trigger the payment of bonuses to themselves.

(195)A

An ineffective control environment does not necessarily mean that fraud will take place, but such an environment has often been seen to be present where frauds have occurred. Specific control activities can be designed to prevent fraud, but if the overall control environment is weak, the potential fraudster may take advantage of control weaknesses that he identifies.

(196)A

For example, no single individual should be responsible for both approving purchase invoices and issuing cheques. It would require collusion or inattentive working by accounts department staff for a payment to be made for a bogus invoice.

(197)D

Teeming and lading involves an employee misappropriating cash and then juggling the accounting records to make everything look normal. '419' fraud (another term for advance fee fraud), **Ponzi** schemes and false billing frauds all originate from outside the business.

(198)B

Credit notes issued at the start of one accounting period may indicate that sales in the previous period had been artificially overstated.

(199)B

During economic good times, high profits are being made and everyone is happy. During a recession there is closer scrutiny of reported profits, so the company can no longer continue its questionable activities. Collapse often follows soon afterwards.

(200)C

The responsibility for the prevention and detection of fraud rests with those charged with the governance of the entity, which in a company is the board of directors as a whole (executives as well as non-executives).

(201)B

If a control is required by law, then it must be implemented regardless of the perceived balance of costs and benefits.

(202)C

Rotation of duties in the payments received department should prevent a teeming and lading fraud from going undetected for long, so should discourage it from happening in the first place. Options **A** and **B** ensure that receipts are correctly recorded at the mail-opening, but it is not the existence of the receipts that is in doubt; it is their allocation against debtor balances. Similarly the fact that a control account reconciliation is carried out has no effect on a teeming and lading fraud.

(203)A

Effective controls depend on the competence and ethical behaviour of the people who operate them. With any control there is a risk that human error or greed will try to subvert the control. That is why an integrated set of controls and an overarching control environment are required for a control system to be effective.

(204)B

Fraud requires an intention to deceive. There may be a genuine disagreement on some matter between the directors and the auditors, with both believing that their view is correct. In such a situation the directors have not behaved fraudulently.

(205)B

First, the Combined Code only applies to listed companies, not all companies. Secondly, none of the detailed provisions of the Code are mandatory (although they do set out best practice). Listed companies must comply with each of the provisions or else explain their non-compliance (the 'comply or explain' rule).

Chapter 25: Recruitment and selection, managing diversity and equal opportunity

(206)A

True

(207)B

Impact comes from Fraser's 5 point plan.

(208)B

False, Psychometric testing measures psychological factors such as personality.

Chapter 26: Review and appraisal of individual performance

(209)E

Coercion

(210)D

(211)D

Chapter 27: Training, development and learning

(212)**C**

(213)**B**

> False

(214)**B**

> False

Chapter 28: Improving personal effectiveness at work

(215)**B**

(216)**D**

> Advisory

Chapter 29: Effective communications and interpersonal skills

(217)**D**

> The actual component is Noise (for Distortion).

(218)**E**

(219)**B**

> False

Index

Index

Index

Index

Index

Index

Index

Index

ACCA

Paper F1

Accountan

Complete T

British library cataloguing-in-publication data

A catalogue record for this book is available from the British Library.

Published by:
Kaplan Publishing UK
Unit 2 The Business Centre
Molly Millars Lane
Wokingham
Berkshire
RG41 2QZ

ISBN 978 0 85732 128 2

Printed in the UK by CPI William Clowes Beccles NR34 7TL.

Acknowledgements

We are grateful to the Association of Chartered Certified Accountants and the Chartered Institute of Management Accountants for permisssion to reproduce past examination questions. The answers have been prepared by Kaplan Publishing.

EXCITING
EXTRA
ONLINE
RESOURCES
INCLUDED

Kaplan Publishing are constantly finding new ways to make a difference to your studies and our exciting online resources really do offer something different to ACCA students looking for exam success.

THIS COMPLETE TEXT COMES WITH FREE EN-gage ONLINE RESOURCES SO THAT YOU CAN STUDY ANYTIME, ANYWHERE

Having purchased this Complete Text, you have access to the following online study materials:

- An online version of the Text which allows you to click in and out of the expandable content and view the answers to the Test Your Understanding exercises
- Fixed Online Tests with instant answers
- Test History and Results to allow you to track your performance
- Interim Assessments including Questions and Answers

How to access your online resources

- **Kaplan Financial students** will already have a Kaplan EN-gage account and these extra resources will be available to you online. You do not need to register again, as this process was completed when you enrolled. If you are having problems accessing online materials, please ask your course administrator.
- **If you purchased through Kaplan Flexible Learning or via the Kaplan Publishing website** you will automatically receive an e-mail invitation to Kaplan EN-gage online. Please register your details using this e-mail to gain access to your content. If you do not receive the e-mail or book content, please contact Kaplan Flexible Learning.
- **If you are already a registered Kaplan EN-gage user** go to www.EN-gage.co.uk and log in. Select the 'add a book' feature and enter the ISBN number of this book and the unique pass key at the bottom of this card. Then click 'finished' or 'add another book'. You may add as many books as you have purchased from this screen.
- **If you are a new Kaplan EN-gage user** register at www.EN-gage.co.uk and click on the link contained in the e-mail we sent you to activate your account. Then select the 'add a book' feature, enter the ISBN number of this book and the unique pass key at the bottom of this card. Then click 'finished' or 'add another book'.

Your Code and Information
This code can only be used once for the registration of one book online. This registration will expire when the final sittings for the examinations covered by this book have taken place. Please allow one hour from the time you submitted your book details for us to process your request.

KVJ2-tcxY-Rdly-NmMu

Please be aware that this code is case-sensitive and you will need to include the dashes within the passcode, but not when entering the ISBN. For further technical support, please visit www.EN-gage.co.uk